LOOKING FOR UTOPIA

LOOKING FOR UT●PIA

WEST IS BEST

The Life and Times of

JOHN C. WEST

Philip G. Grose

The University of South Carolina Press

© 2011 University of South Carolina

Published by the University of South Carolina Press
Columbia, South Carolina 29208

www.sc.edu/uscpress

Manufactured in the United States of America

20 19 18 17 16 15 14 13 12 11   10 9 8 7 6 5 4 3 2 1

LIBRARY OF CONGRESS CATALOGING-IN-PUBLICATION DATA

Grose, Philip G., 1938–
    Looking for Utopia : the life and times of John C. West /
Philip G. Grose.
        p. cm.
    Includes bibliographical references and index.
    ISBN 978-1-57003-978-2 (cloth : alk. paper)
        1. West, John Carl, 1922–2004. 2. Governors—South Carolina—Biography.
3. South Carolina—Politics and government—1951– 4. Ambassadors—
United States—Biography. 5. Ambassadors—Saudi Arabia—Biography.
6. United States—Foreign relations—Saudi Arabia. 7. Saudi Arabia—
Foreign relations—United States. I. Title.
    F275.42.W47G76 2011
    975.7′043092—DC22
    [B]   2010045469

This book was printed on Glatfelter Natures, a recycled paper with 30 percent
postconsumer waste content.

Publication of this volume was made possible in part by a grant from
the Caroline McKissick Dial Fund, University Libraries, University
of South Carolina.

FOR TRICIA

CONTENTS

ILLUSTRATIONS

PREFACE AND ACKNOWLEDGMENTS

The title of this book, *Looking for Utopia,* came from a description of John C. West by his predecessor as governor, Robert E. McNair. McNair knew that West was something of a political anomaly for his time. A Phi Beta Kappa scholar of considerable intellectual power, West had to earn political stripes not only in the sophisticated urban setting of his historic hometown of Camden, but also in the rough-and-tumble backcountry of rural Kershaw County where he was born and raised and made his family home.

"John was an idealist," McNair said, using the term to compare him with another prospective candidate for the office of lieutenant governor in 1966. "[West] was more aggressive and probably more liberal. . . . Camden is what everybody identifies [in Kershaw County], but then you have other parts of the county, and it is tough. It is two different types of people, [and] John was always looking for Utopia."

McNair's description was an apt one for West. It also defined nicely the distinctions between the two men who led South Carolina during the ten years of civil rights transition between 1965 and 1975. McNair was cautious and publicly close-mouthed in style. He took enormous political risks in resisting the die-hard allegiance to racial segregation that characterized much of southern politics of his time. But he was hesitant to extend his commitments beyond what might have been viewed as necessary and prudent. He strove to cloak his progressive initiatives in mainstream propriety, even when it meant diverting the mainstream into new channels. In football vernacular, he did not like to outrun his blocking.

By comparison West was a broken-field runner; he seemed to delight in taking on foes in the open field. In what seemed at the time to be quixotic exercises against entrenched forces such as the medical profession, commercial insurance interests, organizations opposed to serving mixed drinks in public, and powerful prosegregation elements, he was persistent and often prevailed. As the nation's ambassador to Saudi Arabia in the tense years of 1977 through 1981, he was not bashful about championing often unpopular pro-Arab opinions to an American public that viewed some of his thinking as radical.

That was the Utopian side of John West that caught the attention of McNair and other political colleagues. His Utopian tendencies, however, were never equated to "loose cannon" behavior. The other side of John West was that of a negotiator, compromiser, and unifier, in the spirit of most southern political progressives of the time. While he and McNair may have seemed distinctly different and often contrasting in their styles and outward approaches to their jobs, they made a perfectly compatible team in fighting off the common enemy of racial intolerance and violence that beset the South as desegregation was becoming the law of the land.

McNair's theme was that "we have run out of time and we have run out of courts" in persuading disgruntled white South Carolinians to put aside their chains and ax handles and to accept peacefully the legal and constitutional reality of racial desegregation. His fight was against the demons of a South Carolina whose history was anything but moderate on racial matters. In so doing, McNair paved the way for West to become an aggressive advocate of racially progressive initiatives, initiatives he described in the hopeful verbiage of his 1971 inaugural address as things he believed "we can, and we shall" do.

During the decade in which McNair and West governed South Carolina, the state came to grips with the impact of the Civil Rights Act of 1964 (public accommodations), the Voting Rights Act of 1965, and the long-delayed implementation of the 1954 Supreme Court ruling in *Brown v. Board of Education* ordering the desegregation of public schools in the South. It was a decade in which the segregated worlds—the separate and unequal worlds—of racial division in South Carolina were struck down by federal legislation and federal court orders.

It was a time of suspicions among South Carolinians of both races. They worried about the state's willingness to carry out change, its ability to sustain stability and security in such a major transition, and the good faith of its leaders to meet fairly and equitably such enormous challenges. Public anxieties were rampant, and the state lay prey to political exploitation by forces seeking to probe its emotional vulnerability. It was a tough time to be moderates or centrists, but McNair and West held their ground. They labored to maintain order and civil peace and to reshape South Carolina as a New South state of enlightened racial views and progressive economic ambitions. During their terms of office, the state eased back from the brink of civil disorder and racial strife and exhibited the potential for becoming a place where some Utopian ideals—human tolerance and political moderation—could be envisioned.

By the measure of organizational orthodoxy, both McNair and West were limited in the formal power of the office of governor. South Carolina was cataloged as a "weak governor" state because its chief executives could not succeed themselves, did not directly control the agencies of state government, and did not submit an executive budget each year. Even so, both men were powerful in the scope of their influence and their ultimate ability to set the course of the state's immediate future. They were both products of the General Assembly and knew well the potential that lay in cooperative relations with the oligarchic power brokers of the time. They emerged as leaders whose aspirations for change in the state's racial climate were accepted, whose ambitions for economic growth were shared, and whose steadfast insistence on peaceful transitions were embraced.

The author is indebted to the West Foundation and members of the West family for their generous support and participation in the preparation of the manuscript of this book. Governor West reviewed early portions of the manuscript and made himself available for hours of interviews and conversations until the final weeks of his life. Subsequently Lois R. West, his wife; John C. West Jr., his son; and Shelton West Bosley, his daughter, provided critical insight into his life and contributed significantly to the final product.

The book is a product of the Institute for Southern Studies at the University of South Carolina. The author is grateful to the institute director, Dr. Walter B. Edgar, for the kind of day-to-day working environment, support services, and friendly guidance that made this project possible. Also invaluable was the constant assistance and support of Herbert Hartsook, director of the South Carolina Political Collections, who gave the author complete access to the John West Papers and whose staff assisted freely in various research activities. The author is particularly appreciative of the subvention funding provided by the University Libraries and Dean Thomas McNally. An enormous debt of gratitude is owed to Alexander Moore, acquisitions editor of the University of South Carolina Press, for the many ways he found to keep the project on track and to enhance its overall quality.

John West was in many ways a coauthor of this book. In addition to the rich personal insight he offered to the author in conversations and interviews on many occasions, he left for future generations a storehouse of records, papers, and documents that chronicle his generation and the role he played in it. Foremost among those records is the remarkable daily journal he kept during his days as governor of South Carolina and as U.S. ambassador to Saudi Arabia. The journal offers with rare candor an insider's account of some critically important moments in the histories of the state and the nation. It also shows the human side of a man who brought exceptional energy, intellect, and unfailing goodwill to the inordinately difficult assignments that characterized his political career.

West's journal—the Saudi Arabian portion of it—became the object of official scrutiny and reclassification by the U.S. State Department during the years 2005–6. In a nationwide program conducted during the administration of President George W. Bush, some fifty-five thousand documents were included in the reclassification program, many of which had been previously available to the public through libraries and collections. West's journal of his days in Saudi Arabia (1977–81) remained in State Department hands for more than a year, during which time hundreds of passages were removed from the twenty-five-year-old document. In the letter accompanying the returned journal, the State Department said that the redacted portions contained "a large amount of classified and other sensitive information." In the interest of historical integrity, the author is hopeful that the current and future administrations will review this and other similar reclassification decisions and restore these documents to full public access.

Many individuals gave of their time and expertise in the development of this book. President Jimmy Carter was interviewed and provided insight into the working relationship he had with John West. Prince Turki al-Faisal was interviewed while he served as Saudi ambassador to the United Kingdom, and he spoke of the Saudi view of the West ambassadorship. Jim Placke, John Limbert, and Jim Hoagland read portions of the manuscript and offered suggestions on the Saudi sections. Congressman Jim Clyburn, Samuel Tenenbaum, Crawford Cook, Jim Byrd, and Don Fowler were among those who reviewed text or provided information.

Valuable materials on West's days at the Citadel were furnished by Jane Yates, director of the Citadel Archives and Museum. Agnes Corbett was especially helpful in providing access to materials in the Camden Museum and Archives, and other Camden assistance came from Harvey Teal, Rick Todd, and Ann Hutchins. The author is grateful for assistance received from colleagues among West's staff while he was governor: Jim Whitmire, Betty Bargmann Hunter, and Dwight Drake.

Meeghan Kane did much digging in the research trenches to produce credible and useful background materials to support the book's basic themes. Bob Ellis, Gayle Levine, Kate Moore, and Ernie Ellis provided the kind of friendship and support that made the day-to-day work possible and productive.

Inspiration, motivation, and unqualified labor came from the author's editor and critic par excellence, his wife, Virginia, who has performed the indescribably difficult task of seeing two books through to completion at the hands of a basically disorganized author. Without her full edits, textual suggestions, and frequent inquiries as to "which chapter are you on?" and "how are the footnotes coming?" and "are you sure this is how you want to say this?" the book would have died many deaths along the way.

Finally this book belongs completely to the memory of John C. West, for whom public service never lost its passion and personal side. While he has been hailed as a leader and a visionary, there was a further dimension that gave John West a special place among those he knew and served. His story is one of a human soul of wit, charm, and good humor who could build alliances on a grand scale and construct political victories of great public consequence. But his most lasting legacies may well be the lives he touched and inspired among people who knew and treasured him simply as their very good friend.

LOOKING FOR UTOPIA

ONE

A SOUTHERN GOVERNOR IN
THE COURT OF THE SAUDIS

He became the most effective and successful diplomat Saudi Arabia
had ever seen.

Jimmy Carter

On his first two days on the job as America's newly designated ambassador to the kingdom of Saudi Arabia, South Carolinian John C. West gave notice that he would be no ordinary diplomat. These were the tension-filled spring days of 1977, as Americans were discovering the realities and consequences of their dependence on oil from the Middle East, and the issue of Israeli-Arab peace was taking on new dimensions of urgency. The choice of West to the delicate Saudi post had already sent ripples through the State Department's career corps at a time when an experienced diplomat for the post might have been preferred by many.

Instead President Jimmy Carter had chosen a man who was a small-town lawyer by trade and—like Carter—a southern governor by political orientation. West had neither a background in the ways of Muslim nations nor any particular experience in the highly charged world of Middle East conflict or petrodriven economies. He was, in the eyes of some, another of President Jimmy Carter's down-home selections that reflected more his own sense of personal values than it did any degree of political sophistication. Saudi Arabia, it seemed, was hardly the place to break in a rookie diplomat in the spring of 1977.

"To say that West was an unknown quantity when he arrived in Saudi Arabia was an understatement," the chronicler Sandra Mackey wrote. "The professional diplomats were horrified that Saudi Arabia's major ally was forcing a back-slapping, hand-pressing Southern politician on the austere Saudis. Despite the predictions of disaster, the jovial West, seasoned by years on the campaign trail, applied just the right amount of graciousness and diffidence to charm his hosts."[1]

For those alarmed at West's appointment, there was ample reason to believe that the Saudi assignment should have merited a diplomatic professional. The Middle East in general and Saudi Arabia in particular had become places of rapidly escalating economic urgency and inescapable political vulnerability for American interests. While there lingered the popular public image of Saudi Arabia as a place of political intrigue, religious eccentricity, and despotic personal rule, the compelling reality was that Arab-controlled petroleum resources could make or break entire Western economies, a lesson the world had learned painfully only a few years earlier. The term "OPEC," the Organization of Petroleum Exporting Countries, formed in 1960 at the initiative of Saudi Arabia and Venezuela, struck a forbidding tone to many Americans who recognized their nation's dependence on overseas energy sources and their vulnerability to the manipulation of those sources. The very name of Saudi oil minister Ahmed Zaki Yamani set off alarms and anxieties among the gasoline-dependent societies of the affluent, industrialized nations, where memories were fresh of the OPEC-sponsored price increases four years earlier to protest American military support of Israel against Syria and Egypt. The increase had sent the U.S. economy into a tailspin and had been particularly damaging to the travel-oriented states of Georgia and South Carolina, where Jimmy Carter and John West respectively served as governors at the time.

The energy crisis was of such magnitude that the Richard Nixon–Gerald Ford administrations (1972–76) unleashed its biggest diplomatic weapons to address the troubles in the Middle East, including the considerable skills of Henry Kissinger, in the wake of the skyrocketing oil prices of 1973. In this instance even the remarkable Kissinger touch proved less than equal to the task. "Henry Kissinger [lost] credibility with the Arabs," the retired oil executive George Ballou told Jeffrey Robinson, the author of a biography of Saudi oil minister Sheikh Zaki Yamani. "The '73 war ended up with Kissinger's shuttle diplomacy. And the Arabs still feel they were done in by Kissinger. From their point of view, I think they were right."[2]

Onto that stage in May 1977 strode John Carl West, who would have been the first to admit he was not a Henry Kissinger or even a wannabe Kissinger. He sensed the Arab suspicions of Kissinger. "His method of operation," West said of Kissinger, "was to tell each side what he thought they wanted to hear in

Ambassador John West and President Jimmy Carter. South Carolinian West and Georgian Carter served concurrently as governors of their respective states, and when Carter announced his candidacy for president, West was one of his first endorsers. When Carter became president, he appointed West ambassador to Saudi Arabia. Courtesy of the John C. West Papers, South Carolina Political Collections, University of South Carolina

a sufficiently clever way that they couldn't actually say that it was an outright lie. But none of the Arabs trusted him. They respected his capacity, but they didn't trust him."[3]

DIPLOMACY, SOUTHERN FAMILY STYLE

As an antidote to the scowling Kissinger, West may have been short on diplomatic guile, but he was long on personal charm. Carter intended for the appointment of the cheerful southerner to be a bold message to the Saudis not merely of a budding new friendship but of a friendship that carried family-like status. Carter was not only sending his personal friend John West to represent American interests in the eccentric desert kingdom; he was also endowing West with special privilege within American diplomatic circles, direct twenty-four-hour access to the president and the White House.

President Carter said, "When John West went to Saudi Arabia . . . I told [him] . . . that he should relate directly to me . . . and I authorized him to let the Saudi leadership know that whenever there was a crisis or a problem or a personal sensitivity issue that John West could talk directly to me and the White House or write me a personal letter and not go through the vast bureaucracy that might involve dozens of people."[4] This status was extended to only two other ambassadors at the time, the former labor leader Leonard Woodcock in China and Philip Austin in Australia. According to Carter, "We didn't have diplomatic relations with China then and the other one [Austin] just happened to be a close friend of mine . . . [who] maintained the right to communicate directly with me."[5]

What ensued in Saudi Arabia with John West were four years of informal, often unconventional, and at times blatantly unorthodox statesmanship that made West an unabashed Saudi advocate in Washington circles, a trusted insider within the elite society of Saudi royalty, and something of a pariah to powerful pro-Israeli interests in the United States. For all the fractured procedural orthodoxy occasioned by such style and behavior, it was part of an overall Carter initiative to make friends with the world, one nation at a time, and to find new inroads into what had become the abscessed infection of Middle East tensions.

By one count, President Carter met with more than forty heads of state in his first year in office—more than Kennedy, Johnson, or Nixon in comparable periods in their administrations. By another count, the president's first meeting with the shah of Iran in November 1977 was his sixty-sixth personal contact with either a head of state or a head of government that year. At a time when Israel was viewed internationally as the special and favored friend of the United States in the Middle East, Carter was sending signals that he was willing to take risks and to initiate unprecedented overtures to Arab nations in efforts to build American credibility and acceptance as an evenhanded arbiter in the Arab-Israeli conflicts.

Another southern governor who became president, Bill Clinton, followed the Carter precedent of appointing southern politicians as ambassadors to Saudi Arabia—namely, former Mississippi governor Ray Mabus and onetime Georgia senator Wyche Fowler. "In the decades since J. Rives Childs took up residence in Jeddah as the first American Ambassador to Saudi Arabia, the post had generally been filled by one of two types of appointee," Thomas Lippman wrote in a study of Saudi Arabia: "career diplomats who specialized in the Arab world, such as Parker Hart, Hermann F. Eilts, Richard Murphy and Hume Moran; and prominent Southern politicians who lacked expertise but functioned as personal representatives of the president who appointed them."[6]

PERSONAL POLITICS ON A BIG STAGE

Among the Saudis, Carter's newly designated ambassador, John West, would prove from day one to be an early and eager symbol of that aggressive new friendship with the Saudi kingdom. His transparent advocacy of the desert kingdom caused some observers to wonder whether he was the U.S. ambassador to Saudi Arabia or the other way around. He admitted in one of his frequent handwritten letters to Carter five months later, "I recognize that an occupational hazard of an ambassador is to become too imbued with the point of view of the country he represents."[7] Whatever may have been the grumbling among the orthodox careerists at Foggy Bottom, John West made it known from the outset that he intended to be his own man, exploiting his special status with the president when necessary, and that he would carry out the mission as he saw fit, with or without State Department blessing.

His first day on the job set an unmistakable precedent. It was a critical day in the early diplomatic life of the Carter administration, the day when Crown Prince Fahd bin Abdul Aziz and an official delegation from Saudi Arabia arrived in Washington, D.C., for a state visit. It was not the first contact between the Saudis and the new president's administration, but it would provide the occasion for critical head-to-head meetings between the leaders of the two nations. The Saudis' visit was the last of five introductory meetings for Carter with key leaders in the Middle East, beginning with then Israeli prime minister Yitzhak Rabin in March 1977 and followed in succession by summits with Egypt's Anwar Sadat in early April, King Hussein bin Talal of Jordan later that month, President Hafez al-Assad of Syria in early May, and concluding with Fahd on May 24.[8]

West, whose appointment had not been formally announced at the time, accompanied Secretary of State Cyrus Vance to Andrews Air Force Base to greet the Saudi party. While it would be his first experience as the official U.S. ambassador, he had already begun to measure the dimensions of the assignment and to form some personal opinions.

One of them was his belief that the State Department was making a mistake in ordering the retirement of one Isa Sabbagh, a U.S. employee in the Saudi embassy, upon his sixtieth birthday. Sabbagh was a Palestinian, and West had learned reliably that he was the best Arab linguist in the country. He had the confidence of the Saudi community in the delicate—and often diplomatically tinged—task of translations. As it turned out, there was a slight delay in the landing of the Saudi party's plane, allowing just enough time for West to ask Vance to waive the mandatory retirement requirement for Sabbagh. West and Vance had formed a friendship earlier as members of the Southern Center for

International Studies in Atlanta, and the secretary readily concurred in the request. It would prove to be an important step in building West's embassy team and forging the kind of linkages critical to carrying out his assignment of gaining the personal trust of his new Saudi colleagues. It also established that he would not hesitate to incur lower-level State Department displeasure in getting his job done.

Minutes after securing Secretary Vance's support for Sabbagh's continued employment, West stepped out of a flagged State Department limo and met for the first time two of the most important people in the world's petroleum-driven economy: Crown Prince Fahd, who would become king five years later; and Prince Saud al-Faisal, who had been deputy oil minister for five years prior to becoming the nation's foreign minister in 1975.

It was a moment, West recorded later that day in his journal, that gave him the opportunity to make more personal assessments. Saud, he noted, was "a son of King Faisal and bears a striking resemblance to him. Saud is a graduate of Princeton and a very striking looking individual. I am told he is completely honest and extremely attractive to the ladies. I can see why."[9] Friends would later vow that the young Saudi prince bore a striking resemblance to a movie idol of the time, the Egyptian Omar Sharif, "only better, because he was taller," according to the Wests' daughter, Shelton. "He's exactly what you'd think an Arabian Knight would look like. Absolutely stunning."[10]

Day two proved to be even more adventuresome for the fledgling and already-unorthodox ambassador. It began amid formalities and trappings of his new position. As he arrived with his wife, Lois, for the first official visit to the White House, West paused to survey a new perspective, for the first time as an insider, and to admit to himself that he was awed: "Lois and I walked up on the South Lawn where the arrival ceremonies [for the Saudis] were to take place. It was a beautiful day and an impressive sight. From the rear entrance of the White House, you can see the Washington Monument on the left and the Jefferson Memorial on the right. The expanse of green, with shrubs, is truly impressive."[11]

The day would also produce West's first opportunity to participate in upper-level policy talks and to inject his Saudi-friendly opinion into the discussions. A meeting had been called to bring State Department and Defense Department officials together with the Saudi party to discuss a matter of special delicacy at the time, mutual defense interests and, most prominently, the sale of U.S. fighter jets to Saudi Arabia. The issue had been left unresolved by the departing Ford administration, except for an eleventh-hour pledge by outgoing deputy defense secretary William Clement that the Saudis should get the sophisticated F-15 aircrafts, long-range interceptor jets considered at the time to be the best of their kind in the world—and which had also already been promised to Israel and the Iranian government of the shah. The F-15s were the ones the Saudis wanted, and West quickly made it known that they were his choice as well.

THE SAUDI PREFERENCE OF FIGHTER JETS

West wrote:

> I told them I felt we should honor the commitment (of the Ford administration) with the understanding that it did require the approval of the Congress, which we would endeavor to get. I was pleased, surprised and delighted when this view was adopted.
>
> Later I found out that the State Department had recommended a different approach, namely that we would offer them a long-range fighter, but we would try to get them to take the F-16, which they [the Saudis] did not want. The decision [to sell the F-15] was made by the President . . . and the Saudis were extremely pleased.[12]

President Carter later recalled one of the outcomes of the sale. "After I went out of office, Iran launched an air attack against Saudi Arabia. And the Saudis sent up two F-15s and they shot down the Iranian planes before they ever crossed the border," he said.[13]

The sale would not become final until after subsequent congressional battles that brought into play the heavy artillery of the Carter administration and the deeply committed pro-Israeli lobbies. The congressional fight over the F-15 sale to the Saudis would draw deep lines separating the two sides and would prove to be a dramatic turning point in Carter's carefully sketched Middle East strategies.

For the moment, however, in those days of late May 1977, Carter, Vance, and their new ambassador, John West, were making important headway with their friendship initiatives with the Saudis. In recommending the F-15s, West also found himself for the second time in twenty-four hours at variance with State Department functionaries, a posture that he later observed wryly had earned him a kind of rigorous oversight and treatment "worse than my freshman year hazing at The Citadel."[14] For all the torment he was creating for the Foggy Bottom denizens, West was taking the first steps toward an eventual position of remarkable trust and access within the eccentric Arab kingdom.

"He became the most effective and successful diplomat Saudi Arabia had ever seen," Carter later said.[15] West capped off his second day on the job with more personal politics. Walking out of a policy meeting in the company of Crown Prince Fahd and President Carter, West heard Fahd tell the president that his (Fahd's) four-year-old son had Carter's picture and considered him one of his heroes. West turned to the Saudi prince and suggested that he should meet Amy, the president's then nine-year-old daughter, and Fahd agreed. "That night after dinner," West wrote, "the President took the Prince upstairs to Amy's room, woke her, and said, 'How would you like to meet an Arabian Prince?' Amy was sleepy, but gracious, and the Prince was quite taken by her. I knew he would be."[16]

The two days had been productive ones for Carter, Vance, and other U.S. leaders. Talks had ranged from issues of Saudi defense and security to discussions of Arab-Israeli relations and the chances for peace in the region. Fahd had been upbeat and had reported that a recent meeting of Sadat, Assad, an emissary of King Hussein, and Fahd in Riyadh had convinced the Saudi leader that "this would be an especially auspicious year to find a comprehensive solution to the Arab-Israeli problem."[17] Vance later wrote, "The talks ended on a warm and friendly note."[18]

FINDING THE SAUDI COMFORT ZONE

For West his first two days on the job had been heady ones, and he had gained even more confidence from the Saudis by retaining Isa Sabbagh. "In meetings with the Saudis, he was the interpreter," West later recalled. "He had the absolute confidence of King Khalid and Prince Fahd."[19]

For their part, the Saudis were comfortable too and reciprocated in style and in kind. Zaki Yamani's biographer Jeffrey Robinson recalled West's first extended meeting with Yamani, the much-feared broker of oil prices and supplies within the OPEC cartel:

> The Saudi oil minister invited the new American Ambassador to meet with him in a relaxed, informal setting at his summer home at Taif. They sat outside on wicker furniture next to the pool, drinking fruit juice, chatting amicably for about 10–15 minutes.
>
> Once West felt he had paid his respects, he stood up and told Yamani that he'd only stopped by to say hello. He told Yamani that he didn't want to take up any more of his time. But Yamani motioned to West to stay. He said, "I'm happy to see you and anyway you've already spent more time with me than your predecessor ever did."
>
> It was the beginning of an especially warm and long friendship.[20]

West's friendship with Yamani would prove particularly useful as the American ambassador became an increasingly trusted insider among the Saudis and could gain advance knowledge of critical moves in economically sensitive areas such as OPEC's decisions on oil pricing and supply. On a bigger scale, it also fit into the Carter administration's growing realization that the troubles of the Middle East were more than a two-dimensional struggle between Israel and its Arab neighbors. The shadings and the shifting subtleties of relations among the Arab states themselves had also become a matter of interest and concern, and having John West in Saudi Arabia as an active and reliable sounding post, confidant, and communications linkage at the crossroads of Arab financial and political exchanges became a matter of keen value.

Secretary of State Vance would later write:

> The interrelationship between Arab oil, the industrialized West's strategic and economic interests in Middle East stability, the sharpening focus of the U.S.-Soviet rivalry in the Third World, and the incalculable impact of a fifth major Arab-Israeli war on the United States fundamentally altered our stake in achieving a peaceful and lasting solution of the conflict.
>
> Moreover, conservative states such as Saudi Arabia and the Persian Gulf sheikdoms, and moderate leaders such as President Anwar Sadat of Egypt and King Hussein of Jordan, shared concerns that Arab radicalism, feeding on the Arab-Israeli confrontation, could provide a base for the expansion of Soviet influence.
>
> Moderate Arab leaders understood they could not shake the U.S. commitment to the security of Israel, but they believed the clear American national interest in stability in the Middle East gave them significant leverage in seeking an acceptable political settlement.

While the Carter administration agreed with its predecessors on the priority attention given to U.S. political, strategic, and economic interests in the Middle East, it concluded that the step-by-step diplomacy of the Nixon-Ford strategists "had exhausted its potential."[21]

"Carter and his senior foreign policy advisers believed that the time had come to go beyond the Kissinger approach of step-by-step negotiation," Robert A. Strong reported in his 2000 assessment of Carter foreign policy, noting that such a strategy would eventually lead to a U.S. push to bring Middle East states together in a multilateral conference at Geneva. "No one was quite sure what could, or would, happen if all the Middle East diplomatic issues—territorial, political and military—were placed on the same negotiating table," Strong wrote, "but it seemed worth a try. And given the growing importance of Middle East oil to the international economy, successful peace negotiations offered the additional payoff of greater global economic stability."[22]

A MORAL DIMENSION

Carter had also injected into his administration by that time the strain of personal faith and public morality that—coming only three years after the Watergate scandal had driven Richard Nixon from office—had brought to his presidency what some considered to be a refreshing and upbeat component and what others believed to be troublesome and disingenuous distractions. Only days before the arrival of Crown Prince Fahd for the official Saudi Arabian visit in May 1977, President Carter had raised some eyebrows in Washington with a Sunday speech at Notre Dame University that suggested at least to some that the administration was trying "to recapture the high ground of 'moral authority' in the world." One analyst, a *Washington Post* reporter named Murray Marder, likened the speech directly to Carter's campaign swats at the "Nixon-Ford-Kissinger" administration for its "secret deals" and "policy by manipulation," and Vice President Walter Mondale described elements of Carter's policies as being designed to make "most Americans feel good." Kissinger, the analyst noted, "used to dismiss this kind of language in private, and sometimes even in public, as 'moralizing' or 'sermonizing.' In the end, the charge that Kissinger scorned morality became his heaviest burden."[23]

Whatever the impact of the Notre Dame speech and whatever the lingering perceptions of the previous administration may have been, Carter's designation of West as U.S. ambassador to Saudi Arabia was consistent with initiatives interpreted as distancing the new administration from the scarred legacy of its predecessors. "I understand fully the limits of moral suasion," Carter had said at Notre Dame. "I have no illusion that changes will come easily or soon. But I also believe that it is a mistake to undervalue the power of words and of the idea that words embody."[24]

The new strategies for the Middle East might also have contained a significant understanding that "step-by-step" diplomacy had fallen short because, in part, it implied that progress toward peace—particularly among the Arab nations—would follow a linear path. Such would not be the case. It was one thing to understand what lay on the surface of disputes in the Middle East in terms of territorial, political, and military issues; it was quite another thing to fathom the hidden intricacies and nuances of Arab style and diplomacy. Arab nations, and particularly the Saudis, often functioned in ways that defied the application of Western logic or predictability. Theirs was a highly personal and often fatalistic view of the world.

As described by the analyst David E. Long in 1976, "Saudis feel less inclined than Westerners to make their behavior appear consistent; like Orientals, their thinking is compartmentalized. Thus, political, business and personal relationships can be held separate, even at the cost of apparent inconsistency . . . all relationships are highly personalized. It occasionally comes as a shock to Western businessmen that Saudis have rejected their product or service, clearly the most competitive, because of a disinclination to do business with the person representing their firm."[25]

Another writer, in describing the Saudi fatalism, observed, "If you ask an average Saudi what he foresees politically in the next dozen years, he will almost automatically respond with a reference to the Will of God. . . . I have never met a Saudi, no matter how westernized, who would speak about the future, even something that was arranged the following day, without saying *Inshallah* (God willing)."[26]

There was also for the Saudis the awkwardness of sudden wealth and sudden power. The historian William Powell observed in a 1982 study:

> If there is an intensity and an enthusiasm in the Saudi that is rarely found elsewhere in the world, it is nothing in comparison to the size and intensity of the economic and political revolution that has swept Saudi Arabia from the farthest and most isolated reaches of the international backwater to the pinnacle of world power and influence in less than a decade.
>
> Since 1973, Saudi Arabia has emerged as a superpower equal in influence and economic power to either the United States or the Soviet Union. This emergence has taken place with a suddenness that has stunned and stupefied the rest of the world. Never before in human history has an economic and political revolution taken place on the scale of the one that is currently taking place on the Arabian peninsula.
>
> Saudi Arabia has burst through the back door into the twentieth century.[27]

As neighboring southern governors in the mid-1970s, both Carter and West had experienced firsthand the emerging power of the nation that controlled more than one-fourth of the known oil reserves in the world. They had watched the economies of their respective states, and the rest of the nation, go into a tailspin as an angry Saudi Arabia had spurred OPEC, through the oil minister Yamani, to raise unilaterally the price of crude oil by 70 percent, effective in mid-October 1973, and to reduce oil production by 5 percent per month subsequent to that time.[28] This experience would leave a lasting impression on both governors, and four years later both Carter and West recognized how essential a comfortable Saudi Arabia was to the healthy functioning of the U.S. economy, as well as that of the rest of the industrialized world. "The most important domestic issue I had to face was in the energy field, and I recognized that the royal family of Saudi Arabia could either be a very constructive factor or otherwise," Carter said in a 2004 interview. "For that reason, I saw the Saudi Arabian ambassadorship to be a very high priority for me."[29]

Given the daunting economic, political, and sociological complexities of that priority, Carter might have been expected to select for the post a well-seasoned career diplomat or a specialist in Arabic culture. Carter, however, also recognized that the Saudis would be high-maintenance friends whose values were often based on personal—not political—assessments, and whose security fears were based on real, and not imagined, threats to their treasures of oil resources. Building a friendship with the Saudis, it was also recognized, would be at the risk of damaging the long-standing friendship of the United States with the Israelis.

Carter believed, however—naively so, some contended—that a healthy infusion of personal diplomacy could go a long way toward settling disputes where traditional strategies had failed. Such beliefs not only reflected Carter's own style and the human dimension of his administration; they also seemed to fit well with the highly personal and often fatalistic perspective of the Saudi decision-making process. The selection of John West as ambassador to Saudi Arabia proved to be one of those instances in which Carter chose to go with his instincts, and to select a man whose best qualification was his ability to make political friends, sustain them, and build long-term trust and confidence.

"THE PERSON . . . TO MEET MY VERY HIGH EXPECTATIONS"

"There was no doubt in my mind that John West was the person for me to meet my very high expectations and a very specific charge," Carter said. "[He] went to Saudi Arabia . . . and immediately formed a personal compatibility with the King and with the Crown Prince and with other members of the royal family." West's success with the Saudis, Carter felt, could be attributed to "his sensitivity to other people, which I thought his life in South Carolina would have prepared him, especially in dealing with people of different races and different cultures."[30]

For his part, West acknowledged that the special relationship with Carter gave him early entrée into Saudi inner circles. "They saw me not as a conventional diplomat, but one who was Carter's personal choice, which was true, and they felt that if they had a problem, I could pick up the phone and get it resolved. And I did not disabuse them of that perception, although I used it rather infrequently."[31]

It did not hurt West's status with the Saudis that Carter had been the first U.S. president to advocate a homeland for the Palestinians, a distinction that gave him early credibility not just with the Saudis but also with other Arab nations. "It gave me a tremendous advantage going in as President Carter's personal representative," West later said.[32]

John West did not need a short course in Arab diplomacy to understand the vagaries of personal politics. It was a mission he could grasp almost instinctively. He had grown up politically amid the ambiguities of post–World War II South Carolina and had seen firsthand the contradictions of a state torn between its racial prejudices and its own economic ambitions. Given such inconsistencies and uncertainties, West had spent a lifetime investing his political capital heavily in personal friendships, cultivating them richly and hoping that they could withstand the strains and stresses of the unusual times. At his eightieth birthday celebration in Columbia in 2002, the numbers in attendance swelled into the hundreds, and if there was a distinction among personal friends, political friends, and professional friends, it was, as the English essayist and author Henry Fielding once wrote, "a distinction without a difference."

West, in fact, had grown up in a political world not only devoid of partisan politics but also without a great deal of ideology. In the cozy political community known as postwar South Carolina, the legislative process in which he became a master was often a series of shifting coalitions built as much on personality and friendships as it was on issues and philosophy. In that arena favors were swapped back and forth among friends, and power was not so much the fist of authority as it was the handclasp of friendship and trust.

When he announced in 1970 his plans to run for governor of South Carolina, all but one of his Democratic colleagues in the state Senate signed on as his campaign committee, and the only one who demurred did so over a personal grudge. West's slogan in his successful campaign for governor was simply "Elect a Good Man Governor."

If West's politics appeared uncomplicated, however, he was not unsophisticated. The disarming southerner was anything but naive, either as the stereotypically sage "country lawyer" in his hometown of Camden, as the "good man" governor of South Carolina, or as the unorthodox emissary of the Carter administration in the desert kingdom of Saudi Arabia. His ability to gain the personal confidence of disparate parties made him an enduring bridge among political elements who might not trust each other, but who did trust John West.

West's new world contained more than two thousand princes related by blood to all major tribes. The royal family was involved in virtually all aspects of Saudi life, including government, education, military affairs, and business. Such a prospect, formidable as it may have seemed to the political scientist, was less confounding to a practicing politician who was comfortable with the oligarchic style of ruling. West had grown up in a South Carolina dominated by the small-county baronies and fiefdoms that also controlled virtually all aspects of the state's life. As a three-term state senator, a lieutenant governor, and subsequently a governor, West could work adroitly within a system whose dominant figures—men such as longtime House Speaker Solomon Blatt, Senator Edgar Brown, and Senator Marion Gressette—were also men who had converted their mastery of personal politics into enduring political power. The skills West developed in their presence as colleague and friend in politically eccentric South Carolina would be the skills he brought to the job of extending a friendly American presence to the unusual kingdom of Saudi Arabia.

THE POLITICS OF THE HAPPY HOUR

West looked the role. Stocky, soft-spoken, and genial, he seemed more fatherly than bureaucratic, and his blue eyes twinkled at the prospect of a good joke or an anecdote. His open face was disarming and invited confidence, and he had a healthy exuberance for the good life, particularly as it applied to good food, good wine, and good social gatherings of interesting people. From his earliest days, West had the ability and the inclination to turn practically any event into a social occasion, and to use his personal charm unabashedly as an instrument of problem solving.

It was an outlook that hardly seemed suitable for what the State Department classified as one of its "hardship" postings, so designated because of the strict Saudi adherence to Islamic social principles, including no consumption of alcoholic beverages. Such principles were not strictly applicable to U.S. Embassy property, however, which was legally American territory, and that technicality gave West the opportunity to share his view of the "good life" with residents and guests alike. As long as functions were held in the embassy compound, they could include whatever food and drink the hosts desired, and the Wests took advantage of that provision to make the American embassy a place of Western civility and a discreet watering hole for some of the locals, including some who were educated in the United States and had become accustomed to a social cocktail on occasion. "I was the biggest bootlegger in Saudi Arabia," West joked in describing the spirits he imported under diplomatic privilege.[33] He also admitted that the embassy "saloon" was a good place to seek favors and do politicking among the more Westernized residents. It was a role West had spent a lifetime developing. Raised on a South Carolina farm, educated at the Citadel, transformed during World War II into a military intelligence officer, and reared politically in the state's rural oligarchy, West had an affinity for people and could make friends across a broad range of human backgrounds and experiences. He had a way of getting close to people, breaking down inhibitions, and leaving his associates with the feeling that they were not just casual acquaintances with John West; they were close, personal friends.

In that kind of atmosphere, the American embassy at Jeddah became a lot more than just an embassy. West converted it into a place that served up good hospitality, off-the-record diplomacy, consulting services, and business development support and was a way station for visiting Americans and a place of succor where those who had run afoul of Muslim law or custom could seek help or refuge. "John had a disease I called 'invite-itis,'" Lois West later recalled. "He entertained for breakfast, lunch and dinner and sometimes in between. He used it as a tool to do whatever it was he wanted done."[34]

The embassy also became a place where the serious business of transforming American Middle East policy could get the direct attention of a Saudi nation just emerging into prominent international visibility. The Saudis and the Americans actually traced their alliance back to the historic meeting of the two nations' aging leaders, President Franklin Roosevelt and King Abdul-Aziz ibn Saud, at the Suez Canal at the close of World War II. The meeting, held on February 14, 1945, aboard the cruiser USS *Quincy* in the Great Bitter Lake of the Suez Canal, was a personal success in that the American and Saudi leaders charmed each other and developed a friendship that lasted for the few weeks left in the life of the ailing President Roosevelt. For Roosevelt, however, it was considered a diplomatic failure in that he had hoped to win over ibn Saud's support for establishing a Jewish state in Palestine. "Arabs would choose to die [rather] than yield their land to the Jews," the Saudi king told the American president. "Make the enemy and the oppressor pay," ibn Saud told Roosevelt; "that is how we Arabs wage war. Amends should be made by the criminal, not the innocent bystander. What injury have the Arabs done to the Jews of Europe? It is the 'Christian' Germans who stole their homes and their lives. Let the Germans pay."[35]

Nonetheless the friendship outlived the memory of the diplomatic scuffle and proved to be symbolic of the relationship between the two nations over the years. Saudi and American businesses, diplomats, and government leaders would find areas of agreement and common profitable interests, sensing that beneath it all may have been fundamental differences over Israel but choosing to keep those differences obscure as long as there was stability in the region. The Saudis, in fact, one of the world's absolutist regimes, preferred to be viewed as behind-the-scenes players in the politics of the Middle East, and they used their financial wealth in a leveraging role among the Arab states.

All that began to change, however, as the Arab-Israeli feuds burst into wars in the 1960s and 1970s, creating a firestorm of political activity and forcing Western powers to recognize, as Secretary Vance had surmised, that the flow of oil so necessary for their economic well-being was directly dependent on political stability in the Middle East. It was with that recognition that the American embassy in Saudi Arabia was advanced to class A status by the State Department on a par with the rest of the world powers just prior to West's assuming the ambassadorship. Such recognition meant that Western powers had five major players to address in the Middle East, adding Saudi Arabia to the four that had previously been considered the primary influences in the Middle East: Egypt, Israel, Syria, and Jordan.

FELLOW SOUTHERN PRAGMATISTS

In West, Carter knew he had someone who was no stranger to political transformations. Like Carter, West had been part of the most dramatic change of American social, political, and economic life in the century—the civil rights movement and its eventual accommodation by "New South" governors in the 1960s and 1970s. Carter and West not only served as governors together in neighboring southern states, but they also had other elements of a remarkably common heritage. Both had grown up on southern dirt farms, both had served as officers in World War II, and both had their undergraduate degrees from military institutions—West from the Citadel in South Carolina and Carter from the U.S. Naval Academy. Both were moderate southern Democrats who—as fellow governors—steered their respective states and the region away from the racial violence and extremism that had greeted the civil rights movement elsewhere in the Deep South in the 1960s.

Both also represented the staunch practicality born of the wholesome and resourceful agrarianism that had quietly emerged in the South in the 1930s. Stunned by the suddenness of cotton-related economic failures of the 1920s and suspicious of laissez-faire political ideologues who rose to power with swaggering disdain for poverty in their region, southern farmers had become superb survivalists with unconventional ideas about how government could be tangibly and pragmatically helpful to the struggling masses. While political demagogues were fulminating against New Deal programs, likening them to socialism and communism, southern farmers were beginning to discover luxuries such as electric lights, telephones, and indoor plumbing, and they were not too worried about which ideology might have been violated to make it possible.

That pragmatism blossomed into a fresh progressivism in postwar America toward issues of racial tolerance and governmental programs of public assistance, public education, and economic development. West and Carter were in a cadre of southern governors, including Reuben Askew of Florida, Dale Bumpers of Arkansas, William Winter of Mississippi, Albert Brewer of Alabama, and Robert Scott of North Carolina, who were described as "moderate" and "New

South" governors and who did not worry so much about the labels "conservative" and "liberal" as they did about the deplorable living conditions under which many of their constituents found themselves. Roosevelt's aide Harry Hopkins was once told by New Deal critics that such programs could prove to be dangerous in the long run. Hopkins, the consummate pragmatist and insider, is credited with saying to the critic, "People do not eat in the long run. They eat every day."

It was the Depression-era value of eating every day that drove the political pragmatism of not only such initiatives as the New Deal but eventually also the Great Society programs of President Lyndon Johnson, a southerner from Texas, during the 1960s and the massive programs of human assistance and support spawned under that rubric. Fed by a rise in political activism among the nation's blue-collar and minority populations, and encouraged by the nation's postwar economic prosperity, political optimism and confidence were rife. People such as John F. Kennedy could tell the nation with confidence that America could put a man on the moon by the end of the twentieth century, and Lyndon Johnson believed that America could declare a "War on Poverty" and win it.

OUTBURSTS OF PRACTICAL OPTIMISM

That same kind of inordinate optimism had prompted John West, upon taking office as governor of South Carolina on January 19, 1971, to create his own set of impossible-dream goals for the state. "We can, and we shall, in the next four years eliminate from our government any vestige of discrimination because of race, creed, sex, religion or any other barrier to fairness for all citizens," he declared in his inaugural address. "We can, and we shall, in the next four years eliminate hunger and malnutrition, and their attendant suffering from our state," he said on the same occasion.[36] It was quite a leap for a state that had institutionally denied for years the existence of hunger and malnutrition in its midst, despite national reports to the contrary.

It was also quite a leap for a state that had, only seventeen years earlier, led the charge to the Supreme Court to defend its segregated school system, a charge that had resulted in the 1954 *Brown v. Board of Education* Supreme Court decision striking down the institution of racially separate school systems in the South.

"We pledge to minority groups no special status other than full-fledged responsibility in a government that is totally color-blind," he told his inaugural audience, which included many who had actively worked to perpetuate South Carolina's separate societies for decades.[37] When West left office four years later, no one did an audit to see if the goals had been attained, largely because no one really thought they were attainable anyhow. Some dismissed them as only so much political rhetoric from a man whose victory was owed largely to a good turnout of black voters across the state. Others knew that for John West, wishful thinking often found its way into public policy and that there was in him a Don Quixote element that could be fresh and delightful to some and provocative and downright troublesome to others.

West was, at heart, a gambler and risk taker whose mild-mannered countenance belied some radical thinking he was bringing to a very conservative southern state. To the consternation of some of his cautious political friends, he advocated successfully the creation of a state agency that could help moderate-income families afford home ownership. He infuriated his staunch supporters in the Charleston area by leading the fight to create a new medical school at the University of South Carolina in order to increase the number of physicians in doctor-poor South Carolina, a step viewed as threatening to the state's 150-year-old medical university in Charleston. In addition he took up a lonely vigil in opposition to capital punishment, applying to that politically popular legislation a veto he knew would be overridden by the General Assembly. In his veto message he said simply that he did not believe one human being should take the life of another.

In other instances West's political charm could work wonders. For example, he scored a major political coup when he persuaded the longtime segregationist Senator Marion Gressette to sponsor legislation creating a state-level civil rights agency, the State Human Affairs Commission. With Gressette's power behind it, the legislation passed the almost all-white General Assembly without opposition.

EMBRACING THE DISAGREEMENTS

West's against-the-grain initiatives kept things stirring in a state that was still reeling from the 1960s and the powerful upheavals wrought by the civil rights transformation. While the racial tensions of the previous decades had not run their course by any means, West's strategies made him a partner and fellow traveler with the reformers, rather than an adversary. When he made the historic decision to desegregate his own executive staff in the governor's office, he chose a high-profile leader of the civil rights movement in Charleston, James E. Clyburn, who was not bashful about disagreeing with West privately or in public. This disturbed some, but it gave West tons of credibility among the state's black political leaders.

Years later West recalled a query from the press about the differing opinions he and Clyburn had expressed on the same day in separate speeches about the condition of race relations in the state. That difference had found its way into conspicuously contradictory side-by-side stories in one of the state's daily newspapers. "My official response was that people on my staff, as well as people everywhere, were free to speak whatever opinions they might have, whether I agreed with them or not," he quipped. "Down deep, of course, and I did not say this at the time, but I knew full well that nobody was going to tell Jim Clyburn what to say or what not to say."[38] Along the way West and Clyburn formed a close personal friendship, which only grew as Clyburn became powerful nationally as a congressman from South Carolina's poverty-stricken Sixth District.

West's liberalism was not an exercise in doctrinaire conformity. His association with the Jimmy Carter administration was not built entirely on ideology, and it was more than a matter of good-ol'-boy southern friendships. Carter's victory represented the wholehearted injection of pragmatism into presidential politics four years after the worst Democratic loss in fifty years in 1972 by the liberal candidate George McGovern.

Carter was the first American governor to be elected to the presidency since Franklin Roosevelt in 1932, and he would pave the way for subsequent victories by former governors in both parties—Ronald Reagan, Bill Clinton, and George W. Bush. As an ambassador without a Washington background under a president without a Washington background, John West fit nicely into that evolving trend away from "inside the beltway" politics.

West's disaffection with the Washington establishment, however, was not an aggressive, deliberate campaign. It was an inevitable and unintentional outcome for a man whose style was spontaneous and informal, whose politics were personal, and whose values were practical. He was a South Carolinian who had gotten his political upbringing in the racially tinged politics of the 1950s, sharpened his skills and wits in the practice of small-town law, matured within the oligarchic precincts of state government, and whose values grew out of the day-to-day struggles of a Depression-era farming family. These were the values that would guide South Carolina peacefully and progressively through troubled years of racial and economic transformation. And these were the values with which American interests would be represented in the Middle East during the critical years of peace heeping and alliance building with the kingdom of Saudi Arabia.

TWO

WHERE THE NEW SOUTH WAS BORN

I remember my mother saying that she had to make a decision whether to cry or cuss. She decided to cuss.

John West

John West's photo appeared prominently in the March 29, 1971, edition of *U.S. News and World Report,* accompanying an article that proclaimed bravely that the politics of race in the South was virtually a thing of the past. "The South is seen as entering a new era of moderation in politics," the article suggested. "Racial issues are not entirely dead, but increasingly, the growing number of moderate, middle-income whites is represented as being unresponsive to racial appeals."[1]

The rosy—and ultimately naive—picture of southern liberation from its racial obsessions came sixty-two days after West had made the extraordinary appeal for racial justice in his inaugural address on January 19, 1971. His remarks were offered in the context of what was seen by national news analysts as an overall softening of the southern political outlook on race. Part of that softening, *U.S. News and World Report* figured, came from the simple reality that black political power had risen conspicuously in the wake of federal court orders and the Voting Rights Act of 1965 enhancing black access to the ballot box and voter registration.

Blacks registered in the South, in fact, had risen from 2.1 million in the pre–Voting Rights Act year of 1964 to 3.3 million in 1970, a leap of more than 57 percent in six years, the magazine reported. In South Carolina, with the second-highest percentage of black population among the eleven states of the

Old Confederacy, there had been an increase of almost 50 percent in the same period, from 144,000 to 214,000. All the demographic change had left a distinct impact on southern political values. "In the South Carolina gubernatorial race," the article noted, "it is conceded that John C. West . . . won because he pitched his campaign toward the blacks as well as the whites. The Republican, Representative Albert Watson, ignored the black vote."[2]

Racially divisive politics, in fact, had been an early foundation of the two-party system ever since Barry Goldwater's failed bid for the presidency in 1964. That campaign had given new hope to old-line southern conservatives and die-hard segregationists and had triggered the landmark switch of S.C. senator Strom Thurmond from the Democratic Party to the Republican Party during the 1964 presidential campaign. There were many conversions to the Left and the Right during the fluid years of the 1950s and early 1960s, and a number of former segregationist Democrats in the South either changed parties and became Republicans or changed philosophies and remained with the newly moderate Democrats.

BUILDERS, NOT CRUSADERS

Some of the emerging moderates were, in fact, hardly social crusaders on racial missions. They were convinced, however, that racial peace was good business. It opened up vast new labor pools among minorities previously underemployed, and it showed to the world a certain emerging maturity among business, professional, and political leaders in the state.

That argument carried a lot of weight among community leaders, whatever their personal sentiments may have been, and southern governors used it as part of the portfolio they carried into other parts of the nation and world seeking to import new jobs and industry to their states. They were hailed as "New South" governors, largely in a business sense, and among their numbers were onetime segregationists converted by the realities of economic needs and the growing black political power in their region. New South governors were aggressive salesmen whose racial moderation was largely defined by their willingness to accept and implement peacefully the dictates of federal court orders and acts of Congress with regard to the desegregation of public accommodations, schools, and colleges and the opening up of voting processes to black citizens. Among the early generations of moderates, their politics were cautious and they were viewed as peacekeepers as much as overtly racial progressives.

To the nonsouthern world, they were greeted enthusiastically as men of goodwill who were replacing the Claghorn stereotype of southern political eccentrics.[3] The emerging southern image was that of serious, businesslike faces

of political CEOs. The success of men such as Luther Hodges and Terry Sanford of North Carolina, Carl Sanders of Georgia, and Ernest "Fritz" Hollings
and Bob McNair of South Carolina brought billions of dollars and tens of
thousands of jobs to their respective states and paved the way for the emerging South, which would become the economic and political powerhouse of
the nation in the late twentieth and early twenty-first centuries. These were the
governors, the scholar Gordon Harvey would write decades later, who "helped
the region transform itself from Jim Crow South to Sunbelt South."[4]

There was something different about the governors who made up the "Class
of 1971," however. Their New South was a place where there could be open and
candid conversations about the latent issues of poverty, bigotry, and segregation that had characterized southern life for so long. Unlike the restraint of
their recent predecessors, this cadre of governors did not feel it necessary to
address those issues quietly or indirectly, or to package them discreetly as part
of an overall business development strategy. The New South of the Class of
1971 became a place where the residual human failures of the previous generations could be identified in broad daylight, a place where John West could
publicly stare down the specters of poverty, prejudice, and hunger to the appro-
batory cheers of thousands.

That is what caught the attention of *U.S. News and World Report* and
caused its editors to select four rising stars of the Democratic Party—Jimmy
Carter of Georgia, Reuben Askew of Florida, Dale Bumpers of Arkansas, and
John West of South Carolina—for special attention. They were, the magazine
reckoned, future contenders for national prominence who "were not deeply
scarred by the segregation issues of the past. Now they command a degree of
political independence, and are even able to entertain ambitions for second
place on the national ticket."[5]

It proved to be an accurate piece of political speculation, if somewhat under-
stated, for a period when the Watergate scandal of 1972–73 would cast things
in a distinctly anti-Washington condition only about a year later. Three of the
four would run for president with varying degrees of intensity, and one of
them—Carter—would be successful in 1976. The fourth, John West, would
have his own national and international impact as an important player in the
Carter administration.

HOMEGROWN REFORMERS

The four governors of the New South Class of 1971 did, in fact, bring certain
independence to their thinking. None of the four was necessarily a "convert"
to the causes of racial justice; rather their inclinations were homegrown and

intuitive. They were products of a distinctly southern liberalism not developed from ideological dogma or political convenience. Theirs was a liberalism born of personal experience in the economic wastelands of the 1920s and 1930s South. Their political instincts were shaped by seeing firsthand the human suffering occasioned by a "laissez-faire" economic system of brutish indifference to that suffering and a political system that trivialized political rights amid the mythology of historical lost causes and racial bigotry. Each of the Class of 1971 governors had his own personal ordeal that energized his political ambition.

For Jimmy Carter, the New South began on a farm in southwest Georgia, where he and his family lived a relatively affluent life among the desperate sharecroppers and tenants who populated that corner of rural America. The Carters were landowners and operated a farm that—despite Carter's longtime identity as a "peanut farmer"—was diversified and included significant livestock operations. Carter saw firsthand the effects of poverty on his neighbors and friends in Plains, Georgia. "Someone had to be blamed when the ravages of the Depression years struck," he later wrote, "and many of the smoldering resentments against Yankees and the federal government were given new life in my childhood. Yet, with the racially segregated social system virtually unchallenged, it seemed that blacks and whites accepted each other as partners in their shared poverty."[6]

Reuben Askew grew up in outright desperate conditions. He was born to impoverished parents in Muskogee, Oklahoma; was abandoned by his father; and grew up with five siblings in Pensacola, Florida, where they had been taken by their mother. According to Gordon Harvey, "Askew sold magazines, shined shoes, bagged groceries and sold his mother's homemade pies to supplement her income as a waitress and a Works Progress Administration seamstress."[7]

Dale Bumpers, Arkansas governor and U.S. senator for sixteen years, was born and raised in dismally poor Charleston, Arkansas. "I grew up in the depths of the Great Depression," Bumpers wrote in an autobiography published in 2003. "Charleston was little different culturally, economically and socially from thousands of small towns where hunger was a constant threat and often a reality, but it was worse in the South. There was no snob value in being poor. Everybody was poor."[8]

The conditions that would make fellow travelers of the four New South governors were also being played out all across South Carolina in the early 1920s. Like Carter's, West's upbringing was in relative comfort amid families living in conditions of desperate poverty. His home was a relic of the Old South, a 220-acre "four-horse" farm in the Kershaw County community of Charlotte Thompson. "A four-horse farm," West explained years later, "was a farm worked by four mules (not horses). There were four black families who worked on the farm as day laborers and the farm had a substantial mortgage."9

West's father had purchased the farm just prior to the collapse of cotton prices in 1920, when the value of cotton tumbled from an average of forty-two cents a pound to nine cents a pound in less than a year. Then came the boll weevil, an infestation that further damaged farmers' already desperate plight. By the time of John West's birth in 1922, the price of cotton was five cents a pound.

A TRANSFORMING TRAGEDY

The collapse of the cotton economy in the 1920s and the subsequent nation-wide Depression in the 1930s were not the worst disasters that befell the West family in those hazardous times. A catastrophic event that would change for-ever the West family and its farming community struck before John West was a year old. "My early childhood was overshadowed by one great event, 'The Fire,'" West recalled. "On May 23, 1923, the Cleveland School was destroyed by fire, killing 77 people, including my father. From that day forward, all events were dated as either before or after the fire. It certainly influenced the rest of my life."10

The Cleveland School, which lay about one mile from the West farm, was a wooden two-story building, twenty by fifty-six feet, that had been constructed in 1908. There was a single point of entry and exit, no fire escape, and a single narrow stairway that connected the two classrooms on the ground floor to the larger open classroom area on the second floor, a space that was also used for assemblies and other public gatherings. Like most rural buildings of its time, the Cleveland School had no electricity and used a natural spring and outdoor facilities for its water and plumbing needs. Daytime lighting was provided through long, glass-paned windows, and evening events were lighted by kero-sene lamps.

West's mother, Mattie Ratterree West, was a teacher at the Cleveland School, which for its time was considered a model facility. It was described by the his-torian Dale Hudson as being "as sturdy and as fine a school as any built in Ker-shaw County, even in the state. Citizens . . . took education of their children seriously and prided themselves on the achievements and contributions to the community attained by those who had previously attended the school."11

The 1920s, however, were times in which the state was taking an increas-ingly active role in public education, and state officials were calling for the con-solidation of many of the small rural schools. Scheduled for consolidation in 1923 were the Cleveland, Boykin, and McLeod schools, and a wealthy Baltimore native newly arrived in the Camden area, Charlotte de Macklot Thompson, had offered as the location for the new school the home of former governor Stephen D. Miller, recently restored through her funding and support.

The offer was accepted, which meant that the Cleveland School, although only fifteen years old at the time, would be closed after the 1922–23 school year. Acceptance of the offer also meant that the commencement exercise scheduled for May 23 would be the last event to take place at the school. Festivities were planned to commemorate the occasion, including a picnic and an evening performance of a school play, a three-act production called *Miss Topsy Turvy*.[12] The second floor of the building was decorated and lighted for the event and was filled with four hundred students, family members, and teachers. As the third act of the play began, around nine o'clock in the evening, one of the kerosene lamps suspended from the ceiling near the stairs worked free of its fastener, dropped to the floor, and immediately spread a coating of kerosene on the wooden floor. Within minutes the room was in flames and smoke, and the building was quickly devoured. It all happened, it was later determined, in a matter of twenty minutes.

Inside the building were West's parents; his older brother, Shell, age four; and two cousins. John West, nine months old at the time, was too young to attend. As the fire quickly spread across the heart-pine walls and floors and ignited decorative hay and curtains, people rushed for the only exit, the narrow stairs at the rear of the building. The stairwell quickly became clogged and blocked, and when the stairs collapsed under the weight of people, it became a death scene for many helpless victims. John West recalled, "My father was outside, and seeing the flames, he rushed to go upstairs where my mother, my four-year-old brother [Shell], and my grandmother [Mrs. John Ratterree] were. My father was met by a mass of humanity on the stairs, and when the stairs collapsed, he was pinned under them. His body was never identified."[13]

West's mother, brother, and grandmother had actually escaped by then, thanks to the quick thinking of his mother. John West later wrote:

> Mother saw the stairs collapse, and she turned to the second story balcony, which was about 30 feet above the ground. Realizing that people could not jump, she saw that the flagpole in front of the building was close to the balcony. She turned to two men, Alex Bruce and Stony Campbell, and told them to break the flagpole so that people could slide safely to the ground from the balcony.
>
> They did that, and many people on the second floor were saved by sliding down the pole. My grandmother, then 70 years old, was one who was

saved, and later blamed her arthritic condition on the bruises she sustained the night of the fire. My brother, Shell, age four, was too young to slide down the pole, so Mother yelled to people on the ground to catch him, and she threw him to some people below.

Shell often said they didn't catch him, but they broke his fall. I don't know how many people were saved by sliding down the pole, but there were many. Alex Bruce, who remained a dear friend and neighbor (we called him "Squire"), always said Mother was the real hero of the fire.[14]

An account produced years later offered a slightly different version of the West family plight. West's father, according to that account, escaped with his wife, son, and mother-in-law but was still concerned about his nieces inside the building. The nieces, it was explained, had been seated at the front of the auditorium in reserved seats and had become blocked in the narrow stairwell. Standing outside with his wife and mother-in-law, West's father was described as being "bound to save them." Watching in horror as the building burned, "they begged Shell [West's father] not to go back in, but the call to save his relatives was stronger. He kissed his wife and went back to rescue his nieces. He would never have the opportunity to kiss his wife again."[15]

THE LOSS OF A YOUNG FATHER

Shell West was thirty-seven at the time of his death in the Cleveland fire, and he was one of relatively few adults among the seventy-seven people who perished in the horrendous event. Most were children, twenty-eight of whom were students at Cleveland School. Like that of Shell West, most of the bodies were never identified, and a mass burial for sixty-two of the unidentified victims was arranged the next day on the grounds of Beulah Methodist Church. There, Governor Thomas G. McLeod, from nearby Bishopville, delivered an emotional address. Some of the victims, he said, "I have known all my life. They were my best friends and their deaths cause me untold grief. I wish I could say something to convey my sympathy."[16] Among the victims were eight members of the McLeod family.

The governor launched a nationwide fund-raising effort, which brought some one hundred thousand dollars in donations to the small community. He also initiated action to make South Carolina schools safer in the future. In the days before fire codes and mandatory fire escapes, he discovered that two-thirds of the schools in the state were similarly vulnerable to fire.

Things were never the same for the Wests or for the community after the fire. Facing West's widowed mother was the toughest decision of her life: whether to sell the farm and return to teaching or stick it out as a rare single woman head of household on a Depression-era "four-horse" farm. She chose the latter. "She had been a teacher at the Cleveland School," West later wrote, "and presumably would have continued to teach at Charlotte Thompson. However, she made the decision to forego teaching and run the farm. . . . Her reasoning was that her two boys—my brother and I—needed her attention and she could better care for us by staying home and farming than teaching."[17]

For all the long-term benefit the West boys would derive from having a stay-at-home mom who could enrich their educational experience, the decision threw the family into almost immediate economic peril. Nearby farms, many of them smaller "one-horse" operations, were already failing in the wake of the cotton collapse, and foreclosure was becoming a common occurrence. The West farm was no exception. According to West,

> Many people were forced to sell their property for taxes.
>
> The Federal Land Bank was the principal lender of farms, and they foreclosed on almost all in our community. One of my most vivid recollections is the sheriff serving us with an eviction notice. Mother just refused to move. She just sat there and they had to give her notice.[18]

West later wrote:

> Mother, fortunately, had saved approximately $5,000 from her school teaching years and had invested in school bonds. They were the only currency recognized at the time, and she was able—through that—to repurchase the farm. . . .
>
> I remember my mother saying that she had to make a decision whether to cry or cuss. She decided to cuss.[19]

What ensued were years of hardship but not desperation for the West family. "We were never hungry and never lacked adequate clothes," West recalled. With cotton no longer profitable as a crop, the family turned to alternatives. "We didn't make any money out of cotton or corn. . . . I used to pick the boll weevils for a penny apiece. But what really did it [earned money], we kept two or three cows, and I did the milking. We sold butter and had chickens and sold the eggs, and every year we would kill a hog. We also had an extensive vegetable garden. We lived off the farm, and we would generate some income from the side lines there."[20]

West also recalled the uncommon image of his mother riding her horse, Trina, over the farm to supervise activities and to watch farmhands plow, hoe, and pick whatever crops could be raised in the weevil-infested fields. "She soon had a reputation for being a tough woman," West recalled.[21] In addition, "she became one of the most respected farmers and leaders in that decimated community."[22]

A WOMAN TAKES CHARGE

The notion of women being in charge of things remained with West through the years as a matter of accepted practice, and it eventually was a part of his deeply held political beliefs. While he was best remembered by many as a champion of the rights of racial minorities, John West was something of a pioneer in the advocacy of women's rights. He elevated women to positions of seniority on his own staff as governor and vigorously supported the creation of the Commission on the Status of Women as a permanent state agency for addressing gender issues and for promoting and defending women's rights. Even though it was opposed by old-line traditionalists in the state, he successfully advocated the conversion of Lois West's alma mater, Winthrop College, from all-women to coeducation status.

"I remember that my mother was probably the first woman, certainly in that area, actually to run a farm," he wrote.[23] It was also in that setting that young John West, learning the chores of a farm boy, came upon an experience that he contended throughout his life was "a defining moment." As his skills as a storyteller grew later in life, this story became one of his favorites, which he would tell with great relish and detail:

> It was 1937, and one day when [high] school was out, Mother said there was an extra mule and—as she put it—"the grass is growing in the corn." I drew the mule named Maude, which was the poorest of the four mules we had, and was the one that I—as the younger person—was given to plow.
>
> The task on this particular June day was "skimming" corn. This translates into the mule, with a 20-inch steel plow, or "skim," going down between the corn rows plowing the grass, turning it upside down so that it would die, and not choke out the young corn. In this particular field, in front of the house, there was what was known as "wire grass," or "Johnson grass." It was especially hard to plow, because the roots of this type of grass were tough and deep. ·
>
> I struggled with the plow and the mule until about three o'clock in the afternoon. By then, I had completely given out, or—as the country phrase went—"The monkey had me." I looked over to where two hands—both black men—were plowing the same field. Their furrows were straight and they were plowing at about twice my pace. At three o'clock in the afternoon, perspiration was rolling off them, but they were in good spirits and not missing a beat. At that time, their wage was fifty cents a day.

Fifteen-year-old farm boy John West, in his Sunday best. Courtesy of the John C. West Papers, South Carolina Political Collections, University of South Carolina

As I stood at the end of that row, I thought to myself that at that rate, I was worth no more than twenty-five cents a day as a plow hand. So I had better take advantage of educational opportunities. . . .

At any time in my subsequent life, when I became discouraged with studying, I thought back to that incident and said that education would be my only salvation.[24]

West liked to tell the story because he enjoyed poking fun at himself. It also served as a parable—a moment of personal testimony—in support of the homegrown liberalism he shared with the likes of Jimmy Carter, Reuben Askew, Dale Bumpers, and many other southerners of his generation. The two farm-hands who demonstrably plowed better than young John West on that hot June day lacked the fundamental education to advance much further in their lives than fifty-cents-a-day manual labor. One of them was illiterate: "I had to write his name after he 'touched the pen,'" West recalled.[25] The other farmhand had the equivalent of a third-grade education.

Thirty-four years later, in his 1971 inaugural address, West would say, "We can, and we shall, provide a better educational opportunity for all citizens of whatever age or status, from a comprehensive pre-school program for the very young to a continuing educational program for adults, ranging from basic literacy to sophisticated advanced research-oriented graduate programs." It was the moment for West to remember the plight of the two farmhands skimming corn on that June day in 1937. It was also his moment to proclaim that the racially segregated school system in South Carolina, which had operated for the first seven decades of the twentieth century on a so-called separate-but-equal basis, had been a cynical ruse and a political sham that numbered among its victims those two farmhands.

EDUCATING THE FARM BOYS

In those tenuous days of 1937, however, issues of such magnitude were off in the distant future. Of more immediate concern to Mattie West were the successful management of her four-horse farm and—as they grew older—the education of her two sons. For some years the schoolteacher in Mattie West had recognized that both Shell and John were potential college material and that the younger of the two possessed uncommon intellectual capacity. By then she began making a practice of sitting in on classes at the Charlotte Thompson School to assess firsthand the quality of the education her sons were getting. In time she came to believe that schooling at Charlotte Thompson would not adequately prepare her sons for the kind of post–high school experience she had in mind for them.

The place they belonged, she determined, was Camden High School, a larger and more comprehensive institution that she felt would be better equipped to develop the skills and talents of the likes of the West boys. For its size Camden was a sophisticated and historical town. It had been an inland trading center in South Carolina's pre–Revolutionary War days and was the site of a major battle between British Regulars under Lord Charles Cornwallis and American Continentals under General Horatio Gates.

In more recent times it had become popular among wealthy northerners as an off-season home and as a center for steeplechase activities, including the popular Carolina Cup, a fashionable social event for nearby enthusiasts. A number of prominent families wintered there, and it attained some attention as the hometown of the financier and longtime political insider Bernard Baruch. In that kind of setting Camden High School was no ordinary small-town educational institution; it was considered among the best in the state.

As she contemplated enrolling her sons there, however, Mattie West faced obstacles. For one thing, her neighbors in the closely knit community feared—correctly, as it turned out—that the loss of the Wests would eventually doom their school, numerically as well as intellectually. "She didn't give a darn what people thought as long as she thought she was right," John West later said.[26] "Mother had one ambition in life. She had been to college for maybe one semester and had gotten a teacher's certificate. She wanted to see my brother and me get an education, a college education. That was her ultimate goal."[27] The woman who had opted to cuss rather than cry eleven years earlier after the death of her husband was not about to be deterred. Over the objections of neighbors, she enrolled John and Shell in Camden High School because "she was more concerned about her children's education and she knew that neither of us would succeed in college if we did not get better preparation."[28]

As early as the third grade, young John West had begun to display academic aptitude. "I had combined the third and fourth grades in a single year for various reasons, including the one that I was so bad that the teacher in the third grade wanted to get rid of me," West recalled wryly. "My mother's version was that I was not challenged. At any rate, I had developed a fairly quick mind and was able to skip a grade and still meet the school standards."[29]

There was another obstacle, a more logistical one, to the school transfer. The Wests lived six miles from Camden, and there was no school transportation available at the time. To solve the problem, Mattie West dipped into the dwindling savings account and came up with enough to purchase a small, inexpensive import, a British-made Austin. "In 1934 [when John West was twelve], we started driving the six miles back and forth to school over rough, often impassable roads. At least the car was economical; we got about 40 or 50 miles to the gallon."[30]

MEETING HIS MATCH

West's early school years at Charlotte Thompson had been eventful ones, however, and none was more memorable than the occasion on which he met—at age seven—his wife-to-be, Lois Rhame of Camden. According to West's account, it took place under conditions not entirely favorable to the young farm boy, a second-grader at the time, and it left a deep imprint and some specific memories. West recalled:

> There was a speaking contest held countywide for all schools. It was called a "declamation contest" and it was the subject of much rivalry between the rural schools and the Camden schools.
>
> I represented Charlotte Thompson, and my subject was the story entitled, "I Have a Little Shadow." My opponent from the comparable grade in Camden was a little blonde named Lois Rhame, whose subject was "Little Orphan Annie."

She won, and according to my mother's version, I cried, and she comforted me by telling me that the judges favored her because she was a girl.

At any rate, the way Lois tells the story now is that I married her to get even, and since the marriage has lasted well beyond fifty years, maybe it was good retribution for both of us.[31]

Lois Rhame admitted years later that she scarcely remembered young West at the declamation contest, except that he was "tubby. He was fat. His mother fed him well. She fed him pound cake and whipped cream and all that stuff."[32]

Generations earlier the Rhames had been early settlers in the Wateree River area at Spring Hill, and Lois was the youngest of five children born to Boykin Wilson Rhame and Annie Lois Lowrey Rhame. She had three older brothers—Boykin, Walter, and Robert—and a sister, Nora. A sixth Rhame child, Edward, died as an infant. Her mother was born and raised just across the North Carolina border in the town of Monroe, twenty miles southeast of Charlotte in those days and now a suburb of the large metropolis. Her father was a farmer and merchant in partnership with his brothers in the Rhame Brothers company in Kershaw County. "They sold mules originally, and then went to tractors and farm equipment," Lois West recalled.[33] The family owned farmland in Kershaw County, but the Rhame residence was on Laurens Street in Camden, where Lois grew up.

Whatever the memories of the declamation contest may have been, young West was beginning to discover the joy not just of excelling in his school work but also of matching wits with his peers. As his mother was observing, he was growing restless in the Charlotte Thompson setting, where he was not fully challenged intellectually and where he may have been drifting into the kind of habits that made him, in his own joking words, "so bad that the teacher in the third grade wanted to get rid of me."

At Camden High his intellect could be challenged by good teachers, and his view of the world around him could be expanded. He bore out his mother's expectations by taking enthusiastically to the school's broad-based academic program, not only compiling impressive grades but also representing the school in oratorical contests and regional competitions in Latin, English, French, and history. Along the way he also blossomed as something of a schoolhouse politician and journalist, serving as a class officer and editor in chief of the high school paper.

West became fascinated by journalism. Even though the paper he edited at Camden High was produced on a mimeograph machine, it set off in him a passion for the newspaper business in general. This passion would take the form of newspaper ownership later in life and would also shape an important dimension of his political life. West enjoyed writing and devoted much energy and effort to chronicling the events around him, a trait that caused the University of South Carolina archivist Herbert Hartsook years later to observe, "His is one of the best-documented governorships, probably in United States history. He had a remarkable sense of history."[34]

West's journalistic interests also gave him a remarkable appreciation for reporting as a job and as a profession, and he often acknowledged to friends that had he not chosen law for a career, he would have become a journalist. Throughout his public life West was comfortable and natural among reporters; he understood their jobs, and they knew that. He never fell prey to the tendency of political figures to blame reporters for stories they did not like, and he never once issued a "no comment." John West was his own best press secretary and did not hesitate to assume that role on any given occasion.

The mimeographed newspaper gave West another outlet. "I sometimes wrote a gossip column, which caused some concern and threats from friends who didn't want their dates publicized," he later wrote.[35] There was an impishness in the young scholar that would blossom into full-blown wit and a disarming, self-deprecating sense of humor. He liked a good story, and he was particularly comfortable if the joke was on him.

Along the way he became adept in the social world, and while his personality was never flamboyant or charismatic, he had a quiet charm that stood him so well in social and political settings that it was sometimes difficult to separate one from the other. It was not lost on anyone either that John West was becoming interested in his childhood friend, rival, and Camden High classmate Lois Rhame.

Lois considered the friendship to be a casual one and still regarded John West as the "chubby" guy. She recalled, "The first time I remember John was in high school. [He was] ahead of me in high school, and he drove that little Austin. He and [his brother] Shell had a little Austin car. . . . We double-dated. He dated my best friend, Betty Boineau [sister of the future House member Charles Boineau], and I dated Phil Boykin. We double-dated all the time."[36]

AN EMERGING SCHOLAR

For all the new social diversions, however, young John West was a natural scholar. He was not only up to the new academic challenges; he enjoyed them. "The school was excellent according to the standards of the time," he recalled. "We had some dedicated teachers. The principal, L. W. McFadden, instilled in me a love of mathematics which I had never had; Miss Alberta Team introduced me to Latin, and I thoroughly enjoyed that."[37] It proved Mattie West correct; these were experiences that probably would not have occurred at Charlotte Thompson.

West finished Camden High School with a remarkable academic record. His 92.5 average was third best in his class of sixty and the highest for a male student. He was a Beta Club and Honor Society member, and along with his school paper editorship, he was compiling the kind of well-rounded record that would make him a prime prospect for advancement to higher education.

West's older brother, Shell, had enrolled in the state's military college, the Citadel, and as he completed his second year at the Charleston college, West recalled, "Our family savings had been exhausted except for the cash value of a small insurance policy ($250), which was my college nest egg."[38] On April 11, 1938, the sixteen-year-old West wrote a letter to Citadel president General Charles P. Summerall asking to be considered for a scholarship to the military institution. The one-and-one-half-page letter, to which was attached his transcript, summarized his record and concluded, "I am prompted in asking for this scholarship solely because my father is dead and the small income is not sufficient to bear the expense of both my brother and me in college."[39]

West's letter was written with the knowledge that a scholarship had been granted a year earlier for a designated Camden student to attend the Citadel. It was part of a larger scholarship program endowed by one of Camden's wealthy winter residents, the New York financier and philanthropist Clark Williams. Williams, through his wartime friendship with Citadel president Summerall, had established a Citadel scholarship program in 1932 named in honor of the First Division, American Expeditionary Forces (AEF), the unit to which he had been attached as an American Red Cross representative during World War I. The scholarship program came at a time when the state of South Carolina was struggling in its Depression-era economic desperation, and the Williams grants brought to the Charleston institution students from throughout the nation who probably would not have attended the money-strapped state military school otherwise.

In the days before Scholastic Aptitude Tests and other preadmission screening exercises influenced colleges' admissions and grants policies, scholarships had a distinctly personal note. In 1936 Williams had decided to expand his Citadel grant program to include the son of his Camden plantation manager, William Wannamaker Bates Jr., as the recipient of what became the Camden Scholarship. Two years later he decided that the farm boy with the impressive Camden High School records should become the second Camden Scholarship recipient. In his letter of acceptance dated June 13, 1938, West wrote, "I am very

John West graduated from the Citadel in 1942, and six months after the attack on Pearl Harbor he went directly into active duty. Courtesy of Lois R. West and Shelton W. Bosley

grateful for the opportunity of attending The Citadel, which would have been otherwise impossible."[40]

Winning the scholarship from Colonel Williams, as it turned out, proved to be more than an educational opportunity for young John West. It also gave him membership in what amounted to a small but wide-ranging family of scholarship recipients whose members came from such locations as Los Angeles, Cleveland, Chicago, and New York, places far beyond the experience of the Kershaw County teenager. Williams hoped that the scholarship recipients would cohere as his "Citadel Sons," and West remembered some of them decades later. "The other cadets at The Citadel on the Williams scholarship," he wrote, "included Jake Burrows, who was two years ahead of me and became a Cadet Colonel; along with Frank Freeman and Stan Zyndra, all very bright leaders in the academic and military life."[41]

JOINING A FAMILY OF "CITADEL SONS"

Williams sponsored a total of twenty-two scholarships at the Citadel between 1932 and 1943, of which four were for Camden students. Recipients went on to serve militarily in North Africa, the Pacific, and Europe during World War II, and most of them wrote annual letters back to Williams and his wife, keeping them informed of their locations and activities. The Williamses, in turn, bundled the letters and distributed them back to their "Citadel Sons," so that they kept apprised of each other's activities.

Four of John West's letters have been retained at the Citadel in a collection of correspondence from Camp Stewart, Georgia (June 1943); Fort Eustis, Virginia (December 1943); Camp Stewart (May 1944); and Tokyo (November 1945). They tell of his personal experiences and, to the extent possible, the military activities in which he was engaged. They are newsy, personal, and thoughtful letters and reflect his growing ability to write brightly and coherently.[42]

West later acknowledged the Williams scholarship as "a godsend to our family." He wrote that "Shell was able to continue and we both started working on the NYA (National Youth Administration), doing various services at the school at the time. Shell worked in the Armory, and I ended up working in the public relations department."[43]

West by then had become a facile writer and had picked up typing skills along the way (he spent a semester during his senior year in high school taking a typing course), so that he could crank out Citadel news releases and other materials with some speed. The wage, he noted, was thirty cents an hour, "big money for the 1939–41 years," and a far cry from the twenty-five cents a day he was worth as a farmhand.[44]

Lois West's recollection of her husband-to-be was that he was "an eager beaver," working hard and typing papers for the other cadets. "He was brilliant. Fritz [classmate Ernest F. "Fritz" Hollings] said it made him so mad, [that] John was the only one who could ever get everything right."[45]

Besides the correspondence among the "Citadel Sons," the Williams scholarship recipients had other bonding experiences organized by their benefactor, one of them being an annual trip at spring break. In 1940 that spring break trip turned out to be a particularly memorable experience for the seventeen-year-old West: "Col. Williams had usually been having the [scholarship] recipients to his home in Camden for a vacation during spring break, but for some reason, he decided that Cuba was a better choice." What ensued was an eye-opener for the freshman cadet, only a few months separated from the four-horse farm in the Charlotte Thompson community. "General Summerall had called the [Fulgencio] Batista regime in Cuba and we were assigned a military officer, Captain Arubia, to escort us. He showed us through all the military areas, including the prison, which was once infamous, and became so again during the Castro regime."[46]

Captain Arubia also saw to it that the young cadets became acquainted with other elements of Cuban culture, namely the city's nightlife. For Cadet West, who had been born during the nation's Prohibition era and grew up under a mother of strict Associate Reform Presbyterian (ARP) beliefs, it was an eye-opener in more ways than one. Captain Arubia's tour included the "girly shows" and a place called "Sloppy Joe's Bar," where drinks were about twenty-five cents apiece and where Cadet West and his colleagues discovered the joys of demon rum. By then, even at age seventeen, West was beginning to show some political savvy and to see the value of sharing certain of his Cuban treasures in useful places back home. "I brought back a case of rum (50 cents a bottle), which I distributed to some of the cadets, including my company commander, John Harrison of Greenwood, who was rooming with my future brother-in-law, Robert Rhame."[47]

HONING HIS SKILLS OF PERSUASION

The Citadel would prove broadening in other ways for West. From the early days of his crushing loss to Lois Rhame in the second-grade declamation contest in Kershaw County, West had retained an interest not only in young Lois but also in the topic of debate. At the Citadel he became a four-year member of the debate team, serving his senior year as debate captain and manager. "We traveled over most of the East Coast and debated various teams, including participants in several national events," West said. "It was a good way to sharpen my speaking skills, which at first were modest, to say the least. The experience enabled me to think on my feet, and to react to an adversary's point, which was beneficial as I went on to become a litigating attorney and a political person."[48]

It was in debating, in fact, that West began to distinguish himself and attract the attention of others. A letter from Colonel Williams thanked President Summerall for "enclosing the remarkable report of John C. West on the trip of the Debating Team to the National Pi Delta Kappa Convention in Minneapolis, Minnesota." Competition in the Minneapolis convention came in only the second year of the Citadel's chapter of the debating society, and it pitted the school against ten nationally known colleges. "I am delighted with the accomplishments and the promise indicated in the substance of this report," Williams noted.[49]

West, it appears, performed a remarkable feat at that convention, as described in a letter to General Summerall from one of the convention officials: "One of your speakers at the convention, John West, did outstanding work as a member of his panel. Although he did not know until approximately three hours before the panel that he was to be a part of it, his work was rated first of the five participants. Other members of the panel were chosen prior to the convention and each received an outline to be followed. John got his first glance at the outline as we rode to the place of the discussion."[50]

At graduation West had attained the rank of first lieutenant in Company K of the Coast Artillery Unit. The school's 1942 yearbook, *The Sphinx,* listed the following among his achievements: president, Calliopean Literary Society; president, International Relations Club; president, Pi Kappa Delta Debating Society; captain, Debating Team; general editor, the *Bull Dog* (college newspaper).[51]

The young farm boy from the Charlotte Thompson community had gone through a whirlwind transformation, and it was topped off with the fulfillment of another ambition. "During the years at The Citadel, I started dating Lois Rhame on a regular basis," West wrote. "We had a few dates in high school, but the relationship continued and in our senior year [Lois was a student at the then all-female Winthrop College in Rock Hill], we became engaged. She gave me my ring at the Christmas dance, and I—in turn—gave her a miniature, which was a commitment."[52]

Lois West recalled the courtship beginning in earnest while West was at the Citadel. "He asked me to go to a hop his freshman year," she said. "It was just out of the blue." She said she enjoyed dating her high school friend at the dance but was "provoked because my brother was a senior and he was going to take me to the hop, and he invited me. But John invited me first so I had to go with John." Lois enjoyed West's company, but she was still dating others during her years at Winthrop. She was also beginning to notice something special about her Citadel friend. "We just liked each other, and he was persistent," she said. "I think he decided I was the one he wanted and I didn't have a choice after that."[53]

Lois West's account of the ring exchange was somewhat different—and a bit more colorful—from that conveyed in her husband's journal. "He gave me a Citadel miniature at the ring hop," she said years later.

> Except we didn't make it to the ring hop because the car broke down coming over the Cooper River Bridge.
>
> We had gone to Georgetown to visit Ed Bass's aunt for lunch and coming back, the car broke down, and we got a mailman [to push] us over the old Cooper River Bridge [a two-lane narrow iron bridge at the time].
>
> I didn't get to the Citadel hop. But I did get the miniature.[54]

FRIENDS FOR LIFE

John West and Lois Rhame's relationship was hardly a whirlwind romance. Lois West remembered it this way:

> I guess we just liked each other. We were friends. And we stayed friends. All the way through.[55]

Lois West, strong minded and plainspoken, became another powerful woman to influence John West's life, and she had distinct opinions about the woman who would be her mother-in-law for more than thirty years, Mattie West. "A friend in Camden used to say that the reason John had so much tact was because Miss Mattie had none, and he got all of hers," Lois recalled years later.

> Miss Mattie was the kind of person where there were two opinions, hers and the wrong one.
>
> But you had to understand her. She was left a widow with two small boys in the middle of the Depression. She had been a school teacher and she was going to raise those boys. So she went to farming, which she didn't know anything much about. But she managed to do it successfully, and it was a hard life. But she was going to see those children had the best education.[56]

As the decade of the 1940s arrived, Mattie West was seeing the fulfillment of that hard life; both her sons would be college graduates from the Citadel with John's graduation from the military institution at the end of the 1941–42 school year. John West was seeing the promise of fulfilling an ambition of his own, that of wedding his longtime sweetheart, Lois Rhame. Life was good for the bright young Kershaw County farm boy, and the future was filled with bright prospects.

Then one wintry Sunday in 1941 came the news that the planet had been reshaped forever. "The world changed on December 7, 1941," West recalled:

> It was [academic] mid-year, and on that Sunday afternoon, I remember a sophomore named Herman Bates coming down the gallery yelling, "They've bombed Pearl Harbor."
>
> I'm not sure I even knew where Pearl Harbor was, but it was evident that war was a reality. General Summerall spoke to us the next day and said that we could all expect to serve, but he saw no reason for the seniors to be concerned, as they would probably let us graduate, which we did.[57]

THREE

THE CODES OF WAR

Six weeks ago, we would have shot each other. . . . Now we're talking in a friendly way.

John West

"I had an easy war," John West quipped in an interview years after the end of World War II. "I never heard a shot fired in anger."[1] A serious back injury sustained during training at Camp Stewart, Georgia, early in the war kept West off the front lines and assigned to the Pentagon for most of the duration of the combat. His duty was not hazardous.

If it was a relatively safe war, it was not an "easy" or unimportant one. John West's war was the secret war of military intelligence at the Pentagon. He was one of the handpicked officers whose job it was to translate, interpret, and analyze the intercepted code messages from German and Japanese military transmissions and convert them into strategic information to guide the deployment of Allied forces. The failure of military intelligence had been blamed for allowing Japanese aircraft to catch U.S. forces at Pearl Harbor by surprise on December 7, 1941, and Americans were vowing not to let that happen again.

It was the perfect assignment for the zealous Citadel graduate, only three months past his nineteenth birthday when Pearl Harbor was bombed and scarcely three months shy of twenty when the Class of 1942 graduated. West's introduction to military service, however, was scarcely perfect. On his first day of duty as a newly commissioned second lieutenant at swampy, muggy Camp Stewart, near Savannah, West and his colleagues were launched on a twenty-five-mile hike. "I was still wearing my civilian shoes," West recalled. "G.I. boots had not been issued yet. I had too much Citadel pride to complain, but after we had marched 12 miles, my feet were solid blisters."[2]

West's rescuer was his Citadel friend Charles Whitmire, who had graduated two years earlier and was busy shepherding Citadel newcomers into his regiment, the 605th Coast Artillery Anti-Aircraft. "Charlie Whitmire, bless his soul, came along, saw my predicament, and gave me a ride into camp. I may have been crippled for life if it hadn't been for his help," West recalled.[3]

Training was seven days a week at Camp Stewart, owing at least in part to the post commander's having been on duty at Pearl Harbor only months earlier. "[He] reminded us that Japan's sneak attack had occurred on Sunday, December 7, and that we were not going to take any time off. So, we were in the field seven days a week."[4]

Like much of America's military posture at the time, West's early concentration was on the defensive side of operations. The nation was still reeling from its worst single military defeat ever and was buying time until it could mobilize its own offensive capability. Among other things, that meant protecting the nation's shorelines and strategically important coastal installations against potential follow-ups to the Pearl Harbor attack. West's unit lived in pup tents in sweltering Georgia heat at Camp Stewart and trained on long- and medium-range weapons, varying from 90 mm to 40 mm. His unit was called a "searchlight battalion," and its duties were chiefly to illuminate enemy planes should they come into range.

After the work at Camp Stewart and ten days of orientation to new weaponry near Wilmington, North Carolina, West's regiment was shipped to Boston to defend the dry docks there and to replace units of veteran soldiers who were being sent to North Africa to prepare for the Allied invasion of November 1942. The train ride to Boston, West recalled, was a trip "from the heat and insects of Camp Stewart into the coastal regions around Boston, like a transition from hell to heaven, so intolerable was the Camp Stewart heat."[5] In Boston, West was introduced to pleasant summertime weather, the joys of fresh lobster, and even a little precareer lawyering. "I remember some of the smaller things," West wrote, "although they weren't really all that small at the time, such as rationing of coffee. Lobster fishermen in Massachusetts were used to drinking a lot of coffee, and we had a surplus supply of it. Our mess sergeant soon worked out a deal to swap coffee for lobsters. We had fresh lobster practically every night. I gained pounds then and also developed a great, and long-standing, taste for fresh lobster."[6]

West also was assigned the duty of gaining from Boston citizens the "rights of entry" to allow the army to place antiaircraft guns on individuals' private

Lois Rhame and John West were married in August 1942 while she was still a student at Winthrop College. Courtesy of Lois R. West and Shelton W. Bosley

property, much of that permission, as it turned out, coming after the fact. West recalled,

> After the Pearl Harbor attack, the Army simply put antiaircraft guns at locations where needed as quickly as possible, but without getting permission from property owners or other authorities. . . . So my job was to backtrack and arrange to be where they already were, everywhere from the Harvard Yard to individual citizens' property.
>
> So I got a real sense of the people of Boston. Of course, at the time, there were no problems. Everybody was grateful to have the guns there.[7]

MARRIAGE, WITH PARENTAL CONSENT

At about this time John West and Lois Rhame decided that their courtship dating back to the "declamation contest" thirteen years earlier in Camden, South Carolina, should be finalized. Like many couples in wartime America, they saw the prospect of risky days and separation ahead, and they wanted to proceed with marriage vows while it was still possible. They set the date for August 29, 1942, at Fort Monmouth, New Jersey, where Lois's brother, Robert Rhame, was stationed. There were two problems, however. The bridegroom was only twenty, which meant that he required parental permission to be married. In addition New Jersey law required a three-day waiting period, and the couple had only three days for the entire occasion.

As it turned out, Mattie West had come north for the marriage of her son and his childhood sweetheart, and she could sign for her son to be married. It rankled West that he was a second lieutenant in the U.S. Army and still had to have his mother's permission to wed. The three-day waiting problem was also solved, thanks to a sympathetic clerk who agreed to backdate the application for the marriage license. "I've always teased Lois that our marriage probably wasn't legal for that reason," West joked for years afterward.[8]

The work of spotting enemy aircraft and manning the antiaircraft defenses of Boston Harbor proved, to the relief of Bostonians and the men of the 605th Regiment alike, to be a routine and, ultimately, a dry-run exercise. Radar was in its infancy at the time and was a top-secret tool of only limited use. Much of the aircraft-spotting work was done unscientifically by tracking planes on a makeshift grid in the basement of the old Charles Town Armory. Planes could be detected visually or with large listening devices designed to allow spotters to hear the engines before they came into sight. "When they would get within range, [we would] point first the 90 millimeter and then the 40 millimeter guns toward them," West recalled. "It was a rather boring exercise." The toughest part of the system was telling the enemy aircraft from the friendly planes. "There was no adequate communication that could be used," West wrote. "The IFF (identification friend or foe) was a later matter."[9]

During one of West's briefing on the IFF topic, his battalion commander happened to drop in and listen to the young lieutenant's presentation. He was impressed with what he saw. "Lieutenant," he said, "I'm going to send you to aircraft school of recognition so you can become a trainer." The development proved to be an eerily fateful moment. "Fate sometimes changes one's life," West recalled, referring to his selection to attend aircraft identification school.[10]

His departure from Boston for the school, located at Ohio State University in Columbus, Ohio, came on a Friday evening. He would arrive at the destination in time for the opening of classes on December 1.

AN EERIE REMINDER

On the night after West's departure from Boston—November 28, 1942—fire struck a favorite hangout for West and his friends, the Coconut Grove nightclub in Boston. In the worst disaster of its kind in the country's history, 492 people were killed and 166 were injured.

The circumstances of the Boston fire bore a chilling resemblance to those of the fire that claimed West's father, Shelton West, nineteen years earlier at the Cleveland School. The Coconut Grove fire was touched off by artificial palms and draperies around the club's stage, and hundreds died when exits to the building were jammed. More than 1,000 partygoers had been packed into a building whose capacity was 600, and many died attempting to escape the building, piled up at exits that became overcrowded and clogged.

The Coconut Grove fire took a serious toll on the officers of West's unit, the 605th Regiment. A Citadel graduate of the Class of 1940, W. C. Goodpasture, was identified in press accounts as a hero who died saving others. West recalled, "It decimated our officer ranks." His friend Charlie Whitmire barely escaped. Whitmire "crawled out of the fire. The rescue workers said he was too far gone, but he managed to survive. Even to this day, he bears the scars." West continued, "I could well have been with him that night."[11]

The training school in Ohio turned out to be a good experience for the young officer. Being conducted at Ohio State, it made "me a true Buckeye" and offered West and his fellow officers some pleasant off-hours diversions. Nightlife in Columbus, Ohio, was hardly that of Havana or Boston, but West remembered that he and classmates from army and navy units discovered a good after-hours spot. "The hours [of the training school] were not that demanding and we found a place on High Street called 'Cozy Coot' where the hamburgers and beer were excellent," he recalled. "It was actually a lot of fun."[12]

His newlywed bride, who had returned to college at Winthrop for her senior year, made the train ride to Columbus so that the two could be together for Christmas. For all the good intentions, though, things did not work out well for the young couple on that occasion. "I broke out with chicken pox," West recalled, "and at age 20, the chicken pox seemed like smallpox. It was pretty tough." On the Wests' first Christmas as a married couple, the young officer's face was speckled and he was confined to bed in a Columbus, Ohio, boardinghouse. "I had recovered enough by the first of January to take a few days off in Camden," he remembered.[13]

In early January 1943 West's military career seemed to be lapsing into a retracing of earlier steps. First, he returned to Boston, where he was given his first command. While he found the experience of command "interesting" and "exciting," the mission of the unit proved to be less than vigorous. "I became Battery Commander of a 40-millimeter battery that was stationed in the South Boston dry docks," he wrote. "We overlooked the Queen Mary, which was then being converted into a troop carrier."[14]

As 1943 progressed, however, Allied forces were beginning to blunt German initiatives in North Africa, and Russians were stalling German offensives in places such as Leningrad and Stalingrad. The war was beginning to take a turn, and American citizens were getting over some of their anxiety about possible air attacks along the home front. "As the war progressed and the danger of bombing began to diminish," West wrote, "the Army decided to replace the regular troops [in antiaircraft positions] with limited service people, those who had been drafted with physical defects, and were not considered able for general duty. One of my jobs was as training officer for these replacements."[15]

Then came another retraced step, back to the much-disliked Camp Stewart in Georgia. This time West's assignment was with a new unit, the 843rd Antiaircraft Battalion, and its destination was combat overseas. "We were supposed to get troops from the Draft Board and we were scheduled to train them and take the unit overseas," he recalled.[16]

A DEVASTATING INJURY

West would never make it overseas, however. A devastating injury would keep him permanently out of combat and would almost terminate his military service. It could also have caused him to wonder if there was something of a Camp Stewart curse in his life.

On an obstacle course he took a serious fall, fracturing his right wrist and causing compression fractures of his tenth and eleventh thoracic vertebrae. In a Christmas-time letter to Colonel Williams and his wife, West wrote some months after the incident, "One of the horizontal bars in the course wasn't as substantial as it should have been, so when I started to swing on it (maybe it was the 25 lbs. the army has put on me), I came down with a bang."[17]

Lois West had a slightly different account of the conditions leading to the injury: John

> was company commander, and being company commander and a Citadel graduate, he led his men, he didn't just tell them to do it. He said "follow me."
>
> On this particular morning, it was early . . . just after dawn and he went out and they had an obstacle course where you ran up a ramp and grabbed a bar and you'd swing out and drop about eight feet. The bar was too big [around] and it wasn't solid. It rolled and this particular morning, the dew was on it.
>
> He grabbed it, and he went out, and . . . he went out feet first. Then [he] came down and broke his arm and his back.[18]

The injury landed West in the base hospital in a waist-to-neck body cast sweltering in the Georgia heat and enduring a near-tortured existence. "There was little air conditioning," he remembered, "and—above all—there were no showers because of the cast."[19]

By then Lois had graduated from Winthrop—the first married woman to graduate from the all-female institution—and she headed for Camp Stewart in a particularly adventuresome spirit. "She had never learned to drive a car," West recalled, "but we had purchased a car—my uncle had bought it in Rock Hill—and my cousin, John Ratterree, had driven Lois down. He let her drive around the block, went back to the bus station and said, 'Take off.' Fortunately, she was able to get a Georgia driver's license."[20]

Still in the body cast, West was promoted to captain in June, two months short of his twenty-first birthday. He was, according to information sources available to him at the time, "one of the youngest, if not the youngest, captain in the U.S. Army."[21]

The cast came off after West was transferred to Stark Hospital in Charleston, where he was reunited with Citadel classmates Herb Rudnick and Ed Bass, who were at the medical school. "That first shower was the finest thing I'd felt in a long time," West remembered, "but the arm had not healed too well. A young doctor at Stark wanted to operate and reset it, but I refused and he threatened to court martial me. Fortunately, through physiotherapy, I was able to regain use and have had no problem since."[22]

The injury, however, had cost West his overseas assignment, and after several more weeks of hospitalization in Augusta, Georgia, he became an unhappy candidate for retirement from the armed services. It was hardly what the young Citadel graduate had envisioned eighteen months earlier as he and his classmates had set off for what they believed would be serious combat duty overseas. West had been shuttled back and forth among assignments dealing largely with home-land defenses, and once it seemed his combat career was under way, a near-crippling injury had left him in a body cast, in—of all places—Camp Stewart. Even as he recovered, things were not looking good for his military life.

"The question was whether I should be retired," he remembered. "The prospect of being retired as an Army Captain on disability at age 20 wasn't appealing to me, so I told the Retirement Board I wasn't interested, and I could go back on active duty."[23]

West was granted his wish to return to duty but was still in a training capacity. He was sent to Fort Eustis, Virginia, to train another group of "limited service" draftees to replace an antiaircraft battery. For West, an army officer in the middle of World War II, life had become "easy," and the Wests rented a house in Williamsburg for the duration of his tour in Virginia. It was, he said, "one of the more pleasant Army times, and we were there through the Christmas holidays [1943]."[24]

Then came another assignment at Camp Stewart. "I didn't like it any better the third time than I did the second," West said, "but the conditions were better."[25] West's antiaircraft unit [the 841st] had been dismantled and transferred to infantry and was shipped to Fort Benning for training. Captain West remained at Camp Stewart with a staff job this time, as a training center intelligence officer. He and Lois were able to take up residence at a not-so-modern roadside lodging known as the Modern Tourist Court, adjacent to West's assistant, Frank Rector, who had married a Camden native, Helen Stogner, and would later become an attorney and a lifelong friend.

Healthy and back on duty, West was still on the periphery of the war effort, however, dealing with rear-guard activities that seemed to have little influence on the direct conduct of hostilities. Even with his recuperation and promotions, things seemed at a dead end. Then it all began to change.

Shortly after the attack on Pearl Harbor, American military leadership set about to assess the condition of its intelligence services, and—as frequently happened in the wake of such events—there was much second-guessing and recrimination. It appeared, even as early as the initial review and analyses, that there had been missed opportunities for the intelligence service to provide advance warning of the Japanese attack. Among the problems discovered were restrictions on communications among various intelligence units, restrictions that seemed to make the army "oblivious to the Japanese threat" on December 7, 1941.[26]

"ONLY INDIVIDUALS OF FIRST-RATE ABILITY"

The secretary of war at the time in the Franklin Roosevelt cabinet was Henry Stimson, and he decided that what the service needed was a fresh examination from an external, nonmilitary perspective. The man he chose to "examine the implications of the problem" was a strong-willed attorney named Alfred McCormack, a former law partner of Stimson's assistant secretary John McCloy. McCormack wasted little time forming opinions and expressing those opinions. "When the sudden attack on Pearl Harbor occurred," he later wrote, "it became apparent that the event had been clearly foreshadowed in the Japanese traffic [secret communications intercepted by the United States] of 1941. The Secretary of War, and no doubt others, then concluded that the traffic had not been given sufficient close attention, and that some agency should be set up to deal with cryptanalytic intelligence in a more thorough-going fashion."[27]

McCormack, considered an outsider to military careerists who were manning the intelligence posts, became special assistant to the secretary of war on January 19, 1942, a scant forty-three days after the Pearl Harbor attack. Two months later McCormack had studied the fragmentation problem among the various intelligence units sufficiently to produce the recommendation that a special branch of the War Department be created within the Military Intelligence Service "to deal with the processing of communications intelligence."[28]

His recommendation was adopted in May 1942, and in June, McCormack was commissioned as a colonel and was made deputy of the new special branch, serving under Colonel Carter W. Clarke. Before long McCormack was expressing additional opinions, among them the belief that the staffing of intelligence responsibilities lay too low in the military chain and there was a need for an infusion of upper-level brainpower into the service. In a later report describing his study and subsequent work, McCormack wrote, "I disagreed with the notion that any reserve officer, or any civilian who had been graduated from college, was qualified to handle cryptanalytic intelligence. It seemed to me that the job could be done effectively only by persons with special qualifications, that the most careful selection of personnel was necessary, and that only individuals of first-rate ability and suitable training should be taken into the work."[29] The recommendation encountered resistance from within the State Department, including that of South Carolinian Donald S. Russell, who was serving as assistant secretary for administration at the time.[30]

Among those "special qualifications" specified by attorney McCormack was familiarity with the practice of law, and it soon became known that his early recruitment of staff would be from the ranks of lawyers from "elite firms."[31] Years later it would be recalled, "It was only half a joke that, within the War Department, the Special Branch was called 'the best law office in Washington.'"[32]

As the budget, size, and staffing needs of the new branch grew, recruitment efforts expanded, reaching across the country and extending into various military bases and operations. One of those recruiting forays found its way into the swampy precincts of Camp Stewart, where Captain John West had taken up duty as training center intelligence officer. Still disappointed at the prospect that his wartime duty would be spent only in stateside posts, West recalled his introduction to McCormack's recruiter. He later wrote that he was told, "Captain, I was told by our commanding officer we've got this crazy-looking character from Washington and I guess we'd better be nice to him. How about you taking him in tow?" The visitor turned out to be Major Graham Aldis, described by West as "a little on the kooky side."[33] He had been dispatched on one of Alfred McCormack's assignments to recruit and select individuals of "first-rate ability and suitable training" to join the elite new intelligence branch. West wrote,

> Major Aldis told me that he had this mission of going out into the field and finding troops that had common sense and a little brains because the high-powered group they had assembled in Washington needed some "leavening," as he put it. In other words, there was too much brainpower and not enough common sense.
>
> He said he had the authority from the War Department to recruit anyone in the organization.[34]

West spent time with the recruiter from Washington going over files and arranging interviews with prospects for the new intelligence positions. In the process he realized that there might lie before him the makings of an escape from Camp Stewart and even the possible opportunity of doing something more than putting in extended months of routine duties.

By then the lad from the cornfields of Kershaw County, South Carolina, had also begun to display skills that went beyond aircraft recognition or shore battery supervision. John West had begun to take on the bearing and deportment of a budding political operative, schooled in the savvy ways of the Citadel Cadet Corps and buttressed by social skills he had honed in after-hours places such as Sloppy Joe's Bar, the Coconut Grove, and the Cozy Coot.[35] Emerging along with the powerful intellect of the young officer was an undeniable inclination toward a southern style of "social" politics, the disarming meeting-after-the-meeting exercise of persuasion that would stand West in good stead for the rest of his political career.

West recalled his experience with Aldis. "Some of us spent several days with Major Aldis," he wrote. "He was a delightful fellow, what we called a 'retread,' an officer who had originally served during World War I. He was a laid-back sorta fellow . . . [and] he would have a drink with us at night. At the end of one conversation, he said, 'West, there are two or three people here that I want, but they are two of the best people on your staff, a sergeant and a corporal.'"[36]

ANOTHER ESCAPE FROM GEORGIA

West pounced. He realized by then that in Major Aldis, "the crazy-looking character from Washington," there lay a possible route for him into the mainstream of the war.

"Well," West said to Aldis in his disarmingly best southern style, "if you take these two, you've got to take me, too. He [Aldis] scratched his head and said, 'I think that can be arranged.'" It quickly became a sealed deal, and a few days later, after Aldis returned to Washington, West recalled being summoned by his executive officer and being told, "'My God . . . we've got people being transferred directly to Washington, including your only two staff members. Do you think you can handle the job without them?' I said, 'I've already recruited some more, Colonel, and I think I can handle the situation.' Two days later, he called and said, 'My God, West, I've got orders for you, too.' I said, 'Yep, but I've got a successor already selected.'"[37]

West's escape from the steamy confines of Camp Stewart was complete, and he headed into the rigors and demands of a totally new adventure. Despite his self-deprecating observations to the contrary, the army was not looking for people to serve as commonsense "leavening" to offset the "elite" types recruited by Alfred McCormack. It was recruiting from among the ranks of the "best and the brightest" to staff an enterprise that could (and would) affect the very outcome of the war. As it had been with his seven-day-a-week routine when he first arrived at Camp Stewart two years earlier, West was immediately immersed in the process. John West's war had finally begun.

"When I arrived in Washington," he wrote, "they sent me to a school which was in many ways the hardest situation I ever faced in the academic world. As I remember, we had approximately 90 students there and we were put through a 12-hour a day regimen."[38] He also wrote,

> The instructors told us that the purpose of the school was to test our intelligence and our capacities to the utmost; that they only had spaces in the organization for 10–12 people, and that the rest would not be offered assignments in the Pentagon because of the sensitivity of the training.
>
> The school was very competitive and had some very bright people in it. I was motivated, but afraid that I couldn't cut the mustard. Fortunately, at the end of the time, I was one of the eight or ten who made the cut and was assigned to my new position in the Pentagon.[39]

West became one of the special branch "elite," a group that included more than a few future VIPs. His first assignment, in fact, was replacing Philip Graham, later publisher of the *Washington Post,* who was sent to the Philippines and who would rise to positions of prominence within General Douglas MacArthur's air command.[40] As Alfred McCormack had envisioned, "We could recruit, from men who are in the Army—all of whom are in non-combat assignments . . . eight or ten eminently qualified men in very short order; and from similar available personnel, we could build up a working organization to meet almost any demand upon us."[41]

A TIME OF CODE BREAKTHROUGHS

West's arrival coincided with two important developments in army intelligence. In the spring of 1943 Allied cryptanalysts scored a major breakthrough in dealing with Japanese military codes, making the first break into a Japanese army high-level system (the water transport code), which contained information about Japanese shipping and occasionally could be tied to Japanese army troop movements. A year earlier code breakthroughs had led to the major U.S. naval victory at Midway Island. Also in the spring of 1943 a party of army officers visited the British Government Code and Cipher School at Bletchley Park and became aware of the extent to which the British were penetrating high-level German communications in what became known as the ULTRA source.[42]

The British breakthrough had been initiated on May 9, 1941, with the capture of the German submarine U-110 and the discovery of codebooks and a typewriter-looking machine, which became known as the "Enigma" machine. The capture of the German code materials opened entire new realms of intelligence discovery and was credited with major roles in Allied successes in North Africa against German forces under Field Marshal Erwin Rommel, with the securing of Allied convoys in the Atlantic between 1940 and 1944, and with the successful D-day landing of Allied forces on June 6, 1944.[43]

"British efforts in breaking the German Enigma and other ciphers on command links had laid bare many of the most important secrets of the Nazi High Command," a later review confirmed.[44] In April 1944 the United States got full access to material coming from the Enigma-based decoding process, information that would be known in intelligence circles as ULTRA. "Although such intelligence had been provided to Eisenhower during the invasion of North Africa, U.S. Army Intelligence had not been fully aware of its origins. Now the British agreed to share this intelligence with the U.S. Army on an unrestricted basis, in exchange for reciprocal access to American communications intelligence on the Japanese," it was later reported.[45]

Military commanders, traditionally skeptical about intelligence reports, became satisfied that ULTRA-generated materials were so highly reliable that intelligence operations were reorganized and streamlined so that ULTRA information could be quickly disseminated directly to the field. Freed of organizational impediments, the new intelligence units could concentrate almost exclusively on the production of foreign intelligence.

In a matter of weeks John West had gone from the rural backwoods of what he called that "hell hole" Camp Stewart to the inner circles of the code-breaking officers in the Pentagon. While he had been denied the opportunity for combat service, he was now only a matter of several electronic dispatches away from the field headquarters where battle decisions were being made. He was not on the front lines, but information he was developing was directly influencing the plans and outcomes of battle strategies there.

DETECTING THE JAPANESE PLANS

West's first assignment was tracking the organization and structure of the Japanese army air units operating in China, and he worked with British ULTRA specialists. He later wrote,

> The basis of our intelligence was the ULTRA traffic, the interception of messages between planes but more frequently between headquarters. The code-breaking was done at Arlington Hall, a former girls school near Washington, and the results were transmitted to the Pentagon, where it was filtered down to our desk.
>
> The British were still the leaders in our section, although they were technically designated as liaison. Commander Ben King was the ranking British officer, and I was assigned to Squadron Leader Ken Brooke, who was a veteran of the European British intelligence.[46]

The early months of 1944, in fact, saw an acceleration of code breakthroughs, including the capture of the main Japanese administrative code, which contained substantial information about plans and disposition of Japanese forces, as well as additional information about Japanese shipping and oil production, according to McCormack's account. Those breakthroughs, McCormack wrote, made available "a tremendous volume of messages dealing with virtually every field of activity in the Japanese Army. In the spring of 1944, solution of one of the main Japanese air systems began and provided a greatly increased number of messages dealing with Japanese Army air units, including strength and service reports and plan movements."[47]

West's assignment to the Japanese code-breaking section was one of particular complexity and difficulty. McCormack wrote, "The material was extremely fragmentary and, because of the Japanese method of breaking each message into several parts, it was usually the case that only one or a few parts of the message, lacking in context, would be valuable. In addition, even that part of the text which was available would normally be incomplete, because parts of the text would not be completely readable. Both of these factors multiplied tremendously the difficulties of translation and the possibilities of erroneous interpretation."[48]

West recalled, "The work was like a jigsaw puzzle. You would receive a radio transmission intercepted from a Japanese fighter pilot or an intercept from a headquarters being transferred. . . . You would never get the full text, but you would have to take information you had and try to piece it together."[49] He said, "We'd get a mess of translations, anything that had to do with the Japanese army or air force, particularly in the China area. They'd all hit my desk. Well, a lot of times they wouldn't make any sense, but we'd keep them on file anyway. Then, we'd piece them together until we came up with what was a meaningful analysis that showed some significant troop movement."[50]

As he had on other occasions, West was also busy making personal friends. One of them was Colonel Bob Spencer, a former Methodist minister who had been brought on board with the special section because he had lived in Japan and was fluent in the Japanese dialects. "The Japanese language is so complex with so many nuances," West recalled. "We often got an intercept with a sentence that didn't seem to fit in with the rest of the text. I would then call Spencer and ask if there might be more than one translation for the words or sentences. He'd say, 'Yeah, that could be.'"[51]

For all the influence his work had on the war's outcome, however, West had remained during the full extent of the military hostilities remote and emotionally sheltered from the brutality of human ordeal. His had been a war of intellectual dimensions, a high-stakes "jigsaw puzzle" contest conducted in the insular and secure caverns of the Pentagon, where he never heard an unfriendly shot fired.

A SOBERING VIEW OF WAR'S END

At it turned out, however, West would not be spared a firsthand view of war's horrors. Because of his experience and familiarity with the Japanese military operations during the war, he was chosen to be part of the U.S. Strategic Bombing Survey, a postwar study to assess the effectiveness of air strikes over Japanese cities in the waning months of the war and the extent of damage done by those strikes. Only days after the signing of the Japanese surrender on September 2, 1945, West arrived in Tokyo, having flown across the Pacific on what was his first airplane flight. What he saw, as he later described it, was "utter devastation. There was nothing but rubble for miles around."[52] He said, "We landed at Astugi Airport north of Tokyo and suddenly began to realize the true horrors of war. Not a single building was standing anywhere. The B-29 fire raids . . . had killed thousands of people and laid waste the entire area."[53]

What West and his party were observing was largely the result of one of the first firebombings of Japan by U.S. planes six months earlier. A description of that evening of March 9–10, 1945, is provided in this account: "A force of 334 B-29s [bombers] was unleashed—each plane stripped of ammunition for its machine guns to allow it to carry more fire-bombs. The lead attackers arrived over the city [Tokyo] just after dark and were followed by a procession of death that lasted until dawn. The fires started by the initial raiders could be seen from 150 miles away. The results were devastating; almost 17 square miles of the city were reduced to ashes. Estimates of the number killed range between 80,000 and 200,000, a higher death toll than that produced by the dropping of the Atomic Bombs on Hiroshima or Nagasaki six months later."[54]

For West, his assignment to Tokyo had another dimension. Like the fortunately timed trip to Columbus, Ohio, that took him away from Boston on the night of the 1942 Coconut Grove nightclub fire, "there was [another] decision made which may have saved my life."[55]

In those early postwar days in Japan, a number of the members of the Strategic Bombing Survey were assigned to visit the A-bomb sites at Hiroshima and Nagasaki. At the time they had no knowledge of the potentially deadly effects of radioactivity still present in those destroyed cities. "Some even brought back souvenir rocks from the cities which were radioactive," West recalled. The result, West said, was that

> at least half a dozen of those people, my friends, died of cancer within fifteen or twenty years. To me, there must have been a cause-and-effect relationship between their exposure to radioactivity and their deaths some years later. John Palfrey, who was later dean of the Columbia University School of Law, was one who died.
>
> I thought how fortunate I was not to have been among those who were sent on that mission.[56]

Besides assessing the bombing damage, West was also part of the team that debriefed and interrogated Japanese officers to "become familiar with the big picture of the war from the Japanese perspective."[57] One of those "big picture" revelations came from information that had been decoded earlier and that led U.S. officials to believe that there were diehards in the Japanese military who were not willing to surrender.

SENSING A DANGEROUS PLOT

"At the end of the war," West recalled,

> Pentagon intelligence had received a series of messages that just made no sense at all. They were messages between a particular Japanese command

headquarters and a Japanese outpost in Manchuria. It was just a constant flurry of messages, and we couldn't determine what they meant.

Well, I came up with a theory that my colleagues laughed at. I said, "there's a character (Japanese commander) down there who is like some Southerners at the end of the War Between the States. He doesn't want to give up, and he's planning to take a group and break away." . . . They said, "Well, you're way out on that."[58]

Senior officers, however, accepted West's precautionary suspicions and sent bombers to destroy the Japanese outpost in Manchuria. This may have helped avert a Japanese kamikaze mission on the peace-signing ceremonies on the USS *Missouri* in Tokyo harbor. Years later West's son Jack said, "They thought he was crazy, but he stayed on them and convinced them, and they sent some B-17s and B-29s to bomb those bases, which they did. . . . I guess you might say he shortened the war."[59]

Jack West's theory was borne out by a postwar interview in Tokyo. "One Japanese general we were interrogating was very arrogant," John West wrote, "and he started lying about his activities. I had his actual command record, where this had happened and that had happened. That interrogation was an unpleasant experience."[60]

The unpleasant Japanese general brought to mind the flurry of strange messages brought, and West's hunch was confirmed. "Sure enough," he wrote,

I went to find that arrogant Japanese general. I kept asking him about that Manchurian message traffic. Then I started interrogating some of the general's aviators.

One of his aviators was a young kid who spoke English perfectly, so I asked him what the general's plans were. He said, "Well, my father was an American and my mother is Japanese." And he said, "My father died, so I was trapped in the Japanese army." And I said, "Well, tell me more about this general." He said, "Well, at the end of the war, we aviators became Kamikaze pilots. As the American ships came in to Tokyo harbor to sign the peace treaty in September, 1945, we were supposed to take off from bases and bomb the Americans—suicide bombers." And he added, "The night before the planned attack, we went through all of these rituals." And I asked, "Well, what did you think of that?"

He said, "I cried." He said, "I didn't want to do it. Fortunately, fog the next day prevented us taking off."

What he had confirmed was the fact that this Japanese general had a contingent ready to go to Manchuria and not surrender. I turned that over to the Tokyo War Crimes Tribunal and I don't know whatever happened to him. But that general was prepared to send Kamikaze pilots to strike the battleship Missouri in Tokyo harbor on the surrender date, September 2, 1945.[61]

For his diligence in rooting out the suspected attack on the Missouri, West was awarded the Army Commendation Medal. Mention of the medal never appears in any of West's papers or autobiographical sketches.

Even amid the rubble of ruined Tokyo, West was busy making friends, particularly among the defeated Japanese officers. One of the principal subjects interviewed by the U.S. group "was a Japanese major who was very knowledgeable and cooperative," West wrote.

> He was a good source, so we kept talking to him. After about three or four days of interviewing, we stopped, took a break, and had a cup of tea together. In a week or so, we were having lunch together. And one day, I sat and looked at him and I said, "You know, six weeks ago, we would have shot each other on sight. Now we're talking in a friendly way. . . . " He laughed and said, "Yes."
>
> There's a human element no matter how different the culture is. The language and the emotions that were part of my early experience at Camp Stewart contrasted sharply with the experience we had with that Japanese major. During bayonet practice at Camp Stewart, we had Japanese dummies, and [we] taught the recruits how to hate the Japanese. . . .
>
> A lot of old codgers want to tell you how we won the war and what we did to help. But that three-month experience at the end of 1945 was also very touching. It proved that people are the same the world over. There are some differences in people, but it proved to me, looking back, the absolute futility of war. It almost made me a pacifist.[62]

Only eight years had elapsed since John West stood in a cornfield and made his vow to find a life and career beyond the rural reaches of Kershaw County, South Carolina. Still only twenty-two, he headed home matured by a war that had tested his intellect and honed his political skills. The war also left him with a worldly view of human nature and a deep tolerance for the racial and cultural differences that populated the state to which he would return.

FOUR

THE MAKING OF AN ADVOCATE

I began to question the so-called [white] superiority because of the color of skin.

John West

West was twenty-three when he was discharged from the army and returned home to Camden. The enthusiasm for military service and combat experience he carried into the war from the Citadel had been sobered by seeing firsthand the devastation U.S. bombers wrought on Tokyo's civilian population in the conflict's waning weeks.

He also returned home with the memory of at least two experiences that would help shape for him a new outlook on the old racial imperatives that had dominated his native state of South Carolina for generations. As it was with many white southerners, the war had brought West in contact with black men on an even footing for the first time. This was a far cry from his experience with the two barely literate farmhands who had plowed the cornfields with him a scant eight years earlier, and it represented something of a transformational experience.

"In my Charlotte Thompson community," he later wrote,

blacks . . . were servants, and not hated by any means, but they were not considered equal in intelligence and social status to whites. It was a way of life that we did not question.

In my assignment as the intelligence officer of the Antiaircraft Brigade at Fort Stewart, my responsibilities included training intelligence officers of each battalion. As I recall, there were three or four battalions, one of which was black. A lieutenant, whose name I cannot recall, was the intelligence officer of this unit.

We worked with him and the others as a group. I soon found that he was the brightest one of all. It was my first real experience with a college educated black, and I found there was no difference with the whites except that he was smarter.

I began to question the so-called [white] superiority because of the color of skin.[1]

For the social-minded West, the message came home even more clearly in a party setting some months later. He wrote:

As we were leaving Tokyo . . . there was a group of soldiers, some white, some black. One white soldier [was] opening a bottle of beer, took a swig, turned to his black companion, and said, "Have a drink—let's celebrate—we're going home."

His accent was obviously Southern. The black soldier hesitated, and said, "Well, we'd better do it here, Joe, because when we get home, we can't drink like this anymore."

The white boy stood, thought for a moment, and said, "Well, why in the hell can't we? You and I fought and won a war, so why shouldn't we continue to be friends like we've been?"[2]

AN UNANSWERED QUESTION

That unanswered question would frame a social and political agenda for reform-minded southerners in the postwar years and for generations to come. "Being friends" across racial lines would require massive overhaul of a system designed to discourage, and even prohibit, just such possibilities. As black and white servicemen were tossing down beers together overseas, southern political leaders back home were going in the opposite direction, fighting court orders and passing legislation designed to preserve racial separation.

By the time West returned from service in 1946, the desegregation process was in its early stages. By executive order after the war, President Harry Truman desegregated the armed forces, and wartime court rulings had loosened restrictions on black voters in the South, at least legally. South Carolina would continue to fight its own court battle until a 1948 federal court ruling overturned most of the efforts of the state and other southern states to deny blacks the right to vote in the Democratic Party primary, at the time the only meaningful election in the South.[3]

A MATTER OF PRIORITIES

For all the impact they would have in his later life, civil rights issues were not a priority for John West and many veterans like him as they worked to pick up their lives and regain their peace-time directions. By then West had decided on a career in law. During his tenure at the Pentagon, he had enrolled at George Washington University's night law school, following the lead of a Citadel classmate, Frank Martin. "Frank subsequently became an Episcopal minister instead of a lawyer," West later recalled. "At that time, I was torn between law and journalism, but I thought it [enrolling in law school] was a good opportunity. . . . I was fortunate in my first course at GW to get Dean Van Vleck for torts. He was a great professor, gave me an A and caused me to decide that I wanted to be a lawyer. I also had a criminal law professor named Kirkland, whose course was excellent. He infected me with a little of the enthusiasm of a litigator."[4]

A decision to enroll at the University of South Carolina (USC) Law School meant that the Wests would be setting up housekeeping for the first time after their marriage during the wartime years. After West's discharge in Washington, the couple returned to South Carolina in time for him to enroll for the second semester, March 1, 1946. Another decision awaited them, however.

"Lois and I got to Camden and we decided on a big venture," West recalled. "We decided to buy a house in Columbia, rather than to continue to commute. We bought a house on South Edisto Avenue for $5,250, 100 percent financed with a GI loan. It was a two-bedroom house, our first home."[5] The Wests lived not more than a few blocks from another young couple married during the war. Bob McNair, who would precede West as governor twenty years later, and his wife, Josephine, had taken up residence on South Pickens Street in a neighborhood of cottages, all within an easy walk of the USC campus.

West's law class turned out to be a Who's Who-to-Be of state politicians, and he recalled, "Many of us even then were infected with the political 'virus.'"[6] Among his classmates were future governors McNair and Ernest F. "Fritz" Hollings, future congressmen Hugo Sims and James Mann, and Wade Weatherford and Jack Gardner, who would go on to become state legislators and state court judges.

Besides the politically minded young members of West's postwar USC law class, there was a notable older law student, Colonel J. R. Westmoreland, the father of the man who would become commander in chief of U.S. forces in Vietnam, General William C. Westmoreland. West later wrote, "'Rip,' as he was known, had retired as president of a mill in Spartanburg. He had been a long time member of the Board of Visitors at The Citadel, and he said he decided that he wanted to have a little legal training, which would help him preside as Chairman of the Board at The Citadel. He only stayed about a semester, but Colonel Rip, as we called him, was a delightful individual."[7]

BUILDING FRIENDSHIPS

Along the way the small, white, frame house at 507 South Edisto Avenue became a gathering place where West would assume his by-then customary role as unofficial social chairman among his colleagues. "We built some lasting friendships during our law school years," West wrote. "Since Lois and I had a house, it became the central place for study and for parties for our classmates, many of whom were living in government-provided rental units." West also recalled beach parties: "On each school break we would go to the beach, and we had some great times [with] Bill and Patty Horger, Wade and Eleanor Weatherford, Fritz and Pat Hollings, Bob and Josephine McNair. We learned how to crab because that was one of the major items to eat. It was a great time, and the friendships we made there endured."[8]

This was also a time when West would begin to develop what turned into a lifetime passion for the game of golf. It came about through Lois's pursuit of a teaching position with the physical education department at USC. "She taught tennis, swimming, golf and pool," West recalled.

> Lois tells the story that when she was told to teach pool (it was because some disabled veterans had to take Phys. Ed. and couldn't do anything else), she told her boss [Verdanna Craig, the department head], "Lady, in Camden we didn't even go into the pool halls, much less play pool."
>
> The reply was, "You like your paycheck, don't you?" Lois said, "Call me cueball." She did become an excellent pool player, much to our amusement.
>
> Lois had virtually no golf experience, and so we would often go out to the Trenholm Hills Golf Course the day before her class with a book and we would follow the book and she and I would hit the ball. She, of course, became better than I.[9]

For West, golf became an athletic outlet and a social vehicle. While governor he had a pitching green built on the front lawn of the Governor's Mansion, and he was a regular partner with Professional Golfers' Association (PGA) tour players during the pro-am competition that preceded the annual Heritage Golf Tournament at Hilton Head Island. Even during his years as ambassador to Saudi Arabia, he pursued his favorite sport by playing on the sand greens and fairways of the affluent desert kingdom.

West's restless intellect was seeking additional stimulation during his law school years. Even as he was pursuing a full course load in law, he became interested in the relatively new discipline of political science and looked into the possibility of acquiring a master's degree. "I still had an idea of possibly teaching," he wrote. "Instead, I found a great friend in Dr. George Sherrill, the head of the department, who told me that he needed part-time instructors and thought I could qualify, so I became an instructor in political science."[10]

West, who had reaped significant academic recognition during his undergraduate years at the Citadel, was able to add another accolade during his USC experience. His friend Dr. George Sherrill was also head of the Phi Beta Kappa chapter at the university. "When I expressed an interest, I am sure it was his efforts that got me elected to that organization. Fortunately, my grades in Law School were sufficient."[11]

West's experience as an instructor also exposed him to other politically ambitious young men. Among his students was Terrell Glenn, who went on to become a prominent Columbia lawyer and U.S. Attorney in the 1960s. Another student of West's at the time, Albert Watson, would become West's opponent a quarter century later in his gubernatorial race. West enjoyed telling of the instance during the 1970 race when his campaign manager, Harry Lightsey, suggested that West's experience in teaching political science at USC should be listed in the campaign brochure. "No, I don't think so," West recalled telling Lightsey, an attorney who later became dean of the USC Law School and president of the College of Charleston. "My opponent was one of my students." Lightsey still thought it was a good idea until West explained further. The opponent with whom West would have such dire political differences in 1970 was deemed to have had sufficient political wisdom twenty-five years earlier to make an A in West's class. Lightsey lost his point, and West recalled, "Albert and I subsequently laughed about it, but it was never mentioned in the campaign."[12]

Political science became another lifetime interest. As his political career and law practice waned in later life, West became a Distinguished Professor of Political Science at USC and taught young men and women of his experiences and the opinions he developed about the turbulent Middle East during his years as U.S. ambassador to Saudi Arabia.

BREEZING THROUGH LAW SCHOOL

Law school proved to be a joy—and an academic breeze—for West, with his keen intellect and the assorted experiences that helped prepare him for classroom work. He wrote:

We were young, had just won the war, had our whole lives before us and were certainly relieved from the prospect of fighting. It was an exhilarating time.

My experience in the Pentagon had sharpened whatever intellect I had, plus two semesters, part-time which I had at George Washington University, gave me a leg up in the law. . . . I had also clerked for Allen Murchison [a Camden attorney] for several summers and learned a little bit about the practical side of the law, so the books came relatively easy to me.[13]

By the time he had completed a single semester of law school in Columbia, West was ready for the state's bar exam, and "as it turned out, [it] was somewhat of a snap . . . I had a good retentive memory and loved the law. I had read all of the recent cases as reported in the S.C. advance sheets, and found that most of the questions were taken directly from those cases. I was able not only to refer to the cases in many of my answers but give the citation as well. I was later told unofficially that my score was the highest recorded up to that time."[14]

The raw intellect that Mattie West had seen emerging in her son fifteen years earlier was taking form. Fast-tracking a career that had been interrupted by three years of wartime service, West, who was barely twenty-four years old, went into law practice on a part-time basis in Camden on January 1, 1947, ten months after enrolling in law school. His first partner was Allen Murchison, with whom he had clerked in the past. Their office was upstairs over a shop at the corner of Broad and DeKalb streets, the main intersection of downtown Camden. That crossroads would remain a legal address for John West for the rest of his life. Across the corner from his first law office with Murchison would be the three-story office building that housed the law firm he established years later, and where his son John C. "Jack" West Jr. would practice six decades later.

Even after passing the bar exam, West continued in law school, commuting back and forth to Camden and graduating magna cum laude in 1947. One of the advantages of practicing law while still in school, he found, was that "it provided an added zest when I had an immediate problem . . . it made the law so much more realistic."[15]

MAKING A HOME PLACE

The Wests moved back to Camden after graduation, and he went into full-time practice on January 1, 1948. For a while the Wests lived with Lois's mother, Annie Rhame, on Laurens Street in the historic section of downtown Camden. Then came a move that took on an enduring permanence for the family. West's mother, Mattie, deeded them ten acres of the family farm, across the Cleveland School Road from where he grew up and near the cornfields where he struggled with the plow. The site would remain a home and prominent family landmark for the rest of his life.

The first lodging, however, was a less-than-grandiose beginning for the young family. They purchased one of the prefab units that had been quarters for shipyard workers in North Charleston during World War II and that had been surplused in the postwar years for one thousand dollars each "where is, as is," as West described them.[16]

He and a law school classmate, Doug Montgomery, each bought one, and the trucking company owned by the family of another law school friend, Wade Weatherford of Gaffney, hauled the two units from North Charleston to Camden for seven hundred dollars each, bringing the total cost of the new West home to seventeen hundred dollars. "I borrowed the full amount from our friendly dentist, Dr. Williford's wife, Jane," West recalled, "[and we] paid $17 a month house payment. The house was adequate—two bedrooms, small living room, kitchen, and a floor furnace next to the bathroom and bedrooms."[17]

The World War II prefab became the nucleus of the home the Wests would occupy until he became governor in 1971, and it would remain a family residence even after they established a permanent home at Hilton Head following his service in Saudi Arabia. West wrote, "It [the original home] was expanded and renovated ultimately to four bedrooms, swimming pool and fishing ponds being added, but still the basic unit started there in 1948. As I frequently observed, as the family expanded, the house expanded and the mortgage expanded."[18] The house was not sold until 2005, when it was purchased and renovated by a Columbia family.

For the Phi Beta Kappa, magna cum laude law school graduate, the early days of law practice turned out to be just that—practice—and not all that promising. John wrote:

> Allen's practice was largely workmen's compensation with work in the Magistrate's Court, along with domestic cases, a typical country practice. The practice had not been that good historically in Camden. In fact, Janie DeLoach, a neighbor of Lois' mother and wife of John DeLoach (one of Camden's leading lawyers), told Miss Annie at a DAR meeting just after it was announced that I was going to practice in Camden that—something like this—"Annie, I'm sorry to see John coming to practice. You know, every lawyer who has died in Camden since 1918 has died bankrupt."
>
> So prospects were not that good in immediate postwar years in Camden.[19]

A FATHER FIGURE

In Murchison, however, West had found someone who was like the father he had never known. Sixty years old when he and the twenty-four-year-old West went into practice together, Murchison had been a counselor and mentor much earlier. According to West,

> he had been a neighbor in the country and a friend, almost a father figure to me. He had loaned me his new automobile in 1940–41, let me work in his office for several years and in general was one of the kindest, gentlest, most decent persons I ever met.
>
> The relationship Allen and I had was perfect in every way. He gave me all the responsibility that I wanted, and sometimes more. While I was still in law school, he said, "Let's form a partnership, and half the money that comes in is yours." Each Saturday as I would go over to the office, he would pull out his wallet with the week's receipts [and] count out half of them to me. When I told him it wasn't fair, he said, "Don't worry, when you get into practicing law here full-time, I'm going fox hunting."[20]

Murchison was a colorful, lifelong bachelor who, West said, "was perhaps not the greatest lawyer, but he had a lot of common sense."[21] He lived in an old country mansion he had renovated on Black River Road on the banks of Swift Creek, not far from the West farm. The property was purchased by Murchison's father from a black family whose ownership dated back to the land-distribution program for newly freed slaves after the Civil War.

Among Murchison's neighbors were descendants of freed slaves who manufactured moonshine whiskey and who were known popularly as the "Black River Distillers." As a matter of practice, the sheriff would make an arrest of them annually, and they would be represented in court by Murchison. West recalled that Murchison's defense usually was something along these lines: "Your honor, these folks are not real criminals. They are not the Mafia type. They are simply community-oriented people who are furnishing a little cheer for the fellows of the community who cannot afford the store-bought liquor. They only make enough for their own and friends' use. They don't charge much, hardly make any profit, and it's a community enterprise that shouldn't be illegal."[22]

Ordinarily, West recalled, that would be enough for the moonshiners to be released with a small fine. In 1956, however, the Black River Distillers were slapped with a one-thousand-dollar fine because, the presiding judge noted, of new legislation that John West, as the county's new senator, had helped pass. "Is that true?" Murchison asked West with a voice of shock. "I somewhat sheepishly replied, 'I believe so,'" West recalled.[23]

THE COMING STORM

The years of West's early law practice with Murchison were the source of stories and anecdotes that West enjoyed telling. Across the South and the rest of the nation, however, major events taking place would prove instrumental in the young lawyer's long-term future and would transform the state's racial customs, practices, and laws. Judge J. Waties Waring's ruling in *Rice v. Elmore* in 1947 legally gave black voters the right to participate in the Democratic primary, although roadblocks would impede such participation until the passage of the Voting Rights Act in 1965.

Also in 1947 a black farmer named Levi Pearson, in the rural county of Clarendon—forty miles east of Camden—was petitioning for school bus transportation for black children, setting off a series of actions that would lead to the landmark *Briggs v. Elliott* and eventually its successor case, *Brown v. Board of Education,* challenging the entire "separate but equal" principle before the U.S. Supreme Court.

At the federal level, President Harry Truman was not only addressing one of the issues that had confounded West during his military service by ordering the racial desegregation of the armed services but was taking other initiatives as well. Truman was advancing the most ambitious civil rights program of any U.S. president since Lincoln. These initiatives were distressing southern Democrats and led to the presidential candidacy in 1948 of South Carolina's then governor, Strom Thurmond, on the States' Rights Democratic Party, or "Dixiecrat," ticket.

For his part, West was beginning to discover the racial squint of the law. He had already observed early in his practice that "there was still a feeling among the blacks that the whites weren't treating them fairly, and it was certainly justified. To find a young white man who was willing to represent a black with sincerity and a little vigor certainly helped me get a start."[24]

That reality dated back to his early days as a part-time attorney still in law school. In his first month of practice, January 1947, only shortly after he had passed the bar, he encountered what he called "my first major case." Murchison and West, along with two Columbia attorneys, were representing four black men from Blaney, in Kershaw County, in a murder trial in which the Blaney men were charged with murdering one of their colleagues.

Three of the defendants were released, but one—John Brown—was held because he had confessed. West assumed his defense and tried to convince the jury that the defendant had been coerced. "I had gotten somewhat carried away when I cross-examined a Columbia police officer [who] had the nickname 'Hosepipe,' and I asked him repeatedly did he use a hosepipe to beat John Brown. It was good theater, but didn't convince the jury."[25]

West's client was convicted and, despite a series of appeals, served a short sentence on the chain gang, professing his innocence throughout. "Somehow, that case left an impression on me, and one of the weaknesses of my subsequent practice was . . . to become more emotionally involved than I should on my client's behalf. I felt he had been done an injustice and regardless of his inability to pay, we pursued it. Thinking back, I am sure that part of my success as a lawyer is the fact that I gave my clients hope by believing in them, and by going the extra mile to help them, even when the situation appeared bleakest and their financial resources were non-existent."[26]

GAINING A REPUTATION

The John Brown case and West's feisty courtroom behavior also built some early credibility for West within the black community. Another early case West recalled came from an affluent black man and his sister who called on him at his office and asked him to represent the woman's son, a student at Mather Academy, who was charged with rape. He asked about the amount of the fee, and West recalled, "He pulled out a roll of bills and I saw $100 at the top. I said, '$100.' It was more money than I had ever collected and without hesitation, he peeled off the $100."[27]

As West told the story, he was able to have the charges against the man's nephew dropped that afternoon, and a day later he was able to have the charges dropped for a friend who had also been arrested as an accomplice. West also remembered a sobering part of the experience:

> I made a mistake which I never made again in criminal practice. I asked him [the client], "Son, are you guilty or not?" He looked at me, rolled his eyes, and said, "I asked her and just didn't wait to hear whether she said yes or no."
>
> . . . It taught me a great lesson. It is not the role of the lawyer in a criminal case to judge the guilt or innocence of his client. It is to get the facts and to advise him as best you can on those facts. Forever afterwards, when I would be asked how I can represent guilty people . . . I tell that story and I've never tried to form an opinion since that time.[28]

West's quick wit and knowledge of the law were already earning him some courtroom victories and a reputation around the community. He was representing people with names such as June Bug and Mutt and was known as a lawyer who would sue anybody, even if it meant shaking up the town's older establishment. Along the way he was stockpiling the kinds of experiences that would broaden his practical and political abilities and add enormously to his treasured storehouse of anecdotes and homespun stories. He recalled:

Practicing law in a small town in the post–World War era was a great lesson in human nature.

People came in with their problems, no matter what—domestic disputes, stealings, cuttings, fights, disputes over dogs—and, of course, we took any business that came in, whether it was paid or not. It was educational, interesting, sometimes frustrating, but never boring.[29]

It was only a matter of time before formal political opportunity occurred for West, and it came through his mentor and law partner, Allen Murchison. As it turned out, it was a genuine political plum: election to the state Highway Commission.

A POLITICAL BAPTISM

Since its creation in 1917, the Highway Commission had evolved as an agency of rare political influence. Established in the years of agricultural dominance of the state's political and economic communities, its mandate was helping farmers get "out of the mud" and transport their products from farm to market on paved or "improved" unpaved roads. By the 1950s the commission stood as a virtually autonomous agency whose revenues flowed directly from taxes charged at the gas pump and fees assessed elsewhere. Its status, in fact, was so coveted that Governor Olin D. Johnston and the General Assembly all but went to war in October 1935 over control of the agency in a feud that prompted the governor to call out the National Guard to surround the building (now the Calhoun State Office Building on Sumter Street) that housed the agency and to expel its employees. As it did in most tiffs with the governor, the General Assembly prevailed in that one.

Things had cooled down by the early 1950s, but the Highway Commission was still a bastion of governmental independence. The agency was supported by its own dedicated revenue sources, mostly highway user fees in the form of gasoline taxes, and its members were chosen from each of the state's fourteen judicial circuits, elected by members of the legislative delegations of the counties in the respective circuits. Kershaw shared the fifth circuit with Richland County, and it was the custom that the two counties would swap members on the Highway Commission every other term. It was Kershaw County's "turn" in the rotation in 1948, and this provoked a steamy dispute within the county's legislative delegation. West recalled,

The resident state senator was Bob Kennedy and the House delegation was headed by Clator Arrants, both rivals and subsequently bitter enemies. They could not agree on a choice, and finally Bob, who was a friend of Allen Murchison (my law partner), suggested him. Clator Arrants could not really oppose Allen since he had been one of Allen's protégés and Allen helped him considerably.

However, Allen very graciously said, "Take my young law partner John West," and so I was elected.[30]

West, who would later become a political adversary of Bob Kennedy and his wing of the Democratic Party, quickly discovered the remarkable political clout that went with his new position. Each commissioner had an annual discretionary fund of one hundred thousand dollars for road-paving purposes in his circuit, enough to pave ten miles at 1940s–50s costs of ten thousand dollars per mile. The commission held a potential gold mine of political favors to be granted by the incumbent commission member, but for the aspiring young attorney to whom the position fell, his role also meant disappointing those to whom road-paving favors were not granted. "Sometimes deciding where it (the $100,000) went was worse than not having it," West admitted. "At the same time, being a part of the process was a great political experience, plus it enabled me to get around and know not only political people but leaders in the community, all of whom wanted their roads paved."[31]

As a high-stakes agency, the Highway Commission also had high-stakes battles and would provide West with his first direct experience in the rough-and-tumble world of political infighting in a governmental setting. He took office in the midst of a fight over the job of chief highway commissioner, and he jumped into the fray with little inhibition.

The commission had fired Chief Commissioner Stanley Williamson during the year prior to West's election, and the displaced commissioner had appealed the dismissal to the Supreme Court. Upon the court's ruling that Williamson could not, in fact, be fired without cause, West called for a hearing to "bring charges against him."[32]

The case was eventually settled in a quieter fashion, and West went on to befriend Claude MacMillan and Silas Pearman, subsequent chief commissioners. He also made the acquaintance of fellow commissioners from elsewhere in the state, and they would provide something of a bridge for the young lawyer into the world of statewide politics. Among those were Leonard G. Mishoe, commission chairman, who would become a state senator from Williamsburg County, and James J. Wheeler, vice chairman, who had been a longtime House member from Saluda County. West's seatmate on the commission was Boyd Brown of Winnsboro, whose son, Walter, became a House member and subsequently a powerful lobbyist for the Southern Railway.

For all the political schooling he was getting as a member of the Highway Commission, however, West later wrote that at the end of his four-year term,

West (right) served one term on the State Highway Commission (1948–52) and befriended future chief commissioner Silas Pearman. Courtesy of the John C. West Papers, South Carolina Political Collections, University of South Carolina

"I had had my fill of politics. It was a great experience, but I was going to be a lawyer's lawyer and concentrate on the practice of law." Thus committed, he remembered turning down an offer from his old friend Dr. George Sherrill at the University of South Carolina to join the political science faculty as an adjunct professor, even though it would have provided a higher income. "It didn't look as if I had made a good business decision," West said.[33]

West's business plans, in fact, were taking on a more long-term nature, and he was sinking his roots deeply into the Camden community. As his law practice with Murchison grew and expanded, he undertook, along with friends Doug Montgomery and Edwin Boyle (Allen Murchison's cousin), the construction of what he called Camden's first modern law office, a modest three-story structure across the corner from his former offices over the Fashion Shoppe. It would include numerous other offices, including space for another friend, the dentist Dr. J. L. Williford. The law practice prospered, and West enjoyed his reputation as the brash upstart in Camden's staid legal community.

West's absence from Camden politics, in fact, did not last long. Within months after the end of his stint on the Highway Commission, he was back in the fray, this time in a more contentious role than that of doling out road-paving dollars. The issue was health care and specifically whether the county should build a new hospital, and this was sufficiently urgent in West's mind to impel him into his first race for public office.

CHAMPIONING A CAUSE

The decision had a distinctly personal angle. The Wests had become the parents of a young son, John C. "Jack" West Jr., three years earlier, and they watched nervously as a dangerous virus attacked children in the community. As it reached near epidemic stages, the virus hit young Jack one evening at about 11:00 o'clock. West later recalled:

> For young parents to see a child in convulsion was as frightening an experience as one can imagine. We rushed him to the Camden hospital . . . and there was only one private room for pediatrics, which—of course—was filled. There were two wards, one for male and one for female children . . . Lois took Jack into the boys' side while I paced the floor. Every so often nurses would come in and give all the children shots of penicillin, which created bedlam. At 7 o'clock the next morning, my uncle, Dr. Carl West (for whom I was named), came in for his morning rounds.
>
> I greeted him by saying, "Uncle Carl, this hospital is a disgrace; the facilities are inadequate." He looked at me and said, "Son, we know that—we're trying to get a new hospital, or get this one renovated, and we're looking for members for the new board. Would you serve?"
>
> At that stage, I was agreeable to anything, so I said, "Of course." Soon thereafter, the board was constituted and I was elected chairman.[34]

The hospital issue had been simmering for some years, and it would divide the county painfully along political, economic, and social lines in the months ahead. The Camden Hospital was housed in a gracious colonial-style home, to which wings had been added to bring its capacity to sixty-eight beds. Its governing board was a self-perpetuating one, as West recalled, composed mostly of "old Camden residents," and he noted that the venerable Camden native and wealthy statesman Bernard Baruch annually wrote a check to cover whatever operating deficit the hospital might incur.

At the time that the Wests had the frightening experience with their son Jack, there was already a significant movement under way to address the hospital issue, and legislation had been passed to replace the aging Camden board with a newly constituted county board. By then Baruch—in his eighties—believed that the area needed more than the makeshift approach to hospital operation that characterized the situation at the time. According to West, Baruch had made it known that given his age, "the hospital could no longer count on him for an annual contribution to make up deficit."[35] While he was leaving the hospital a substantial sum in his will, he also believed that the time had come when the delivery of hospital care should become a countywide public responsibility.[36]

Such was easier said than done. Some Camdenites had become comfortable with the informal arrangement by which their hospital was annually underwritten by Baruch. A new hospital or even the expansion of the old one could require a sizable chunk of new money, and in postwar Camden, even with its influx of wealthy northerners in wintertime, such a prospect was a daunting one.

West's presence on the newly constituted county board became an influential and aggressive one, and a consulting firm was retained to put dollar figures to the various options emerging to address the area's hospital needs. Renovation, the firm said, would cost $1.2 million; a new hospital would cost $2 million. "While the difference [did] not appear to be too great," West recalled, "in 1952–53, it was a substantial, meaningful difference."[37]

SHAPING THE ISSUES

The issue was thus divided along three distinct lines politically and publicly among (1) those who would support no changes to the old hospital, (2) those who would favor renovation of the old hospital, and (3) those who would support the construction of a new hospital on a new site. A referendum, in fact, had been held in 1952 to determine public sentiment about the issue, and it proved to be an omen of the confusion to come. Voters approved bonds amounting to $2 million for a new hospital, but legal and constitutional questions entangled the issues. In the same referendum in which the hospital bonds were approved, voters turned down a constitutional amendment necessary to permit the board's bond capacity to be increased, a move that nullified the approval vote.[38]

The legal brambles would continue to be used as strategic and diversionary devices as Kershaw County's political forces settled into hand-to-hand combat over the hospital. It would not be, as it turned out, the only issue that would divide and provoke voters and the public in general. Events that unfolded during the course of 1954 would make it a year of immense consequence to South Carolina and the nation, and a year in which the political neophyte John West would be buffeted by forces within and beyond the borders of South Carolina.

In Kershaw County the season of political uproar officially got under way on February 9, 1954. On that day Clator Arrants, the county's state senator, announced that he would run for lieutenant governor in the June Democratic primary. Arrants, thirty-seven at the time, had graduated from Charlotte Thompson High School in 1933 and was a World War II veteran and classmate of West's at the USC Law School. He had served in the S.C. House before and after the war, was completing his first term in the S.C. Senate, and was generally viewed as a moderate in what would become an increasingly polarized political community.

Arrants's announcement left the Senate seat open and set off a series of politically conspicuous events. West, as the clearly defined hospital advocate, filed for the Senate at the deadline of March 16, along with other county office candidates. West later wrote:

> It was put to me that the only way we could get a new hospital on a new site was for me to run for the state senate. I am sure this was an overstatement, but I bought it at the time, and talked to Lois about running. It was probably the most strained time of our marriage. She was reluctant for me to get into politics.
>
> However, I was finally persuaded (probably didn't take too much) and I announced for that office.[39]

A LOOK AT THINGS TO COME

Lois's version of the story went something like this:

> He [John] asked me about it, and I said, "Well, I really don't want you to . . ." and he didn't want to go into politics, and I didn't want him to. I said, "Well, I tell you what. You get . . . about twelve people to publicly endorse you and ask you to run, take an ad in the paper. And if they'll do that, then I'll agree to run."
>
> Instead of that, his friend, Doug Montgomery, announced that he [West] was going to run. . . . I said, "Well, I'm not going to be put in a position of you having to say I can't run because my wife won't let me." I didn't like it, which was true.

He got trapped into it. But I knew what was ahead of me. I knew right then where he'd go, because I knew him. It was the only time I cried.[40]

West's opponent would be Arthur Jones, the feisty mayor of Kershaw, who had lost by thirteen votes to Arrants four years earlier in a heated race, from which the wounds had not healed. West remembered that election and the role he played: "Clator Arrants [was] elected State Senator in 1950. Bob Kennedy [the incumbent] had decided not to run, and Doug Montgomery and I persuaded Allen Murchison to run, while the most conservative groups chose Arthur Jones . . . as their candidate. Allen, along with George Nicholson, a lawyer-professor, were eliminated in the first race, and the second race was a battle between Clator and Arthur. Allen and I were supporting Clator, who was our neighbor in the Charlotte Thompson community. Donald Holland and John Baker of Bethune were elected to the House. Clator's election was a close one."[41]

In the 1954 race for lieutenant governor, Arrants would be challenged by Ernest F. "Fritz" Hollings, the Charleston attorney who had served three terms in the S.C. House, the last two as Speaker pro tempore, and was making his first statewide race. Running for governor were two Democratic Party veterans: George Bell Timmerman, who had served two terms as lieutenant governor, and Lester Bates, the Columbia mayor and insurance executive who had lost in a 1950 race for governor to Byrnes.

While local issues and political rivalries were steamy, each race had as part of its virtually built-in agenda a matter that was nearing a judgment before the U.S. Supreme Court that spring—the decision as to whether the state's segregated public school system would be upheld in the *Brown v. Board of Education* case. On November 11, 1949, black parents in Clarendon County had filed suit in federal court challenging the state's notoriously imbalanced "separate, but equal" education system. The suit would become *Briggs v. Elliott,* which was combined with four others to form the *Brown* case. In an effort to head off a potential court finding that the state's schools were indeed separate and not equal, South Carolina had instituted a 3 percent sales tax in 1951 to provide for a quick upgrading of black public school buildings, and many South Carolinians believed that step would protect the segregated school system. Part of that sentiment stemmed from the fact that the state was represented in court by the onetime solicitor general and presidential candidate John W. Davis, whom West later called "probably the outstanding lawyer of the 20th century."[42]

AN UNEXPECTED BOMBSHELL

Whatever the outcome, South Carolinians sensed that a Supreme Court decision might be near in spring 1954. However, as late as May 3 the *Camden*

Chronicle published a Charleston news account that reported, "There is increasing speculation in Washington that the Supreme Court will let its current term expire without reaching a decision on the momentous issue of the legality of race segregation in public schools."[43] The speculation proved incorrect. *Brown v. Board of Education,* with its unanimous ruling that school segregation violated the U.S. Constitution, arrived on May 17 and was tossed squarely into the already heated political contests of Kershaw County, which would be settled less than a month later in the June 16 Democratic primary.

Political campaigning in South Carolina in 1954, under any circumstances, was no place for anyone suspected of being "soft on race." With the *Brown* decision arriving as such a fresh—and somewhat surprising—issue, it lay as a political imperative to be addressed by both candidates for the Kershaw County Senate seat. West, the man who would sixteen years later make a "color-blind administration" the chief political pursuit of his gubernatorial administration, chose to take an unmistakably firm but diplomatically careful stand in favor of segregated schools. On May 19—at the first stump meeting of the campaign—West delivered his encomium on the topic at rural Blaney, saying, "Seven days ago today, a group of men in Washington put upon the South the greatest problem we have been faced with since 1876. By an edict of a court sitting in Washington, it has been determined that our children cannot go to segregated schools. The solution to that problem will rest on the shoulders of the man you send to the legislature. I cannot offer you a wrapped up solution to the problem. But I can tell you that I will work with all the talents at my command to see that the races are not mixed in our schools."[44]

West tried to sound statesmanlike as he addressed what would turn out to be a pro-Jones, hostile audience. He called his presentation "my maiden political speech" and added,

> It is not my purpose to stand here tonight and recommend myself highly. I am not running on the demerits of my opponent, if he has any. I shall sling no mud.
>
> Look us over. If you think my opponent is better qualified to handle that problem [the *Brown* decision], vote for him. Because we need the wisdom of Solomon and the help of God in this crisis.[45]

TAKING OFF THE GLOVES

Jones was having none of that rhetorical civility. He dismissed the *Brown* decision on that occasion by saying, "From now on my feelings are that the august body [the U.S. Supreme Court] has been lowered to the level of a cheap political body."[46]

While both candidates toed the line in support of segregated schools, West believed that there were conspicuous differences between him and Jones in style and tone. He later wrote, "My opponent, 'Mush' Jones, was a strong segregationist . . . I had taken a much more moderate view on the Supreme Court decision."[47]

Once it was established that the candidates did not disagree substantively on *Brown,* at least not at the Blaney stump meeting, Jones turned his attention to the issue on which they had their most serious disagreement, the proposal for a new hospital. He came out swinging. "I do not care to blaspheme my opponent," he said, "but he [West] was chairman of the hospital board, which has done everything within its power to cram down your throats a two-million dollar hospital and did a good job of it."[48]

Blaney, a community known for its drag-racing strip, was clearly Arthur Jones territory. If there had been any question about that preference, most doubt was removed at the outset of the meeting when one of those in attendance presented Jones with an American flag and a printed statement, which was read publicly. "We present this flag to you, Arthur Jones," the statement said in part, "believing that you will keep faith with the people of Kershaw County and that, through you, we will have fair and impartial representation and bring freedom and liberty back to Kershaw County."[49]

During the course of the short campaign, West absorbed a lot of punishment from Jones and began to get scrappier. Responding to comments that Jones made about family members at a stump meeting at Bethune (West's uncle, Dr. Carl West, was a staunch supporter of the new hospital and a Jones target), John West called the remarks "a low blow" and said, "it hurt me deeply. I want to tell you here and now. If you can't say something good about a man, keep your big mouth shut!"[50]

Jones was a political brawler and did not keep his mouth shut. He said, "I've been accused of attacking my opponent. As long as I'm running for this office, I can say what I please. If I have offended his relatives, I'm sorry, but what is my friend, a tattletale? Will he run and tell his kin that I said something to offend them?"[51]

Paralleling the street fighting in the Senate race was a series of events that carried the hospital issue to the brink and back several times. The county's legislative delegation sought to avoid another public referendum on the issue by gaining passage of legislation authorizing the hospital board to issue bonds without public approval. The action set off another firestorm in which the bill was vetoed by Governor Byrnes, the veto was overridden in the General Assembly, and in the melee the delegation agreed to provide for another referendum.

It would be held at the same time as the Democratic primary, making the hospital issue and the individual political races directly connected.

FRIENDS AND NEIGHBORS

During the course of the battle, sides were drawn along somewhat familiar lines among the county's political leaders. Although it was his first race for elected office, West had gained some political attention as highway commissioner and was clearly identified as the prohospital candidate. That made him allied with some of the political insiders and opposed by others. It also became evident that he bore no particular fondness for his pugnacious opponent Jones, whom he enjoyed calling "Mush." West later wrote, "It turned out that I was aligned with the then 'Courthouse crowd,' including a chief of the rural police, the auditor, treasurer and Clerk of Court. They were all suspicious of Arthur 'Mush' Jones, who was my opponent. . . . 'Mush' was a former . . . baseball player . . . [and] it was said he had a short career because of a stubborn nature and hot temper, characteristics he still enjoyed in politics."[52]

Harvey Teal, a Kershaw County historian who worked in the 1954 campaign, recalled that the West alliance extended to incumbent House members John Baker and Don Holland. "John Baker lived north of the town of Bethune," Teal recalled, "and [Don] Holland, although practicing law in Camden at the time, was from Cassatt. Those three [including West] ran as a sort of ticket."[53]

Jones's chief backer was Bob Kennedy, a former Camden mayor and former state senator who made no secret of his dislike for the prospect of a new hospital. Early in the campaign, Kennedy orchestrated a unanimous resolution from the county Democratic Party's executive committee praising Governor Byrnes for his veto of the legislation authorizing the county to issue hospital bonds without a referendum. Kennedy's resolution, carried prominently at the top of page 1-A of the *Camden Chronicle,* also resolved that the General Assembly be "rebuked for its action in over-riding the . . . veto, which is in opposition to the will of our people."[54]

The race was thus divided along several lines, among them (1) urban v. rural, (2) prohospital v. antihospital, (3) moderate v. conservative, and (4) the Bob Kennedy faction v. the Arrants-West faction. In some minds, West later recalled, it also had a moral angle. He wrote about a sermon delivered at his home church, Bethesda Presbyterian in Camden, on the Sunday before the election. It "was probably the most meaningful I had heard in terms of its effect on my life," he wrote. "It was two days before my first election. Reverend [Douglas] McArn, the minister, was a conservative soul who seldom strayed from the scriptures, and on that Sunday he didn't. But he preached about 'good and evil,' and holding up a slip of paper, said, 'This is the ballot you will cast two days from now, and you will have a choice between good and evil.' He was obviously referring to me."[55]

Two days later South Carolinians cast their ballots, and the outcome in Kershaw County was just as it had been four years earlier, razor thin. West had this recollection of the experience: "It was the only election I ever went into feeling confident I was going to win. I had campaigned all around the county and found no one who was going to vote against me. However, when the votes were counted and recounted . . . I had won by a total of three votes. . . . The referendum question was whether to build a new hospital on a new site or renovate the old one. The new site won by 36 votes, and some interpreted that to mean that the [hospital] issue was 12 times more popular than the candidate who espoused it."[56]

SQUEAKING BY

The three-vote margin came from election-night returns, 3,239 for West and 3,236 for Jones.[57] A subsequent recount boosted West's actual victory margin to eight votes, 3,249 to 3,241.[58] As it turned out, West was the only successful candidate among those on his "ticket." Both of West's "running mates" for the House, Don Holland and John Baker, were losers, falling to L. P. Branham and James Sweet. Clator Arrants was defeated by Fritz Hollings in the lieutenant governor's race.[59]

In the hospital referendum, election-night results were deemed inconclusive among the three options: (1) a new hospital; (2) renovation of the old hospital; or (3) no expenditure. A second vote was set to decide between the $500,000 renovation of the old hospital and the $1.25 million construction of a new hospital. In that vote the new hospital was carried by a margin of 43 votes, 1,353 to 1,310.[60]

West actually carried only ten of thirty-one precincts in the election, and the new hospital was approved in only thirteen boxes. City voters supported both West and the new hospital, and the new state senator did surprisingly well in boisterous Blaney, losing by a 62–38 percent spread. In the second hospital referendum two weeks later, Blaney residents actually supported the new hospital in a much lighter turnout.

Timmerman beat Bates in the race for governor by sixty thousand votes, a wide margin by South Carolina standards. Timmerman had demonized Bates by intimating that the Columbia mayor had support from two of South Carolina's political scapegoats, the National Association for the Advancement of

Colored People (NAACP) and the national labor organization, the Congress of Industrial Organizations (CIO). While Bates drew support from party regulars, Timmerman capitalized on the bitter racial sentiments of the segregationist Dixiecrats who had supported Strom Thurmond in his run for the presidency in 1948.

Timmerman would set the state on a four-year crusade to fight school desegregation, joining the Virginia-sponsored "interposition" movement, which contended that states could resist federal court orders, namely *Brown v. Board of Education*. Bates, as mayor of Columbia, would later become the first South Carolina elected official to negotiate a settlement with civil rights protestors, leading a peaceful effort that desegregated the city's lunch counters and opened job opportunities for blacks in city employment in August 1962. Hollings won his first statewide race and put into motion a career that would take him to the governor's office and the U.S. Senate over the next five decades. His initiatives in economic development and racial peace would move the state toward a position of moderation in the 1960s and 1970s.

THE UTOPIAN CANDIDATE

For West, the seeds of future political activity were being planted in several ways. His style reflected the amiable personality he had been showing the world through his education, military, and legal careers, and he would remain, sometimes painfully, a "nice guy" candidate and officeholder. The "Mush" Joneses of the political universe would continue to make a target of him.

West also found himself running not just as an individual but as a candidate with a cause—the hospital issue—and the identity of candidate and cause were at times inseparable. West would continue to be an advocate, and in his biggest political victory sixteen years later in the race for governor, his championing of civil rights was similarly viewed as being inseparable from his individual candidacy.

The development of nuances in the approach to race as a political and public issue characterized the 1954 elections. While both candidates declared their support for segregated schools, West was not a race-baiter, and in the racially obsessed politics of the 1950s there were clear distinctions among the various levels of segregationists. As he evolved into a moderate on racial matters, and as moods turned darker among more extreme elements, West would find himself pitted openly—and dangerously—against elements that preferred violence to the diplomacy of "nice guy" candidates.

In a bare-knuckles political brawl, Kershaw County had elected to the state Senate a Phi Beta Kappa, magna cum laude intellectual whose political career would belie his backcountry upbringing. He would, in fact, never be a comfortable fit for rough-and-tumble rural politics.

Governor Robert E. McNair, West's friend and future political ally, was one of those who saw the anomaly in West's makeup. "He was articulate and bright and good," McNair said years later.

> John was . . . an idealist . . . aggressive . . . and liberal. . . . Camden is what everybody identifies [in Kershaw County] but you get out into other parts of the county, and it is tough.
>
> It is two different types of people and John was always looking for Utopia.[61]

POLITICS IN THE ROUGH

> When we decided to continue our strong stand against them [the
> Klan], we felt it was probably the end of us as a newspaper.
>
> *John West*

Utopia would prove to be a particularly elusive objective in 1950s South Carolina for the newly elected senator from Kershaw County. "It was a mean time," David Halberstam wrote, and "the nation was ready for witch hunts."[1] South Carolina was feeling that spirit. It was a place of uneasy political suspicions about everything from racial upheavals to communist conspiracies, and West's early years in the S.C. Senate would be shaped by those extraordinary influences.

He would not be a bystander. John West would find himself caught up in some of the rough-and-tumble gyrations of a state squirming, scheming, and plotting to resist the political transformations that were overtaking the rest of the nation. The daunting presence of such elements as Ku Klux Klan night riders, Joseph McCarthy anticommunist zealots, and other southern eccentricities would be among the political realities the new senator would encounter as he embarked on a career of service at the state level.

For sheer political theater, however, nothing among those sideshows would match the spectacle that would unfold in the summer of 1954 and draw him into one of the state's landmark historical events. This was a write-in campaign for the U.S. Senate, an option usually viewed as an exercise in political folly, futility, or desperation. In this case, however, it would escalate into a full-voiced expression of the state's highly personal style of political warfare. While race and communism tended to dominate much of the political thinking of the time, this contest turned out to be purely personal. Two powerful figures traded haymakers until only one was left standing.

THE MAKINGS OF A DONNYBROOK

It all began with the unexpected death of South Carolina's U.S. senator Burnet R. Maybank of Charleston on September 1, 1954. Suddenly vacant was the supreme prize of the state's political and electoral system, as a seat in the U.S. Senate had come to be recognized. The vacancy came at a time when South Carolina was endowed with an array of political celebrities, and their ambitions were quickly drawn to the rare and coveted political opportunity.

One political celebrity was Strom Thurmond, a former governor who had achieved heroic status among many white South Carolinians by his 1948 run for the presidency on the States' Rights, or Dixiecrat, ticket in opposition to the civil rights plank that year of the Democratic Party and its candidate, Harry Truman. Two years later, in 1950, Thurmond had lost a bitterly fought race for the other U.S. Senate seat to the incumbent, Olin D. Johnston.

Another was James F. Byrnes, the state's sitting governor, resident political celebrity, and master strategist, whose opposition to the desegregation of public schools had cast him in a national role of leadership for that cause. Byrnes had also gained some attention as a discontented Democrat by organizing "Democrats for Eisenhower" in 1952 to support the GOP presidential candidate in South Carolina and to block the election of the Democratic nominee, Adlai E. Stevenson, with his civil rights advocacy.

Another political notable was Edgar Brown, the powerful state senator from Barnwell County who had failed in two previous attempts for the U.S. Senate and who—at age sixty-six—saw his years of political potency slipping away. While Thurmond and Byrnes had achieved some national recognition and status with their highly visible roles as dissident Democrats in fighting desegregation, Brown had become the consummate insider. He was known as "Mr. Democrat" for his inordinate loyalty to the party and his experience as a legislative leader and political power broker.

Among Brown's several political bailiwicks was the State Executive Committee of the Democratic Party, a committee that he chaired and where he had served as a member since the days of Woodrow Wilson's presidential nomination in 1914. In the days before two-party politics in South Carolina, the Democratic primary was the decisive election in state and local matters, and the Executive Committee was the arbiter of matters dealing with that defining event.

Among the three prospective front-runners for the U.S. Senate seat, Brown made the first move. Maybank's death, as it turned out, had come at a particularly awkward time for the Democratic Party, largely because of a state law requiring the certification of party candidates for placement on the November general election ballot no later than two months before the general election. That meant that the state's Democrats had to come up with a candidate to replace Maybank by September 4, three days after the senator's death and one day after his September 3 funeral. Under those conditions, Brown reasoned, there was neither time nor money to hold a primary or a convention to select a nominee. Only by action of the state's Democratic Party Executive Committee could such a choice be made in time to meet the legal deadline, he contended.

"Anybody that had any sense knew that you couldn't have a convention," Brown later told the biographer William D. Workman Jr. "And you couldn't have a primary. And you couldn't have an interim primary. You couldn't raise enough money. Nobody but a millionaire could set up the expense of running a primary at a time like that. It was out of the question."[2]

A MOMENT OF AWKWARDNESS

However logical that conclusion may have been, the awkwardness of the process played out graphically when members of the Executive Committee wheeled their vehicles directly from the funeral service for Senator Maybank in Charleston up the road to Columbia to meet only a matter of hours later to nominate his successor. Thurmond biographer Alberta Lachicotte wrote, "Following the church service, the cortege formed for the slow funeral procession uptown to Magnolia Cemetery. Before the cortege reached Magnolia, however, Senator Edgar Brown's long Cadillac pulled out of line and sped to Columbia. In close pursuit was *The News and Courier,* which had sniffed the air . . . and pricked up its ears at what seemed to be a too-hasty departure. Like a hound on the scent of a fox, the Charleston press took off behind that Cadillac."[3]

The press feasted on the remarkable turn of events; the state's Democrats squirmed uncomfortably at the timing; Byrnes and Thurmond stewed. The Columbia meeting proceeded balkily, with the party's leaders eventually falling in line behind Brown as the Democratic nominee. This meant that his was the only name to appear on the printed ballot for the November election.

The nomination came, however, only after the Executive Committee tussled for several hours at its September 3 meeting, eventually abandoning the idea of staging another primary. Even then the nomination was by a 31–18 vote. The decision to empower the Executive Committee to name the nominee was even closer, 29–18.[4]

Then the party regulars took over, and Brown, sensing that the nomination was his, signaled to Berkeley senator Rembert Dennis to make the motion. "After an afternoon of intense discussion and debate, and legal positions explored," Dennis later recalled, "it was decided . . . that [the] committee, before midnight that night, had to have a candidate. . . . Edgar looked at me and there wasn't any hesitancy on my part. I nominated him as a man of great national stature who would make a great U.S. Senator."[5] Brown, in turn, accepted, saying, "I feel as humble as I did in the old days when I was a youngster in old Aiken County. Little did I think I would ever be chosen for this high honor."[6]

In making the Executive Committee nomination sound like a coronation, Brown hoped to stem the ambitions of the other prospective candidates, namely Thurmond and Byrnes. However, he was a savvy warrior and knew the risk he was taking. "There was Strom Thurmond who had just been beaten by Olin Johnston [in the 1950 Democratic primary for U.S. Senate], had a terrific organization and was itching," Brown later wrote, "and [Byrnes] didn't like anything except public life . . . he didn't want to retire and twiddle his fingers."[7]

Brown also believed that Thurmond and Byrnes had somehow disqualified themselves in the public mind from consideration because of their actions against the Democrats' national candidates. In that context Thurmond and Byrnes "had eliminated themselves from being nominated," he said, and "a good many people had talked about it and told me they'd be for me ahead of Strom Thurmond, or they'd be for me ahead of Jim Byrnes."[8] The Executive Committee, he noted, "was composed of more complete loyalists to the old party than otherwise."[9]

Brown, in fact, to many Democrats may have seemed the natural choice for the nomination. The author Nadine Cohodas observed in her 1993 biography of Strom Thurmond, "The question was never whether Edgar Brown was qualified to go to the United States Senate, only the route by which he would get there. In 1954, he was banking on the assumption that [South] Carolina voters shared his respect for party loyalty and its corresponding political reward."[10]

THE GATHERING STORM

Within hours of the committee's late-night decision to nominate Brown, however, things began to grow testy. Questions arose about the political propriety of the method by which Brown was chosen, and Workman wrote, "Here was Brown, at the age of sixty-six and with forty years of party service behind him, seemingly with his long-sought prize within his grasp. . . . Had the people of South Carolina shared his own values of party loyalty and political reward, he would have been a shoo-in. But other values were involved, along with a strong resentment against anything which seemed to deny the people a right to be heard in the selection of a candidate."[11]

A few days later Thurmond made known his sentiments. In a September 7 announcement, he said,

> It is still not too late to hold a primary. All that is needed is for the [executive] committee candidate to withdraw and agree to run in a primary which, under the law, can be held legally and for which there is ample time.
>
> If those who put over the committee nomination continue to ignore the demand which has swept over South Carolina for the people to be given a right to choose their senator, then I shall permit my name to be used in a write-in campaign to be aggressively conducted between now and the November election.[12]

A week after that (September 14) Governor Byrnes joined those calling for a primary "to settle the political brushfire which was sweeping the state." According to Workman, "The . . . proposal from the governor called for the withdrawal of Senator Brown from the general election as a committee-named nominee, and his subsequent re-entry into a Democratic primary against anyone else who wished to run."[13]

Brown, however, chose not to accede to the demands of his former political colleagues, Thurmond and Byrnes, men he believed had "eliminated themselves" from consideration for the nomination. "Battle lines began to form," Workman wrote. "This time, more than personality was involved. On Brown's side was the factor of party regularity, exploited to the maximum by those who contended that 'all true Democrats' owed him their allegiance in the general election. On Thurmond's side was the massive wave of reaction against the committee's having 'hand-picked' a nominee, rather than letting the voters do so by Democratic primary."[14]

Brown, party chairman Neville Bennett, and other Democratic officials met on September 15 to give consideration to the positions taken by Thurmond and Byrnes. Their decision remained unchanged: no primary and no convention. They would stick by the decision of the Executive Committee. Edgar Brown would be the only name printed on the ballot as the Democratic candidate for the U.S. Senate.[15]

With that decision, the fight was on. Thurmond, who had run for president on an unorthodox third-party ticket six years earlier, would challenge Brown in an even more unorthodox manner, as a write-in candidate for statewide office. He was, in fact—as Brown had noted—fresh from an unsuccessful campaign for the Senate against Olin Johnston, and he quickly organized. By mid-October he was described as being "at the helm of a well-staffed campaign team."[16]

By then the state's newspapers, which had "sniffed out" a good story earlier, began to make their editorial sentiments known, and they were solidly with Thurmond. Of the state's sixteen daily newspapers, fourteen were with Thurmond, and of the eighty-six nondailies, seventy-three favored the write-in candidate.[17]

ENTER JOHN WEST

Entering the picture at this point was John West, a neophyte to statewide campaigning who had not yet taken his seat in the S.C. Senate. He already had reason, however, to consider Brown a political friend and ally. According to Thurmond's biographer Cohodas, West was "brought in late in the game to manage Brown's campaign (and he, West) considered Thurmond's write-in effort to be '100 percent expediency. Strom has never been loyal to anyone but Strom,' West asserted."[18]

West later wrote about his selection to run Brown's campaign: "The chairman of the party at that time was Neville Bennett of Bennettsville, who had won a reputation before World War II as a very bright young legislator and who had made an unsuccessful run for governor in 1946. He was a talented, yet somewhat hardheaded individual, and Edgar and others decided they needed a younger face, probably World War II vintage, to offset Strom's war record. . . . At any rate, I was given the job, and Lois joined me at the Wade Hampton Hotel [in Columbia] running the headquarters in a suite there. Clarence Ford [a Camden businessman friend] contributed the office furniture, and we supplied the nucleus of some sort of organization."[19]

From the outset the ominous sense of political revolt was palpable. "Many old political alignments began coming apart," Workman wrote. "Men and women who had stuck with the South Carolina Democratic Party through thick and thin in years past declared that the Executive Committee's action was not representative of party sentiment."[20]

For West's part, some of the explanations lay in exploring political genealogy, including the dissolution of one longtime personal friendship. West wrote,

Byrnes' and Edgar's friendship went back for nearly half a century. Byrnes had been a court reporter in Aiken, where he got his start in the law, and Edgar was one of the leading lawyers in the judicial circuit. Edgar, in fact, had been Byrnes' best man in his wedding.

However, Byrnes decided to support Thurmond, much to everyone's amazement. The explanation going around at the time and it's the only one that made any sense, is that Byrnes himself wanted to go back to the Senate,

James Byrnes, Strom Thurmond, West, and Edgar Brown (left to right) at the 1964 Carolina Cup. West is credited with bringing Thurmond and Brown together for a photo for the first time since Thurmond beat Brown in a 1954 write-in campaign for the U.S. Senate. Courtesy of the John C. West Papers, South Carolina Political Collections, University of South Carolina

where he had served, and that he resented Edgar's taking away the nomination through the Executive Committee nomination.[21]

Thurmond had no such residual friendship with Brown. In his successful 1946 campaign for governor, Thurmond had made Brown and his Barnwell legislative colleagues the target of some of his most powerful attacks, singling out for special attention what he termed the "Barnwell Ring." Brown and House Speaker Solomon Blatt, his Barnwell colleague, were the rhetorical objects of his assault.

The historian Ernest M. Lander wrote, "The 1946 campaign . . . featured Strom Thurmond's onslaught against the 'Barnwell Ring . . . ' [and] government 'of the Barnwell Ring, for the Barnwell Ring and by the Barnwell Ring.' Thurmond's Democratic Party convention nomination was seconded by another gubernatorial hopeful, Dr. Carl Epps, who called Brown, Blatt, and state Senator Richard Jefferies 'three political devils.'"[22]

From its earliest moments, the Brown campaign was plagued by misadventure and political pratfalls, some of them coming from well-intended and/or insensitive Democrats from outside South Carolina. In mid-October an unneeded and uninvited endorsement came from President Truman, accompanied by a statement from his aide that the president could "forgive little things like rape and murder but (could not) forgive a guy that goes back on his party." Brown had to issue a statement denouncing the Truman comment as "misleading, untrue and vicious."[23]

Then came snickers about the dubious level of schooling attained by South Carolinians and whether they could successfully execute the writing in of a candidate's name. National Committee chairman Stephen Mitchell of Illinois told the National Press Club, "They may have a different level of education down there, but in Illinois, if a man had his name printed on a ballot and if the people had a choice of marking an 'X' or writing in the name of Strom Thurmond, the man with the printed name would win." Thurmond feasted on the comment and said, "Evidently this friend [of Brown's] thinks the people of South Carolina cannot write. . . . Our people can . . . and will write the name Strom Thurmond."[24]

West recalled a similar incident. It came in the form of what West called,

> some unexpected and unintended help from an old friend of Edgar's, Jim Farley, Roosevelt's Postmaster General who had broken with the New Deal when Roosevelt offered for a third term.
>
> He and Edgar Brown had been friends since the 1920s and had been to every Democratic convention since that time. He [Farley] was then chairman of the board of Coca-Cola and was asked by a reporter what he thought about "States Rights" Thurmond running for the Senate against his old friend, Edgar Brown.
>
> Farley allegedly said, "There's not enough people in South Carolina who know how to write in Strom Thurmond."[25]

PARTY TO A POLITICAL DISASTER

The comment and Stephen Mitchell's gaffe quickly found their way into Thurmond's campaign and became a rallying cry. Along with the embedded in-state political rivalries and resentments, the out-of-state snubs helped stir a full-blown uprising within Democratic Party circles, and for his part, about all West could do was watch the downfall of his good friend Brown. In fact, from the suite in the Wade Hampton Hotel, which served as Brown's campaign headquarters, West could see the windows of Governor Byrnes's office, across Gervais Street on the north and west sides of the first floor of the State House. From that vantage point West suspected that he had a firsthand view of the emerging political shifts that would cost Brown the Senate seat. He wrote:

> We suddenly found that political leaders out in the counties throughout the state were beginning to switch to Thurmond. We suspected that Byrnes was

a key factor, as we could see the lights on in the Governor's Office . . . each night until midnight or later.

Jim Smith was the State Auditor and as such he had access to long distance [telephone] records of the Governor's Office. He was an old buddy of Edgar's, so periodically, sometimes each day, he would give us a list of the telephone numbers that had been made the previous day and night from the Governor's Office. We in turn would identify those numbers as county individuals who suddenly switched to Thurmond.[26]

For West, it was like watching fuel leak from the Brown campaign vehicle. "Perhaps the most vivid example of how things changed came from the football season. In one of the first [University of South Carolina] home games, both before and after the game, our headquarters was lined with people from all over the state coming by to greet Edgar and wish him well. As the season progressed, and the November election came closer, fewer and fewer people came by on the Saturday afternoons before the football games."[27]

The Thurmond victory was overwhelming. "South Carolina voters went to the polls on November 2 in greater numbers than they ever had done before, for a general election in a non-presidential year," Workman wrote. "It was the year of the 'un-secret ballot,' for thousands upon thousands of voters were openly flourishing pencils as they entered the voting booths—pencils which often bore special imprints calling for write-in votes for Thurmond."[28]

The final margin was 143,444 votes for Thurmond and 83,525 for Brown,[29] producing a historical victory that not only resuscitated Thurmond's flagging political career but also turned him into an almost instant political legend. He would serve almost half a century as the state's senator, retiring as the then-longest-serving senator in the nation's history in January 2003 at age one hundred, five months before his death in June of that year.

Brown would return to his role as "Mr. Democrat" in South Carolina, president pro tempore of the state Senate, and chairman of the Senate's Finance Committee. He would harbor bitterness against his onetime friend Byrnes and would accept his defeat, according to West, only "somewhat gracefully." West wrote, "The feeling between Byrnes and Edgar continued and Edgar for many years never really forgave Jim Byrnes."[30]

For West, there was little in the way of consolation in the defeat. It did produce, however, a lifelong friendship with the avuncular Brown. "During this time, my association as a State Senator, Lt. Governor, and Governor ripened into a friendship," West later wrote. He particularly enjoyed telling anecdotes about that friendship. Like West, Brown enjoying politicking over a cocktail, and West later recalled one particular moment in that friendship: "[It] came in the 70s in an evening session at the Governor's Mansion after two or three drinks; Edgar turned to me and said, 'John, you're one of the best friends I've ever had in the world.' I said, 'Edgar, that's nice of you to say and I appreciate it.' He said, 'You know you saved my life one time.' I looked at him a little questioning and said, 'Edgar, I don't know what you mean.' He said, 'You remember the campaign of 1954?' I said, 'How in the hell could I forget it?' He replied, 'If you'd been worth a damn as a campaign chairman, I would have won the election and going to Washington at my age, and liking to drink liquor and . . . [enjoy life] . . . as I do, I wouldn't have lived five years . . . and that's ten years ago.'"[31]

Brown's election to the U.S. Senate would have deprived West not only of a good friend and mentor in South Carolina politics, but also of a defender and protector in the South Carolina Senate. For all its deeply rooted adherence to the past and its conservative traditions, the state Senate was also a place where civility and personal politics were important and where members accorded each other extraordinary courtesies, official and unofficial. The Senate would prove to be a vital part of the political environment in which the idealism of John West and the political realities of South Carolina could find an enduring, if sometimes rocky, compatibility.

Whereas the tradition-bound South Carolina Senate was a place of civility, Kershaw County presented some rough-hewn realities of life for the new senator. His race with Arthur Jones had exposed clearly defined divisions in the county—not just political or geographic but philosophical and economic as well. Much of his narrow victory margin had come from urban Camden, the educated and comfortable families who occupied the broad avenues of the town's treasured historical neighborhoods and who supported their Phi Beta Kappa senator. Out in the countryside, in the smaller crossroads communities, Jones spoke the language of emotion that suffused the rural precincts where West had not done well. In that context, West saw two major obstacles to his continued political success in Kershaw County: the Ku Klux Klan, whose numbers had burgeoned since the *Brown v. Board of Education* decision, and the *Camden Chronicle*, the twice-weekly local newspaper whose editorial policies were described by West as being "to the right of Genghis Khan."[32]

West set about early in 1956—less than two years into his first term as senator—to address the newspaper issue. On March 3 of that year he became owner of the *Chronicle* along with two partners: his longtime friend Clarence Ford, a Camden businessman; and Ben F. Davies, owner of newspapers in Barnwell and a supporter of West's mentor, Edgar Brown.

The plan of operation, according to West, went something like this: "Ben would furnish the newspaper expertise, Clarence [who owned an office supply business] would develop the printing business, and I would do the legal work." The transaction amounted to $120,000, all but $1,500 of which was borrowed. West recalled that each of the new owners put up $500 apiece, and a "bridge loan" from a friend and political supporter, Talmadge Bowen, accounted for another $20,000. That left almost $100,000, which the departing owners agreed to finance. "The *Chronicle* was deeply in debt," West wrote, "and was not making any money. Most small country papers at the time were not profitable."[33]

Whatever the business and financial risks of the transaction may have been, West believed that he had rid himself of a political tormentor in the former leadership of the *Chronicle*. He also believed that his newspaper should become a voice for new enlightenment in the community, particularly in matters dealing with race. That new policy, naturally enough, would closely track the emerging moderate beliefs of the newspaper's new owner, the young senator from Kershaw County.

The first expression of that new policy took the form of an article on the editorial page of the *Chronicle* for March 13, 1956, a week after the purchase of the newspaper by West and his partners had been announced. The article assailed the Ku Klux Klan and contended that

> every now and then, in scattered sections of South Carolina, the KKK comes out of hibernation and pops up its hooded head like a cobra.
>
> South Carolina has been notorious for the production of . . . terrorists and demagogues and the KKK seems to be a descendant of a similar breed of animal which pestered our forefathers many years ago.[34]

The Klan was likened to the Regulators of eighteenth-century upcountry South Carolina. The article bore the byline of Robert Raymond, but its sentiments bore the distinct imprint of its new owners, John West in particular.

For its time the article was an exercise of considerable journalistic and personal risk. Only two days earlier and forty miles to the east, the *Florence Morning News* editor Jack O'Dowd had written a final editorial, "Retreat from Reason," lamenting the conditions that were causing him to vacate his home and newspaper position after having advocated editorially that the state comply with *Brown v. Board of Education*. The historian Ernest Lander wrote that O'Dowd and two members of his staff were subjected to threats and attempts to force their cars off the road, and that the newspaper had suffered declining circulation and mounting complaints.[35]

West believed that a similar economic fate might lie in store for the newly acquired *Chronicle*. Its strong stand against the Ku Klux Klan, he fretted, would leave the paper vulnerable to economic reprisals from disgruntled subscribers and advertisers. More worrisome to him and his partners, however, was the report that Camden would have a rival paper for the *Chronicle,* the *Camden News,* with the former editor of the *Chronicle,* Harold Booker, at the helm. Financing would come from William F. Buckley Sr., the Texas millionaire whose family members were among Camden's powerful residents and whose son, William F. Buckley Jr., had just published, in 1954, a defense of the stormy anticommunist Joseph McCarthy entitled *McCarthy and His Enemies: The Record and Its Meaning.*

Besides the new competition for advertising and subscribers, staff defections from the *Chronicle* to the new publication were significant. West wrote, "The competition was devastating, particularly when the advertising manager [also] began working for them. Much of the advertising was split, and, of course, the *Chronicle* had not been making money anyhow. Clarence and I had no capital . . . [Ben Davies had by then dropped out of the ownership], so we came very close to folding on several occasions."[36]

As the *Chronicle* fought for its economic life, racial sentiments in the community were fanned from many quarters, and West gave at least part of the credit to the rival newspaper. The *Chronicle*'s stand against the Ku Klux Klan had become an issue, West recalled, and he contended,

> *The News* capitalized on it as being "a white man's newspaper."
>
> When we decided to continue our strong stand against them [the Klan], we felt it was probably the end of us as a newspaper . . . that public sentiment in the white community was so supportive of the Klan that we probably wouldn't survive.[37]

West believed that the stand against the Klan "in the end turned out to be good business," and he credited his partner Clarence Ford and the newly hired editor Bill Calk for keeping the paper alive.

At about that time the full force of the South Carolina legislative wrath came to bear on the *Brown v. Board of Education* decision, and the conservative newsman Bill Workman of Charleston dubbed the 1956 General Assembly "the Segregation Session."[38] Acts passed by that all-white body authorized everything from closing public schools to shutting down a state park (Edisto) to avoid desegregation.[39] The assembly even banned state employees from belonging to the NAACP and authorized the creation of a special committee to investigate NAACP activities at the all-black South Carolina State College.[40]

Besides giving his support to such legislative efforts, Governor George Bell Timmerman had initiatives of his own. He joined Governors Thomas B. Stanley of Virginia, J. P. Coleman of Mississippi, and Marvin Griffin of Georgia in supporting the doctrine of "interposition," a mechanism by which states' rights advocates contended they had the authority to "interpose their sovereignty in the face of a federal action they regarded as beyond the government's constitutional authority."[41] It was a replay of the nullification issue that had divided the nation (and the South Carolinians Andrew Jackson and John C. Calhoun) a century earlier, and it caught the attention of South Carolina's segregationist legislature. The state Senate passed a resolution unanimously, presumably including the senator from Kershaw, supporting Timmerman's popular stance.[42]

The S.C. House of Representatives took time to commend South Carolinians who had organized White Citizens' Councils in some forty communities, praising them as entities "to propose and maintain proper relations between the races residing in South Carolina."[43] Members of the council in Kershaw County turned out in force in midsummer 1956 to hear First District congressman L. Mendel Rivers lambast the Eisenhower administration, the Fourteenth Amendment, labor unions, the Ford Foundation, and the American Newspaper Publishers Association, among other targets. "I voted for Eisenhower," he told the group, "and I apologize for it tonight."[44] Besides attacking what he considered "liberal" targets, Rivers worked in some raw racial material. "I have been in Washington so long, I now call it 'Knee-grow,'" he said, to the delight of the overflow audience at Camden's grammar school auditorium.[45]

The Ku Klux Klan, in the meantime, was attracting widespread attention. In the summer of 1956 a Klan rally north of Camden drew an estimated forty-five hundred people to hear a red-robed, unidentified "Wizard" speak. He told the audience, according to a press account, that "many people are misinformed about the Klan." The revised Klan, he said, "did not condone violence and was mainly concerned with maintaining segregation." The news account reported him as saying, "Many acts of violence blamed on the Klan were committed by non-members."[46]

John West believed otherwise. Not more than a mile from his home on Black River Road was the meeting place of the "Black River Club," a group that had been linked to the Klan and whose organizing, West later wrote, coincided with acts of violence in the area. "Things began to happen during this period," he wrote. "There was at least one death of a white man who [it was] alleged [had] been living with a black woman. There was a series of burnings of black churches in the community which stopped only after the remaining churches went together and insured their buildings for at least their full worth."[47]

In that setting of vigilante violence and incendiary behavior of public and political leaders, one event brought Camden residents face-to-face with the demons in their midst. It was a cold December night in 1956, two days after Christmas, and Camden High School band director Guy Hutchins was on his way home from Charlotte, where he served as a conductor of the Charlotte Symphony Orchestra. According to a press account in the *Chronicle,* Hutchins was changing a tire on the side of the road near Westville when a car carrying five men with "tow sacks" over their heads stopped, threatened Hutchins with a pistol, forced him into the car, and drove him to an isolated place some fifteen miles away. There, Hutchins said, he was tied to a tree, was beaten "at least 80 or 90 times" with boards and branches, and was freed only after he promised to leave town the next day. "I asked them how I could leave town when I could not even walk," Hutchins was quoted as saying. "They told me I could 'crawl out of town.'"[48]

In the ensuing days, weeks, and months the Guy Hutchins beating would take on magnified proportions. It would become a drama in which the many elements of the community would come to light and play out in complex and conflicting roles. For John West, it would become a painful lesson in the realities of 1950s South Carolina and would—in his own words—be "the turning point in my life."[49]

Explanations for Hutchins's beating varied, but in the years immediately following *Brown v. Board of Education,* there was reason to believe that it had something to do with race and that the Ku Klux Klan, or some offshoot thereof, might be involved. Hutchins said that he was told by the masked men that he was beaten because of a speech he had allegedly made to a Lions Club in which he "favored integration." He had not appeared before the Lions Club in six years, Hutchins said, and then it was to "play wind instruments."[50]

The more likely cause for the beatings was Hutchins's service as a temporary music teacher at Mather Academy, a highly regarded black preparatory school in Camden. "Are you beating me because I taught a class of Negro children at Mather Academy?" Hutchins said he asked the men. He was given no answer, but—he said—the beatings continued with "new energy."[51]

For those attending Mather Academy at the time, there was no doubt as to the connection. Enrolled at the school was a young Jim Clyburn of Sumter, the son of an evangelical minister, who would graduate from the academy in 1958. Clyburn recalled years later that a cross had been burned in front of the school, which—he said—was of no particular concern to the South Carolina students but "scared the daylights out of the northern students."[52]

The Camden community, populated at Christmastime with many of its wealthy winter residents, reacted with alarm and indignation at the spectacle of one of its prominent citizens being subjected to such brutality. A reward of one thousand dollars was posted by an aggregation of public and private sources, including the Camden City Council, for information concerning the beating. A news account in the West-owned *Chronicle* stated that "public sentiment deploring the flogging reached a fever pitch in Kershaw County and appeared to be spreading throughout the state, as aroused citizens called on authorities to conduct round-the-clock investigations until Hutchins' assailants are arrested."[53]

West, who knew Hutchins only casually, recalled learning of the beating from a mutual friend the next day and followed up with a visit to the sheriff's office to gather details. There he found what he later described as a laconic treatment of the incident. West wrote, "I was outraged and put in a call to Pete Strom [of SLED, the State Law Enforcement Division]. He came over and immediately started an investigation."[54]

Even in racially troubled South Carolina, where the Klan retained some degree of respectability, the Hutchins beating took on a visibility of exceptional proportions. The involvement of SLED and its chief, J. P. "Pete" Strom, brought the case to the attention of South Carolina's segregationist governor, George Bell Timmerman, who said that Strom should "use every man and every means available in assisting Kershaw County in solving this [flogging] case."[55] Fifth Circuit solicitor T. Pou Taylor, whose job it would be to handle the case, promised that he would "prosecute vigorously anyone indicted for the crime," and he speculated that the assailants could receive up to twenty years' imprisonment.

It did not take long for arrests to be made. Strom, who had become SLED chief only six months earlier after serving as lieutenant under O. Lindsey Brady during the administration of James F. Byrnes, was instrumental in rounding up six suspects a week after the beatings. Working with local law enforcement, Strom said, "Investigating officers are satisfied that these six men are the ones who participated in the masked beating incident."[56]

For its part, West's *Chronicle* beamed editorially, "An aroused public said the case MUST be solved, and two of our own county law enforcement agencies (Camden County Police and Kershaw County Rural Police), with a helping hand from SLED, came through in one week after the flogging took place. The *Chronicle* salutes you on behalf of a grateful public. Now it's up to the solicitor to finish the job."[57]

Then came conspicuous signs that things were changing and that other forces were arising in the community. It began to appear that in place of public indignation at the beatings and self-congratulations over the handling of the case, there might be some interruptions in the locked-step march to justice. Within days of the "solving" of the case, there came the hint that the prosecutors anticipated some resistance in pursuing the matter and might seek a change of venue. "Authorities have reported an 'alarming' number of county citizens appear to be in sympathy with the action the six men are accused of taking," the *Chronicle* reported.[58]

By February that resistance had come to the surface. A Kershaw County grand jury was asked to bring three charges against the six men: (1) conspiracy; (2) assault of a high and aggravated nature; and (3) pointing and threatening with firearms. Instead the grand jury exonerated two of the men and reduced charges against the other four to simple assault, a magistrate's court offense.

Reaction from West's *Chronicle* was steamy. "We shall, in the strongest words our mind can bring into print," the paper stated in a March editorial, "continue to remind our citizens that our laws—those things which insure us all, including the floggers of Guy Hutchins, a fear-free society in which to live and raise our children—have been broken and the guilty must be brought to justice else we invite more violence of this nature."[59]

Three months later Solicitor Taylor tried again, bringing to a June session of the grand jury the same charges against four of the men and charging with conspiracy the two who had been exonerated earlier. This time presiding judge G. Duncan Bellinger told the jurors, "Lawlessness begets lawlessness, and if left unpunished, those who take the law into their own hands in one instant will take it in other instances."[60]

John West later called Bellinger's statement "as strong as I've ever heard." By then, however, the momentum for prosecution so prominent months earlier had dissipated. For a second time the grand jury refused to indict, and West later wrote that Solicitor Taylor "had little choice but to dismiss the indictments."[61] For all the exhortations from the *Chronicle* and Judge Bellinger, and for all the community spirit that had been expressed in the wake of the post-Christmas brutality, other forces had prevailed in those pivotal days of June 1957, and Guy Hutchins's beating went unpunished.

For the young senator who had won election by a scant six votes a little more than two years earlier, it was clear that Kershaw County was still a deeply divided place and that his political survival would remain in a precarious balance for the foreseeable future. The night riders who had assailed Guy Hutchins would escape consequences for their deeds. For Hutchins and West and their families, there would be both immediate and long-range outcomes growing from the incident and its aftermath.

For Hutchins, one outcome was the destruction of a career. Even before the final judgment from the grand jury, Hutchins resigned as band director and took a temporary position in Charleston. A year later he became a member of the music faculty at Syracuse University in upstate New York, where he and his family remained until 1967. "He got tired of shoveling snow," according to his daughter-in-law Ann Hutchins, and they returned to South Carolina, where Hutchins took a position on the USC music faculty for two years before his retirement. He spent the rest of his life in an assortment of jobs, working at music stores in Columbia and Camden and managing a motel owned by his son in Pageland. Ann Hutchins remembered him as "a warm and wonderful man . . . a good Samaritan, always trying to help people."[62] In a 1981 *Clemson World* article, which carried a description of the 1956 beating, Hutchins was called a "Johnny Appleseed" of music who "led the state out of the Dark Ages of music."[63]

Hutchins lived to be ninety-two, and in his obituary in the July 21, 1997, *Chronicle* he was called a "distinguished musician, pioneering music educator and humanitarian, [who] devoted a lifetime to advancing music education and enjoyment."[64] No mention was made of the December 27, 1957, beating that altered the course of his life and career.

For John West and his family there were also consequences. There had been an ongoing current of threats and dangers, and West recalled having been advised by Chief Strom to carry a pistol. "In retrospect, I don't know what good it would have done me," he said. "It was a small weapon I carried in my pocket, and I doubt that I could have hit anybody six feet away, but it gave me a feeling of confidence." He continued, "The most heartening thing that developed was Lois' action. She had developed a reputation as a young girl of being a crack shot. Her brother, Walter, had taken great pride in teaching her to shoot, and she would go to the fair . . . as a young girl with long hair, and win all the prizes. Her reputation was well known."[65]

According to Lois West, "I was just a good shot. He [Walter] would take me down to the county fair. You know, they'd have those shooting galleries there. He'd tell his friends . . . 'I'll let my sister shoot for me.' He'd win all the money because I'd just go bling, bling, bling, bling. But he would sucker them in, and let his sister shoot for him."[66]

West found Lois's shooting skills to be more than a matter of anecdotal entertainment. He said, "After the [March 1957] Grand Jury refused to indict, Lois sent word through the community that if anything happened to me, they did not have to worry about a Grand Jury indictment, because she would go out and kill [the responsible party]. This was discussed at least at one of the Klan meetings, and was perhaps the biggest factor of all in my protection."[67]

Lois West confirmed that she could "kick a tin can in the air with a .45." She recalled one particular instance when she and John had to pass through crowding and shoving people who had gathered outside his law office one evening. "They were jostling us," she said, and she worried for their safety as the two of them prepared to leave for their home on Black River Road, some six miles away on lonely roads. They were driving separate cars, and once they were on the road, some of the hostile crowd at the law office pursued them in cars. "They tried to separate us," she recalled, "but I'm a pretty good driver. John was in front, and I was on his bumper, and they were trying to separate us [so they could] get John. They wouldn't attack a female as such, but if they had gotten me away from him, they would have tried to get him. I had a pistol on the seat next to me, and if they'd run me off the road, they'd wished they hadn't."[68]

John West survived the back roads of Kershaw County and the back alleys of South Carolina politics. By the time he was halfway through his first term in the South Carolina Senate, he was no longer a rookie legislator. In the early years of the state's dyspeptic reaction to civil rights initiatives and court orders mandating racial desegregation, he had seen the powers that could be unleashed in resisting those changes.

He had witnessed firsthand—albeit from the losing side—how the raw power of political protest in the form of a write-in candidacy could energize an often lethargic South Carolina electorate to support an anti–civil rights champion. He had seen how the forces of vigilantism could penetrate the processes of criminal justice and leave unpunished a heinous roadside crime. He had found how those energies could be translated into personal threats and dangers for himself and his family. It was a painful crash course in political realities for the man whose power was often derived from the persuasion of newspaper editorials and the civility of cocktail-party politics.

A QUIET VOICE OF REASON

After a time, we saw that there were no communists . . . in South
Carolina.

John West

ohn West's residence and place of business would remain in Kershaw County,
but his political and sentimental home quickly became the South Carolina
Senate. It was a place of inordinate civility and decorum, where members addressed each other with third-person formality when speaking from the podium,
and where a single objection could delay or scuttle a piece of legislation under
what was known as "senatorial courtesy."

In the days before one-man, one-vote rulings caused both legislative bodies
to be apportioned on the basis of population, there was one senator per county,
regardless of population. A senator from a smaller county had as much (and
often more) power than a large county's senator did. Senators served for years
and years, and many became close friends. The South Carolina Senate had all
the trappings and characteristics of an exclusive men's club. It was a perfect fit
for John West.

It did not hurt, either, that West arrived as Edgar Brown's protégé, having
met many of his new colleagues during the unsuccessful U.S. Senate campaign
only months earlier. West adapted nicely to the environment, and for all the
rough-and-tumble politics of Kershaw County, the Senate became a place of
comfort and refuge for the newcomer. He was assigned to the Judiciary Committee his first year, a plum designation for a freshman and one that no doubt
involved his friend Edgar Brown. As a member of that committee, West came

under the tutelage of its chairman Marion Gressette, the keen-minded senator from St. Matthews who headed the legislature's efforts to carry on the fight against racial desegregation. "He was one of the great legislative leaders of our history," West said of Gressette. "While I frequently disagreed with him, I came to respect him as a most capable and honorable individual. Our friendship existed until he died."[1]

Twenty-six of the Senate's forty-five members (one seat was vacant at the time) were lawyers, and ten were farmers, giving West some common ground and common interests with most of the senators. Its presiding officer was Ernest F. "Fritz" Hollings, a Citadel classmate and friend who had been elected lieutenant governor in the 1954 election. Two of the Senate's members, L. G. Mishoe of Williamsburg County and James Wheeler of Saluda, had served on the Highway Commission with West. Timmerman, the newly elected governor, was also a Citadel graduate, and West recalled, "I had . . . come to know him pleasantly, but not too well. Few people ever got close to George Bell."[2]

West made friends quickly. "My desk mate was the newly-elected senator from Richland County, Fletcher Spigner Jr. He and I, along with George Mc-Keown [of Cherokee County], constituted what we called the 'Just Made It Club.' I had been elected by three votes, Fletcher by 18, and George McKeown by one."[3]

McKeown, West remembered, had been elected only after numerous ballots in the Democratic primary in Cherokee County had been contested. As was the procedure at the time, the election wound up in the hands of the party's Executive Committee, where Edgar Brown held sway. The committee was presented with numerous contested ballots, and state law required that a vote would be counted only if the voter's intentions were clear. "The critical ballot [which had been counted in favor of McKeown] had the letters 'MM' written after his [McKeown's] name on the paper ballot," West later wrote. "Edgar looked at this ballot, which was about to be thrown out, and said, 'Oh, the voter's intention is clear . . . MM stands for My Man, meaning McKeown.' The vote was counted and it was the margin. George, however, did not appreciate being called 'My Man.'"[4]

West enjoyed an early—and lasting—friendship with Allen Legare, the senator from Charleston County. "He had been elected [two years] earlier, and soon became known as one of the 'Young Turks,' [but] he also maintained a close friendship with Edgar Brown." That close friendship helped Legare engineer what West called "one of the most far-reaching pieces of legislation passed during my time."[5] This was a major bond bill for the expansion of the State Ports Authority, most of whose facilities were located at the Port of Charleston. As was often the case with West's political friends, Legare would become a close personal friend, a business associate, and a legislative ally in a number of enterprises.

THE SENATE WORKAHOLIC

West became a workhorse in the state Senate. His quick wit and charm made him popular with his colleagues, and his intellect gave him early acceptance and confidence from the likes of Gressette and Brown. By then he was also feeling the quickened pulse of political ambition.

Viewing the Senate seat as a potential step toward higher office, West was glad to have opportunities to extend his visibility beyond the borders of Kershaw County and the confines of the South Carolina Senate. For the rest of his Senate career, he would toil at a breakneck pace on project work, usually in the form of study committee and joint committee leadership in the General Assembly. Such work cast him comfortably in the role of advocate for causes, as he had been with the Kershaw County hospital bond issue during the Senate race in 1954. These causes appealed to his sense of personal priorities—public education, health care, economic development, and constitutional reform, among others—and he could bring enthusiasm, energy, and the power of his considerable intellect to them.

They also introduced him to new, statewide constituencies of teachers, nurses, businesspeople, chambers of commerce, and others with whom he could discover common cause and for whom he could become something of a champion. The issues he addressed through such projects would be mainstream and political—education, health care, economic development—in the state in the 1950s and 1960s, and his role in furthering such causes would give him visibility in the press and leadership positions in the General Assembly. Given West's penchant for converting work assignments and tasks into social events, they also gave him the opportunity to add to his growing community of personal and political friends.

One such experience came from a committee assignment he had not sought and did not particularly relish: the chairmanship (of all things) of the Committee to Investigate Communist Activities in South Carolina. This was a puzzling task for the man who would in later years gain attention for defending a prime target of McCarthyite red-baiters, the North Carolinian Frank Porter Graham. In 1956—West's second year in the Senate—the young Kershaw senator was approached by one of the Senate Brahmans, Richard M. Jefferies of Colleton County, who had served briefly as governor during the war year 1942.

FIGHTING COMMUNISTS

The chairmanship of the committee "was recognized early on as a 'hot potato,'" West later recalled. "These were the days of the Joe McCarthy hearings in Washington [and] the responsible leaders did not want it to degenerate into that." In offering West the unwanted assignment, Jefferies

> explained that he wanted the committee to function, but did not want it to become a "witch hunt." Since I had no real responsibility in the Legislature, and since this was an opportunity to become chairman of a committee, I accepted without any hesitation.
>
> I soon found, though, that there were many emotions involved, and that they were inextricably tied to the anti-integration sentiment. Any disparagement or any negatives which could be put on the efforts to integrate the schools were seized upon and the communists made, of course, a convenient and highly acceptable target.[6]

Even in the drudgery of that committee assignment, West found some solace. "There were two fortunate events," he said, "the first being that I really got to know Pete Strom [J. P. Strom, chief of the State Law Enforcement Division, or SLED]. I called Pete in and said, 'We have to find a communist to justify our existence,' and he said, 'I'll do my best.'"[7]

West's other "fortunate event" was meeting the Far East scholar and diplomat Richard Walker, who subsequently served as U.S. ambassador to South Korea. "Dr. Walker had been brought to the University by President Donald Russell to head the Byrnes Institute, named for Jim Byrnes, who had been Donald's law partner. He was a bright young professor out of Yale who had served in World War II as a Chinese interpreter. This was the beginning of a friendship that . . . lasted over the years and . . . [became] meaningful to us both."[8]

For all the associated benefits of personal friendships that West derived from the experience, there remained the business of carrying out Dick Jefferies's directive to keep the committee's activities from becoming a "witch hunt." To avoid such a bloodletting, the committee decided to direct its attention and energy to developing a program to educate South Carolina students about the hazards and dangers inherent in the communist system. West said,

> After a time, we saw that there were no communists per se in South Carolina, so we turned the committee's investigative charge to an educational effort, i.e., to teach about communism. Fortunately, the American Bar Association had started to sponsor such a program which had been planned in some parts at least by Dick Walker and his [USC] colleagues.

So we joined forces with the American Bar Association, which gave us credibility. The thrust of the committee became education about communism and contrasting it to the free market capitalistic system.[9]

The strategy satisfied the desire by Jefferies and the leadership to avoid a "witch hunt," but it did not satisfy others. From Frank Best of Orangeburg, the state's voice of the John Birch Society, came a ringing attack on the USC professors for their support of such Birch Society targets as the United Nations and the admission of mainland China to the UN, among other things.

"The 'experts' at the University of South Carolina to whom Senator West refers," Best intoned through his radio station, WDIX in Orangeburg, "are those professors who organized a three-day seminar at the University last winter for 250 college students from three states at which the principal subject was 'United Nations Should be the Cornerstone of U.S. Foreign Policy' and the themes that Red China should be admitted to the UN, that the UN could be reorganized and that Portugal is an oppressor in Angola."[10] The Best critique aside, the committee's report was accepted, and in his first legislative assignment, West had dutifully saved South Carolina from witch hunts and communists.

A PLATEFUL OF PROJECTS

West's other study committee work would prove less vulnerable to Right-wing sniping and more in keeping with his own interests and ambitions. During his three terms in the Senate, he chaired committees that (1) studied public school curriculum and recommended standards and revisions, (2) made recommendations that resulted in a revamping and expansion of nursing education, (3) studied the feasibility of establishing a two-year college system, (4) made proposals for the revision of the state's 1896 constitution, and (5) developed recommendations that resulted in the overhaul of the state's economic development structures and strategies.

Out of these activities came a number of lasting proposals. In the nursing field, West chaired a nine-member committee appointed by Governor Donald Russell and authorized by the General Assembly in 1964. The committee, composed of legislators and representatives of the medical and nursing fields as well as nursing education, found "an acute shortage of adequately trained nurses in the state" and made recommendations designed to broaden nursing education beyond its traditional hospital base. The state's nurses were primarily being produced from a three-year program at the University of South Carolina and from a diploma program at the state's hospitals, from which "there has been an alarming number of diploma school graduates who failed the State Board Examination on the first attempt."[11]

The West committee's answer to the nursing inadequacies was a strengthening of nursing education ties to academic institutions. Among the committee's recommendations were the establishment of associate degree programs in conjunction with state colleges and universities, the continuing of the baccalaureate program at USC, and the creation of a graduate program at USC. These recommendations subsequently formed the basis of future expansion in the field.

The Florence TV station WBTW, noting that the Florence campus of USC could be a beneficiary, hailed the report as "good news out of Columbia" and commented that "money spent to improve the educational standards of our state is rarely wasted. The two-year associate degree nursing course has received widespread support from the medical and nursing professions."[12]

West's committee work produced other notable outcomes, some conspicuous for their role in preventing prospective damage to the state's school system in the wake of the *Brown v. Board of Education* decision. One such instance occurred in 1958 during his first term in the Senate, when he chaired what was called the Public School Curriculum Committee, whose membership included then USC president Donald Russell and Gordon Garrett, the well-respected superintendent of schools in North Charleston.

A DEFENSE OF PUBLIC EDUCATION

In terms of its formidable title, the committee chose to interpret its role broadly and not to deal in specific course recommendations for high school graduation. This disappointed the *Charleston News and Courier* editor Tom Waring. In a response to a critical editorial, West wrote Waring, "My feeling . . . was that the responsibility of deciding what courses should be offered and what courses should be required for graduation is basically the responsibility of educators and not the General Assembly." Typically, West appended to the letter of disagreement with Waring a friendly postscript that read, "During 1941–42, I recall a most pleasant and interesting telephone acquaintance with you. At that time, as a Cadet, I was working in the public relations office at The Citadel and had an occasion to talk with you almost daily. I hope that we will have the opportunity of renewing that acquaintance at some future time."[13]

While the committee avoided potential squabbles over specific courses to be required of high school students, it did not sidestep an issue that had arisen in the General Assembly and elsewhere, the reduction of the state's school program from twelve to eleven years, as it had been prior to 1945. The proposal to cut back schooling to eleven years prompted a letter to West from another of the state's highly regarded educators, George C. Rogers, a longtime educator whose son would become one of South Carolina's preeminent historians and scholars at the University of South Carolina. Rogers Sr., who had become director of Coastal Carolina Junior College in Conway, wrote in January 1958: "I am moved to give you the convictions of a school man with 47 years of experience in the schools of South Carolina, in Charleston and 3 here in Conway." Rogers cited the 59 percent rejection rate of South Carolina men for the military draft, half of them for lack of educational requirements, and urged rejection of the eleven-year proposal. "There are some people in South Carolina who would like to see all grades eliminated. They do not like public education," Rogers wrote.[14]

The West committee report stated simply, "On the basis of its work, the members of the Committee are unanimous in their belief that the 12-year program should be retained." In the heat of the post-1954 turmoil of public education, cooler heads prevailed, and the General Assembly rejected the eleven-year proposal that year.[15]

In June 1965 West was appointed to chair a fifteen-member committee to study the feasibility of establishing a junior college system in the state. At the time there was a scattering of public and private two-year institutions in the state, most of them regional campuses of the University of South Carolina. The committee, whose Senate members included Robert Hayes of York, Marshall Parker of Oconee, W. G. "Willie Green" DesChamps of Lee, and Edward Cushman of Aiken, visited the community-college system in California and came back enthusiastic about modeling a South Carolina program after the one they had seen on the West Coast.

Donald Russell, who had become governor in 1962, shared that enthusiasm and was ready to push for such a development at the time. The death of Senator Olin D. Johnston in April 1965, however, and Russell's ascendancy to the U.S. Senate to replace Johnston cut short that initiative. Russell's successor as governor, Robert E. McNair, was less enthusiastic about the community-college concept and did not pursue the initiative at the time. Incorporated into McNair's "Moody Report" recommendations in 1968, however, was a proposal for a third tier of higher education in South Carolina, which would essentially have been two-year institutions.

By then the junior-college, or community-college, proposal had become entangled in the debate over the direction the state's highly popular technical education system should take. McNair and others believed that a community-college component would weaken the technical orientation of the system. They worried that technical colleges would allow academic ambitions to interfere with their commitment to industrial growth.

Not until West's term as governor, 1971–75, did the California "community college" system appear, at least in name, in South Carolina with the renaming of the state's technical college system as the Technical and Comprehensive College Board. The debate over the technical- and community-college aspects of the system would continue vigorously into the twenty-first century.

AN ECONOMIC DEVELOPMENT TOOL

Of all the projects West undertook during his twelve years in the state Senate, none could approach the significance and impact of that with the weighty title Committee Studying the Needs of the State Development Board on the Subject of Vocational and Technical Training, of which he was chair. This assignment came early in West's second term in the Senate (1958–62), which coincided with the years of Fritz Hollings as governor.

"Since I had been a classmate of Fritz's at The Citadel and Law School, and we had worked together during my first term in the Senate when he was Lt. Governor, the presiding officer of the Senate," West later wrote, "he turned to me and a small group of other senators to work with him on his legislative program." Included in the group, he noted, were his Senate colleagues Marshall Parker of Oconee, William "Billy" Goldberg of Marlboro, his good friend Allen Legare of Charleston, and House members Bob McNair of Allendale, Rex Carter of Greenville, Barney Dusenbury of Florence, and others. "We became the legislative engine, or quarterback, of the Hollings proposals," West wrote.[16]

This engine, the committee learned, would require a lot of horsepower. "One of the early sessions I recall," West later wrote, "was a luncheon at the Governor's Mansion at which time Fritz invited the CEOs of several major corporations who had their plants in South Carolina. I recall asking one of those present this question: 'Sir, if you could wave a magic wand and help South Carolina achieve our goal of industrial development, what single action would you take?' Without hesitation, his answer was: 'I'd move MIT to Columbia.' I shall never forget that remark because it emphasized to me how important education was to our future."[17]

Short of transplanting MIT from Cambridge, the study committee took a big-picture view of its assignment and set about to find large-scale solutions to the state's economic troubles. Committee members discovered early that South Carolina had fallen behind other southern states in the rush for new industry. Whatever strategy the committee might recommend, it was clear that it would require a "catch-up" approach. Particularly conspicuous to committee members was the success of the state's next-door neighbors, Georgia and North Carolina, which had become pacesetters in the quest for the gold of transplanted industry.

Northern manufacturers had, in fact, been coming south for decades, usually in search of the "three C's" of southern industrial appeal—cheap land, cheap water, and cheap labor. In the postwar years those commodities were still available, but southern leaders were becoming more aggressive than before in seeking out new plants and new jobs for their constituencies. World War II had produced some new notions in southern minds. Traditional assumptions about life on the farm as a given part of the southern culture were giving way to ambitions of economic growth based on something that paid better than sharecroppers' wages or textile mill salaries.

With that incentive, southern states began competing for manufacturing plants with the zeal usually reserved for high school running backs or linebackers. The southern distaste for "Yankee dollars," which could be traced back to the days of Reconstruction and its influx of carpetbaggers, was being transformed into a welcoming invitation to bring the once-distasteful northern industry into the heart of Dixie.

ANOTHER KIND OF "SOUTHERN STRATEGY"

From the earliest days of industrial recruitment in the South, various types of inducements became a part of the competitive scene among states and among localities in order to give their respective jurisdictions an advantage. Besides the appeal of cheap land, cheap water, and cheap labor—which still played a major role in decisions to come south—manufacturers were being offered such advantages as tax breaks, discounts on water and utility costs, publicly supported infrastructure development, and many others. Industrialists were also keenly aware that much of the South's labor pool was nonunion, and they were impressed by "right to work" laws enacted across the South after the passage of the Taft-Hartley Act by Congress in 1947. Such state laws forbade "closed shops," an arrangement in place in the more unionized states by which all workers in a given plant or unit were required to pay union dues if workers voted to accept union representation.

In the expansionist economy of postwar America, manufacturers were also undergoing transformations. Traditional, labor-intensive operations were giving way to automation and the profitable processes of sophisticated technology. In states such as South Carolina, such a transformation posed its own set of problems. As John West put it, "Automation was hitting the textile mills and eliminating the need for manual labor. Persons who worked eight-hour shifts and came out tired and sweaty were being replaced by machines."[18]

A similar impact was being felt in agriculture, West recalled, and South Carolina was faced with the reality that its workforce could not meet the needs of the rapidly changing economic engines of American business. West said that there was "continuing and increasing unemployment among unskilled laborers in our state. A survey made shortly after Fritz [Hollings] took office showed that nearly two-thirds of our workforce was functionally illiterate. Our state was at a crossroads."[19]

The West committee's findings not only provided a refreshing degree of candor about South Carolina's educational deficiencies but were also breaking some new ground in terms of institutional and jurisdictional boundaries. The state's efforts at technical or vocational training had traditionally been housed in the various public school entities at the state and local levels and were contained in programs of industrial arts or basic vocational courses, activities generally carried out at the high school level.

What the West committee envisioned was something brand new. After visits to other states, and after special concentration on North Carolina and Georgia, committee members realized that the state would not be able to compete with its neighbors by simply adjusting or adapting existing programs. South Carolina needed a separate entity that could meet the special needs of incoming industries and also provide a general program of technical training and education beyond the high school level. Out of those conclusions came what was envisioned by the committee as the Advanced Technical and Vocational Training Facilities and Program, to be governed by a new board that was initially called the Advisory Committee for Technical Training.[20]

Key to the proposal, according to West, was what he called a "three-pronged approach," the most critical of which were the "special schools." The provision would make it possible for a new Technical Education Center to provide state-sponsored job training for workers to learn the specific skills needed to handle the requirements of a new industry. In some instances it might have been viewed as a program to replace the apprenticeships offered by unionized industry elsewhere in the country. The availability of special schools, committee members believed, offered the most substantial incentive to prospective new industries that could be developed by the state. A neighboring state, the report said, "is currently recruiting new industries at the rate of one per day. It is said that the Technical Training Program proves to be the decisive factor in ⅔ of the decisions."[21]

Of the other two "prongs," the most significant was the establishment of a system of technical-education schools to provide post–high school education for students within commuting distance of virtually every section of the state. The other was envisioned as a massive adult-education program for those who had dropped out of school before completing high school.

BORROWING FROM NEIGHBORS

The legislation proved to be a blockbuster. It launched South Carolina on an industrial recruitment effort that quickly made the state competitive with its neighbors. Part of the reason for its success, West admitted, was its outright copying of the North Carolina system and the recruiting of at least two of its leaders. "We actually borrowed, or plagiarized, from North Carolina the idea of technical training," West later wrote. "We revised it and improved upon it, thanks to the input from John Cauthen, with whom I spent many hours."[22] (Cauthen was the executive director of the powerful S.C. Textile Manufacturers Association and a longtime high-level influence in South Carolina political and governmental circles.)

Wade Martin was hired from North Carolina to head the fledgling South Carolina program, and Walter Harper was hired from the Tar Heel State's industrial recruitment effort to direct the enriched State Development Board. The two became effective partners and a dynamic sales duo for the Palmetto State during the 1960s and 1970s. "It was out of one of the meetings with him [Martin] that we devised the three-pronged approach which subsequently became the basis of our TECH program," West wrote, and "we still say immodestly [it] was the best in the world."[23]

West, in fact, had a special pride of authorship in the technical education legislation. "Actually, the act creating the Technical Education Commission was written by me on a yellow pad and [was] added as an amendment to the state's appropriation bill. It had an initial appropriation of $250,000," West later wrote.

> While all of us loudly proclaimed we were the authors, I guess we all could claim credit. It was during Fritz's administration and our committee was the legislative vehicle. In fact, as I have often said with a laugh, the legislation itself was poorly drafted. I did it rather hastily and introduced it during the second reading of the appropriation bill in the Senate.
>
> Billy Baskin, who was the senator from Lee County, an ardent segregationist and a former vocational teacher, was opposed to it. The vocational [teachers], i.e., agricultural and shop instructors, saw it as a threat to their turfdom and he made a fiery speech against it. I flushed, got up, and was about to answer it when Edgar Brown pulled my coat and said, "John, if you'll sit down, I'll pass your bill." And he did.[24]

The legislation, as crafted by West on a yellow pad, had one major flaw. It "completely overlooked having expiration dates for [commission member] terms. Years later, someone questioned when the original appointees' terms expired and found the legislation failed to address that point."[25]

Flawed or not, the legislation proved a powerful moment in West's political life. He called it "one of the bright spots in my political career. Without it, I doubt that I would have been elected to statewide office."[26]

Even before the work on technical education, however, West's political career was beginning to develop some continuity in other circles. The new hospital he had advocated during his first race in 1954 was taking shape and giving his political résumé something of a substantive record. It was also continuing to serve as an issue of debate from his longtime protagonist Arthur Jones.

A POLITICAL REMATCH

As campaigns heated up for the 1958 election, Jones was quoted by the *Camden Chronicle* as saying that the hospital rates were "too high" and that he intended to work for legislation insuring "the most needy of necessary medical treatment." West countered by saying, "No Kershaw County citizen has been denied medical care because of lack of funds," and he went on to contend that "the people of the county had voted to spend $1,250,000 on a new hospital, and we spent a quarter of a million less and got a hospital valued at twice as much [$2 million]."[27]

Jones and West got into a tussle at a stump meeting over the segregation of the chain gang at the county prison, and Jones was quoted in the *Chronicle* as saying, "No white convict will be required to work with 'darkies.' I didn't say the chain gang was integrated now! I just said it would never be with me as your senator." West toed the 1958 politically safe segregationist line and said, "There is complete segregation at the Kershaw County chain gang and the Kershaw County Medical Memorial Hospital, and anyone who circulates rumors that the two institutions are integrated is not only telling falsehoods, but insulting your intelligence."[28]

By then the differences between the "polite segregationists" and the more vehement, emotional variety were becoming an issue as well. Jones was described in the *Chronicle* as being one of six candidates who "denied any connection with the Ku Klux Klan. He stated hotly, 'That little Jew [unidentified] who circulated that list . . . had my name on it . . . I am not a member of the Ku Klux Klan, but I won't say I didn't solicit their support. I have no war with the Klan.'"[29]

It appeared that the divisions that had characterized their earlier race were still deep, and it was speculated in the local press that the contest between Jones and West in 1958 would be a close one, similar to that which West and Jones waged in 1954 and the one between Jones and Arrants in 1950. In both races a handful of votes decided the winner.

The 1958 contest, however, turned out to be a surprise. West sailed to a 59–41 percent victory (5,076 to 3,339 votes), and the *Chronicle* observed, "The senate race in yesterday's election wasn't a shadow of the race political prognosticators had envisioned as West carried all the county's larger boxes with the exception of Jones' home box at Kershaw." (Jones carried the box 485–69.) West outpolled Jones in the six Camden city boxes 2,004 to 417, and he carried his home box of Charlotte Thompson 120 to 24.[30]

For the first time in his legislative career, West felt some breathing room, and that energy was converted into an expanded role as newly elected governor Ernest Hollings's go-to guy in the General Assembly. West's hope for establishing himself as a productive and aggressive legislator in areas of new enterprises was becoming a reality, and he was emerging as someone with political potential beyond that of a state senator. As early as 1960, in the middle of his second term in the Senate, he was attracting favorable attention. The prominent Columbia attorney C. T. Graydon wrote to West on October 19, 1960, "I cannot think of anyone in the entire state I would rather vote for. . . . People who know you know your character and ability and will vote for you."[31] West answered cagily, "'62 is a long way off. My thinking is certainly not definite."[32] West's comment on "'62" was a reference to the next general election year—1962—for statewide offices.

The 1962 elections may have been "a long way off," but there were already signs that it would be a year of conspicuous tremors to the political landscape of the state. Even before passage of the 1965 Voting Rights Act by the U.S. Congress, registration of black voters was rising in the wake of federal court decisions declaring that the Democratic Party primary could not be an all-white affair. Republicans, viewing the popularity of Dwight Eisenhower in the South as the GOP presidential nominee in 1952 and 1956, and remembering the experience of Strom Thurmond in carrying four southern states in 1948 as the anti–civil rights Dixiecrat candidate for president, were entertaining ambitions for greater roles in state and local affairs.

On January 2, 1962, West received a letter from the longtime Charleston journalist and legislative reporter William D. Workman Jr. informing him that he intended to run for the U.S. Senate against the Democratic incumbent Olin D. Johnston in the 1962 general election. "I have a deep personal conviction," Workman wrote in a letter of broad distribution, "that the policies of the National Democratic Party, as they are now being carried out under the Kennedy Administration, are no longer in the best interests of either the South or the nation. For that reason, I am willing to meet the threat head-on, believing that the presence of a Conservative Republican senator from South Carolina in Washington would help safeguard our form of government while enhancing our state's standing in both major political parties."[33]

Workman was a Citadel graduate whom West had befriended as a journalist and also as a member of the committee studying revision of the S.C. Constitution. West responded to Workman's letter in a conciliatory tone, saying that he was "disappointed" at his friend's decision because "I feel that the Democratic Party needs the influence of persons such as yourself."[34]

As in his letter to Tom Waring, however, West found a way to personalize the message and give it a positive note. "Your decision will not affect the friendship which we have enjoyed for well over 20 years," he wrote.[35] In subsequent years Workman and West's close friend Charles Wickenberg would become part of a major overhaul of Columbia's *State* newspaper in the early 1960s. In addition West's friendship with his two Citadel compatriots would form part of the wide journalistic support he enjoyed throughout South Carolina during his years of statewide service.

In the 1960s more and more South Carolinians of Workman's conservative persuasion would find political homes in the Republican Party. While Workman's race against Johnston resulted in a one-sided defeat, it was a respectable showing for the party's first statewide contest in the twentieth century. The 1962 elections would continue to be dominated by Democrats, but it was clear that the days of South Carolina as an all-white, one-party state were rapidly drawing to a close.

For his part, West was maintaining the "precarious balance" between discreet conservatism on social issues and aggressive activism on economic, education, health care, and other matters dealing with the state's long-term well-being. As the *U.S. News and World Report* would subsequently observe in its March 1971 article, West tailored parts of his campaign to black voters, but he never abandoned conservative white friends such as Waring and Workman.

ISSUES OF CONSCIENCE

Along the way West worked hard to keep his moral compass and his political compass as closely aligned as possible. As early as 1956, halfway through his first term in the Senate, he began to feel more secure and comfortable expressing his views on some heartfelt matters, among them racial issues and other human rights matters. One of those issues of conscience for West took the form of what he viewed as a First Amendment right, although it had clear racial applications. In March of that year a resolution sponsored by Representatives Henry

Stuckey of Williamsburg County and Albert Watson of Richland (later West's opponent in the 1970 governor's race) directed the State Library to have removed from its shelves certain books that were believed to be supportive of school desegregation. Although the resolution passed, West spoke up against it, and he gained attention from librarians around the state for his stand.

"I could appreciate all you said about Hitler's Germany," wrote Estellene Walker, director of the State Library Board, "and the burning of books, for I served as Materials Supply Librarian during the last months of the war and the following year. Even the sting of defeat [the passage of the resolution] was less sharp knowing how many defenders South Carolina had for the Freedom to Read."[36] Similarly, Robert C. Tucker of Furman University, president of the state's library association, wrote, "It took courage to stand for the traditional American principle of free access to information when the resolution's supporters had confused the issue by injecting the race issue."[37]

Five years later West once again took a stand on an issue that was ostensibly a matter of free speech but that had the usual racial overtones. This time the legislative resolution took exception to a March 1961 speech given on the Winthrop College campus in Rock Hill by longtime University of North Carolina president Frank Porter Graham. The speech supported the sit-in demonstrations being carried out in Rock Hill by students at two local all-black colleges in protest of segregated lunch counters. The subsequent legislative resolution branded Graham "a known agitator" and stated, "It is the sense of the General Assembly that our state institutions should avoid a recurrence of similar situations, and more thought on their part be given to anyone who may be invited to address the institutions of this state."[38]

The resolution encountered little opposition in the S.C. House, but when it came up for a voice vote in the Senate, a journalist sitting at the back of the Senate chamber detected a soft "no" vote. West later recalled, "Dr. Graham, a noted educator [who] served briefly in the United States Senate, was accused of being a communist, as well as a supporter of equal rights for blacks. The resolution came before the senate, was read, and on a voice vote, was passed. I instinctively said no, and the press, including my friend Margaret Wickenberg, then a reporter on the *Charlotte Observer,* recognized this small voice from the rear, and she reported that I voted against the resolution."[39]

Margaret Wickenberg's husband, Charles—West's good friend from the Citadel and head of the *Observer*'s Columbia bureau—expanded on the story later in the week in a two-column story on the front page of the paper's South Carolina section. "No maverick legislator," Wickenberg described his friend West, "the 38-year old Camden attorney is an effectively practical man with intense loyalty to his friends and to his own ideas. He is an influential senator."[40]

In the clubby atmosphere of the Senate, West had so endeared himself to his colleagues in his seven years of service that they tolerated even an occasional foray into the world of liberal viewpoints. His demonstrated independence, Wickenberg wrote, was something "his colleagues knew well." West was careful not to endorse the sit-ins themselves. However, "he saw in the resolution something more important—the legislature stepping into a role of arbitrating freedom of speech."[41]

West also remembered expressing his opposition to a bill that would have required the closing of any state college or university that had been ordered to desegregate and, at the same time, the closing of S.C. State College, the state-supported black institution in Orangeburg:

> I recall being at Clemson for a conference, sitting in a car with then-President Bob Edwards and John Cauthen, who was head of the Textile Manufacturers Association, and one of the most influential business persons in the state. Bob, with his usual vehemence—he being a person of strong convictions—made this statement: "If Clemson College is forced to close its doors for one day, it will be ruined forever."
>
> When the bill came up for consideration, there was a recorded vote, and I voted against it. Later, in one of my political campaigns, the question was raised in the black community about my commitment [to civil rights]. There was a meeting in Orangeburg and some of my friends, including James Akin, who was principal of the schools in Camden, took the record of this vote to Orangeburg and told me later that it was a deciding factor in convincing the black community that they should enthusiastically support me [in the 1970 governor's race] against the . . . black candidate [Thomas Broadwater].

That vote, West never doubted, "cost me dearly in the redneck community."[42]

FIGHTING THE SPEAKER BAN

Some South Carolina legislators still believed as late as 1965 that it was a good idea to control whom and what students could hear on state-supported college and university campuses. Following the lead of North Carolina and its notorious Speaker Ban Law (1963–68), which prohibited the appearance of communists on state college campuses in the state, South Carolina introduced similar legislation in 1965.[43]

A speaker-ban bill was introduced in the 1965 South Carolina General Assembly, and West became a visible opponent. Once again the Kershaw senator attracted attention for his stand on the issue of free speech and renewed the position he had taken almost a decade earlier in fighting the book-banning resolution of 1956. This time he could do so with some experience under his belt and claim some hard-won expertise on the subject. He wrote in response to a letter urging his opposition to the resolution: "This problem is not a new one as I served as Chairman of the Communist Investigating Committee for seven years. During this time, numerous groups urged our committee to sponsor a law similar to the North Carolina Act. We declined to do so on the basis that the Presidents of our state-supported institutions were quite capable of judging and regulating the character of the speakers appearing on the campus."[44]

By the end of his second term, West was already entertaining thoughts of running for statewide office, and his eyes were on the office of lieutenant governor. The 1962 elections were no longer off in the distance, and they were shaping up with some interesting variables and uncertainties. West was confident that his star was in the ascendancy and later wrote, "The question was being debated long and hard about which one of our group [Hollings's legislative support team] would run for Lt. Governor. Because of my seniority of two years and the recognition which I had received as Chairman of the Committee which had shepherded most of Hollings' legislation, it was felt that perhaps I was the one to run."[45]

Elsewhere other dynamics were at play. In the S.C. House one of West's colleagues in the economic development initiative, Bob McNair, was also testing the statewide political waters. Initially primed to succeed Solomon Blatt as Speaker of the S.C. House in 1962 after the latter announced his intention to seek a seat on the S.C. Supreme Court, McNair was left casting for other options when Blatt subsequently changed his mind and chose to run for Speaker again. One of the options available to McNair was the lieutenant governor's race.

SOME POLITICAL SHUFFLING

There was, in fact, more than the usual shifting and jockeying taking place as candidates sized up their chances in what was still the only meaningful race in the state, the Democratic primary. In the days before South Carolina governors could seek two consecutive terms, Hollings was not eligible to run for reelection, and assumptions were made that Lieutenant Governor Burnet Maybank Jr., son of the late U.S. senator from Charleston, would be a candidate for the top spot. The two previous governors, Hollings and George Bell Timmerman, had been elected from the lieutenant governor's office, fueling the belief that the number two position could be used as an effective stepping-stone to the top.

Some, however—including West and McNair—believed that Maybank was politically vulnerable, that he did not have the political wheels to win the governor's race. Maybank, West said, was quiet, unassuming . . . but somehow lacked that spark that makes a difference in a political campaign.

I became fond of Burnet and came to respect him as a decent, kind individual. However, he did not have the so-called charisma. (I hate that word, because I was accused of not having it, either.)[46]

McNair was thinking the same thing: "It became obvious that Burnet was going to have trouble getting elected [governor]."[47]

As the candidates eyed each other, McNair made a feint toward the governor's race. It was flattering, he acknowledged, to be considered for the post, and he "began to look at the opportunity."[48] The move did not go unnoticed in other camps. "As the political battles shaped up for the 1962 elections," West recalled, "Bob's name was used more and more as a candidate for Governor. He did not deny his interest in seeking that office, and for that reason, Allen Legare felt he had to look out after his friend Burnet for the governor's office, and Bob began to appear as his chief rival. Allen, as I recall, tried to get Bob to agree to run for Lt. Governor and support Burnet for Governor, but he would not do so, causing Allen to work even harder in Burnet's behalf."[49]

The Legare-McNair exchange began to engender some intensity and even bitterness, which also did not go unnoticed. McNair was aware that his interest in the 1962 governor's race, and his unwillingness to support Maybank,

> caused some of Burnet Maybank's close friends, notably Allen Legare, who had been a strong supporter of mine, to get offended. He and a few others got very upset with me because I was toying with the idea of running against Burnet for governor.
>
> So they started looking actively for somebody to run for Lt. Governor to force me to make a decision.[50]

At about that time Donald Russell's name appeared in the governor's race. With the prospect of Russell as Maybank's foe and with the knowledge of the personal wealth the former USC president could bring to the race, McNair rethought his plans and opted for the lieutenant governor's race. By then, however, other pieces had already begun to fall into place.

Stung by McNair's refusal to commit to Maybank and determined to proceed with plans to field a candidate for lieutenant governor, West's political friends talked among themselves about their options. Making up the core of those friends were Senate members of the special committee that had advanced the economic development legislation under Hollings and who considered themselves Hollings's "legislative engine." The friendships became even more binding when they purchased together a small house on the as-yet-undeveloped barrier island Kiawah, below Charleston.

West wrote:

> Actually, Allen Legare, Marshall Parker [of Oconee County], and I had become the closest of friends and [were] sort of the core of the "young Turk" crowd. We had bought a house together at Kiawah along with Earle Morris [from Pickens County], and Billy Goldberg [from Marlboro County]). Billy and Marshall were the other two senators on the special committee. Other co-owners were John Martin, Tommy Welch and Banny Jones, who died shortly after the house was purchased.[51]
>
> Allen kept insisting we needed to make a decision on who would run and to get to work on a statewide campaign. We had several sessions at Kiawah, and the option was given to me on running. However, I had real problems at the time. I had developed an excellent law practice, but did not have the organization in place that would run it in my absence. With three young children, I did not have the financial cushion necessary, and I just felt I was not ready.
>
> On the other hand, Marshall Parker had independent wealth (a dairy farm he had others managing) and he was anxious to run. Finally, the decision was made during a weekend at Kiawah that Marshall should run. It was interesting that Allen and I in helping to plan a statewide campaign found that we knew more political figures than he [Parker] did, partly because he had gone to UNC and was not a lawyer with contacts such as Allen and I had developed at The Citadel and Carolina, along with our practices as lawyers.[52]

The decision at Kiawah to support Parker for lieutenant governor, West noted, was made while McNair was still mulling over the race for governor. "Bob McNair had been a friend since our days in Law School together," West recalled, "and had also been a friend of Allen's. However, as the political battles shaped up for the 1962 elections, Bob's name was used more and more often as a candidate for Governor. He did not deny his interest in seeking the office, and for that reason, Allen Legare especially felt that he had to look after his friend Burnet [Maybank] for the Governor's office, and Bob began to appear as his chief rival."[53] McNair, who had actually considered running against Maybank in 1958 for lieutenant governor, had gained status as a protégé of Speaker Blatt's in the South Carolina House and had won attention as a champion of the probusiness "Right to Work" statute, which banned closed-shop labor-union organizations.

A RACE TURNS BITTER

In the sequence of events that ensued, Parker's announcement came ahead of McNair's, and McNair acknowledged, "By holding back, I sort of generated opposition. I had to announce later on, and that gave him [Parker] something of a head start."[54] West remembered, "Suddenly it was Bob McNair who was going to run. . . . One of Allen's greatest assets was his complete loyalty. His word was his bond, and we had agreed to support Marshall, so unfortunately, we found that we were opposing our friend of longstanding in many ways, Bob McNair."[55]

Whatever the sequence or order of events may have been, a remarkably intense race was thus put in place for what might otherwise have been considered a lesser office. "It turned out to be," McNair acknowledged, "one of the toughest races for Lt. Governor . . . that has ever been run in this state."[56]

On the surface it did not appear to be so, at least not in the beginning. One Democratic Party veteran, Attorney General Daniel R. McLeod, described it as "just a powder puff campaign . . . like a couple of people running for student body president."[57] However, the campaign heated up, and before it was over, the candidates were trading verbal haymakers. Accusations late in the campaign that Parker had advocated a tax increase to benefit the state's municipalities sent the two candidates into spirited personal exchanges. In the course of the combative race, deep political wounds were inflicted on both candidates and their supporters.

McNair scored a convincing victory, and this proved to be something of a surprise to those who believed that senators usually beat House members in statewide races. Winning a statewide race from tiny Allendale County was a political upset of the highest magnitude. As surprising as the victory itself was the overwhelming margin, 58 percent to 42 percent (191,429 to 138,463 votes). McNair carried thirty-seven of the state's forty-six counties, including Charleston and a number of the upstate counties where the Oconee senator had been expected to do well.

The residue of bitterness remained long after the contest ended. McNair had tapped the "courthouse gangs," many of whom he had befriended during his five years in the S.C. House of Representatives, and he had also found some support from party regulars such as senior U.S. senator Olin D. Johnston. Parker, whose North Carolina roots had become a source of some McNair attacks, had conducted much of his campaign through advertising and media strategies. In the end, McNair's claim that Parker was advocating a sales tax increase was the final blow in a campaign that had become deeply personal on both sides.

PUTTING THINGS BACK TOGETHER

In the wake of Parker's defeat, the Kiawah friends tried to regroup. Not only had McNair beaten Parker, but Donald Russell had also defeated Maybank, and the "Broad Street Gang" led by Legare had seen its hold on Charleston politics damaged. West remembered the postelection gathering of the Kiawah friends:

> The week after the election, we all met and I well recall the evening we spent at Point Farm, Allen's place on Wadmalaw. Marshall was licking his wounds and Allen was again the upbeat quarterback of our little group. He said to Marshall, "OK, you didn't start soon enough, things were bad, but you still have a good future. Don't you want to try it again four years from now?"
>
> Marshall said, "Absolutely not."
>
> Then Allen turned to me and said, "Well, John, do you want to try it?"
>
> I said, "I do," and he said, "Well, let's profit by the mistakes that have been made, namely getting a late start. Let's plan now for you to begin to run."[58]

West had to hear one more commitment before he was comfortable. He recalled turning to Parker and saying, "'Marshall, are you sure you don't want to run, because you are entitled to a second bite of the apple?' He said, 'Absolutely not. I will support you as you have supported me.' With that, I began my third term [in the S.C. Senate] planning the race for Lt. Governor."[59]

Being tapped to run for statewide office by a small group of friends and political cronies on a barrier island off the South Carolina coast hardly constituted a draft nomination. But like so many other decisions in the world of John West, social, political, and personal matters tended to blend into a seamless process. West trusted his instincts, and Legare's words and Parker's assurances were all he needed to proceed. With the backing of a handful of Kiawah friends, the race was on as far as John West was concerned.

Even as the handshakes were being exchanged, however, there were obstacles already in place. The bitter 1962 fight for lieutenant governor had left an impact, and West and McNair had become politically estranged. McNair later recalled that as he made plans to run for governor in 1966, West would not have been his first choice as a running mate in the lieutenant governor's race. That designation would have belonged to the Greenville attorney Rex L. Carter, who had become Speaker pro tempore in the S.C. House in 1955. McNair had become politically allied with Carter when Speaker Blatt announced plans to run for a seat on the S.C. Supreme Court, and he had made it known that

McNair would be his choice as a successor. McNair and Carter decided to run as a ticket for the Speaker and Speaker pro tempore positions, respectively.

When Blatt changed his mind and decided to run again for Speaker, McNair dropped out of the race, but Carter remained in the Speaker pro tempore contest and won the number two position over the incumbent Tracy Gaines of Spartanburg. McNair and Carter maintained their political friendship, and McNair said of West, "The Parker campaign divided us . . . [it] caused very strained relations. It put me in a position that if Rex Carter had wanted to run for Lieutenant Governor, I had let everybody know that I had an obligation to him, and intended to carry out that one because I felt I owed him one."[60]

As it turned out, Carter chose not to run, and McNair and West eventually patched things up and became political allies. Some of the wounds from the Parker-McNair campaign never fully healed, however, and the two campaign forces that collided on that unlikely battlefield would keep their distance for years to come.

Aside from healing political wounds, West would have larger issues to confront. Between 1962 and 1966 the political world in South Carolina would undergo changes of enormous proportions. The year 1962 would prove to be the last in which Democratic candidates could view their party's primary as the main electoral contest for the state. Buoyed by the conservative candidacy of Barry Goldwater for president in 1964 and the party switch that year of West's old nemesis Strom Thurmond from the Democrats to the Republicans, the GOP would field candidates for most of the statewide seats in 1966 and would be competitive. The rise of the Republican Party meant, in essence, that Democratic candidates would have to win two elections to gain office: their own primary in June and the general election in November against Republican candidates.

This would make political races for Democrats veritable marathons from early spring until late fall. In addition the rise in importance of media advertising—particularly radio and television—would drive the cost of running for public office considerably higher and would make the role of fund-raising a considerably higher priority in serious political campaigns.

Of even more long-term significance would be the changing demographic of the South Carolina electorate. Federal court tests in Texas during World War II and Judge J. Waties Waring's ruling in *Rice v. Elmore* had opened up the Democratic primary to black voters, and the Voting Rights Act of 1965 would provide monitoring and protection to black voters in registering and casting their ballots. The 1966 elections would not be all-white Democratic contests as they had been for half a century in South Carolina. They would be lengthy, expensive, and diverse. Parties would run what amounted to unofficial tickets for major public offices, and as never before, candidates would be viewed on the basis of their party as well as their individual merits.

For John West, it would be a major test of his long-standing effort to maintain a precarious balance in charting the course of his public life. A stronger presence of racial and partisan interests in the electoral process would make the middle ground more difficult to define and maintain. The soft voice of protest would have to be amplified into an articulated voice of progressive policy and direction. The politics of personality and friendship would have to be expanded into a public persona that generated confidence and credibility.

No one was looking for a new John West. It was simply time for John West to take his place near South Carolina's political center stage.

AN EXPLODING POLITICAL UNIVERSE

The Lt. Governor's office was seen by many to be somewhat useless
and a symbol more than an effective part of state government. To me
it never fit those stereotypes.

John West

The political world of the 1960s was becoming the battleground for deep
divisions in America—divisions by gender, by generation, by lifestyle,
by an unpopular war in Southeast Asia, and, most powerfully in the
South, by race. In South Carolina those divisions were reflected in the emergence of at least two powerful forces reshaping the political terrain. White voters, increasingly unhappy with the civil rights movement and heartened by the
1964 presidential candidacy of Republican Barry Goldwater, were becoming a
source of new and long-term conservative energy within the GOP. Black voters, enfranchised by court rulings of the 1940s and 1950s and fortified by the
Voting Rights Act of 1965, were flocking to the Democratic banner and reshaping the party as a politically moderate/centrist entity.

The rush to populate the Left and Right wings of the state's enlarged political community sent voter totals soaring. Between 1960 and 1966 registrations
in South Carolina rose by nearly 50 percent, from 585,989 to 888,090, an almost
unheard-of development in a state more known for its personal politics, political nonchalance, and downright apathy. Even in its most hotly contested races,
South Carolinians rarely cast more than 350,000 votes. The race between Olin
Johnston and Ellison "Cotton Ed" Smith for the U.S. Senate in 1938, won by
Smith, attracted 336,956 votes;[1] Thurmond's write-in victory over Edgar Brown

in the 1954 race for the Senate had drawn 216,969;[2] and McNair's win over Marshall Parker in the 1962 lieutenant governor's race saw 329,892 South Carolinians going to the polls.[3]

Suddenly, as the 1960s evolved, the political universe began to explode. Goldwater alone captured 309,048 votes in the 1964 presidential race out of a total of 524, 771 votes cast. This was a 35.7 percent increase over the number cast four years earlier in the presidential race between John Kennedy and Richard Nixon and more than two and a half times the number of South Carolinians who voted in 1948, the year Strom Thurmond ran for president.

Year	Voters Registered	Pct. Increase over Previous Year[4]
1958	536,205	—
1960	595,989	11.1
1962	666,694	11.8
1964	772,572	15.9
1966	888,090	15.0

Statistics aside, there were other cosmic developments influencing the political awakening. The desegregation of the University of Mississippi in 1962 and the violence that accompanied the event showed Americans that there were tragic consequences to the incendiary political behavior of racially obsessed leaders such as Governors Ross Barnett of Mississippi and George Wallace of Alabama. A year later President John F. Kennedy was assassinated in Dallas, Texas, and Americans lost not only their leader but also their sense of political and emotional security.

Before the decade was out, the nation would witness more political assassinations—Dr. Martin Luther King Jr. and Senator Robert F. Kennedy in 1968, most notably—and people would watch on their television sets as rampaging mobs brought destruction to their own cities and towns. They would also see the unfiltered brutality of a jungle war in Vietnam and form opinions not just about the Asian conflict but also about war in general. For South Carolinians, the reality of public protest and upheaval would be brought home in Charleston, Columbia, and elsewhere, and the tragedy of violence and death would become forever associated with the town of Orangeburg and the campus of South Carolina State College.

NEW COMBAT, NEW WEAPONS

For John West, the new political arena would be a far cry from the intramural sparring with the likes of Arthur Jones. The universe was larger, the stakes higher, and the combat more savage. In scale alone he was moving from a one-county political community where a few thousand votes decided elections to a statewide venue where he would be trying to reach prospective voters by the hundreds of thousands. It was an enormous new universe in terms of geography, in terms of population, and in terms of the length and magnitude of campaigns.

The real distinction, however, between the campaign for state senator and the statewide race for lieutenant governor lay in the political agenda and the issues and strategies on which the campaigns would be based. In his senatorial campaigns the issues had been local and mostly one-dimensional, such as hospitals and chain gangs. By 1962, in fact—the year he was elected to his third state Senate term—West had so cloaked himself in local political clout and civic respectability that he was unopposed and therefore virtually immune to issues of any kind other than those of his own choosing.

In many settings that would have made him a political "boss," and he looked the role—chubby, balding, and usually agreeable to a round or two of social beverages. There was nothing of the "boss" in his manner however. He spoke softly and engaged listeners with a blue-eyed sensitivity that made him more comfortable in small groups or one-on-one settings than in larger gatherings. He was not boisterous, and he was not one to arouse the passions of a large crowd.

As he made the rounds across the state in precampaign tours to promote his statewide visibility, West's appearances were usually before groups such as chambers of commerce and civic clubs, and he stuck to an agenda of "safe" issues such as economic development and public education, which chambers of commerce and civic clubs could appreciate without feeling particularly political or partisan. West came across as being bright, witty, self-deprecating, and thoroughly acceptable to establishment audiences who were anxious to avoid taking risks or setting sail on hazardous political adventures. He rarely sounded partisan or emotional, and he designed his comments to be acceptable to the political Left or the Right, preferring to stake out the center for himself. He spoke with the confidence and self-assurance of someone who had spent his Senate years working hard and earning something of a "Most Likely to Succeed" image among his peers.

His friend Bill Calk, whom West had hired as editor of the *Camden Chronicle*, noted as early as 1964:

> The Kershaw County senator, whose senate and professional background qualifies him as an authority on many subjects, is accepting practically

every invitation that comes to him to speak to groups across the state. At present he is averaging three out-of-town speaking engagements a week.

Observers view his willing, but physically taxing jaunts on the state's banquet circuit as a means to an end—to build up a strong "public image" in all sections of the state, preparatory to his bid for statewide office.[5]

For all the effort being expended by West to steer a centrist campaign, however, the dynamics of the political explosion taking place in South Carolina in the 1960s had one basic theme, the politics of race, and that made neutrality impossible. Democrats had initially dismissed the Goldwater success in South Carolina as a temporary thing. McNair called it "Goldwater hysteria," and newly appointed U.S. senator Donald Russell said that it was a "unique and isolated" occurrence.[6]

There was permanence in the Republicans' Right-ward march, however. The GOP was providing a haven for white voters unhappy with the civil rights initiatives of the Democrats, and the Democratic Party, in turn, was becoming the home for new black voters determined to push the civil rights issue with all their freshly won political clout.

The racial issue in its many iterations was defining the difference between the political Left and the Right in South Carolina and between liberalism and conservatism, and race was providing the basic public definition of Republicans and Democrats. As Bob McNair noted, "Conservatism began to take on new meanings. . . . It became how you felt about civil rights. . . . The integration question emerged as . . . the more dominant factor in determining whether somebody was a conservative or a liberal."[7]

SOME MOMENTS OF TRUTH

For many of the state's political leaders, such overt exposure of the race issue promised some degree of discomfort. For years racial segregation had been a political assumption in a state in which only a relative handful of black citizens were registered or could vote. The distinctions on the race question among white political figures of the time were the differences between "polite segregationists" and the more emotional "firebrands." Fritz Hollings, Bob McNair, Donald Russell, and John West would have been considered in the former category. They were political leaders who had taken stands and cast votes to retain the state's segregationist laws and traditions but who had rejected some of the invectives and violence that had become associated with more extreme elements in the state's Jim Crow society.

Racial violence offended West's sense of decency, as reflected in his angry eruption over the beating of Camden High School band director Guy Hutchins by night riders and in his own public defiance of the Ku Klux Klan. At the same time, however, West remained staunchly segregationist in defending the racial separation of prisoners on county chain gangs and patients in the Kershaw County hospital.

Even in his denunciation of book banning in libraries, speaker bans on college campuses, and witch hunts against perceived communists, West examined the issues from an abstract and intellectual perspective and was careful to address them in the context of First Amendment rights primarily and their racial implications secondarily. West found ways to stay in contact with conservatives such as Tom Waring and Bill Workman and to maintain a certain degree of acceptance and respectability among white conservatives in general. He was navigating carefully within what he deemed to be the political tolerances of the day, drifting occasionally to the Left on issues of personal freedom but remaining essentially a centrist. West knew that even with the significant increase in the number of black voters registered in the 1960s, whites maintained an almost 80 percent majority through the decade. His politics, as *U.S. News and World Report* would observe in 1971, were keyed to blacks but did not ignore whites, while his GOP opponent in the governor's race confined his appeal to whites alone, a pattern already established in the 1966 statewide races.

As late as the spring of 1965, West was cautious about taking positions overtly friendly to the civil rights movement and its supporters. In response to a letter from a friend recommending that a state-level civil rights commission be created, he wrote, "I agree with you that the Legislature should take some action with respect to the Civil Rights Act, and although this idea is somewhat distasteful to many of us, it seems the lesser of two evils. I am taking the matter up with Senator Gressette, Chairman of the Segregation Committee [whose formal name was the South Carolina School Committee], and others, and hope something can be worked out."[8]

While Democrats were worrying over their strategies for dealing with the newly emergent prominence of civil rights as a political issue, Republicans were finding themselves in some turmoil over their incipient role as the white people's party. Their supporters had come from all manner of segregationists—the polite brand and the not-so-polite brand, the ideologically zealous and the politically pragmatic. It was not always a happy family, as it turned out. Harry Dent, the Strom Thurmond aide who became a key White House operative in the Nixon years, later wrote, "Some southern Republicans are so ideologically motivated they cannot be practical enough to either nominate a moderate conservative for public office or adapt to some moderate positions on issues in seeking mainstream votes."[9]

Even as the architect of the "Southern Strategy," which swept Nixon into office in 1968, however, Dent fretted about extremism in the ranks of the segregationists. He identified the John Birch Society as being among those zealous elements and wrote that its members "exert an undue influence within the Republican Party. . . . There needs to be less Birch influence in the Republican Party."[10]

A LAST-MINUTE SURPRISE

For West, however, before any of his new statewide political challenges could be addressed, there was some unfinished business to be conducted among his close political friends. As it turned out, his selection as the candidate of the Kiawah group for lieutenant governor was not quite sealed. One more conversation would take place, and it was a surprise, eleventh-hour inquiry from Marshall Parker. West later wrote:

> I began to sense . . . that Marshall was reassessing his political future, and . . . that he had changed his mind about the Lt. Governor's spot in the '66 election.
>
> Marshall called and said, "John, let's get together on a Tuesday night of the legislative session." I went to his motel room, we had a drink, he looked at me and said, "You really want to run for Lt. Governor?" I said, "Marshall, that was our plan and I've been following it for nearly three years now. Do you want to change your mind? If so, let's talk about it."
>
> He looked at me and said, "No, I gave you my word and that's it and here's a contribution for your campaign." He handed me an envelope and it was $300, which was a substantial amount at that time. I thanked him and we left, but [I] asked before leaving what his plans were and he said, "I'm not going to run for reelection to the State Senate, but I don't know what I'm going to do."[11]

What was actually taking place in those cloak-and-dagger days in the spring of 1966 was the recruitment process by Republicans to lure high-profile Democrats over to the GOP side as candidates. Neither West nor Allen Legare could get their friend Parker to divulge his plans, but rumors were circulating that he would become the Republicans' candidate to run for the U.S. Senate against Fritz Hollings, a decision that could seriously divide the Kiawah group and other Democrats who had supported both men in previous primaries. Hollings "had asked Marshall to run his '58 campaign for Governor and they had been close friends," West recalled. "Hollings was particularly miffed."[12]

The first reliable word on Parker's decision came from a man who had no such mixed feelings about Parker, Bob McNair, who had won the bitterly

John and Lois West with Harry Lightsey Jr., who was West's campaign manager in his successful 1966 race for lieutenant governor against Marshall Mays. Lightsey went on to become dean of the University of South Carolina Law School and president of the College of Charleston. Courtesy of the John C. West Papers, South Carolina Political Collections, University of South Carolina

contested lieutenant governor's race over Parker in 1962 and held no particular fondness for the Oconee senator. "I was having lunch at the Palmetto Club," West recalled, "and ran into McNair, who called me aside and said, 'You see what kind of so-and-so your friend has turned out to be—a turncoat.'"[13]

Parker would be the most prominent Democrat to join the Republican ranks that year, and—except for Strom Thurmond, who had changed parties in 1964—he would be the only one with statewide experience. The other two GOP candidates for major statewide office that year were also former Democrats: S.C. House member Joseph O. Rogers of Manning, who would take on McNair in the governor's race; and former S.C. House member Marshall C. Mays of Greenwood, who would be the Republican candidate for lieutenant governor against West.

There remained another hurdle for West before he could turn his full attention to a contest against Mays. It was the Democratic primary, once the main event on the election card and now a preliminary before the general election main event. Two small-town political figures from the Pee Dee region—Dero Cook, a perennial candidate from Conway, and Roger W. Scott, a state senator from Dillon—had filed for lieutenant governor. While neither represented a serious threat to defeat West, he could ill afford a nonchalant performance against what would have been considered lightweight opposition on a statewide basis. "I ran scared," West wrote, "because I thought if I were defeated by a combination of Cook and Scott, I would never get over the embarrassment."[14]

As it turned out, West was not embarrassed. With neither Hollings nor McNair facing primary opposition in their bids for U.S. Senate and the governorship, respectively, West was the party's top vote getter, disposing of Scott and Cook in sufficiently impressive fashion by polling 217,722 votes (71 percent) against 63,959 for Scott and 26,657 for Cook.[15]

That brought West into what was uncharted political territory for him, a statewide general election contest against a formidable Republican foe with the potential electorate numbering more than 830,000. West's statewide debut would be on the biggest political stage South Carolina had ever seen, with two candidates for virtually every state and federal elective office on the ballot for the first time in anyone's memory. Both U.S. Senate seats were being contested because Donald Russell's interim appointment to fill the vacancy created by the April 1965 death of Olin Johnston lasted only until the next general election, putting the seat on the 1966 ballot. Russell was defeated by Hollings in the Democratic primary, setting up the Hollings-Parker match in November. Senator Thurmond was up for regular reelection as his six-year term expired. All S.C. Senate seats were on the ballot because the Senate had been reapportioned under the one-man, one-vote provision of federal court order, and that order required that all senators be elected under the terms of the new plan.

A POLITICAL SWEEPSTAKES

The veteran Associated Press reporter Al Lanier wrote, "Except for an aging handful with recollections of Reconstruction, nobody in South Carolina can remember a political year like this one. The state Republican Party, for 75 years a minuscule organization remote from the public pulse, is now riding a wave of anti-administration sentiment that could conceivably sweep the GOP into control of the state capital and the Congressional delegation."[16]

The political sweepstakes also promised to bring South Carolina's biggest political stars—Thurmond, Hollings, and McNair being the most prominent

Mattie Ratterree West raised John West and his brother, Shelton, as a single mom after their father was killed in a school fire. She was on hand for the opening of West's campaign office when he ran for lieutenant governor in 1966. Courtesy of the John C. West Papers, South Carolina Political Collections, University of South Carolina

among them—into action. They had risen to prominence as veterans of statewide skirmishes and would remain politically influential in the state for the rest of the twentieth century.

In that supercharged political arena, John West's race with Marshall Mays would attract a voter turnout the likes of which neither candidate had ever seen before. It also meant, however, that the West-Mays race would probably not be the centerpiece of public and journalistic attention that year. That kind of scrutiny would belong to three other races: Strom Thurmond's first race as a Republican against Greenville state senator Bradley Morrah for Thurmond's U. S. Senate seat; Fritz Hollings's race against his old political friend Marshall Parker for the other U.S. Senate seat; and Bob McNair's race against Clarendon County S.C. House member Joe Rogers to retain his hold on the governor's office, the position he had assumed eighteen months earlier after the death of Senator Olin Johnston.

Since Thurmond was a heavy favorite to defeat Morrah, the Hollings-Parker and McNair-Rogers contests quickly became the crowd favorites. It was where the Republicans were concentrating their most intense efforts and where they took their most aggressive stances, particularly on the issue of civil rights. As basic strategies GOP candidates would target President Lyndon Johnson, a civil rights champion, and seek to establish associations between the South Carolina Democratic candidates and LBJ.

McNair's opponent, Rogers, was only too pleased to remind voters that he had been a member of the School Committee, chaired by Senator Marion Gressette and tasked with the job of warding off school desegregation. Rogers described the civil rights movement as having come under "mass hysteria" and was quoted in a Charleston newspaper as saying, "Aside from the racial question in such areas as housing, medicine [and] schools, congressmen seem to be in a state of mass hysteria when the President sends anything down with the heading of civil rights."[17] For his part, Parker busied himself linking his opponent, Hollings, with other civil rights advocates, namely the surviving Kennedy brothers, Robert and Ted, and he conceded any interest in appealing to the newly enfranchised black voters in the state. "I will have to have 80,000 to 100,000 [white] votes to start off Election Day even," Parker was quoted as saying.[18]

As Harry Dent was realizing, the segregationist forces had many forms, shapes, and sizes in South Carolina. Not all of them were respectable, and some of them were downright ugly. One of the less respectable ones was a GOP-published circular called *"Had Enuff?" News,* whose editorial content was such that it considered it politically advantageous to carry a front-page picture of Governor McNair shaking hands with a black attorney in the town of Cheraw.

Most of the publication was devoted to the McNair-Rogers race, and a number of entries in the two-page circular were designed to connect McNair financially and politically to President Johnson and his civil rights agenda. In one item, the reprint of an Associated Press article by Kent Krell, Rogers said that McNair lacked the "political courage" to oppose the federal government, and in another he called McNair's support of LBJ "reprehensible."[19] West's opponent, Marshall Mays, was notably absent from the publication, appearing in one picture with other GOP candidates but otherwise escaping attention.

Mays's disassociation from the more aggressive of the GOP efforts was no accident. While never making a public declaration of such, his campaign of moderation was attracting attention. An editorial in the *Florence Morning News* in late August stated:

> On numerous occasions, Mr. Mays has shown his willingness to base his case for lieutenant governor upon a frank discussion of important state matters.

In contrast, his Republican colleague seeking the governorship has shown no such willingness, choosing rather to latch his campaign to such trivia as Gov. McNair's succession to the governorship following Donald Russell's elevation of himself to the U.S. Senate, McNair's support of LBJ in the 1964 campaign, and his financial contributions . . . to that campaign.

AVOIDING THE LOW ROAD

"Both Republican Mays and Democratic West have set a tone of high-level campaigning in keeping with progressive thinking on what will improve state government."[20] In another editorial only days before the election—this one in Mays's hometown *Greenwood Index-Journal*—Mays was separated from the race baiters. Entitled "Politics at Its Vilest," the editorial addressed "a political appeal distributed by the South Carolina Independents making the most blatant appeal to racial hatred in the name of Republican candidates. . . . Apparently nothing was too low or vicious for this group, because it would be hard to imagine a more scurrilous political broadside."[21] The latter editorial, however, singled out Mays as being "conspicuously absent from the sheet. South Carolina Independents had omitted Mays from the list it was supporting, and we had no idea how much credit was due him until the work of this group became apparent."[22]

For all the attention for good behavior the West-Mays race was getting, it was not without its moments of combat. True to his party's strategy of associating Democratic candidates with President Johnson, Mays lobbed one toward West, claiming that the lieutenant governor had distributed forty thousand dollars of campaign funds in the 1964 presidential campaign in support of LBJ.[23] In an October 22 statement West responded that he would prove "the complete falsity of this ridiculous charge," and two weeks later he held a news conference and produced letters from managers of three Kershaw County banks and a letter from a certified public accountant that, he said, "showed nothing to indicate any role in distributing campaign funds in 1964."[24] The dispute proved to be a political standoff, unproved and unresolved, leaving little damage on either side.

Aside from the charge of being a friend of the president of the United States, whom Thurmond had called a "traitor," West was spared much of the wrathful campaigning being conducted elsewhere. Reports of the Mays-West race would be found on the inside pages of the daily newspapers, while the Thurmond-Morrah, Hollings-Parker, and McNair-Rogers races got front-page attention.

In the final outcomes, the intensity of the racial campaigning did not seem to make much difference. McNair won 58.2 percent of the votes to Rogers's 41.8

percent (255,854 to 184,088), and West was a winner over Mays by a similar 57.2 percent to 42.7 percent (250,041 to 185,042). In the only other constitutional office race that the Republicans contested heavily, state superintendent of education, Cyril Busbee was a winner over Inez Eddings, 54.3 percent to 45.7 percent (233,623 to 196,953). The margins of victory in the three top state-level races were similar enough to suggest that there may have been a pattern to the voting and that McNair, West, and Busbee may have had similar political bases around the state.

The U.S. Senate races, however, defied any such categorization. Marshall Parker almost got the white votes he said would be necessary to defeat Hollings, losing by 51.3 percent to 48.7 percent (223,790 to 212,032), while Thurmond— as expected—easily defeated Morrah, 61.2 percent to 37.8 percent (271,297 to 164,959). The close victory would not be the last for Hollings, nor would Thurmond's overwhelming win over Morrah be his last landslide.[25]

The Democrats could attribute their victories to several factors: (1) most of the newly registered black voters would have been strongly Democratic in their sentiments, given the anti–civil rights position of the Republicans; and (2) the fact that all 170 seats in the General Assembly were up for election would have produced a heavy, pro-Democratic turnout at the local level, given the tendency of the state's "courthouse crowd" to favor incumbents and to support their long-time friends McNair and West. A third possible factor was the fact that for all the campaigning the Republicans had done against President Johnson, it was not a presidential election year. Had disgruntled GOP voters been able to cast their ballots against the demonized LBJ, the turnout among whites may have been higher.

A BIG-TIME VICTORY

Whatever the reason for the election results, John West was taking another giant step along his political career with the November 8, 1966, victory. The turnout, in the range of 440,000 to 450,000 voters, was the largest in the state's history, and West put up big numbers amid that explosion of the state's political interests. He had attracted the bulk of new black voters in a campaign in which neither he nor his opponent had gotten into political mud wrestling over the civil rights issues. In many ways he was still a "Mr. Clean" of the South Carolina political scene, and this image meant that his potential for the governor's race in four years was still attractive among white and black voters alike.

The state Senate over which he would be presiding was historical for several reasons. It was the first one in which senators were not elected on the one-senator-per-county basis. That had been struck down by federal courts and replaced by a population-based system in which senators were elected from population districts. Some counties would be without resident senators. Other counties—such as Greenville, Richland, and Charleston—would have as many as four resident senators.

There was another unusual characteristic of the 1967–68 state Senate. It had fifty members instead of forty-six. In the painful process of drawing the new apportionment lines for the population-based districts, the 1966 General Assembly had opted to increase the total number from forty-six to fifty in order to reduce the number of incumbents who might lose their seats in the newly drawn districts. The S.C. Supreme Court, however, rejected the notion of the fifty-member Senate, ruling that by requiring one senator per county, the state constitution had set the number of senators at forty-six, and there could be no more. That meant that in addition to presiding over the only fifty-member Senate in the state's history, West would be overseeing another political bloodletting that pitted senator against senator in a virtual civil war for survival. The ensuing reapportionment battle would mean that at least four senators, no matter how the lines were drawn this time, would be eliminated. As Bill Rone of the *State* newspaper wrote, "Hanging over the whole scene was the thought in the minds of many small county senators that they might be setting forth to legislate themselves out of office."[26] That, of course, was precisely what they would be required to do.

There were twenty-eight newcomers among the fifty senators, an unprecedented turnover in the tradition-bound chamber. Among those not returning would be West's good friend Allen Legare, who was defeated in a Republican uprising in the populous Charleston County in which the GOP won three of the four resident seats.

Republicans were also elected from Newberry, Lexington, and Aiken counties, bringing the total of GOP members to six. Another new senator, Thomas A. Wofford of Greenville, declared himself an Independent but voted often with the Republicans. Wofford had defeated the incumbent P. Bradley Morrah for the Senate seat in a rare election in which Morrah had contested Strom Thurmond for the U.S. Senate seat and Wofford for the state Senate and had lost them both.

While the newcomers outnumbered returning senators and urban senators outnumbered small county members, the Senate was still governed by the seniority system, which meant that senators with the most years of service chaired standing committees and continued to exercise dominance in the chamber. West's colleagues and mentors—Edgar Brown of Barnwell and Marion Gressette of Calhoun—retained their chairmanships of the Senate's most powerful committees, Finance and Judiciary, respectively, and their power over the chamber, while challenged frequently, remained undiminished.

Even as the Old Guard held its influence over the day-to-day business in the Senate, the new "class" was filled with prospective stars in the new political order in the state. Elected to the Senate that year was Richard W. "Dick" Riley of Greenville, who would serve two four-year terms as governor (1979–87), becoming the first governor in the state's history to do so. Riley would be named secretary of education in the cabinet of President Bill Clinton. Also from Greenville in that distinctive 1967–68 Senate was Nick A. Theodore, who served as lieutenant governor (1987–91) and lost a race for governor to another Greenvillian, Republican Carroll A. Campbell, in 1990.

Among the Republicans in the new state Senate was Floyd D. Spence of Lexington, who would be elected sixteen times to the U.S. Congress from the state's Second Congressional District. Other energetic newcomers were Eugene N. "Nick" Zeigler of Florence, a Harvard-educated attorney who would take on the Senate establishment on reform issues and would run against Strom Thurmond for the U.S. Senate in 1972. John W. Drummond, a feisty war hero from World War II, became the senator from Greenwood, and his rebellious nature was such that it earned him a reputation as a renegade. His occasional decision to vote with the new Republicans also created what some called the "Six-Pack and Drummond" caucus, although Drummond, who liked to call himself the "Senator from Ninety Six" (his hometown), would later become chairman of the Finance Committee and president pro tempore of the Senate.

West could also identify some especially familiar faces among the members of the class, including his law school friend Wade Weatherford, a first-year senator from Cherokee County, and James M. Waddell, a fellow Citadel graduate who had already served six years in the Senate from Beaufort County. Waddell, a rising star among younger senators, would become an important political friend in West's upcoming endeavors, and he was one with whom the new lieutenant governor could share a glass of red wine in the evening hours. Also in the group was Earle Morris of Pickens, who—at age thirty-eight—had already served sixteen years in the legislature, twelve of them in the Senate. Morris went on to become lieutenant governor during West's term as governor (1971–75), lost a bid for governor in 1974, and served twenty years as the state's elected comptroller general (1979–99).

DISPROVING THE STEREOTYPES

As the new lieutenant governor, West saw his job as having two major components. He would preside over the Senate, as prescribed by the Constitution, and he would also make himself available to manage on the floor of the Senate whatever programs Governor McNair would propose to the General Assembly, as McNair had done for Russell earlier. "The Lt. Governor's office was seen by many to be somewhat useless and a symbol more than an effective part of state government," he later wrote. "To me it never fit those stereotypes."27

The next four years would bear out West's contention. In his constitutional role, West presided over the fading days of the old Senate he had cherished as a member. Eliminated in the process would be the office of the "county senator," that old southern legend of the rural political baron who was typified in the personages of men such as Edgar Brown of Barnwell and Marion Gressette of St. Matthews, for years the two most powerful men in the Senate. Brown and Gressette would remain in the Senate under the new arrangement, and their authority would linger into the early years of the urbanized Senate, largely through the exercise of their personal political skills.

House Speaker Solomon Blatt and Lieutenant Governor West ratified the act that overhauled the state's juvenile justice system. Attending the ceremony were (left to right) Sen. Travis Medlock, Rep. Ernest Carter, Sen. John Drummond, and Sen. Nick Zeigler. Courtesy of the John C. West Papers, South Carolina Political Collections, University of South Carolina

The reapportionment fight also pitted some of West's longtime friends against each other and occasionally put him in a position of wielding the gavel and deciding procedural questions that could sway things affecting the careers of those close friends. At one point in the prolonged struggle, West noted that a proposed plan would have put Edgar Brown's Barnwell County in a district with its larger neighbor, Aiken County, which was becoming staunchly Republican. West wrote at the time,

> Senator Brown opposes [it] so vigorously (and) . . . many persons did not want to, in effect, eliminate Senator Brown.
>
> He had told Bob McNair and me that he would resign from the Senate if this plan passed as he would consider it a personal affront to him. I think this position is a little strong . . . but I can understand his feeling. It is unfortunate that both he and Mr. Blatt do not announce their intention to retire at the end of this session.[28]

Blatt, seventy-two at the time, continued to serve as Speaker until 1973, stepping down to assume the honorary position of Speaker Emeritus and continuing to serve as a S.C. House member from Barnwell County until 1987. His service in the S.C. House stretched across forty-four years. Brown, seventy-nine, continued to serve as president pro tempore of the Senate and chairman of the Finance Committee until his retirement from the Senate in 1972 after forty-eight years of legislative service.

For all the hundreds of hours of legislative wrangling and personal suffering that took place during the reapportionment fight, the biggest problem with the ordeal was that—outside the political careers of fifty individuals—it did not really matter much in the larger scheme of things for the state of South Carolina. Most members of the public could not have cared less which counties were grouped with which other counties in electoral districts. There was little to show to the public or to the state's political community for the life-and-death combat; for most people outside the Senate, it was a waste of time.

SOME PAINFUL DIPLOMACY

Even after the districts were finally drawn and agreed on, the reapportionment fight lingered, this time over the "definition of a legislative delegation." This was essentially a battle between S.C. House members and senators over who would wield the power over local government in the absence of the "county senator" hegemony. The issue remained unresolved for the rest of the session, and the Senate tucked its version in the state appropriation bill, the final piece of legislation passed each year by the General Assembly.

The Senate action infuriated the S.C. House, particularly Speaker Blatt, and as the hours ticked down to the end of the fiscal year (June 30), the appropriation bill remained unsigned by Blatt, thus preventing its ratification and submittal to the governor for his signature. Some people, including West and McNair, worried that if an appropriation bill was not adopted by the start of the next fiscal year (July 1), questions could be raised about the state's fiscal responsibility and its credit rating could be damaged. Blatt was not buying that theory, and when West approached him on June 29 about signing the bill, Blatt was at his iciest. "I went over to the House to ask Sol Blatt when he would be willing to ratify the [appropriation] act," West wrote in his journal. "I had to run down the stairs and caught him in the hall just as he was leaving the State House. The press was all around. He told me in a rather loud tone that they would not ratify the act the next day, [and] because he was tired, he was going home to Barnwell and would be back next Wednesday."[29]

A newspaper account the next day reported the confrontation and also disclosed that Speaker Pro Tempore Rex Carter of Greenville had agreed to sign the appropriation bill in Blatt's absence the next day. Learning of the plan, Blatt stormed back to Columbia the following day and told West that he would resent Carter signing the bill "until his dying day" and would resign as Speaker if he did.[30]

There ensued a standoff for hours that day—West in his office in the S.C. Senate, Blatt across the State House in his House office, and members of the press seated strategically in the lobby between the two. West made the next move, striding glumly across the lobby, head down, followed closely by reporters. Blatt met him at the office door, and one of the reporters remembers West asking if the Speaker would sign the bill and Blatt responding, "God strike me dead if I'll sign that bill!"[31]

With that West, Carter, and Blatt went into the Speaker's office and closed the door, and for the next few minutes things simmered. Then they reappeared, a calmer Blatt having invited them to lunch. By four o'clock that afternoon the appropriation bill was signed, and West, the diplomat, had scored a humbling victory. West and Blatt were never close, unlike the friendship the crusty Speaker had with West's predecessor as governor, Bob McNair. McNair was an avowed protégé of Blatt's, representing a county (Allendale) in the same area of the state as Barnwell and growing up politically in the S.C. House under the tutelage of Blatt. West, on the other hand, never served in the House, and his political tutelage came from Senator Edgar Brown, the man with whom Blatt had developed a bitter political rivalry over the years.

West's diplomatic skills had also been tested only days earlier over the issue of legalizing mixed drinks in the state. Under McNair initiatives, South Carolina was launching a major effort to attract vacationers to its borders for more than overnight or pass-through business, and included in those initiatives was the creation of a new state agency to promote tourism. A stumbling block, however, was a state constitutional provision that forbade the serving of mixed drinks in bars or restaurants in the state, a provision that many thought would withstand a direct challenge through referendum. Many of the state's potential tourism customers were arriving in South Carolina from places such as New York, New Jersey, Pennsylvania, and Florida, where mixed drinks were part of everyday life. McNair, fearing the loss of tourism business because of the state's inability to serve a cocktail with dinner, came up with a legislative proposal he thought might solve the problem, at least on an interim basis. Under the proposal the serving of cocktails in restaurants would become legal if customers brought their liquor with them, customarily carried in a wrinkled "brown bag." This would not require an amendment to the Constitution, its backers felt, and could improve the state's tourism potential.

The proposal met stiff opposition from the Charleston area, where open bars had been flourishing for years with virtual impunity, and from the upcountry, where influential church groups opposed the consumption of alcoholic beverages in public or otherwise. Even so, the bill made it through the S.C. House, but it encountered difficulty in the S.C. Senate. In early June, McNair appeared at a legislative breakfast to present the case for his "brown-bag" bill. West wrote:

> We had invited all the senators we felt might vote against brown-bagging. . . . Bob McNair really laid it on the line.
> He said if we refused to relax the law [and pass the brown-bagging bill], he would expect the legislature to set the example with no more drinking, even in hotel rooms. He also said, privately, that he would put SLED agents in the counties where the delegations voted against the law to make sure that the laws were enforced to the letter. I believe he changed a good many votes.[32]

West also proved handy with the gavel eight days later when the brown-bag bill came up for a crucial second-reading vote on the floor of the Senate. "No one is sincerely opposed to it," West wrote in his journal, "but a few ministers have put terrific pressure, especially upon the Piedmont senators, who feel obliged to oppose it. The question is whether or not a roll call will be had [requiring that five senators request it]. Finally, it was figured that 5 members would not ask for a roll call, and sure enough, they didn't. Dick Riley and Harry Chapman [senators from Greenville] demanded it, but I could never see more than three or four hands, so I put the question and brown bagging passed."[33]

Brown bagging gave the state some temporary, if awkward, relief from its stringent constitutional provisions against public drinking, and it offered some solace to those promoting the state as a travel destination. In practice, however, it was discovered that customers bringing full bottles of liquor into restaurants were more inclined to overindulge than those buying liquor by the drink. By the time West became governor and pursued a constitutional amendment to permit bars and restaurants to practice a more conventional sale of mixed drinks, it was argued that liquor by the drink was actually something of a temperance measure, as opposed to liquor by the bottle. Under the leadership of Ben Morris, publisher of the *State* newspaper in Columbia, the referendum passed, but with the quirky provision that cocktails could be sold only from "minibottles," small containers that held about 1.7 ounces of liquor. Each of the minibottles amounted to a stiff drink—almost a "double"—but bars and restaurants soon discovered that they could charge a stiff price for such a libation. For the next three decades South Carolina—along with commercial airlines—would be one of the few places in the nation that offered drinks in such an unusual manner.

West's tenure as presiding officer of the Senate got mixed reviews, some worrying that he was too lenient with procedural practices such as filibusters. In a *State* newspaper article after the stormy 1967 reapportionment session ended, the staffer Paul Clancy wrote, "West endured more filibusters than most who have held the office and although he declared an end to irrelevant debate, [he] decided to allow filibusterers to read about sharks when they were talking about reapportionment." Clancy also noted, "Some thought the lieutenant governor could have been firmer during the session. But what he did not do with the gavel, he did with diplomacy."[34]

In the meantime West was proceeding to crank up an unofficial campaign for governor, much in the same way he had run for lieutenant governor, crisscrossing the state in speaking engagements and addressing issues in which he could now claim some political proprietorship. News accounts told of visits to Bennettsville, Greenwood, Charleston, and elsewhere across the state, during which he registered his opinions on topics such as public education, economic development, health care, law enforcement training, urban pollution, and any number of other issues. This, as Bill Calk had written earlier, qualified him "as an authority on many subjects."[35] Midway through his diplomatic presiding over the Senate and the carefully orchestrated centrist campaign for governor, however, there interceded a series of events that changed everything in South Carolina.

ERUPTIONS IN ORANGEBURG

As an outgrowth of the civil rights movement that was empowering black South Carolinians in a wave of legal and constitutional reform, students were becoming active and heavily invested in public protest activity. Beginning with lunchcounter sit-ins in the early 1960s, student demonstrations became increasingly frequent. Things reached a new level of intensity in 1967, when student leaders at South Carolina State College (now University) organized a classroom boycott to protest academic standards and college governance, among a number of issues presented to state leaders. The boycott was supported by almost the entire student body.

Noting the boycott's effectiveness and feeling pressure from black political leaders, Governor McNair interceded and took steps to advance the students' causes, including improved funding for the college, the loosening of some of the college's outdated student rules, and the eventual removal of the college's president, who was identified by students as being unwilling to meet with them to address their concerns. In the atmosphere of the 1960s, communication among students and educators was becoming a major area of sensitivity for the protest movement, and South Carolina seemed to be averting major troubles along those lines.

Months later, in the wintry days of early February 1968, a demonstration by S.C. State students against a segregated off-campus bowling alley in Orangeburg grew tense and then erupted out of control. On the fourth night of the protest, February 8, state highway patrolmen fired into a crowd of protesting students on campus, killing three and injuring twenty-nine. The incident shocked a state that did not believe it could happen and left the college community angry and bitterly distraught.

A month after the shootings, aggrieved students carried their outrage to Columbia and descended on the State House in midmorning. The protesters were organized into three groups, one visiting the House, one the Senate, and a third paying a call on the governor's office. Governor McNair, who had met two days earlier with representatives of two S.C. State student groups, hurried back from a meeting across town and conveyed to the demonstrators that he would meet with a representative group of those who had camped outside his office. That did not satisfy the group leader, Wayne Curtis, and the protesters settled into his outer office for a lengthy stay.

According to news reports, the students visiting the House chamber entered quietly and left after a few minutes. In the S.C. Senate, however, demonstrators burst into the visitors' upstairs gallery and began shouting their grievances to the stunned senators below, whose regular session had suddenly become chaotic. As presiding officer, West rapped his gavel and told the students that no one could speak from the gallery. After several more students attempted to shout their grievances, six of the group were arrested and escorted from the chamber. West told the students that their petitions could be presented to the Senate in written form and would be printed in the Senate journal.[36]

The students took him up on his offer. Six days later a much larger contingent of students—estimated at one thousand—arrived at the State House equipped with petitions for presentation to McNair and West. While most of the students remained outside and paraded around the capitol building, a delegation of fifteen to twenty students met with McNair and later with West and Greenwood senator John Drummond. Drummond was singled out because in the earlier demonstration, as students milled around the State House lobby, he recognized one of the demonstrators as being from his hometown of Ninety Six and told him he would see that the grievances were brought to the attention of the Senate members. "The second contingent of students particularly sought out Drummond," a news account reported.[37] Drummond and Marion senator J. Ralph Gasque had walked freely among the angry student demonstrators while most of their colleagues avoided the crowd and some of the senators reportedly carried firearms.

The next day West took things one step further. At the motion of Senator Gressette, he agreed to have the petitions not only read and published in the journal but also referred to the various standing committees of the Senate. This was a significant—and not overly popular—step with his Senate colleagues, some of whom had responded negatively to the students' behavior in their gallery. To the students and faculty at S.C. State, however, it was a sign of interest on the part of a high-ranking state official, and West would shortly become one of the objects of a letter-writing campaign from students and faculty.

The letters received by West, most of which were handwritten, ranged in tone and intensity. Some called West "stupid" and a "patsy" or "sucker" for Governor McNair; others thanked him for his attention; and several called for specific actions, including those from student government officers Robert V. Scott and Alexander Nichols. Scott and Nichols called West's attention to the students' petition, which listed among its primary objectives an "open hearing" on the February 8 shootings, a significant increase in S.C. State's budget, a restructuring of the governing board to make it an all-black body, and the dropping of charges against the six students arrested in the Senate chamber, as well as those against Arthur Dodson—a student charged in the bowling alley protest—and against Cleveland Sellers Jr.—arrested in connection with the February 8 demonstrations. The petition also called for the naming of the college's new athletic facility after the shooting victims, Henry Smith, Samuel Hammonds, and Delano Middleton, a request that received favorable action from the college's board.

Among those writing letters to West were two students who would years later become presidents of S.C. State, Leroy Davis and Andrew Hugine Jr. Both letters carried strongly worded messages. "I wish you would get out of your private, segregated world and do something to help our cause," Davis wrote. "I know not whether you have any children or grandchildren, but if you do, I'm sure you wouldn't want them to be murdered in school. You would do everything in your power to see that the murderers are brought to justice, and you would find the causes and try to resolve them. This is what we are trying to do."[38] Hugine urged West to use his influence to "have this incident investigated by the Civil Rights Commission." He wrote, "Their findings should be made public. I am sure that if the findings, along with those of the FBI, are made public, and the facts are presented uncensored, it will do much to quiet racial tension in South Carolina."[39]

West received some fifty letters, and he answered each of them personally and responsed directly to the issues raised in the individual letters. Within weeks after the February 8 shootings, West and several members of the Senate visited the S.C. State campus and spent time talking with students, faculty, and administrators. In the course of those exchanges, West came to know two faculty members in particular. One of them was Rubin F. Weston, chairman of the social sciences department and faculty adviser to the Black Awareness Coordinating Committee (BACC), an activist student group that was founded by Cleveland Sellers Jr. and that had sponsored several speakers and programs on campus. Weston invited West to speak to his class on April 20, and the lieutenant governor accepted the invitation. West spoke at length to a Saturday morning gathering and answered questions afterward. In a follow-up letter Weston wrote:

The class and many of the invited members of the State College family were deeply impressed with your sincerity and concern for all citizens of our State.

We feel that, in you, we have found a friend who is interested in the well-being of all higher education in our State. We are aware that your acceptance of responsibility on the part of state officials to provide the best possible opportunity for the optimum educational development of all citizens . . . will redound to the benefit of South Carolina State College.[40]

West also became acquainted with Charles H. Thomas Jr., a member of the political science faculty, the state chairman of the Voter Education Project, and a prospective candidate for the open presidency of the college. A fourteen-page letter from Thomas to Governor McNair dated March 6, 1968, a scant four weeks after the shootings, outlined what he described as "my thoughts and recommendations on what the role and function of State College should be, now and in the next ten years."[41] Curiously, in addition to the formal, typed copy of the letter, the document appears in the archived files of West papers as a handwritten draft in West's familiar scrawl on a legal pad, indicating that the letter may have been a collaborative effort of the two men and represented the sentiments of West as well as those of Dr. Thomas. However it may have been composed, Thomas's letter to McNair was a none-too-subtle presentation outlining how Thomas would approach the job if he were chosen as the next president. West made no secret that he favored Dr. Thomas for the presidency, a position that eventually went to the interim president, M. Maceo Nance. Nance was the institution's longtime finance officer, had wide-ranging support among legislators, and had impressed McNair with his cool-handed performance as interim president during the harrowing days of the February crisis. This was another instance where the governor and the lieutenant governor had their differences, but West and Nance remained on good terms.

West's apparent empathy for the S.C. State cause did not go unnoticed within conservative quarters. His old nemesis Frank Best, the John Birch Society spokesman from Orangeburg, broadcast on his station WDIX that West was "sweeping under the rug the incipient pattern of destructive race relations that have marked the Negro revolution since May 17, 1954 [date of the Supreme Court decision *Brown v. Board of Education*] and that have sparked the successive hot summers and that promise an attack by the Rev. Martin Luther King and Stokely Carmichael on 20 major cities. . . . Good race relations begin with good people and the kind of people who contrived and executed the February riots in Orangeburg are still with us and they were among those who laid siege to the State House on March 13 and they won't go away because Lt. Gov. West shuts his eyes."[42]

On June 23 Nance officially became president of S.C. State, and among his early actions he invited John West to speak to a student assembly on September 20. It was West's third visit to the campus since the student shootings, and while he made no specific reference to the February shootings, he did address the matter of student unrest in general:

> The youth of today have become involved in society's problems to a degree far beyond what fathers and mothers ever expected or can understand. This

involvement and concern has taken many forms, including protests, demonstrations, marches and even—in some instances—actual revolts on the campuses of major colleges and universities.

All of these occurrences have made communication between college presidents and students—as well as between parents and children—difficult at best and impossible at times. The main purpose of my appearance here today is to attempt to bridge, in a small way, some of that communication gap which probably exists between you and your state government.

Much of the dissent, turmoil, misunderstanding and violence which exists in our society comes from the desire by young people to be recognized and involved in the problems of our age. Every person in every generation needs a goal and a challenge. Without it, life can be flat and meaningless.[43]

There was nothing flat or meaningless about West's experience at S.C. State. It gave him prominent presence and status in the state's civil rights community at a time when it was considered politically risky to venture too close to the volatile political environment in Orangeburg. As West was learning, his identification with S.C. State made him vulnerable to attacks such as that launched by Frank Best, and while Best and the Birchers were viewed as extremists by some Republicans, Best's message was one that resonated among the state's racially oriented conservatives. There was a widening chasm between South Carolina's political Left and Right—its conservatives and liberals—and for a man who had spent years trying to keep feet planted in both communities, the feat was becoming increasingly precarious.

In the months ahead South Carolina would experience an escalation of tensions, driven in large part by events that brought the realities of the state's long-standing racial alienation into full view and to the public attention of every South Carolinian. In a state known for its racial separation, things were becoming even more polarized, socially and politically. These were hardly the conditions under which John West had hoped to run for governor.

EIGHT

"WE CAN, AND WE SHALL"

We pledge to minority groups no special status other than full-fledged
responsibility in a government that is totally color-blind.

John West

The South Carolina governor's race was still two years off as tumultuous
events erupted across America in what would become the historically
discordant year of 1968. Against a backdrop of violence in cities and on
college campuses, the incumbent Lyndon Johnson withdrew from the upcoming presidential race in the turmoil over the Vietnam War, and in subsequent
months the assassination of Dr. Martin Luther King Jr. and Senator Robert F.
Kennedy shook the nation further. By the time of the political conventions that
summer, America's nerves were shattered.

The Democrats met in Chicago in mid-August, and to most Americans,
the convention proved to be a shocking display of a political party in disarray.
Televised accounts were beamed around the world of violent clashes between
police and antiwar demonstrators in Grant Park, and within the convention
hall backers of the late Senator Kennedy and Senator Eugene McCarthy were in
bitter combat with the delegates supporting Vice President Hubert Humphrey.
West, McNair, and most of the South Carolina delegates—originally backers of
President Johnson—supported Humphrey, and the Minnesotan emerged the
winner. South Carolinians and other southerners, however, came away from the
convention worried that their party had been damaged by the Chicago chaos
and that their candidate would be a hard sell in their respective states.

Two weeks earlier the Republican Party convention in Miami Beach had
been—by comparison—a model of decorum and far more attentive to South

Carolina interests. South Carolinians, in fact, dominated the proceedings. To the surprise of many traditional GOP regulars who may have expected the party to take a centrist turn after the Goldwater defeat in 1964, the party did quite the opposite. Led by Strom Thurmond and his South Carolina strategists Fred Buzhardt and Harry Dent, the party chose to pursue a "Southern Strategy" that made Richard Nixon the champion of efforts to slow down the racial desegregation of southern schools. The Nixon forces not only overcame the candidacies of New York moderate Nelson Rockefeller and California governor Ronald Reagan; they also chose as Nixon's running mate another staunch conservative, Maryland governor Spiro T. Agnew.

The rallying cry for segregationists by that time was "freedom of choice," a code phrase among southern conservatives for minimalist desegregation. Cyril B. Busbee, state superintendent of education at the time, later contended that freedom of choice was "a system whereby black children and their parents were permitted to request assignment to previously all-white schools." The placement of white children, Busbee said, was generally unchanged.[1]

Under those conditions freedom of choice was only one small step beyond the token desegregation of previous years. White parents, fearful that busing plans would send their children far from home and perhaps into heavily integrated or even majority black schools, clung to the hope that somehow Nixon could reverse things and leave their children only marginally affected by the state's long-delayed compliance with the *Brown v. Board of Education* ruling. "Mr. Nixon will give the South just about what it wants," wrote the columnists Rowland Evans and Robert Novak, "token integration under the 'freedom of choice' plans."[2]

The summer of 1968 thus passed with the national Democratic Party in apparent disarray, the Republicans in the hands of South Carolina operatives, and the nation distressed and despairing over what seemed to be the imminent collapse of its social order and stability. There was plenty of reason for anxiety for John West as he took stock of what seemed to be deteriorating conditions for a Democratic candidate for governor in South Carolina.

NIXON VS. WALLACE

The liveliest part of the 1968 presidential race in the South turned out to be the fight among segregationist interests, part of them supporting the newly energized conservative Republicans and the candidacy of Richard Nixon, and others moving toward the more strident campaign of Alabama governor George Wallace, the candidate of the American Independent Party. Amid the swirling violence of 1960s America, Nixon hammered at the theme of law and order and satisfied many southerners with his support for freedom of choice. In his more transparently racial campaign, Wallace worked vigorously and probably took votes that would have gone to Nixon—those of white segregationists in the South and blue-collar workers in the East and the Midwest.

As it turned out, Wallace carried five states in the Deep South—Arkansas, Louisiana, Mississippi, Alabama, and Georgia—four of which had gone for Goldwater in 1964 and three of which had supported Strom Thurmond's Dixiecrat presidential bid in 1948. The one state missing from Wallace's total was South Carolina, which had supported both Goldwater and Thurmond. Nixon's victory in the Palmetto State could be attributed to Thurmond's political power there and also to the growing organizational strength of the South Carolina GOP, which had one full election campaign of statewide races under its belt in 1966.

Whatever the cause of the South Carolina outcome may have been, it was not good news for John West. Between them Nixon and Wallace polled more than 70 percent of the total vote, a resounding protest against the wave of demonstrations and public violence sweeping the nation and a loud statement for slow, or no, school desegregation. The Democratic candidate, Hubert Humphrey, was left with less than 30 percent of the South Carolina vote, much of it coming from loyal black voters who cheered his early and steady support of civil rights reform. The Republican Nixon tallied 254,062 votes (38.1 percent) to Wallace's 215,430 (32.3 percent), and Humphrey finished third with 197,486 (29.6 percent). Nixon's victory in South Carolina, coming on the heels of Goldwater's win in 1964, would be part of a skein of more than four decades in which Republican presidential candidates would carry the state in eleven of twelve elections. Only Jimmy Carter from neighboring Georgia carried the state for the Democrats in 1976. For John West, the 1968 numbers translated into the uncomfortable reality that less than 30 percent of the South Carolina electorate had voted for the presidential candidate of his own Democratic Party.

As sobering as that outcome was for West, however, there was another, more heartening reality in the 1968 election outcome. Even as South Carolina voters were turning out in large numbers to cast their votes for candidates other than the Democrat for president, the pattern was not holding up in other elections around the state. South Carolina reelected the Democrat Fritz Hollings by a wide margin to the U.S. Senate in a return match against Marshall Parker, and the five Democratic members of the six-member delegation in Congress were returned to office.

In state legislative elections things were even more interesting. All seats in the S.C. Senate and House were up for election—as in 1966—because a new forty-six-member Senate reapportionment plan was in place. In both houses, as it turned out, Democrats actually picked up seats in the 1968 election. Two years earlier in the fifty-member Senate, Republicans held seven seats, including all four of the Charleston County places. In the 1968 election Democrats won back the four Charleston seats, and the GOP total in the Senate fell from seven to three.

In the S.C. House, Democratic gains were even more conspicuous. The number of Republicans in the House shrank from 17 in 1966 to 5 in the 1968 elections. All told, Republican legislative seats in the General Assembly dropped from 24 in 1966 to 8 two years later, and Democratic seats rose from 146 to 162. For John West, the message was mixed but hopeful. For all the partisan hoopla at the national level, it appeared that a lot of South Carolinians were splitting their tickets at the local level, supporting Democratic incumbents and the "courthouse crowds," who often went along with the incumbents. This provided some reassurance to a man who had spent years cultivating the courthouse denizens and winning the friendship of the long-serving incumbents who still held the strings to power in the state.

A LOW-PROFILE CAMPAIGN

The West campaign, in fact, would not be a high-profile enterprise, in keeping with the style and personality of the candidate. It would stick to the pattern of his lieutenant governor's race, issues-oriented and measured in tone. His chamber-of-commerce-type speeches continued, as he pledged in Columbia to fight pollution, supported expanded health care in Charleston, stood up in Bennettsville for law and order, and bragged about the state's technical education system in Cheraw. Quietly, West was also seeking to shore up his right flank on school desegregation by taking an anti-Washington stance and expressing his support for freedom of choice.

In keeping with his low-key and noncombative style, West's slogan was "Elect a Good Man Governor." He would eschew the bright red, white, and blue campaign colors traditionally favored by candidates and would choose instead the muted look of a soft medium blue and pale yellow. His pictures were not assertive or aggressive. They depicted the wholesome, friendly look of a round-faced man who could pass for someone's uncle or the corner pharmacist.

West's opponent was Albert Watson, a congressman whose credentials among the segregationists were undeniable. He had followed Strom Thurmond from the Democratic Party to the Republican Party during the Goldwater campaign of 1964, and he had a record of resisting the civil rights initiatives of

John West's campaign slogan in his 1970 race for governor was a simple, low-key appeal, and it worked. Courtesy of the John C. West Papers, South Carolina Political Collections, University of South Carolina

Democratic presidents during a career in Congress that began with his election as a Democrat in 1962. Watson was West's opposite in looks and style. He was tall, dark-haired, and aggressive, and his evangelical voice could fire up—or perhaps even incite—a crowd. His campaign slogan was "Our Kind of Man," an exclusionary line that seemed to suggest that there were others who might not be "our" kind.

Even before he was nominated as his party's candidate for governor, Watson was going on the attack and was making things personal and emotional. "It is high time," he said in a January 1970 statement, "that the elected leadership of this state . . . show determination and courage in protecting the rights of our local school systems and our children."[3] It was a curious ploy for the Republicans, who only two years earlier had convinced South Carolinians that Nixon could slow down the desegregation process with his advocacy of freedom of choice. Watson was now calling on "the elected leadership of the state" to resist the very administration he had helped to elect in 1968. To Democrats, it amounted to something of a political bait-and-switch exercise.

Harry Dent claimed that some of the problems came from "desegregation booby traps," cases that had been under way before Nixon took office and that were reaching final stages.[4] There were other complications, he said, which were preventing the kind of relief Nixon had offered in his simple freedom-of-choice advocacy. Desegregation orders were coming from many quarters—various courts and various federal agencies—and to make matters even more confusing, there was internal friction within the White House between "Southern Strategy" staff and others. For whatever reason, Watson was trying to make

South Carolina Democrats the scapegoats for actions over which the Nixon administration now had ownership.

One particular court case was getting attention in South Carolina. Two of the state's school districts—a large district that encompassed all of Greenville County and a smaller, rural district in Darlington County—were under order from the Fourth District Court of Appeals to desegregate in February 1970. That meant that the districts would be required to implement their plans in midyear, shifting thousands of students and teachers from one school to another in the span of one weekend. Even though the court-ordered desegregation was coming sixteen years after *Brown v. Board of Education* had ruled against segregated school systems, it was called "instant integration" because it came during the course of a school year.

The timing of the "instant integration" also became crucial to the West and Watson campaigns. West had scheduled the formal announcement of his plans to run for governor on a Monday, February 23, a week after the court orders for school desegregation in Greenville and Darlington counties were to be carried out. The timing of the "instant integration" order brought the school issue front and center as a matter of campaign attention.

As it turned out, there was relative calm in both school districts as the desegregation plans went into effect. Unhappy white parents in the Darlington County town of Lamar had launched a classroom boycott to express their displeasure, and it was beginning to take effect among the white students. There seemed little threat of violence, however, at least for the moment.

Less than a week after the desegregation orders had gone into effect, boycott leaders scheduled a rally at the Lamar High School football stadium. It would be on Sunday, February 22, and the boycott leader, Jeryl Best of nearby Lydia, invited both West and Watson along with Governor McNair, Congressman John L. McMillan from the state's Fifth District, and Arthur Ravenel of Charleston, who was vying with Watson for the GOP nomination.

A SUNDAY SPEECH

All but Watson declined, and West did so in a cordial note to Jeryl Best, reminding the boycott leader that he supported freedom of choice.[5] People did not need to be reminded of Watson's position, however. He made it amply clear in a resounding affirmation of his dedication to freedom of choice, as well as his support for the classroom boycott. "I choose to be with you and those concerned with quality education and freedom of choice," he said to the cheering crowd. He urged his audience to ignore people who call you racist, bigot and redneck. I've been called a racist, a bigot and a buzzard, but I intend to tell it like it is. On controversial issues, it is often best not to take a stand, but you don't elect people to public office who refuse to take a stand on political issues.

There are some people who will criticize me, but even if it means my defeat, I will stand up and take a stand and tell people where I stand as regards freedom of choice. God bless anyone who is interested in their children. I'll stand with them and applaud them.[6]

It seemed a heroic moment for Watson, squaring his shoulders against the alien forces in Washington, D.C., and invoking divine inspiration to support the segregationists of Lamar, South Carolina. The next day, in announcing his plans to run for governor, West weighed in sympathetically with those opposing the midyear integration that had been carried out in Greenville and Darlington counties:

The Supreme Court decision to integrate at this time, in the middle of a school term, is wrong. It's stupid and senseless.

One thing is certain, however. Freedom of Choice is the best solution available and I will continue to do everything I can to see that we get it.[7]

As he had earlier in his political career, West was pursuing a center-Right strategy, making himself as conservative as he felt was politically prudent. He would not be winning over the Lamar boycotters or the Frank Bests of the world, but he hoped he could provide enough conservative credibility to satisfy the chambers of commerce and courthouse crowds he had worked so long to win over and sustain. It was a hazardous course and one in which he would find the centrist channel an increasingly elusive route.

In the meantime conditions were not growing any calmer in Lamar. The boycott was picking up support daily as measured by the empty desks in classrooms, and unrest among the parents grew stronger. On Monday evening, March 12, about a month after the desegregation order had been put into effect, around two hundred white men gathered at the Lamar High School armed with chains and clubs and were confronted by law enforcement officers. Violence was sporadic and quickly suppressed, but the next morning—March 13— the armed protesters returned in force with mayhem in mind. They attacked school buses as they pulled into the parking lot carrying black students to the high school, and scarcely moments after the students had escaped, two of the buses were overturned. The ensuing melee between demonstrators and law enforcement produced no deaths or serious injuries, but it left the community bruised and angry and the state caught in a firestorm of political reactions.

The Lamar incident attracted national news coverage, and officials from President Nixon and Vice President Agnew on down dutifully deplored the incident. In South Carolina, Republicans and Democrats exchanged accusations and law enforcement proceeded with the arrests of Jeryl Best and others involved in the activity. Within two weeks schools were beginning to return to normal in Lamar. On March 21, Republicans met in convention in Columbia and nominated Watson as their gubernatorial candidate. No mention was made of Lamar, but Watson renewed his attack on Governor McNair for his "surrender" on the school desegregation issue.[8]

Through it all the one thing that did not go away about the Lamar violence was its association with Watson and the Sunday speech at the football stadium. Days after the incident, state senator J. P. "Spot" Mozingo of Darlington, a longtime leader in state Democratic circles and a friend of West, attributed the Lamar trouble to a small group rooted in the Ku Klux Klan and said, "A lot of people think this is a severe blow to Albert politically, but I don't want to make that judgment." The Darlington NAACP president, Arthur Stanley, commented, "You might as well say that Watson poured gasoline on the fire."[9]

ON THE HUSTINGS

The campaign slogged into the summer months, and at least one columnist—Charleston's Hugh Gibson—was making an interesting observation. He wrote, "One would have supposed the democratic nominee, Lt. Governor John C. West, enjoying a long head start over Republican opponent Albert W. Watson, now would be coasting. And that Watson, faced with the challenger's traditional task of dramatizing issues and galvanizing voters, would be the one sweating on the hustings. Instead, West is out beating the drums and Watson has been off poking around the Asian combat zone [Vietnam]."[10] West's "Elect a Good Man Governor" strategy required the kind of steady, persistent, and sometimes punishing regimen described by Gibson and seemed well suited as a counterbalance to West's aggressive, racially oriented Republican opponent. The contest was shaping up as a good test between the conservative and the moderate elements of South Carolina's political community. Then came a shockingly unexpected moment that caught even some of West's strongest supporters by surprise.

Commenting on the filing of suits by the Justice Department to force the ten remaining noncompliant school districts in the state into compliance, West erupted at a news conference on July 8. An Associated Press account said that West "promised that South Carolina will not accept federal school integration without an all-out legal fight."[11] Another account quoted West as saying that

South Carolina "must continue to fight to prevent the massive disruption of our public school system threatened by the actions of the federal government."[12]

While the comment may not have been all that different from his description of the Greenville-Darlington suits as "senseless and stupid" or his steadfast support of freedom of choice, something about the tone and intensity made this one different and objectionable across a surprisingly wide range of political interests. West's opponents in the Republican Party seemed the most surprised, and party chairman Ray Harris said, "The sudden switch to a diehard segregationist qualifies Lt. Governor West as the biggest political phony that I've ever known."[13] At the opposite end of the political spectrum, state NAACP field secretary Isaac "Ike" Williams said that West's statement appeared "designed to appease white bigots and racists," and he added that black voters may be driven into a state of apathy. McNair, who believed that West's statement undermined his own position that the state had "run out of time and run out of courts," seethed. "When he wants my help, he can ask for it," he told an aide.[14]

One immediate impact was a shift of attention to a third-party contender, Thomas Broadwater, who ran as a write-in candidate of the United Citizens Party (UCP). The UCP was a black political initiative launched a year earlier in Charleston. Broadwater, an outspoken Columbia attorney, was considered more of a protest candidate than a viable competitor for the position, but he offered an alternative to disgruntled black Democrats.[15]

A RESCUE MISSION

A survey conducted in September by the West campaign indicated the extent of the damage. About half the black voters polled indicated that they were "undecided" over their choice of a gubernatorial candidate, a drastic piece of news for West that set off alarms and led to some repair efforts. Jim Waddell, the Beaufort County senator who was friendly to both McNair and West, was brought into the campaign as an intermediary between the governor and the lieutenant governor. In addition Democratic Party chairman Don Fowler set off on a statewide campaign with retired NAACP field secretary I. DeQuincey Newman to mollify and win back unhappy black political leaders. It was an effort that would continue until the weekend before the November election.

According to Clyburn, Newman convened a meeting in Camden in early October to shore up West's support among black voters. Represented at the meeting were critical elements of the black political leadership at the time, including Newman, who could reach out to the ministerial community as well as the NAACP; Billy Fleming of Manning, a prominent funeral home director who also was a leader in the NAACP; and I. P. Stanback, a Columbia business-man who was a committed West supporter and a major figure in the politically powerful black Masonic lodges. "It became very clear that West had only one chance of being elected governor of South Carolina," Clyburn recalled, "and that was to get almost all of the black vote. But the black vote had to turn out. The big point was to get black people to the polls. So Newman did his thing with the ministers, Billy Fleming with the NAACP, and I. P. Stanback with the Masonic lodges."[16]

One final drama would have an impact on the West-Watson race. It took place in the early days of the 1970–71 school year at A. C. Flora High School in Columbia in the heart of the fashionable suburb of Forest Acres. Skirmishes broke out on the school grounds on October 13 between black and white students in the newly desegregated school, and tensions escalated the next day, with some fifty students throwing sticks and rocks and creating what school principal Clinton B. Harvey called "pandemonium." Learning that the first day's violence had not been reported in the local press, Watson called a press conference and said, "I have the courage to take a stand on this issue," and he called for immediate investigations into "spreading violence and disruption in our schools."[17] News reports, however—later disputed by Watson—laid part of the blame for the escalation of violence on Watson staffers who had stopped to take pictures of white and black students mingling on the school's campus. A Watson aide said that he was in the area with a fellow staff member and saw police cars at A. C. Flora. They stopped, out of curiosity, he said, and his friend "likes to take pictures."[18]

The Flora incident actually proved helpful to West in several respects. For one thing, it brought McNair back into the campaign in a forceful way. He held a news conference on October 16, two days after the A. C. Flora violence, and if anyone had failed to link the Lamar and Flora incidents to Watson, Mc-Nair did it for them. He said, "I think the gentleman [Watson] should have learned from Lamar that inflammatory statements [and] over-reaction only add to the problem, rather than lessening it."[19]

At least one prominent Republican had already drifted from the Watson camp for racial reasons. A month earlier the Republican mayor of Greenville, Cooper White, withheld his support of Watson, at least partially on the basis of campaign ads featuring scenes of riots that had taken place in the Watts section of Los Angeles. The *Spartanburg Herald* urged candidates to drop school desegregation as a campaign issue. For his part, West vowed never to "inflame or polarize class against class, rich against poor, color against color."[20]

West began to gain newspaper endorsements around the state as election day neared, and one of them—the *Florence Morning News*—notably picked up

The West family gathered to watch the television account of his victorious 1970 election, with son Doug (left), son Jack (center), and daughter Shelton (right). Courtesy of Lois R. West and Shelton W. Bosley

on West's low-key style. "He has avoided emotional appeals," the editorial stated. "Possessing no flare for showmanship and no special charismatic gifts to capitalize on politically, he is nevertheless a strong, solid, intelligent person whose dedication to South Carolina has been proved over 16 years of public service."[21]

ELECTING A "GOOD MAN GOVERNOR"

On November 3 South Carolina voters elected the "Good Man" of West's campaign ads as their next governor, rejecting the self-proclaimed man of courage for a "strong, solid, intelligent person." West won by a healthy 51.6 percent to Watson's 45.6 percent. The turnout was almost five hundred thousand voters, slightly higher than the number of votes cast in West's 1966 lieutenant governor's race. It was a good night all around for the Democrats, in fact. Earle Morris of Pickens was elected lieutenant governor, and the Democrats won all the constitutional offices, retained their five congressional seats, and kept healthy margins in both houses of the General Assembly.

West carried thirty-six of the forty-six counties, including the heavily white upcountry counties of Spartanburg and Anderson, traditional Democratic strongholds among textile workers. Watson carried three Pee Dee counties—Florence, Darlington, and Lee—possibly because of his locally popular stance at Lamar. Among black voters Newman, Fleming, Fowler, Clyburn, Stanback and all the others who went across the state to turn out the vote got their job done. UCP candidate Tom Broadwater got only 3,315 write-in votes.

In fact West got a lot of white votes too; he would not have won otherwise. In addition he swayed some conservatives along the way. A GOP-leaning columnist for the *Columbia Record,* Harrison Jenkins, wrote of West:

> No arm-waver, no hellfire-and-brimstone orator, he accomplishes his logical goals with a patient persuasion worthy of a British member of the House of Commons. In a General Assembly that is not particularly noted for good listeners . . . John West is a splendid example of one who has developed that communications skill to an art.
>
> Power corrupts or changes some people; others, it does not. John West has not been contaminated; he remains an undemonstrative public servant; a practical and perspicacious politician of humanistic convictions, capable of conscientious reasoning with all sorts of people, unwilling to sacrifice basic morality to expediency.[22]

There were no such things as "transition teams" or "transition offices" in 1970. Governor McNair assigned staff and provided some working space for the governor-elect, and West began the process of accepting applications and interviewing prospects for his administration almost immediately. One of the worst-kept secrets was that West intended to hire a black staff member. McNair had broken the color barrier in his office by hiring Margaret Percell from the Urban League in an administrative position. West, however, let it be known that he planned to hire a black professional for his executive staff. This became big news, and there were plenty of prospects. One of them was Clyburn, the young Charleston activist who had run for the S.C. House of Representatives that year and had lost in a close race, finishing twelfth in a contest for eleven seats. "I went to bed thinking I had won," he later said, and "I woke to learn that I had been declared a loser."[23]

The actual selection of a black executive staff member represented an early and interesting policy decision for the governor-elect. There were candidates for the job who represented "safer" choices than Clyburn, as far as West's more conservative, white supporters and friends were concerned. Clyburn was a 1962 S.C. State graduate who had participated in the sit-in demonstrations of 1960,

West made South Carolina history by appointing future U.S. congressman James E. Clyburn as the first African American to serve on a governor's executive staff. Courtesy of James E. Clyburn

and who had been hosed by the police and spent time in jail as a result. He not only had been among the founders of the United Citizens Party but also was active in support of the one-hundred-day strike of black workers at the Medical College (now University) of South Carolina in the summer of 1969 and had been a community organizer with the Neighborhood Youth Corps. Clyburn moved in politically active circles that made even some of the older black families in Charleston a little nervous. He clearly represented a risk for the usually cautious West, but other factors influenced West's choice of his first black staffer. South Carolina was just coming out of a decade of unprecedented unrest and civil disturbance, much of it coming from blacks and unhappy young people of both races. In the eighteen months before the election, demonstrations had rocked two of the state's largest cities—Charleston and Columbia—and there was no guarantee that more of the same would not be forthcoming.

As it turned out, West opted for Clyburn, thereby sending a message that not only did he intend for there to be racial diversity on his executive staff but he also wished to have someone regularly in touch with the major political leaders of both races. Clyburn was reluctant to take the job, telling West

West was escorted to the inaugural platform by his predecessor, Gov. Robert E. McNair. Behind the governors are patrolman Harry Coker (left) and L. K. Martin. Courtesy of the John C. West Papers, South Carolina Political Collections, University of South Carolina

that he "was a little too outspoken for his administration." He later attributed his acceptance of the appointment to a strategic leak to the Charleston press from a West staffer.[24]

Clyburn's selection would prove to be only the beginning of the powerful messages West would articulate on behalf of the state's minority population in the coming weeks. Whatever ambivalence or equivocation he may have expressed about civil rights or public school desegregation during the campaign for governor vanished somewhere between his election on November 3, 1970, and his inauguration on January 19, 1971. "I knew that I would never run for public office again," West later said. "I felt that I could say what was really on my mind and not suffer any political retribution for it."[25]

A SPEECH FOR THE AGES

Speak his mind he did. His inauguration, on January 19, 1971, took place on a cold Tuesday morning that one reporter described as a "frozen vigil," noting that "a sharp wind [was] turning faces red and lips blue."[26] However, there was nothing chilly about the words John West delivered from the north steps of the

State House that morning. Forty-seven years before a charismatic young man named Barack Obama would thrill Americans with the words "Yes, we can," John West stunned South Carolinians with a litany of pledges, each beginning with the words "We can, and we shall."

His delivery was not loud, but the words were powerful. They carried a message that South Carolinians were not accustomed to hearing from their political leaders, words about things such as poverty, racial discrimination, hunger, and illiteracy, for example. West's was a "politically incorrect" speech for its time in a state where even enlightened leaders chose their words carefully in addressing the state's grim racial past and grievous human deficiencies. Speaking in his soft, modulated conversational tone, West violated whatever customary restraints there may have been in addressing certain of the state's realities.

In his "We can, and we shall" canon, he enumerated ten prescriptive items, most of them addressing historically painful elements of life in South Carolina. Some of the proposals were preposterously optimistic, and others fell well within the range of being politically doable. The first pledge fell into the former category: "We can, and we shall in the next four years eliminate hunger and malnutrition and their attendant suffering from the state." The pledge was the product of his friendships with longtime NAACP chief Reverend I. De-Quincey Newman and Senator Fritz Hollings, whose publicized "Poverty Tours" had brought attention to places in the state where living conditions were particularly poor and malnutrition among children was evident. Hollings's and Newman's claims had been scoffed at by some of the state's political leaders, who claimed that they were either exaggerations or plays for publicity. West's statement contained the message that he not only believed the problem existed but also disagreed with the doubters and scoffers, some of them political friends.

Whatever surprise may have been evoked by his hunger pledge, the next item in his inaugural address received the most attention and became an enduring theme for the administration and for John West's place in South Carolina history. He said, "We can, and we shall, in the next four years, eliminate from our government any vestige of discrimination because of race, creed, sex, religion, or any other barrier to fairness for all citizens. We pledge to minority groups no special status other than full-fledged responsibility in a government that is totally color-blind."[27]

South Carolinians had never heard a governor speak so openly and frankly about racial matters, and after a stunned moment, applause broke out among the huddled thousands. The sound was muffled by gloves and mittens worn by the chilled assemblage, but there was nothing muffled about the response

With temperatures in the twenties, bundled up South Carolinians gathered on the chilly north side of the State House to see John West sworn in as the state's governor. Courtesy of Lois R. West and Shelton W. Bosley

(right) West stunned South Carolinians in his 1971 inaugural address by pledging to attack ignorance, illiteracy, and poverty in the state and to eliminate discrimination from the practices of state government. Courtesy of the John C. West Papers, South Carolina Political Collections, University of South Carolina

West's words received around the state and around the nation in subsequent days. The *New York Times* accorded his "color-blind" statement headline attention and linked him with Jimmy Carter, who had taken office in Georgia the day before with a similar statement of racial justice.[28] West also got the attention of the *New York Post,* which contrasted his progressive racial statement to the recalcitrant position of U.S. attorney general John Mitchell, who was described as having "resorted to his customary sophistry in warning against 'forced integration.'"[29] James "Scotty" Reston of the *Times* identified Carter and West as new "Voices of the South" and wrote prophetically, "we are beginning to create a new national politics in which good men, from whatever region, and even from the smaller states, may in the future have an equal chance to get to the White House."[30]

Closer to home former governors Hollings and McNair had words of praise. Hollings said, "He really talked as a governor leading his people rather than the head of a militia defending them from Washington." McNair called the speech "well done and very good. It set the tone for what we know will be a fine administration." Strom Thurmond offered a partisan harrumph: "The Democrats have been in power all these years, and if there was any discrimination, they could have ended it."[31]

West's longtime friend Reverend Newman, who helped rescue his candidacy in the waning weeks of the campaign, called the speech "an emancipation proclamation for all those bound by those traditions which should have been relinquished a long time ago. It was a clarion call to all citizens from all walks of life for positive participation in state government."[32]

For West, the speech was the completion of a journey, from the cornfields of Charlotte Thompson with his scarcely literate workmates, to the racially tinged campaign with Arthur "Mush" Jones, to the outrage over Guy Hutchins's beating and the subsequent acquittal of his accused assailants. It was the loudly spoken statement from a governor, amplifying the small, quiet voice of a senator speaking out from the back of the chamber on behalf of constitutional rights a decade earlier.

There were other "We can, and we shall" items. A key message was the pledge to "initiate new and innovative programs which will in our time provide adequate housing for all our citizens." Clyburn recalled having recommended this proposal to the meeting of black political leaders in Camden in early October as an issue that could be used to generate grassroots support among the state's rural poor.

Another item that would gain much attention was West's pledge to "initiate far-reaching programs to provide more doctors, nurses, health personnel as well as better systems for the delivery of health care to each citizen." Innocent sounding in its intent, this would set off a political firestorm over the implementation vehicle West chose to recommend: a new medical school at the University of South Carolina.

A DIFFERENT EDUCATION MESSAGE

There was no mention of freedom of choice, or anything resembling it, in the speech. West's education references were general ones, aimed at issues that were felt deeply among the state's minority families. Saving education for the last of his ten priority items, he said, "Finally, and perhaps most importantly, we can, and we shall provide a better educational opportunity for all citizens of whatever age or status, from a comprehensive pre-school program for the very young to a continuing educational program for adults ranging from basic literacy to sophisticated, advanced research-oriented graduate programs."[33]

Along the way West did not ignore the chamber of commerce and civic club faithful who had heard eight years of his speeches addressing the various issues he believed important. Among the "We can, and we shall" priorities were items such as industrial development, agricultural improvement, the quality and support of law enforcement, and the emerging issues of environmental protection. While those did not receive the kind of audience response accorded the other more provocative items, they would prove to be important parts of his administration's focus, particularly industrial development. "The time has arrived," West told his chilled listeners in linking all his proposals, "when South Carolina—for all time—must break loose and break free of the vicious cycle of ignorance, illiteracy and poverty which has retarded us throughout our history."[34]

The inaugural address was not the product of a clever speechwriter. It sprang almost word for word from the fertile yellow legal pads that West had used from his earliest days to record important messages and thoughts. The speech draft got a close review from friends and family and a polishing from a staffer, but little—if anything—of substance was altered. It was intended to be the personal expression of his own values and beliefs, a call to arms for his administration, and the blueprint for the formation of his recommendations to the General Assembly in future years. "I was a little concerned about the way the speech would be received," West wrote in his journal the next day, "as it was radical by many standards . . . especially in pledging that the state would be color blind for the next four years. Amazingly enough, the reaction, even from the strong conservative segregationists[,] has been good."[35]

Eight days later, in a far more prosaic address, West delivered his first State of the State speech to the General Assembly. While it was expected that he would begin to lay out the steps by which he hoped to achieve the goals he had articulated on the frozen north steps of the State House on his inaugural day, the second speech had other purposes. By custom the State of the State speech was not an address on the state of the state at all. It was the presentation of the governor's legislative program to the General Assembly for the upcoming session.

For West's 1971 presentation, much of that program would come from holdover issues from the previous administration, items such as state budget priorities and the hot-button issue of the times, teacher salaries. The General Assembly appropriated on a year-to-year basis the amount that the state would pass along to local school districts in the form of a state supplement to the

Formally attired Governor West and the First Lady led the way at the 1971 inaugural ball. Courtesy of Lois R. West and Shelton W. Bosley

locally generated salary moneys. The supplement constituted a significant portion of the total salary funds and was a matter of keen political importance and sharp disagreement among legislators each year. South Carolina teachers had traditionally earned less than their counterparts in neighboring states, and under the leadership of its director, Carlos Gibbons, the teachers' professional organization—the South Carolina Education Association (SCEA)—had become increasingly aggressive and politically active. Teachers for the most part had supported West in the November election, and they expected to see something tangible in return. The SCEA, in fact, had requested a $1,500-per-year increase, and the State Department of Education had recommended a $1,000 hike for teachers.

It was not a good year for West to be meeting such expectations, however. Midyear budget cuts had left state agencies strapped, and a first-year governor could hardly run the risk of proposing a tax increase after being in office only a little more than a week. His recommendation for a $250 average increase in the state supplement for teachers hardly satisfied anybody, and West's battles with Gibbons and the state's teachers would be an ongoing struggle for most of his term.

West would not return to his "We can, and we shall" list until the end of the forty-five-minute speech, and he announced almost casually what was something of a political and historical blockbuster. "Within the next two weeks," he said, "I will announce the formation of South Carolina's first Commission on Human Relations as an adjunct to the Governor's Office. This commission will be comprised of outstanding citizens from throughout the state and will be staffed on a full-time basis to direct its full attention toward the elimination of discrimination . . . and the improvement of relations among all the people of the state." West also told the General Assembly that he planned to introduce legislation that would lead to the creation of the State Housing Authority, an entity he described as providing "the tools for making adequate shelter a reality for every citizen in this state."[36]

ACTING SWIFTLY ON HUMAN RIGHTS

It was the civil rights proposal that caught the public and legislative attention. For a state that liked to take its time in making decisions, even if that meant all-night debates and filibusters, West's swift action came as both a surprise and a statement of conviction. He did not quite make his two-week time frame, but five weeks after the State of the State message, he established the Governor's Advisory Commission on Human Relations by an executive order, the wording of which stated: "The essential quality of life in South Carolina is dependent upon the maintaining of harmony, understanding and mutual respect among all people. Ours is a state comprised of men and women of different races, religions, national origins, age groups, economic levels, political persuasions and other diverse interests. It is a state which treasures its individual freedom and liberties, and respects the basic dignity of each citizen. Such dignity and personal liberty require that each person be free of the injustice of discrimination."[37]

West's decision to create the new commission by executive order, while limiting its powers to that of an advisory role, preempted some of the anticipated opposition to the proposal in the General Assembly and provided time to prove that maybe a state-level civil rights agency was not such a "radical" idea after all. Legislation would not be introduced for another year, and by then, he hoped, the commission would have won the confidence of the state's conservatives as well as of the legislative moderates who had cheered West's proposal from the beginning.

West staked his hopes for winning broad-based support for the civil rights agency on the makeup of the commission. In his executive order he described the commission as comprising nineteen members, which "shall at all times reflect the broad concerns of all people of the state, particularly with a view toward representing the basic ideological, economic, geographic, racial, religious and age interests within the state."[38]

The commission was composed of ten white and nine black members. West's idea was for the black members to be sufficiently in tune with the state's racial problems to be able to identify discrimination issues as they arose. White members, he believed, would be the problem solvers. For that to happen, he packed the first commission with a powerful cross section of the state's business and professional establishment, corporate CEOs, journalists, and the Republican mayor of Greenville, Cooper White, who had supported him against Albert Watson in the just-completed governor's race. Black members represented a cross section of professional, religious, and academic leadership and also included some community organizers and protest leaders who might have been considered somewhat on the militant side by 1970s standards. Andrew Hugine, the S.C. State student with whom West had exchanged correspondence after the February 1968 shootings, was among West's appointees to the commission. The first chairman was Bill Travis, the South Carolina CEO for Southern Bell, and the vice chairman was Dr. Benjamin Payton, an Orangeburg native who was president of Benedict College at the time and would later become the long-serving president of Tuskegee University in Alabama.[39]

Grumblings were heard from several activist members of the civil rights community. West's decision to load the board of his human rights agency with establishment types seemed a slight to organizations such as the Quaker-based American Friends Service Committee and the Council on Human Relations, two organizations that had held a long and historic stake in South Carolina's race relations. Particularly rankled was Hayes Mizell, the American Friends director who had proposed the creation of a human rights commission during the McNair administration. Paul Matthias, of the Council on Human Relations, called Mizell's exclusion from the council "a real shame" and said that "it created suspicion among many who fully shared the goals and objectives that Gov. West set forth."[40]

For all his advocacy of civil rights issues, John West was at heart an establishment guy. He wanted to make civil rights part of that establishment and not a perpetually fringe issue that relied on the courts and legislative bodies for enforcement. Such mainstream status could happen only, he believed, if the men and women who populated that establishment made it happen.

In South Carolina in the 1970s there was not much in the way of racially integrated activities. Blacks did not belong to downtown city clubs, civic clubs, or country clubs, and there was little interchange through such institutions as churches or even athletic events. Blacks and whites met generally under crisis conditions as part of ad hoc committees to deal with emergencies. One initiative to combat such racial separation came from Columbia's civic leadership in the form of an entity called simply the Luncheon Club. Its driving force was Reverend Howard McClain, a Baptist minister who was executive minister of the racially progressive Christian Action Council, and who served in that position for thirty-five years.

By design and at Reverend McClain's insistence, the club never had programs or agendas. Its meetings were intended to be opportunities for black and white people to get to know each other on something other than crises bases, McClain said at the time. Fifty years later the club was still functioning on that same nonstructured basis. For a number of years, however, there was one notable exception. Columbian Hyman Rubin, a longtime state senator and a founding member of the Luncheon Club, remained active long after his retirement from political life, and he closed each meeting—at members' insistence—with some words of wisdom from his vast stores of erudition and warming morsels of Jewish humor.

Such initiatives were in their early stages, however, and in the early 1970s racially oriented efforts such as affirmative action, voter registration drives, minority business contract set-asides, and others were considered by white establishment types as being at best out of the ordinary and at worst downright nuisances and impediments. John West wanted to change that, not just through the actions of a civil rights agency, but also through the interactions of black and white commission members who would gather regularly in a work setting to address problems he hoped would be viewed as issues of common interest. Less than a decade earlier, an editorial in the *State* newspaper had wondered, "What does the Negro community want?" and "Who speaks for the Negro community?"[41]

It was that separatist, us-and-them perception that West hoped to dispel by creating a mechanism through which racial problems could be viewed as community issues in general and not just as issues for the "Negro community" or, for that matter, the civil rights community to identify and articulate. If race relations, like public education and economic development, were to become part of mainstream South Carolina, he felt that both blacks and whites should be their champions—bank presidents, utility company CEOs, mayors, college presidents, journalists, doctors, and attorneys among others, and not just civil rights advocates. West actually recruited most of the commission members himself, and those he did not were brought in by Clyburn with West's authorization.

AN ACTIVE BEGINNING

The commission came together nicely, as it turned out, and hit the ground running. Its first meeting was held on February 18, a month after the governor's inaugural address, and on April 2 the commission selected an executive director, George Hamilton of Walterboro, a candidate heavily backed by Clyburn. Since the commission functioned as a part of the governor's office in its early days, Hamilton's selection brought to three the number of black professionals in the office. From its earliest days the commission wished to assert its independence and separation from the influence of the governor's office. When Clyburn and another staff member took up seats at the rear of the conference room for the first commission meeting, they were asked by Chairman Bill Travis what business they had with the commission. When the answer was that they were there "just to observe," both were asked to leave, which they did.

At the April 2 meeting the commission undertook its first inquiry, an effort to seek the return to the state of Reverend J. A. De Laine, an AME minister who had been a major civil rights champion from Manning. Reverend De Laine had been active in organizing the first comprehensive challenge to the state's segregated public school system, the *Briggs v. Elliott* suit in Clarendon County, which eventually was combined with four other suits to form the landmark *Brown v. Board of Education.* During the course of his activities, his home became the target of night riders, and during one of the attacks De Laine fired back, winging one of the cars and allegedly one of the occupants.

Warrants were sworn out for De Laine's arrest, and he fled to New York City, where he was sheltered from extradition efforts by an AME bishop. Learning of West's racial initiatives, De Laine requested that the new Human Relations Commission look into the possibility of having the charges against him dropped so that he could return to South Carolina. Working through Attorney General Daniel R. McLeod, the commission learned that the solicitor for the judicial circuit that included Clarendon County was not willing to drop the charges against De Laine, thereby sustaining the civil rights pioneer's status as a fugitive. With no statutory power at the time, the commission was unable to pursue the matter further and so informed De Laine. He was never able to return to his native state.[42]

On another front the commission was more successful. At a meeting on August 6 it got directly to the heart of West's promise to be color blind, authorizing a study of employment patterns in state government. The study, conducted by Dr. Gerald E. Breger of the University of South Carolina, was reported to the commission seven months later, and its findings were not surprising. In the lowest two pay grades of state employees, black men and women occupied 80 to 88 percent of the positions. In the highest nine pay grades, only 8 of the 447 employees were black.[43]

The Breger study made West realize how far South Carolina had to go to carry out his "color-blind" promise. He also recognized that if he were to make that promise a reality, the agency would need to be created by the General Assembly with full statutory authority.

Legislation was introduced in 1972 to create what became the State Human Affairs Commission. To his conservative legislative friends, including the staunch segregationist senator Marion Gressette of Calhoun County, West sold the legislation as a way to "keep the Feds out of South Carolina" in the investigation of civil rights complaints. To others, including the state's first three black legislators since post-Reconstruction days, West sold it as a fulfillment of his inaugural address. Either way the bill passed both houses virtually without opposition, which was considered by many to be a political miracle in a state as deeply rooted in racial segregation as South Carolina.

Many of the members of the new statutory commission were reappointments from the advisory board, but one new appointment held a particularly symbolic significance for West. It was Guy Hutchins, the Camden High band director whose beating two decades earlier had brought to West's eyes the reality of racial violence in his state and in his own hometown. Hutchins's appointment did not close the book on the unpunished incident, but it did bring some sense of awareness that attitudes had changed a bit in South Carolina between 1954 and 1971.[44]

By the end of his second year in office, West was being hailed around the nation for his aggressive attack on discrimination. In addition he was building momentum within the state to get tough with state agencies that had compiled such a dismal record of minority employment. In May 1973 he was ready to make his frontal assault on the agencies, most of which did not report to the governor under the state's decentralized boards and commissions system. His primary weapon in dealing with the semi-independent agencies would be the new affirmative action program developed under the administrations of Presidents Lyndon Johnson and Richard Nixon. According to an account in the *New York Times:* "Gov. John C. West bluntly warned state agency and department heads that if they did not cooperate with the South Carolina Human Affairs Commission to end discrimination, their practices on minority hiring would be turned over to the Federal Government for possible action. I don't like the idea of the Federal Government having to come down and tell us to do what we know is legally and morally right . . . I don't mean this as a threat . . . but any state agency that refuses to cooperate, we'll simply tell the Feds, 'this is your baby.'"[45]

There was reason to feel that the "color-blind" initiative as described in West's inaugural address was well under way, and with a good smattering of political hardball, it was generating confidence and gaining surprising acceptance in the world of political reality. However, that was only one of the promises West had made to South Carolinians on that wintry day in 1971.

MAKING THINGS HAPPEN

As long as there is a single South Carolinian unemployed or under-
employed . . . then I shall ask you to join me in a resounding rejection
of the status quo.

John West

olitical observers may have been poised to paint John West as the most
liberal governor ever to grace the chief executive's office in South Carolina after his stunning inaugural address. It seemed to contain all the
standard ingredients of what southerners would consider a leftist agenda: civil
rights, public education, health care, nutrition, and housing for the poor,
among other issues.

What they would discover, however, was that John West did not travel an
ideological superhighway. His journey was not one to discover some sort of
philosophical perfection or political orthodoxy. John West's mission was a personally shaped human-scale Utopia that defied political categorization and
invited contradictory and conflicting assessments. While he was being hailed as
a prototypical New South governor of a progressive stripe, civil rights groups
and women's organizations sometimes found his actions frustrating for failing
their litmus-tests. In addition, while he championed the cause of quality public schools in fully desegregated settings, he shook his fist at federal officials in
resistance to requirements that students be bused to achieve racial balance. John
West lined up comfortably with moderate forces within the Democratic Party,
but he also embraced the politics of George Wallace. At any given moment, it
seemed, West could be a populist, a reformer, a traditionalist, an opportunist,

or a maverick. Restrictive terms such as "conservative" and "liberal" were not applicable in that setting, and by then those had lost their meanings in South Carolina in anything other than a racial context.

If West's politics seemed befuddling on occasion, there was nothing puzzling about his overall approach to the job of governing South Carolina. West was a builder, and where he saw long-neglected needs and deficiencies, he worked to construct something to address them, whether it was a program, an agency, an institution, or a new statute. Unlike latter-day exponents of small government and tax cuts who would leave it to "market conditions" to address social needs, West used whatever resources were available, governmental or otherwise. If that meant "growing government," a term of disdain popular with antigovernment ideologues, West did so with gleeful abandon. Midway through his term in office, he was asked to comment on the fact that his office staff had grown from 116 to 244 in the two years since the McNair administration and the fact that the budget had increased from less than $1 million to $2.4 million in that same period of time.

Unapologetically he said, "I think it is fair to say that the $28 million we have generated in federal funds is not an inconsequential factor in the fact that we now have a budget surplus in the state."[1] What the reporters and political critics were leaving unaddressed with their questions about numbers and dollars was the considerable force being built within the governor's office with that staff and budget. They were also missing the major financial changes taking place that would alter not only the moneys available to state government but also the political relationships among the various players.

SOME SPENDING MONEY

For the first time in anyone's memory, South Carolina was not strapped for cash. Federal moneys were flowing in, in many forms, including Great Society program moneys of the Johnson administration and generous revenue-sharing dollars that had been initiated by the Nixon administration. The state was seeing healthy revenue streams, partly because McNair's "Moody Report" recommendations had been funded with a 13 percent tax increase in 1969 and partly because the state was enjoying success with its industrial development initiatives and the various revenues being produced as a result.

These were energetic times for South Carolina. During the West years as governor, per capita income rose by an average of almost 11 percent per year, and total personal income in the state increased by 75 percent between 1971 and 1976, offset somewhat by inflation. The state could look down its economic nose not only at Mississippi but also at Arkansas and Alabama, and it was fast gaining on Tennessee and Kentucky. South Carolinians were in a good mood, and in the days before taxation was represented to them as a mortal sin, they seemed satisfied that their tax dollars were part of the reason that schools were improving and better-paying jobs were coming their way.

The new revenues were changing attitudes and relationships within the governmental structure as well, particularly in the ways the governor and the legislature viewed each other. Traditionally the governor's budget proposals were just that—proposals—and before they could be enacted, they would undergo the scrutiny of at least two major bodies, the State Budget and Control Board and the General Assembly. While much of that procedure remained in place during the West years, some interesting options and strategies were emerging. For one thing, with his new financial resources West did not need the Budget and Control Board or legislative authorization for some new programs, at least in their early stages. That is what made the Human Relations–Human Affairs initiative so effective. He not only created the agency under his own executive authority, but he staffed and funded it fully for two years with moneys from federal sources he controlled: the Economic Development Administration and the Office of Economic Opportunity.

The governor was gaining a second advantage with his financial clout. The new Division of Administration handled a substantial amount of grant money for programs at the local level. That fact alone made the governor something of a funding broker and created potential leverage for him with legislators. Included in programs administered by the governor were such locally popular commodities as new fire trucks and police cars, water and sewer lines, and manpower training programs, items that secured local political approval for legislators who could help deliver them. While there is no recorded evidence that political favors were ever traded over such transactions, it is known that John West could be a pretty good horse trader.

Yet another dimension was created by the governor's new financial clout, and it gave him the opportunity to be something of a "full service" governor. In a state where governors had little in the way of direct statutory or constitutional authority, South Carolina chief executives could basically do as much, or as little, as they pleased, and they could direct their attention to areas where they had particular interests.

In the years prior to and following the *Brown v. Board of Education* decision, for example, the S.C. governor's office was primarily devoted to fending off the desegregation of public schools required by the *Brown* decision. As governor, Hollings broke out of that confinement by making the governor the state's lead salesman in the industrial development program he helped to create.

Russell sustained that initiative, and McNair expanded the economic growth effort into new areas, such as tourism promotion and development. He also took major roles in higher education and public school innovation and helped to reshape and modernize the state's financial management and planning systems. It fell to West to build on those precedents and to extend the reach of the governor's office even further. This expansion of executive authority, however, was not the kind that gave the governor direct control over agencies and their operations, as was carried out in later years. It was, instead, the application of influence and pressure that made things happen without the political bloodshed of firing a lot of people or moving around the boxes on the organizational chart.

AN ACTION PLAN

This was the kind of activity that West enjoyed. He was not building empires; he was creating and activating processes by which his priorities could be addressed, using existing agencies and programs and applying whatever political skills or incentives were available to him. That is how he set about to implement his social agenda. He was taking what many viewed as radical ideas and processing them through the state's conventional organizational structure so that they became imbedded in the state's operational mainstream. Anyone thinking that his idealistic inaugural address was simply the abstract statement of broad visions misunderstood his meaning entirely. His intent was for each of the items in his "We can, and we shall" canon to be followed up by specific, tangible action, usually involving the governor himself.

This was a far cry from the days of Governor James F. Byrnes (1951–55), who believed in a limited role for the governor and once wrote that he found it "surprising that the Governor should be asked to give time to the recruitment of new industry."[2] Byrnes would have been even further stunned to find a governor involving himself in such an extended range of interests as health care, housing, and nutrition activities. By the end of his administration, West's influence had been felt in virtually every major aspect of state government operation, and he had altered significantly the notion of a governor's role in the broad fabric of state government operations.

In the 1970s South Carolina governors could not succeed themselves in office, and many believed that after the first two years of their terms they became "lame ducks." West did not intend for that to happen to him. He sought to sustain the momentum of his aggressive inaugural address initiatives by urging legislators in the 1972 State of the State address to stay on course. He said: "As long as there is a single South Carolinian unemployed or under-employed—

Throughout his senatorial and gubernatorial days, West maintained a close political and personal friendship with John Drummond, the senator who hailed from Ninety Six in Greenwood County. Courtesy of Lois R. West and Shelton W. Bosley

and there are thousands of them; as long as there is a single family living in sub-standard housing—and there are some 200,000 such units; as long as there are citizens of this state who must go elsewhere for career opportunities—and there are 150,000 of them who left in the last decade; as long as these situations, or any one of them, exist, then I shall ask you to join me in a resounding rejection of the status quo."[3]

The elevated rhetoric got loud applause and generated the kind of support he had hoped for. By the end of the 1972 session, West had made a significant down payment on fulfilling his inaugural address promises:

- In addressing the issue of hunger, West was able to expand the Food Stamp program statewide and had initiated services that would make it possible to receive food stamps by mail. He had also recommended expansion of the school lunch programs.
- To address housing deficiencies, West got his requested legislation creating a State Housing Authority. Its early priorities were to sponsor housing in

areas where no local authority existed and to provide technical assistance to contractors and nonprofits. Like the Human Affairs Commission, the Housing Authority was chaired by a strong businessman, the Charleston banker Hugh Lane.

- In the area of education, West launched an innovative program using federal money to employ welfare mothers as paraprofessionals in day care centers. During the first six months of his administration, the state-funded kindergarten program launched under Governor McNair was made permanent and was expanded significantly.
- In the area of employment, the state expanded its Emergency Employment Act moneys from $6 million to $11 million to employ 2,500 people in public service jobs.

The report card was quite impressive for a governor whose ambitious agenda was unlike anything South Carolinians had seen before. Programs and services were patched together in sometimes unorthodox ways, and federal dollars were sprinkled strategically where there were gaps or deficiencies. It was also quite a display of financial muscle for a poverty-ridden state that had once been so desperately poor that it had to pay its schoolteachers in scrip.

West also got his statute creating the State Human Affairs Commission in 1972, and it came after the fledgling advisory agency had put in an impressive performance in its first year. Civil disturbances had slowed down significantly after West took office, in part because the McNair administration had absorbed much of the fury of the desegregation process and had set a precedent for peaceful resolution of differences. Credit also went to the fledgling Human Relations Advisory Commission, created by West's executive order, which had defused several potentially troublesome racial incidents. One in particular gained West's attention. It took place in Clarendon County, site of the *Briggs v. Elliott* suit, which became an important component of the *Brown v. Board of Education* case argued before the U.S. Supreme Court. In this instance racial trouble had flared when the school board in the town of Summerton had planned to hire a white school superintendent to oversee a mostly black district. Angry parents and residents demonstrated in the streets, and Human Affairs commissioner George Hamilton was dispatched by West to investigate. When he returned, Hamilton recommended that West appeal to the county legislators and use his influence to reverse the board's decision. Through a series of political steps and initiatives, Hamilton's recommendation was carried out.

With the adoption of a substantial portion of his 1972 legislative proposals, West had reason to believe that he was making headway on his ambitious social agenda. One item had become a stumbling block, however, and it proved to be a major one. He had expressed in his inaugural address the pledge that he would "this year initiate far-reaching programs to provide more doctors, nurses and health personnel . . . for delivery of health care to each citizen." This pledge was backed up by the dreadful statistical evidence that South Carolinians lived shorter lives, had a greater incidence of infant mortality, and died from strokes and heart disease at a much greater rate than most Americans did. In fact, the state ranked near the last in most of those categories.

There was also evidence that South Carolina ranked near last among the states in the number of doctors per capita, and West knew in particular that there were poor, rural counties in which the doctor population was scarce and inadequate. Although circumstantial, the connection between doctor population and health care quality seemed more than coincidental.

As a senator West had been involved in recommendations to increase the nurse population by expanding nursing education opportunities, but he knew that educating doctors was a far more complex and expensive process. He had been hinting about the topic for a while, telling a Charleston audience during the campaign that he considered health care "a basic right"[4] and suggesting to an audience of Charleston doctors a year later, as governor, that "perhaps we need to ask ourselves most seriously why the life span of the average South Carolinian is so much shorter than that of his counterparts in other parts of the nation."[5]

HIS TOUGHEST BATTLE

Even so, it came as a shock to many when West not only recommended the establishment of the new medical school at the University of South Carolina but also said that it should be done "immediately."[6] In his column the next day, West's friend Charles Wickenberg wrote, "Anyone who had been thinking that the governor of South Carolina, John C. West, is bland must have done a double-take Wednesday during his State of the State message."[7] Less generous was the *Charleston News and Courier,* which grumped, "Surely a practical study of the needs and costs of a second medical school, and the prospects of adequate return on the investment in terms of improved medical care, indicate [that this] is a doubtful, if not completely bogus proposition."[8]

Predictably the Charleston legislators howled, threatening to "fight to the death" and vowing to "block passage of any other meaningful legislation this season."[9] Cooler heads separated the combatants, and Chester County House member John Justice told the reporter Jack Bass, "The boys from Charleston and Columbia will fight and fight and it will be bitter and everyone will get tired of it, so we'll probably end up appointing another committee to study it."[10] Justice proved prophetic, and the appointment of a study committee ended the bloodletting. From all appearances it seemed that the fight was over and that the issue would be given a quiet burial in the study committee. Sure enough, a year later the committee report came out, recommending that the medical school not be built unless federal money was available. As it turned out, that suited everyone. Charleston senator Allen Carter, a vehement and vocal opponent of the new medical school, said, "I think we would be highly foolish to say we would not take a new medical school if the federal government would give us one, but I think as a matter of reality, that's not going to happen."[11]

It suited John West just fine too, and he said so. He was already working on another plan, typically involving a federal funding source. West and the backers of the USC Medical School had been tracking the progress of a piece of legislation making its way through Congress, the Teague-Cranston Act, which would create and fund the start-up of five new medical schools attached to Veterans Administration (VA) hospitals. The act was based on original proposals from Congressman Olin E. Teague of Texas and Bryan Dorn of South Carolina's Third Congressional District.

Knowing of Congressman Dorn's close association with the bill and his long-standing relationship with the VA, West had every reason to believe that South Carolina's chances of being one of those five states were good. He was optimistic that the awarding of a grant to South Carolina would make the establishment of the medical school at USC, attached to the VA Hospital in Columbia, a reality. So did Dr. Donald E. Saunders Jr., a Duke-educated cardiologist who had been one of the early advocates and promoters of advanced medical education in Columbia in the postwar years. In his book chronicling the campaign for a medical school at USC, Saunders wrote, "We were ready. We had twelve years of data and reasoned arguments [and] . . . we had an in-depth knowledge of the purpose of the [Teague-Cranston] law."[12]

Thirteen months after the issuance of the legislative committee report opposing the new medical school, West announced to the General Assembly that the Veterans Administration deal had been sealed. The state would be required to put up only $391,000 the first year, the amount would increase to about $1 million the next two years, and in the ninth year the cost to the state would be about $7 million.

The bargain could not be refused. The House Ways and Means Committee quickly authorized the first-year appropriation, and in late May the Senate Finance Committee voted unanimously to follow suit. Among those supporting the measure in committee was even Allen Carter, who said, "When

The signing of the bill creating the Medical School at the University of South Carolina represented a major accomplishment of the West administration. In attendance were (left to right) Sen. Marion Gressette, Sen. Rembert Dennis, Sen. Robert Lake, State Auditor Pat Smith, Rep. O. H. Wienges, Sen. Frank Owens, and Dr. Donald Saunders, the Columbia cardiologist who spearheaded public support for the effort. Courtesy of Dr. Donald E. Saunders Jr.

you're beat, you're beat."[13] The full Senate, with dissenting votes from seven members (including a still-bitter Carter and future governor Richard W. Riley of Greenville), approved the measure, and Governor West gleefully signed the Appropriation Act, which contained the USC Medical School funds, on June 18, 1974. Among those in attendance at the signing was Dr. Saunders, to whom West stated that the medical school fight had been the toughest of his administration.

A RISING TIDE

In the parlance of twenty-first-century America, West's initiatives could be termed part of an "economic stimulus" package. Lifting the fortunes of the poor was not simply an exercise in charity and goodwill. It was an attempt to build for the state a healthy, well-educated population that could sustain long-term economic growth at a high level of productivity and sophistication.

While never saying it, West was working to build in South Carolina a middle class, a class that had never really been prominent in the state. To some extent this was what set the state apart from close neighbors such as North Carolina, Georgia, and Tennessee, where prospering cities had given rise to prospering merchants and businessmen who built good schools, good colleges, good hospitals, and good transportation systems.

South Carolina had no such urban tradition, and its public policies were, in fact, deliberately anticity. As places such as Atlanta, Charlotte, and Nashville blossomed into centers of commerce, South Carolina cities such as Columbia, Greenville, and Charleston were hemmed in amid a hodgepodge of disconnected suburbs, detached governments, and underfunded inner cities that bickered among themselves endlessly. In that kind of urban vacuum it was difficult to find and sustain a community-wide and politically significant sense of urgency about the condition of the state's schools, colleges, hospitals, and other institutions of community service.

At least part of West's Utopian vision was that South Carolina would become a place with a thriving biracial middle class that would expect and demand quality in their public institutions and services and would provide political support and continuity for such values. To that end he tried to bring clarity to the state's deficiencies and energy to addressing its needs. Nowhere was this more evident than in the industrial recruitment effort. Like McNair and Hollings before him, West and his economic development team worked to sell South Carolina as a good place for northern and midwestern industries to build plants to accommodate their need for new and expanded capacity in a growing national economy. The South, they contended, was also a good place to automate and modernize facilities and to create new manufacturing efficiencies.

To those strategies West added a new component. As lieutenant governor under McNair, West had headed a South Carolina trade mission to Europe and had seen a transformation taking place there. Western European nations were recovering from the downtrodden postwar days and were looking for expanded industrial capacity themselves. South Carolina, with a decade of industry-hunting experience, made a perfect fit for the European—and later the Asian—manufacturers. As an architect of the state's strategies and programs, West knew them better than most, and he made the European initiatives a centerpiece of his overall industrial recruitment efforts. "Reverse investment" was the term used, contrasting the strategy with the traditional investment of U.S. moneys in Europe in the postwar year. West was also aware of labor shortages in Western Europe, and he realized that the weakness of the U.S. dollar against European currencies made it a good time to spend French francs and German marks in the United States. South Carolina opened a sales office in Brussels, and later one in Japan, and threw itself full force into "reverse investment."

By the end of the West administration, South Carolina had become an important place on the map for overseas investors, particularly from Germany. Even before the construction of the BMW auto assembly plant in Greer in the 1980s, South Carolina held the single largest concentration of German industrial investment anywhere in the United States. Much of it was located in the state's only real concentration of manufacturing, the Greenville-Spartanburg area, and West's resident expert on such overseas investment was a chamber of commerce executive from Spartanburg named Dick Tukey. Within only a few years the German resident population in Spartanburg was sufficient to create its own Oktoberfest, an event that became a permanent part of upcountry culture.

The "reverse investment" effort had some stunning results. By 1975 roughly 10 percent of the entire European industrial investment in America resided in South Carolina, a fact that laid nice groundwork for the arrival of the BMW plant a decade later. All told, industrial development during the West years amounted to more than $3 billion, exceeding significantly the total of the entire previous decade. New jobs totaled more than fifty thousand, and they were helping to break South Carolina from its dependence on the low-wage jobs of the textile industry. The criterion by which the value of the new jobs could be evaluated, West told an interviewer late in his administration, was the amount of money invested per job. That amount, he said, had been $5,000 a decade earlier. The new industries were spending around $9,000 per job.[14]

COMPONENTS OF UTOPIA

In West's Utopia racial equality was the fundamental component, but without the jobs, education, and governmental pieces it was only a partial step. West believed that racial progress was more than a guarantee of human rights; he saw economic opportunity as the cornerstone of racial progress in the state, supported by and dependent on publicly supported education, health care, and other institutional systems. Public and private sectors were not distant—and sometimes opposing—forces in communities. The success of either, he believed, was dependent on its ability to cooperate and even to merge its interests with the other. Ideology in the sense of a singular, narrow orthodoxy did not drive this Utopia; this was an idealism in which distinctions and boundaries were blurred.

As with most Utopias, however, the component pieces were not always in harmony. Externally the advocates of the various pieces of the vision did not always care about all the other pieces and did not share the abstraction and sub-tleties. Internally the pieces occasionally fell out of balance and became com-petitive with each other. So it was with West's fragile coalition of potentially conflicting interests. Increasingly the power of the federal funding machine seemed to dominate policy, and West found himself occasionally refereeing conflicts. Within his own staff the mix of retired military officers, long-haired young people of both genders, old-line Camden friends, energetic minorities, and long-term governmental functionaries made for some interesting working conditions. "The governor doesn't manage his staff," one senior member once said; "he presides over it."[15]

In time Clyburn became disenchanted with what he called "the bureau-cracy" and decided to enter law school. Earlier the Human Affairs Commission staff had departed the governor's State House suite to set up operations in its own offices across the street, and one day West awoke to find in the morning paper his longtime critic Ike Williams of the NAACP taking a swing at him. "What used to be the ebony suite," Williams told a reporter, "has now become a lily white flower garden."[16]

West was stung that his seemingly unassailable record of racial fairness was being challenged. With the subsequent departure of Hamilton from the Human Affairs Commission to return to the family funeral home business in Walter-boro, he became even more vulnerable. Even with his vision of racial progress tied to economic growth, there were those who were not ready for that particu-lar Utopia yet. Critics within the civil rights community had surfaced earlier, and they were quick to jump this time, seeing in the West administration what seemed to be an internal shift of priorities. As staff and the governor mulled various options, it became clear that West's credibility problems were serious and required more than just another black face in the executive suite. It became increasingly likely, in fact, that a reuniting with Clyburn was the best—and possibly the only—solution to the sudden tempest of racial troubles that threat-ened him. The vacant Human Affairs Commission offered the best solution, but West had two sales jobs to make that happen. First, he had to persuade Clyburn to give up his law school interests and to accept a position he had rejected earlier in the administration. Second, he had to persuade the increas-ingly independent-minded Human Affairs Commission, which had already chosen a successor, to reverse itself and choose Clyburn.

In the latter undertaking, West got some powerful assistance from a strong-minded young woman named Jean Hoefer Toal, a member of the commission whose diplomacy and powers of persuasion won over her colleagues to the gov-ernor's position in support of Clyburn. Toal would later carry her considerable powers into the legislative and judicial branches of government and would become chief justice of the S.C. Supreme Court in 2000. As for winning over Clyburn, that was left to West, and with his usual flare for diplomacy he was once again able to reach agreement with his spirited friend. Clyburn went on to serve seventeen years as Human Affairs commissioner until his election as the Sixth District congressman in 1992, and he and West remained lifelong friends.

A MATTER OF CONSCIENCE

Not all of the governor's actions followed a grand scheme or plan. Some were purely personal, and West was nothing if not personally motivated in most of his actions and decisions. Such an occasion arose late in his term when the General Assembly enacted a bill authorizing capital punishment with provisions that brought the state into compliance with the recent U.S. Supreme Court decision in *Furman v. Georgia*. The bill arrived on his desk in late June 1974, his last full year in office, and there it lay while West deliberated. It was clearly a matter of conscience, as had been the decisions earlier in his career as a state senator to oppose both legislation dictating to libraries the content of their books and the censuring UNC president Frank Porter Graham for his support of the Rock Hill lunch-counter sit-ins. This time, however, he could not be the quiet voice at the rear of the chamber expressing a personal opinion. He was governor of the state. He had to do something, and the public was watching.

It was an agonizing decision. He told a reporter, "I question the right of society to take away the most precious gift—life. It's a gift society can't create."[17] A lifelong Presbyterian who taught Sunday school at Columbia's downtown Arsenal Hill Presbyterian Church, West examined his options. He could sign the bill, he could let it become law without his signature, or he could veto the bill.

He chose to veto the bill, sending to the General Assembly the message, "I cannot accept the premise that man can end a life that God has created. . . . Reinstatement of the death penalty would not, in my opinion . . . serve as a deterrent to crime, but would rather be a return to a barbaric, savage concept of vengeance which should not be accepted, condoned or permitted in a civilized society." The General Assembly overrode West's passionate veto, as expected. He said afterward that any decision other than vetoing the bill would have made him a party to future executions. "If I had made the other decision [not to veto]," he said, "I would have been all torn up. But I am at peace with the world."[18]

Other issues nagged at him and brought out the trial lawyer–populist side of his makeup. One of them was the massively complicated business of automobile liability insurance, made even more complicated by legislation that made it mandatory for all drivers to carry liability insurance. Such legislation, as it turned out, vested in the insurance companies wide latitude in determining which drivers constituted good risks and which did not. Those not deemed good risks wound up in "assigned risk," a state-created pool that charged high rates and offered minimal benefits.

Having young drivers in his own family, West worried that companies were dumping drivers with good records into assigned risk because they fell into certain demographic categories, and it infuriated him. West's sense of injustice, it was clear, was not limited to racial matters, and he brought to the governor's office a determination to do something about the one hundred thousand drivers—some good, some bad—in the assigned risk program.

The companies offered in his first year in office a "voluntary" plan to reduce the number of good drivers in assigned risk and to increase benefits to those in the pool. West agreed, with some skepticism, but he never took his eyes off the "voluntary" plan. Two years later it was his sense that nothing much had happened, and he blew a gasket.

"THEY . . . LIED AND CHEATED"

"I have no sympathy with [insurance] companies," he told a newsman. "They have literally lied and cheated."[19] In his State of the State speech of 1973, he asked the General Assembly for insurance reform that would create "a full insurance availability plan," making it possible for each driver to obtain coverage at a "fair and equitable rate" and "to lay to rest forever the assigned risk plan, that great monument to insurance inequity."[20]

A year later, about the time West was celebrating the creation of the USC Medical School, the General Assembly presented him with an insurance reform package that abolished the assigned risk plan and replaced it with a reinsurance facility that would write policies for drivers who could not obtain coverage on the open market. There was even a provision for modified no-fault coverage of accidents in which damages were less than one thousand dollars. In crusty old South Carolina this provided a surprisingly happy ending to a three-year fight that many of his friends thought he would never win.

For an otherwise cautious and prudent man, West seemed to delight in addressing political issues and taking political risks that others before him might have considered best left alone. Such was the case with a close-to-home matter in which he had a personal stake: the conversion of Winthrop College, the state's women's college, into a coeducational institution.

The presence of Senator Marion Gressette as a staunch opponent had been enough to discourage earlier advocates of coeducation, but West's family stake gave him strong incentives to enter the fray against the formidable Calhoun County legislator. There was, in fact, ample evidence to argue for coeducation. The General Assembly was spreading four-year colleges around the state geographically—Florence, Charleston, Aiken, Greenwood, and Spartanburg— to go with its established senior universities, and Winthrop could serve the rapidly growing upper tier of counties near the North Carolina border. Winthrop's conversion could even give the college a toehold in the large Charlotte market, only twenty miles away. If there was a formidable presence to counter Gressette, it was Lois West, the well-liked First Lady and Winthrop alum who had set something of a precedent by returning to campus after her wartime marriage to Citadel cadet John West.[21]

Additional forces were building this time. The prominent Charlestonian Ruth Williams joined the fray on West's side, and Rock Hill businesses— noting that enrollment was declining at Winthrop—took an interest in the issue and raised money to retain West's friends Crawford Cook and Lee Ruef to lobby the General Assembly. York County senator Lew Wallace became the point man on the floor of the Senate. The battle was waged through most of the 1972 session, and Gressette finally agreed to a phased-in admission of male students to the all-women's college. "Co-education does not mean less education for women," West told a Winthrop graduating class that year, which included six men; it "means better education for everyone throughout South Carolina."[22]

Another prickly issue awaiting resolution was the long-deferred question of whether mixed drinks should be served in public establishments around South Carolina. As the tourism industry became a high-ticket item in the 1960s, pressure built on Governor McNair to find a way around the restrictive constitutional provisions so that South Carolinians and the increasingly large number of visitors to the state could enjoy cocktails in restaurants, hotels, bars, and clubs as well as in the posh resorts being developed around the state. Fearing that the Puritanical upcountry would outvote the more free-wheeling lowcountry in a referendum to amend the Constitution, McNair had opted for an interim statutory measure that allowed customers to carry their own liquor into restaurants and have it served back to them in cocktail form, the so-called brown-bag law.

As compared to McNair, a Baptist, no one enjoyed a civilized cocktail in a civilized restaurant more than John West, and he decided to run the risk of letting the voters decide the issue in a statewide referendum on mixed drinks. Rather than argue with the Baptists over the morality of the issue, West decided to put it on a business basis. Simply stated, mixed drinks meant big bucks for the state in the form of pricier restaurants, swankier resorts, better entertainment, and lots and lots of new jobs. To mollify the temperance interests, however, West and his cohorts came up with a quirky wrinkle. If approved by the voters, mixed drinks would be served in South Carolina only in 1.7-ounce containers, known as "minibottles," which most South Carolinians had seen only on commercial airplane flights.

Promoting the mixed-drink proposal was an austere-sounding group called the Foundation for Modern Liquor Regulations and Control. It was headed by another West friend in the newspaper business, *State* newspaper publisher Ben R. Morris, who was also known to enjoy a cocktail on occasion. In the month before the November 1972 referendum, West admitted that "pouring [mixed drinks] is going on all over the state."[23] The proposed law, West argued, would have a temperance effect because it would cost more to buy a minibottle drink than it would to have drinks poured from a big bottle contained in a brown bag.

CHEERS!

For all its decades as a Bible Belt prohibitionist state, South Carolina approved the minibottle constitutional amendment in November 1972, and the General Assembly ratified the act early in the 1973 session. Just as West was somberly vowing strict enforcement of the new law in a midday news conference on the first day of legal mixed drinks in the state, members of his staff were celebrating the occasion over lunch with Bloody Marys in a nearby watering hole, which, it is said, had been "pouring" all along.

Whatever the effect of the minibottle approval may have been, tourism was booming in South Carolina. During the West years in office, annual travel-related expenditures in the state increased from $425 million in 1971 to $675 million by the end of his administration.[24] Tourists were no longer using South Carolina simply as a stopover en route to Florida from populous areas elsewhere. They were traveling along nearly completed interstate highways such as I-95 from the Northeast and I-26 from the Midwest in their air-conditioned cars heading for air-conditioned destination resorts in places such as Myrtle Beach, Charleston, and Hilton Head. They were playing golf and enjoying luxury accommodations comparable to those farther to the south, and they were enjoying as part of their vacation experiences civilized cocktails from legally licensed bars and restaurants. It was John West's kind of world.

One of the reasons for West's good relations with the General Assembly lay in the fact that both houses of the legislature were overwhelmingly in Democratic hands, and partisanship had not reared its head to any great extent in

The golf course was the perfect place for West to practice his brand of personal politics, here chatting with Idaho governor Cecil Andrus during a governor's conference at Hilton Head. From the author's collection

carrying out business at the state level. For all the upheavals at the national level, South Carolina Democrats continued to win elections at the state and local levels, at least partially because they had been able to keep a safe distance from their Left-leaning, raucous colleagues at the national level. That polite detachment became more difficult as a parade of mainstream Democratic candidates moved through the state in the spring of 1972 seeking the party's nomination to challenge Richard Nixon in November. Among the luminaries who paid visits to Columbia that year were George McGovern, Henry "Scoop" Jackson, Ted Kennedy, Edmund Muskie, and Hubert Humphrey. Each visit was brief because South Carolina was considered a no-man's-land for national Democrats, but West and the candidates were cordial to each other, and the S.C. governor made it known that among the front-runners, Humphrey would probably be his choice.

Wherever West's real preference may have lain, however, he believed that there was an important opportunity emerging for his party to slow its leftward drift, a development that would make him and other southerners comfortable. It lay in the potential influence that Alabama governor George Wallace could exert within the party. Wallace had run for president in 1968 as an Independent, and his segregationist campaign found some ready listeners and adherents in white southern hearts. As the 1972 race for the presidency got under way, Wallace was running again, but this time as a Democrat. For all his progressive, New South credentials as a governor, John West began talking up the candidacy of the Alabama governor, an archsegregationist who had gained national attention by defying federal court orders to desegregate the University of Alabama in June 1963. While Wallace had run for president as an Independent in 1968, he was entering Democratic primaries in 1972, and West believed that gave him new respectability, credibility, and potential influence within the party. A reinvented Wallace, newly styled as a conservative Democrat rather than a rebellious segregationist Independent, West believed, could also help South Carolina Democrats counter the power of Strom Thurmond within the state.[25]

Even as prospective national Democratic candidates were making their way through Columbia, West told a convention of Young Democrats in New Orleans in March 1972 that Wallace's support of the national Democratic ticket was necessary for victory. Wallace was "no longer a segregationist, but a populist," he said. Even Clyburn, who had become president of the S.C. Young Democrats, agreed, saying, "It's the only way I see we can win. I believe blacks are sophisticated enough to accept an endorsement by Wallace of the Democratic ticket."[26]

THE WALLACE APPEAL

Wallace was doing well in the primaries, and—as West had speculated—he was bringing independent and conservative voters into the Democratic contests. Wallace carried Florida on March 14, getting 42 percent of the vote in a large field and winning every county in the populous state. On May 6 Wallace scored another impressive southern victory, winning the North Carolina primary and overwhelming the popular senator and former governor Terry Sanford in the process.

Important primaries were looming in mid-May in the "border" state of Maryland and the midwestern industrial state of Michigan, as Wallace tried to break out of his all-southern identification. However, on May 15, a day before the Maryland primary and less than a week before Wallace was to speak to the S.C. General Assembly, the Alabama governor was gunned down while campaigning in a shopping center parking lot in Laurel, Maryland. The gunshot wounds damaged his spine, leaving his legs permanently paralyzed and effectively shutting down his campaign.

Even so, Wallace won the Maryland primary and stunned the nation by getting more than 800,000 votes in blue-collar Michigan, outpolling the eventual Democratic nominee George McGovern by almost two to one and providing the political muscle for the Democrats to outpoll the Republicans by 1.5 million to 337,000 in the same-day primaries in that state. For whatever dubious pleasure it may have provided him, West could have told his Democratic colleagues, "I told you so."

A little more than a month after her husband's shooting, Wallace's wife Cornelia told the South Carolina General Assembly that unless Wallace won the nomination, "The Democratic Party will spend the next four years on the outside looking in."[27] Her remarks proved prophetic. McGovern won the party nomination and lost forty-nine of fifty states to Nixon, leaving the Democratic Party in further disarray and setting up the moment four years later when the Democrats would turn to another southern governor, John West's good friend Jimmy Carter of Georgia, to return them to the White House.

West and Wallace got along well, and when southern governors convened in September at Hilton Head for their annual conference, Wallace made one of his rare trips outside Alabama to attend the event. To honor the paralyzed governor, West had arranged to decline the chairmanship of the conference so that Wallace could be elected to the largely honorary position. The veteran Mississippi newsman Bob McHugh wrote, "There it was: the wounded Wallace feeble and obviously deeply moved emotionally as his colleagues took the podium to praise his courage and to acknowledge that [he] had indeed made 'a great contribution to the American political system.' These were the same guys who only a couple of years ago avoided Wallace like the plague, fearing that his political incursions into their states would upset political party balance. Now they were wooing his support."[28]

Governors' conferences, by their nature, were places to exchange ideas. They were also places where governors' staffs loaded down their colleagues and friends with souvenir paraphernalia from their respective states—key chains, luggage tags, tie tacks, and various assortments of garish certificates that designated the recipient an "Arkansas Traveler," a "Kentucky Colonel," a North Carolina "Tar Heel," a Tennessee "Volunteer," and so on.

South Carolina had no such merchandise, and Governor West mentioned to a staffer that it would be nice to have developed a commemorative certificate that "might look a little nicer than the others."[29] The idea was taken to the S.C. Department of Parks, Recreation and Tourism for its development of concept and design. Within a few weeks a rich-looking mock-up was submitted with draft language that proposed to designate its recipients as members of a fictitious fellowship known as the "Order of the Palmetto." Recipients would be known as "Palmetto Ladies" and "Palmetto Gentlemen," and the distribution of the certificates would be solely at the discretion of the governor.

West loved it, and as soon as the new certificates became available, he spread them around by the hundreds. Visitors, friends, guests, and families were all prime recipients of the new "Order." The first one went to the grandmother of the staff coordinator's wife on her ninetieth birthday, and from then on the Order of the Palmetto became the currency of friendship and goodwill for the state. In addition to its stern-looking design (some said it looked like a cross between a stock certificate and a college degree), the new certificate had other distinctions. All names and dates were hand lettered in Old English (done by a talented inmate artist at the Central Corrections Institution), and all governors' signatures were original (no stamped facsimiles). Such requirements made for some interesting production problems, particularly when the governor placed orders on short notice and the inmate artist had to be made available, also on short notice.

From its humble beginnings, the Order of the Palmetto would become sanctified as the "state's highest honor" years later. A strict process of application and criteria for awarding the certificates was put in place, and mention of the Order of the Palmetto began appearing solemnly in résumés, eulogies, and obituaries. In the meantime thousands of South Carolinians had one or two of the certificates on their walls or stuffed away in closets. They had been given to them not necessarily as the state's highest honor but simply as recognition that they were friends of John West.

In South Carolina in the early 1970s, there was a sense that things had calmed down from the turbulent 1960s. The divisive Vietnam War was winding down, the civil rights fury seemed to be abating, and there was a president in Washington who had carried forty-nine of fifty states. All that made for some sense of political security. Then it all began to come apart. To their shock and dismay, Americans learned in a nightmarish set of revelations that the man who had carried forty-nine of fifty states had also been a party to some sleazy campaign activity and an even sleazier cover-up of the dirty deeds. The series of events became known as the Watergate scandal after the location of the Democratic National Committee office where a late-night break-in had occurred, setting the entire ordeal in motion.

Within a month after Nixon's inauguration for a second term, the Watergate burglars had pleaded guilty to the break-in, and suspicions were being raised about possible linkages of the burglary to the Nixon campaign and ultimately to the White House. Nixon was beginning to feel the pressure, and he decided that this would be a good time to travel to a friendly place such as South

Carolina and make a speech. The speech was scheduled for February 1973, and upon his arrival in Columbia, he got the good welcome that organizers had hoped for. Crowds along the route from the airport to downtown Columbia were estimated at twenty thousand, and the newsman Kent Krell wrote, "Stoic-looking hard hats and flag-waving youngsters mingled with other archetypes of Middle America to greet President Richard M. Nixon on his historic visit to South Carolina's State House."[30]

The speech proved to be undistinguished, except for some observations made by West in his journal. "I introduced him [to the General Assembly] and he made an extemporaneous speech for about 20 minutes. He amazed me because he had no notes or prepared text. It was mostly about Vietnam, etc., [and] he received a warm reception," West wrote.[31]

Warm receptions would become scarcer and scarcer for the embattled president. Within two months of his visit to South Carolina, Nixon was forced to fire his two top aides, H. R. Haldeman and John Ehrlichman, both of whom would serve prison sentences. From that point forward the president's Watergate troubles would accelerate. They would also divert the president's attention from other pressing issues.

THE OIL WEAPON

One of those pressing issues, it has been speculated, was a crisis of enormous proportions building in the Middle East. Analysts have contended that Nixon officials knew as early as the spring of 1973 that oil-producing Arab nations in the Middle East were becoming restive and were preparing a plan to use their "oil weapon" against nations that aided Israel in its ongoing fight against Arab neighbors. Whether the White House did not believe the warnings or was too occupied with Watergate troubles to notice, the reports of the threatened oil reprisals from unhappy Arab nations went largely unheeded. Americans awoke one morning in October 1973 to discover, to their dismay, that gasoline prices had skyrocketed and supplies had dwindled to a relative trickle. The Organization of Petroleum Exporting Countries (OPEC), the cartel of oil-producing nations, had raised prices and was organizing an embargo of Israel's friends.

All of this happened within days after the October 6, 1973, attack on Israel by the joint forces of Egypt and Syria—with the full support of America's friend Saudi Arabia—in what became known as the Yom Kippur War. It was the fourth Arab-Israeli conflict since the founding of the Jewish state in 1948. Less than a week later the United States, as it had in the past, came to Israel's assistance, airlifting weapons and supplies to its longtime friend. This time, however, Americans and their pro-Israel allies got a surprise. On October 16 the oil-producing states of Saudi Arabia, Iran, Iraq, Abu Dhabi, Kuwait, and Qatar raised prices by 17 percent, and a day later OPEC agreed to an embargo on nations assisting Israel, including the United States.

The impact was sudden and enormous. Gasoline prices rose from thirty-cents-plus per gallon to fifty-cents-plus—not much by later standards but staggering in the 1970s—and gasoline became scarce almost overnight. Lines stretched from service stations for blocks, and commuters found that getting to and from work and running errands were tedious and expensive chores. By year's end Nixon had gotten an emergency appropriation of $2.2 billion from Congress and was putting an allocation system in place. In South Carolina and other states, energy-saving plans were enacted, and for the first time since World War II, Americans found that gasoline was being rationed.

West put South Carolina on a voluntary plan of sorts. Motorists with license tags ending in even numbers would buy gasoline on even-numbered days, and those with odd tag numbers would fill their tanks on odd-numbered days. In addition the speed limit was lowered to fifty miles per hour as an efficiency measure. For all their unhappiness, South Carolinians were relatively compliant with the restrictive conditions being placed on them. By March 1974 the embargo was lifted, and things returned to some normalcy. But two longer-term impacts remained after motorists sped up again and resumed their usual driving practices.

South Carolina's travel economy—booming on the crest of the state's new prosperity—would not recover for years. Expensive resorts dependent largely on motoring guests suddenly found that their customers could not keep their reservations or make new ones, and months of severe downturn ensued. The results were devastating for a business that had grown heavily dependent on the automobile.

There was another important outcome, this one of a most unlikely nature. Within four years of the first fully effective oil embargo imposed by the Arab states against the United States, the governors of two neighboring southern states, who struggled to keep their states afloat during the politically imposed shortage, would be dealing directly with the sources of the nation's new economic torment. Jimmy Carter would become a conspicuously Arab-friendly president, and John West would become his ambassador to the kingdom of Saudi Arabia.

In the meantime Nixon's Watergate dilemma only worsened. There were not, as it turned out, enough "archetypes of Middle America," such as he had found in South Carolina, to rescue his presidency. On August 9, 1974—amid U.S. Senate plans to impeach him and eighteen months after his visit to

Columbia—Nixon resigned, the first American president to do so. He was succeeded by Vice President Gerald R. Ford.

DEALING WITH RAVENEL

As it turned out, South Carolina was only weeks away from a political upheaval of its own in those waning summer months of 1974. A political newcomer, Charles "Pug" Ravenel, had stormed through the Democratic primary and runoff in June and July with an energetic and imaginative campaign and had emerged as the surprise Democratic candidate for governor. Along the way he had knocked off party regulars such as Earle Morris and Bryan Dorn and was poised to take on a little-known Charleston dental surgeon James B. Edwards, the Republican candidate, in the general election. There was a lingering question, however, about Ravenel's legal qualification to serve as governor. The state's constitution required that a candidate for governor reside in the state for five consecutive years before taking office. A Charleston native who had earned an MBA degree from Harvard and played quarterback for the Crimson football team, Ravenel had spent his post-Harvard years in New York City as an investment banker. He had returned to Charleston in 1972 to launch his campaign for governor.

Suit was filed by two Columbians challenging his eligibility, and on September 23, six weeks before the general election, the S.C. Supreme Court ruled Ravenel ineligible. As had been the case twenty years earlier with the death of Senator Burnet Maybank in September of his reelection year of 1954, the party was thrown into turmoil, and its options were not good. There was not time for another primary, and the hastily called convention was fraught with divisiveness and bitterness. Dorn emerged the winner, and he had a mighty struggle on his hands to pull together disheartened elements of the Morris and Ravenel camps.

Ravenel was not through, however, and he came up with a proposal that thrust John West squarely into the middle of the dilemma. Under Ravenel's plan, the General Assembly would be called back into a special session by the governor to consider adopting a constitutional amendment that would make Ravenel eligible. The amendment would be placed on the November 5 ballot, and Ravenel would offer himself as a write-in candidate for governor at the same election. If the amendment were approved—and subsequently ratified—and if Ravenel won as the write-in candidate, then, as the plan projected, he could still become governor. There were those zealous Ravenel supporters who did not find that improbable succession of events any more outlandish than the belief twenty years earlier that Strom Thurmond could beat Edgar Brown as a write-in candidate for the U.S. Senate.

There were a lot of ifs to the Ravenel plan, however, and before making a response, West decided to explore the first if. Would the General Assembly, if called back into special session, vote to amend the constitution to accommodate Ravenel's candidacy? This would require a two-thirds vote of each house, and after about forty calls to senators and House members, West decided that there was a notable lack of enthusiasm for the amendment. Far fewer than half of those he called, West said, would support the constitutional amendment, so he decided to reject Ravenel's proposal.

Weeks earlier, after Ravenel's victory over Dorn in the runoff primary, West had said of the Democratic newcomer, "I'm tremendously impressed with him. I think he has the potential to be a great governor."[32] Now he was telling a live television audience in a rare Saturday evening press conference that he was not going to call the special session, thus dooming Ravenel's chances. "Nothing would have pleased me more than for the events of the past week [the Supreme Court decision] to have turned out otherwise," he said.[33] For his part, Ravenel dismissed the decision by saying, "Once again, the few have decided that the many shall not decide."[34]

There is little way of knowing what role Ravenel and his supporters may or may not have played in the subsequent general election. What is known is that Edwards, who garnered 20,177 votes in defeating General William C. Westmoreland in the Republican primary, increased that number by more than thirteenfold in the general election and defeated Dorn by 266,338 votes to 248,861. The gubernatorial election was one of the closest in the state's history and elevated to the governor's office the first Republican in South Carolina since Reconstruction days a century earlier. "When I saw that I had won," the affable Edwards enjoyed joking with friends, "I felt like calling for a recount." Typical of his style and personality, West formed a lasting friendship with Edwards, and the administration's transition from Democratic to Republican was remarkably smooth.

A DIFFERENT KIND OF STORM

John West spent a lot of time in the eye of storms, political and otherwise. One in the latter category arrived unexpectedly in the winter of 1973 in the form of a ferocious snowstorm that blindsided the state in the late afternoon and evening of Friday, February 9th. Besides its magnitude, the storm's special danger lay in the fact that it blew in from the east and south and smacked the low-country, the Pee Dee, and the midlands, areas more accustomed to warm-weather hurricanes than cold-weather snow and ice. Unexpectedly in the path of the storm were northern tourists headed for Florida on Interstate 95, the busy north-south artery that dissected the eastern part of the state. Also surprised were travelers on Interstate 26 heading east for winter weekends at the beach. The farther south and farther east the traffic flowed, the worse it got, and finally things ground to a halt. As much as twenty-three inches fell, accumulating in drifts up to five feet high, unheard of for subtropical parts of South Carolina.

In all, some sixteen thousand motorists were stranded in the worst snow-storm to hit the state in a century, and the state was ill-prepared to handle such an emergency. News accounts described the airlifting of motorists to shelters in the small towns along the highways and the provision of food, fuel, and medical supplies by helicopters and military trucks to areas where such necessities had run short. This was a full-blown crisis, and West designated thirty-one of the state's forty-six counties as disaster areas.

He also paid a helicopter visit to some of the more heavily hit areas, with some memorable results. At one stop he took a spill on the pavement getting out of the helicopter, injuring only his pride but affording newsmen and photographers some entertainment. At another stop, in the town of Manning, he accompanied Mayor Pansy Ridgeway to a local National Guard armory, where stranded motorists had been sheltered for more than a day on army-issue cots. Having little else to do but play cards, eat sandwiches, and take naps, a number of the temporary residents had turned to various varieties of recreational beverages for diversion during the boring hours. As West and Mayor Ridgeway entered the building, they were immediately hit with the unmistakable odor of those alcoholic refreshments. They were also greeted with one volley after another of angry and often incoherent blasts from the unhappy occupants, most of whom were complaining about the state's lack of preparedness. After absorbing several of the verbal attacks, West and the mayor turned to leave, and he said to her quietly, "I think it's time to close the liquor stores, Pansy."[35] This was done, by executive order of the governor.

Not all things in the West administration were raucous and front-page news. The relative calm that had descended over the public school system was the result of many influences, not the least of which was the no-nonsense toughness of the McNair administration, as well as the presence and vigilance of the newly created Human Relations Commission in addressing racially oriented troubles. Internally, and less visible, there had also grown up within the state's public education community a remarkable communications network. While the McNair administration had the burden of absorbing the first shock of most of the desegregation plans at the start of the 1970–71 school year, it fell to West and the state's education leaders to deal with the follow-up details of the actual implementation of those plans. West's files are filled with correspondence among the various parties involved: district school superintendents, local board members, Washington officials, state superintendent Cyril Busbee, and others. West's education assistant, Robert E. "Jack" David, was a former school superintendent and retained credibility among his former colleagues. Topics addressed included a wide range of concerns, such as teacher assignments, school bus routes, team nicknames, and the Confederate flag, as well as just plain disagreements over the terms of the desegregation plans. Through it all, however, communication seemed to remain open and reasonably civilized, and differences were settled short of violence.

Of pressing concern at the time was the matter of teacher salaries. Elements of the South Carolina Education Association, the teachers' professional organization, were growing increasingly militant under the leadership of their executive, Carlos Gibbons, also a former school superintendent. Threats of work stoppages, called "sanctions," were heard frequently.

West had sparred with Gibbons early in his administration, notably during the 1972 session, when state funds were too scarce to meet Gibbons's and the SCEA's expectations. S.C. teacher salaries were measurably lower than the average for southeastern states, and attaining that regional average became a goal of the teacher advocates. West, however, was concerned about another dimension of the salary issue. As all-white private schools sprang up around the state in defiance of—and in competition with—the desegregated public schools, West worried that the new schools would lure not only students but also teachers away from the public school system.

As the state's economy improved, and as state funds became more plentiful, West gave the teacher salary issue priority. By the time he left office, the South Carolina average had risen from its 1970 level of $6,883 to $9,340 for the 1974–75 school term, an increase of more than 35 percent.[36] South Carolina teachers' salaries were near the southeastern average, and after all the years of desegregation tension and combat over salary levels, relative peace reigned in the state's education community. In 1975 Gibbons even accepted a position on Governor West's staff.

Another quiet piece of business with powerful long-range impact came as a result of West's years of work on constitutional revision. The state's constitution dated back to January 1, 1896, when a convention under the leadership of onetime governor Benjamin R. Tillman (1891–95) created a document that—among other things—severely limited the rights of the state's black population. While federal court rulings had subsequently invalidated many of the racial provisions, other sections were outdated as well.

The most important proposed amendment, in West's view, was presented to the electorate in November 1972 on the same ballot as the mixed-drink provision. It became known as the unified court system provision, and it permitted the chief justice of the S.C. Supreme Court to assign judges to various areas of the state, depending on the size of the dockets. The amendment not only helped spread the caseload more evenly but also opened the door to significant, ongoing reforms to the court system by management-oriented leadership from the Supreme Court in the years to come. The judicial amendment was adopted by the electorate in November, and West wrote that it "will play an important part in reducing court congestion and speeding up trials."[37]

THE BUSINESS OF GOVERNMENT

There were other quiet initiatives under way. Early in his administration West sought to balance perceptions of his social-oriented, big-government approach by inviting business executives to come into government as a team, explore and review its methods of operation, and make recommendations for businesslike improvement. It was called the Management Review Commission. While public and political attention was focused on such early agenda items as civil rights, hunger, poverty, and public schools, a team of thirty-two business executives, on loan from major South Carolina corporations, combed their way through the operations of eighty state agencies, interviewing agency leaders, analyzing documents, reviewing fiscal records, and applying their own sense of business values to the world of public operations.

The commission was chaired by Columbia mayor Lester Bates, a veteran of the state's political wars, who bridged the business-government gap nicely. Bates was chairman of the board of New South Life Insurance Company, a firm he had built to prominence, and he had also run for governor twice. Under the staff guidance of the senior executive Jim Whitmire, the brother of West's longtime friend Charlie Whitmire, the commission produced its report after six months of work. This report turned out not to be the kind of adversarial diatribe pitting business against government that would characterize much of the fractious relationship of the two sectors later in the century.

Instead the commission's report made proposals for internal operational changes that, it said, could produce annual recurring savings of $73.8 million and new revenues of $29.6 million. Most of the changes, the report contended, could be implemented without great public controversy, legislative action, or authorization. In South Carolina's decentralized system, the agencies would be expected to carry out the changes themselves. In a report issued at the close of the West administration, savings from the commission's recommendations were estimated at $80.0 million.[38]

The report had just the effect West had hoped it would. It reached out to a business community he had long valued and considered a major part of his

West and his executive staff: (left to right) Vernon Pate, James Clyburn, George Hamilton, James Whitmire, Nettie Bryan, West, Mary Jean Todd, Kelley Jones, Kathy Cecil, Philip Grose, and Robert "Jack" David. From the author's collection

political universe. Just as he had placed key business leaders—such as Bill Travis, Ben Morris, Arthur Williams, John Lumpkin, Hootie Johnson, and Hugh Lane—in key leadership positions in his administration, so too he hoped to convey that his government could be run like a business.

The commission's report also attracted favorable attention from the press. The *Greenville News,* whose readership included much of the state's major industrial community, wrote, "The commission . . . found a good many little and not-so-little grains and drops of financial sand and came up with recommendations for a mighty amount of saving to the taxpayers. . . . It was a mighty effort, and if only a fraction of the savings projected by the Commission can be realized, the study will be of tremendous benefit to the state and the taxpaying public."[39]

West, in fact, got a remarkably good ride from the state's newspapers in general. In an article published near the end of his administration, the reporter Bill Starr wrote that West "has for the most part enjoyed a 'good press' in the nearly 27 months of his administration." He quoted the executive staffer Philip Grose as saying, "On a personal, one-to-one basis . . . the governor has an excellent relationship with the press of South Carolina." Starr quoted Grose as attributing West's comfort with reporters to his own interest in journalism. "I think . . . down deep he is a newsman at heart," Grose said.[40]

Jack Bass echoed the sentiment, writing in January 1973, after West's well-received State of the State speech, that "the governor's office perhaps is more open than ever. West is accessible to the press, holds frequent press conferences with no holds barred, and is probably more candid than most politicians. His office also is open to legislators, whom he treats with respect."[41]

West's "good press" carried over into end-of-the-term praise from many of the state's daily newspapers. The *Orangeburg Times and Democrat* wrote, "Governor West's greatest single success was in the field of economic growth. . . . As a result of the state's growing income and new jobs, the historic trend of out-migration . . . was halted."[42] According to the *Florence Morning News,* "much has been accomplished toward providing equal opportunity to state employment and other segments of public life."[43] The *Greenwood Index-Journal* probably hit the closest to West's own theme, writing, "The state moved forward in many areas . . . each had its own ingredient to add to the mix, and for Governor West, it was the uplifting spirit to free us from limited expectations, the intolerance for mediocrity and a restlessness for pursuing the unattainable."[44]

Accolades came from elsewhere as well. Marion Gressette, the veteran Calhoun County senator, sponsored a Senate resolution praising the governor, saying that West was able to get many of his programs through the legislature not by the threat of executive power "but because of his persuasive manner and his knowledge of state government."[45] Coming from the man who had wrought terror in the minds of many a reformer in the past, the resolution shed light on how West had been able to get Gressette, the staunch segregationist, to champion the legislation that created the State Human Affairs Commission in 1972. Marcia Duffy, a longtime Democratic Party leader, said, "I thank the Governor and his family for decency, dignity and respect for humanity which has set a pattern for our state."[46]

Along the way West lost two mainstays of his life. Mattie Ratteree West, the mother who decided to "cuss instead of cry" after her husband was killed in a school fire, died after a lengthy illness at age eighty-five. After living fifty years in the farmhouse where John West was raised, she had spent the last several weeks of her life in the Governor's Mansion, where she could get round-the-clock care. The governor noted in his journal that a large crowd turned out for the funeral, and the services were "very touching."[47]

Eight months later his longtime mentor Edgar Brown died in an automobile accident. Brown had retired from the Senate the previous year, having served in that chamber for forty-five years. In the eulogy West delivered on June 29, 1975, in the Senate chamber, he said of his old friend, "He had visions of greatness, but what separated him from the dreamers was the fact that he also had the courage when the going got rough, and was willing to square off, and punch, and counter-punch, for what he believed in."[48] West later wrote, "I gave the eulogy at Edgar's funeral, regretting that I could not share with his friends and the persons attending some of the stories which made him such a unique and loveable character."[49]

There was a finality about things. Events were combining to seem like a valedictory for a soon-to-be political has-been. Then some unusual things began to happen.

MAKING THE ARAB CONNECTION

Early in West's final year in office, the Kuwait Investment Company from the oil-rich Persian Gulf state of Kuwait purchased Kiawah Island off the South Carolina coast below Charleston for $17 million. The purchase was completed in February 1974, and the Kuwaitis made it known that they planned to build a luxury resort on the undeveloped barrier island. Six months later the Kuwaiti financial manager Abdlatif Al-Hamad visited South Carolina, and West, who knew the island like the back of his hand, was among those who gave the Arab leader a helicopter overview of his new purchase. He immediately befriended Al-Hamad, and the island tour proved to be a turning point in John West's life.

West's residence on the island, where he and the other six co-owners had hatched so many political plans, was not part of the sale to the Kuwaitis. While the governor did not invite the Arab financier to his small island house, he did extend the hospitality of the state to Al-Hamad, inviting him to the Governor's Mansion in Columbia. "I found that in the Middle East, inviting people to one's home is a mark of real friendship—far more significant than it is here," he told the reporter Jan Stucker (Collins). "We gave them the VIP treatment and told them that they were welcome and . . . [that] there was no prejudice against foreigners. . . . as a result of this, they invited me to Kuwait and I went just before leaving office."[50]

West visited Kuwait and Lebanon in January 1975. He had made a trip to the Holy Land in 1971, but this was his first experience in the Arab part of the stormy region, and it had a profound impact. Even though he was no longer governor, he and his successor, Republican governor Edwards, had formed a good friendship, and West felt comfortable inviting the finance and oil ministers of Kuwait to visit South Carolina as guests of the state. At a time when partisanship did not divide the state into mindless political camps, Edwards and West entertained the visitors at the mansion, and they made such a good impression that Kuwait's neighbor Saudi Arabia sent two officials to the state a month later for more South Carolina hospitality.

A year later the South Carolina–Middle East connection was becoming serious enough that Edwards named West to head a fifteen-member trade mission to Saudi Arabia, Kuwait, and Jordan. Also appointed to the delegation was

West's friend John Drummond, the senator from Greenwood County. By then it was clear that John West was no stranger in Arab circles. "We had a private audience with several members of the royal family in Saudi Arabia and met with King Hussein of Jordan," Drummond later recalled. "The Saudis seemed to have great confidence in John West. They knew him well and knew of his interest in the Arab world."[51]

West followed up on his rising status in the Middle East by forming, along with three associates, the Arab-American Development Services Inc., a company designed to promote economic ties with the Middle East. Shortly thereafter he became chairman of the board of trustees of the Southern Center for International Studies in Atlanta. The organization was created by former secretary of state Dean Rusk, and another member of the board was Cyrus Vance, who would become a key player in the next chapter of John West's interesting life.

It appeared that West was setting up what could become a lucrative law practice and business that could sustain him comfortably for years to come. Life, however, was just about to become even more complicated. Jimmy Carter, West's good friend and fellow governor, had decided to run for president. This announcement was greeted in most quarters with caution, even among his fellow southerners, but John West, who had not been bashful about his admiration for George Wallace, became one of the first major southern leaders to endorse Carter's candidacy. Whether it was insightful or instinctive or both, it proved to be one of John West's best political decisions.

Carter, seeing how McGovern had risen from the status of dark horse to front-runner by campaigning hard in the primaries, chose to enter all the caucuses and primaries, and he proved early that he could become a national candidate. He made impressive showings in New Hampshire and Iowa, and by convention time his continued state-by-state success had made him the surprise nominee. He carried that momentum into the fall, nosing out the Republican Ford by a narrow margin and becoming the first president from the Deep South since 1848. Carter's success made John West seem the most astute of political prophets, and it put him in an enviable position for a future role in the Carter presidency.

There was only one position on his mind. The friendships he had built up in the Middle East, the promise of a major role in international affairs, and the prospect of a long-term career in Middle East–related business pointed in one direction: Saudi Arabia.

West's new position would become one of Carter's appointments of "southern friends" and would draw its share of critical attention. "John West's most esteemed credential as ambassador to Saudi Arabia is an autographed picture of

President Carter on the paneled wall of his office," one newsman noted.[52] The *Economist* pronounced stuffily that "Mr. John West . . . would not seem as well placed as a career diplomat to take on the difficult job of ambassador to Saudi Arabia."[53]

Even so, John West was brimming with confidence. He believed that he not only had the kind of Middle East experience to win him early credibility but that he also had a good track record in bringing people together. "If I had any qualification to take on this job, it would be my background in the area of race relations," he said. "I've lived with that all my life and I've been involved in it politically for 25 years. . . . If you're able to sort of be a referee between blacks and whites, maybe you've had some test in refereeing human differences. I like to think so, anyway."[54]

With the approval of his friend Cyrus Vance, West was formally nominated as ambassador on May 23, 1977, and shortly thereafter he cleared Senate confirmation with little discussion. He was sworn in on June 16, and within weeks he and his family would be embarking on an adventure of a lifetime.

TEN

AN ARABIAN ADVENTURE

We [were] met by Ahmed Wahabi, the Royal Chief of Protocol.
I reminded him of our golf date and asked him how many strokes
he was going to give me.

John West

On Monday, June 27, 1977, Lois and John West left the comforts of
home, the security of friends, and the familiarity of virtually every
aspect of their day-to-day lives. On that day they embarked on a
journey that would take them thousands of miles from home and light years-
away from the only culture they had ever known. That journey would deposit
them in a place not only different from but often alien to their own values,
beliefs, and customs.

An overnight TWA flight from New York took them through London and
on to their Saudi Arabian destination of Jeddah, an ancient trading city on the
Red Sea. Even the location there of the American embassy, some 560 miles
across desert country from the interior Saudi capital of Riyadh, contained an
implicit message of Arab reservation about the very presence of their Western
allies. Jeddah was in the Hijaz, the Muslim Holy Land, where the holy cities
of Mecca and al-Madinah were also situated. According to one description, it
"long served as a kind of religious quarantine area in which foreign diplomatic,
consular and commercial representatives were allowed to live on a strictly temporary basis."[1] Jeddah would be the Wests' home for the next four years, and
it would be where he would conduct the business of the Carter administration
in the unconventional southern style they both knew so well.

The Saudi Arabia most Westerners encountered was puzzling. It defied predictability and resisted application of the very logic on which customary decision-making processes were based. The historian William Powell wrote, "Depending on who and what you read, you will discover that Saudis are the most polite, most hospitable, most generous, most philanthropic, most idealistic, most devout, most fatalistic, most cynical, most hypocritical, most corrupt, most racist, most barbaric people on the face of the earth. In short, you will learn that the Saudis are like most people in most places, except more so."[2]

A brochure produced in 1976 for American professional and corporate newcomers to the kingdom similarly described some of the rigorous conditions to be encountered and suggested that the new arrivals be prepared for a "culture shock." Among some suggested dos and don'ts for living in the Saudi kingdom was the recommendation that before leaving the United States, it would probably be a good idea to "update your Will and leave copies with responsible people."[3]

If that was not daunting enough, there was the admonition not to "speak or write anything derogatory about the country, its religion or customs." The expatriates' brochure described some good shopping opportunities for visitors but warned, "If a shopper is in a shop when the call [to worship] is given, he or she should leave. The religious police may signal the merchants to lock up by rapping against the store fronts with their sticks." Failure to observe the call to worship, the brochure noted, could cause the merchant to "suffer the revocation of his license to do business."[4]

It was into that world that the Wests descended on that June evening in 1977 as if dropped into a surreal late-night Arabian fantasy. Lois West recalled the moment of arrival as they left the airplane: "The door opened and that heat just went 'Wham!'"[5] "We were bedraggled," recalled staff assistant Betty Bargmann Hunter, who accompanied them on the trip and remained for the duration of the Wests' stay.[6] The new ambassador and his wife were met at the airport by the entire embassy staff, lined up by rank at the foot of the airplane steps. The Wests were then whisked in an aging Chrysler limousine through streets lined with stunning Old World Mediterranean architecture and crumbling building fronts.

The Wests actually did not get a good view of the city because of the thickness of the bulletproof glass in the limousine. As they would discover in daylight hours, a vast treeless horizon lay beyond the street fronts, and the city's skyline was shaped by an occasional domed mosque or sharply pointed minaret. Their new residence would be in a starkly white, walled-in compound, which covered a city block and was patrolled on a round-the-clock basis by a contingent of U.S. Marines.

Within the compound were the official residence of the ambassador and his family, living quarters for staff and attaché personnel, working offices for the various embassy operations, a swimming pool whose waters were constantly warm but still provided some refuge from the heat, and tennis courts, which got little attention because of the heat. Temperatures in Jeddah rarely fell below 70 degrees Fahrenheit, and the year-round daytime temperature ranged from the mid-80s to the low 100s. Elsewhere in the desert kingdom the heat climbed to the 120 to 140 degree mark on a regular basis.

The ambassador's home was divided into formal rooms and living quarters. Upon first viewing the residence, West cheerfully proclaimed it to be "luxurious," although staff member Betty Bargman Hunter later said that it was modest compared to other Western embassies. On that steamy June night in 1977, the American travelers arrived weary and anxious for a good night's rest. What they found, however, as they arrived at their "luxury quarters" was a formal dinner party. Lois West recalled, "I'd been traveling how many hours, something like twenty hours, and we got to the residence and they had a formal dinner set up."[7] It was one o'clock in the morning, or eight A.M. South Carolina time, when they finally turned in, "tired," John West wrote, "but still excited."[8]

REPORTING TO WORK

Three and a half hours later West arose, still tired, still excited, and facing a flurry of activities that would allow little time for adjustment or settling in to his new assignment. By late that afternoon, less than a full day after the family's arrival from South Carolina, West was en route by small plane to the Saudi capital, Riyadh, for the ceremonial presentation of his credentials to King Khalid the next day. This trip would foretell much of the tone and spirit of the activities that would engage him for the next four years, and it would offer him another opportunity for some personal politicking. With boyish glee and detail, West offered this account of his visit to the palace:

> We left the hotel [the Riyadh Intercontinental, where he had spent the night] at precisely 10:35 [A.M.]—all signals go. First was a police car— (Chevrolet, naturally) with red lights blinking—a series of them stopped at each intersection—followed next by a red Jeep with six soldiers—four in the back manning a machine gun. Then a Rolls (600) with me and the protocol officer in back and officer plus driver in front. Next was chase car followed by all the staff—two to a car.
>
> We wheeled into the palace and I reviewed the guard of honor in the courtyard. The palace was a magnificent structure—tile, marble with green

roof. We then [went] into the main hall where we [were] met by Ahmed Wahabi, the Royal Chief of Protocol. I had met him in Washington and he had sat by Lois at one of the dinners. I reminded him of our golf date and asked him how many strokes he was going to give me.[9]

West may not have had the swankiest embassy in Jeddah, but he soon learned what it was like to be the most important ambassador in town. While some ambassadors cooled their heels for hours and days waiting to present credentials, West not only was given VIP treatment upon his arrival but also garnered some valuable personal time with the king. While some officials had warned that the aging king was in poor health and that the meeting would probably be very short, West wound up talking with Khalid, through an interpreter, for a half hour in a setting that included only two other people, Khalid's doctor and Prince Saud al-Faisal, the young foreign minister whom West had met in Washington.

Khalid, sixty-five years old, was the fourth Saudi monarch to rule the desert nation and the third son of the kingdom's founder, Abdul-al Aziz al Saud (known to Americans as "Ibn Saud"), to hold the crown. As such, Khalid was among the last of the Saudi leaders whose roots went back to the days before the discovery of oil propelled the kingdom into a position of international prominence. He would prove to be a transition figure between the old and the new in the rapidly changing desert kingdom, and he would also serve as a compromise leader among rival factions vying to set a future course for the nation. Emerging from the oil-driven economic surge that had brought sudden wealth and enormous influence to the House of Saud in the 1970s were two powerful elements within the family. One, headed by Khalid's younger half brother Fahd ibn Abdul-Aziz, was a largely pro-Western group that favored accelerated modernization and progressive approaches to the nation's political and economic policies. The other, led by Abdullah bin Abdul-Aziz, was more conservative and traditional, representing tribal and nationalistic interests.

Fahd and Abdullah accepted Khalid as the compromise choice, and Khalid, in turn, installed Fahd and Abdullah as next in line respectively to the throne. To seal the deal Khalid restored the position of prime minister to the Saudi hierarchy, making Fahd crown prince and prime minister, and Abdullah was made second deputy prime minister while retaining his position as head of the Saudi Arabian National Guard (SANG).

Khalid succeeded Faisal ibn Abdul-Aziz, whose assassination by a distraught relative in November 1975 brought to an end twelve formative years of Saudi history. Faisal had asserted the kingdom's continuing role as a U.S. ally, but he

Upon his arrival in June 1977 as U.S. ambassador to Saudi Arabia, West struck up a friendship with King Khalid. Khalid was a political moderate whose reign was marked by an easing of travel restrictions on American Jews and the quietly allowed the practice of some non-Muslim faiths. Courtesy of the John C. West Papers, South Carolina Political Collections, University of South Carolina

also fostered its emergence as an Islamic state that was not bashful about its support of Pan-Arab activities and associating itself with such anti-Western influences as those of Egypt's Gamal Abdel Nasser. Faisal was "shrewd and visionary, with a keen sense of the country's needs."[10] The turnout of Arab heads of state at his funeral "was a measure of the stature gained by the Kingdom by virtue of its oil resources and Faisal's authoritative influence. . . . The Arab heads of state present symbolized the achievement of the King in establishing Saudi Arabia in a secure position in the diversified and divergent Arab family of states."[11]

Some felt that the new king, Khalid—besides bridging some generational and political gaps in the House of Saud—provided the kingdom some time to catch its breath after the energetic rule of Faisal. "Khalid's warmth and sympathy . . . was in contrast to the austere and forbidding demeanor of Faisal," the historians David Holden and Richard Johns wrote. Khalid "commanded affection, as well as a measure of esteem, and was the prince least likely to become involved in factional disputes. According to most accounts, he was the most agreeable of the senior princes and the best loved. His face reflected a genuine sense of humour uncommon in his solemnly self-important clan."[12]

The author Sandra Mackey, a close observer of the Saudi scene in the 1970s, wrote, "As it turned out, he [Khalid] proved to be an excellent choice. During his seven years on the throne, Khalid reigned and Fahd ruled. Khalid had the demeanor of a true sheikh, a kind, generous, pious man, whose bearing was regal but not haughty. He exhibited great patience with his subjects and chose to spend his happiest hours on the desert with his beloved Bedouins. Hundreds flocked to his weekly *majli,* and, like his father, he sometimes shared his dinner with a thousand of his male subjects."[13]

GOOD OL' BOY POLITICS IN THE DESERT

It was clear from the beginning that West and Khalid would hit it off, Khalid clad in the traditional robes and headdress of his Arab heritage and West wearing one of the suits that the Columbia tailor Larry Washington had made for him a month earlier. After exchanging formalities and pleasantries, West chose to use the occasion to sound out his new acquaintance on the most sensitive of topics, Jewish relations and the state of Israel. There ensued a friendly conversation in which the king declared that the Saudi position toward Jews had been misunderstood and that they welcomed visits from Jewish lawmakers from the United States. Until three years earlier there had been an absolute ban on issuing visas for Jewish visitors to Saudi Arabia, and Khalid's predecessor, Faisal, had made it clear that he made no distinction between American Jews and citizens of Israel. Khalid instituted an easing of that policy, making it possible for Jews to visit under conditions negotiated with the U.S. State Department.[14]

West's meeting with Khalid was sufficiently encouraging for the new U.S. ambassador to record an account of the session in his scribblelike handwriting and to head back to Jeddah with the sense that he had scored something of an early diplomatic and personal breakthrough with the Saudi king. En route, as he was dashing off his notes, the time lag caught up with the excited but tired ambassador, and he drifted off to sleep.[15]

Having established a personal relationship with Crown Prince Fahd during the Saudis' visit to Washington in May, West had reason to believe that he was now on sufficiently close terms with number one and number two in the Saudi hierarchy (Khalid and Fahd) not only to carry out his function as Jimmy Carter's personal emissary but also to pursue his own agenda of bringing American Jewish leaders into a conversational relationship with the Saudis. He also felt comfortable addressing issues that represented particularly onerous aspects of Islamic law for the Western expatriate community. Foremost among them for the Wests, pillars in their Presbyterian churches in South Carolina, was the ban on the practice of non-Muslim religions in Saudi Arabia.

INTO THE CATACOMBS

Secure in his relationship with Khalid, West went to the king on behalf of his fellow churchgoers, who found themselves deprived of a regular religious service. He was, according to Mackey,

> less hesitant than his predecessors had been to approach the Saudis about the plight of the Christians in the kingdom.
>
> Using his access to King Khalid to speak on behalf of the Christians, West is said to have told the King that Americans had great respect for Islam and he was sure that the king had respect for Christianity. Furthermore, because the Saudis were such religious people, he knew that they wanted to attract morally upright people to their labor force.[16]

The Saudi king accepted the argument, and he responded with a set of ground rules that essentially amounted to a "don't ask, don't tell" arrangement. Christians could practice their religion under certain circumstances, as long as nobody found out about it. Services in Jeddah, which the Wests attended, were called "welfare" meetings. Permitting the Christian services, Mackey wrote, "exhibited a great deal of moral courage" on the part of Khalid "in risking the rage of the religious zealots."[17] Some years later the *Christian Science Monitor* wrote of the arrangement, "In Saudi Arabia—the most conservative of the Islamic countries—the existence of a functioning Christian community was a feat in itself. Much of the credit for its presence goes to John West, former American Ambassador to Saudi Arabia under the Carter Administration."[18]

In time the "rage of the religious zealots" caught up with the Saudis. With the fall of the shah of Iran in 1979 and the rise of Islamic militancy in Saudi Arabia, the arrangement was suspended, and worship in large groups was forbidden. Religious services could be held only in private homes, which the Christians dubbed the "catacombs." "All organized activity among the Christians . . . has ceased," the *Christian Science Monitor* reported in 1983, "with little hope that it can be resumed in the foreseeable future."[19]

For his part, West made only one journal entry regarding his championing of the Christian cause in the Islamic nation, and it was a self-effacing one-liner. Referring to the so-called welfare meetings, he wrote, "I laughed . . . what a field day the *News and Courier* [the conservative Charleston morning paper] would have had with the headlines that one of West's first actions was to go to a meeting about welfare."[20] West was becoming the still, quiet voice in the inner sanctums of Saudi policy making. As he had in the South Carolina Senate, he was gaining the confidence of his senior colleagues and using that confidence to challenge the system from within. As Edgar Brown and Marion

Gressette had done years earlier, the Saudi leaders seemed to trust his friendship and judgment sufficiently to give the affable American some latitude.

The Wests were joined a few months later by their daughter, Shelton, who had remained in the United States for a wedding. She was twenty-three at the time and a graduate of the University of South Carolina after transferring from Winthrop. Shelton became a full-time Saudi resident, while the Wests' sons, Jack and Doug, remained in the United States and became frequent visitors.

The three South Carolina women—Lois and Shelton West and Betty Bargmann Hunter, the ambassador's administrative assistant—became familiar presences in Jeddah's diplomatic and social life. One of their frequent calls was at the regular Thursday night open house at the home of Carmen bin Laden, wife of Osama bin Laden's half-brother, Yeslam. In her book *Inside the Kingdom,* bin Laden wrote, "Our Thursdays were open house—anything from twenty-five to seventy people. There were regulars, like the American ambassador, John West, and his wife, Lois, friends who have stood by me to this day. Their daughter, Shelton, was about twenty years old. I could imagine how difficult Saudi life must have been for her, a young, single American girl in such a closed society."[21]

Shelton became friends with Carmen bin Laden. When the West daughter was married at Hilton Head some time later, Carmen's two daughters, Wafa and Nadjia, were flower girls in the wedding. "She was young and loved Americans," Shelton recalled. "She felt like Mom [Lois West] was another mother."[22]

The bin Laden book chronicles Carmen's unhappiness as a Saudi woman in the closed society for women within the kingdom. However, Shelton denied that she shared that unhappiness: "All of us went over there with the idea that it's a different culture and that it would be a learning opportunity and experience for us, that it would be an adventure. We didn't expect it to be mainstream U.S.A, but the Saudis were lovely to us. We didn't do anything to offend. We didn't parade down the middle of downtown in a mini-skirt. We all went out and had long dresses made, just cotton prints that you could wear down to the souk [market]. Nobody was offensive; everybody was very cordial, very welcoming, from the affluent Saudis all the way to the shopkeepers. They couldn't have been nicer or more respectful."[23]

Jack West, like his dad a Citadel graduate with a law degree from USC, became knowledgeable in the Saudi customs and their ways of business. "In practice, you had to have a partner," he remembered:

> American companies usually had either a partner or an agent, and the cut for the agent was usually five percent. The commercial section of the American Embassy in Jeddah had a list of people—say—in the widget business. If you were in the widget business, they'd be glad to help you and arrange

interviews with three different widget companies. There were trade missions from the U.S. Commerce Department, as well as the State of South Carolina.

Daddy wanted to increase business for South Carolina. He encouraged South Carolina businessmen to come to Saudi Arabia.[24]

BRIDGING SOME GAPS

Within a week after presenting his credentials and befriending the Saudi king, West set about to build bridges between American Jewish leadership and his new Saudi friends. He hosted a second Jewish senator to visit the Saudi kingdom, New York's formidable Republican Jacob Javits. The first had been Senator Richard Stone, a conservative Democrat from Florida, who visited Saudi Arabia prior to West's becoming ambassador. Javits would be a guest at the embassy for four days, during which time West hoped to bring Javits into friendly conversations with the Saudi leadership. He also hoped to create the kind of favorable impression for Javits that might lead to his support for the crucial congressional action on the sale of F-15 fighter jets to the Saudis.

Whatever diplomatic business might lie ahead, West soon discovered another challenge with the veteran lawmaker. Javits was a robust seventy-three-year old physical-conditioning enthusiast whose daily exercise regimen left the plumpish fifty-five-year-old West huffing and puffing. West wrote on Javits's second day at the embassy, "Javits and I went for a swim, although he can swim about a dozen laps without breaking stride or appearing winded and I could do no more than two or three."[25] The day after the New York senator departed, West wrote, "Javits has shamed me to the point that I jogged, then went swimming, ate breakfast and was at the office at 8:00."[26]

Elsewhere during the Javits visit West kept pace with the energetic senator as he led him through a busy series of diplomatic engagements—some tense, some cordial, and some probing. "Sparks flew" at the meeting with oil minister Ahmed Zaki Yamani, West wrote, but sessions with Foreign Minister Saud al-Faisal and Monetary Agency head Abd al Aziz al-Qurayshi proved productive and caused West to believe that Javits "might have some of his predetermined thoughts shook."[27] It all led up to sessions with Khalid and Fahd, which took on the tone of summit meetings. "I am your friend," West quoted Javits as telling Khalid, "and we hope that Saudi Arabia is a friend of ours." Khalid was quoted as responding, "No doubt about it."[28]

The meeting with Fahd left West even more pleased. "The chemistry began to work in great fashion," he wrote. After a cordial discussion of world affairs and after finding common positions between the two, West wrote, "The most

JOHN C. WEST

AMERICAN EMBASSY

APO NEW YORK 09697

July 1, 1977   # 1

Dear Mr. President:

From time to time, I'm going to take the liberty of writing you to give you observations and impressions that may be useful. These communications will be informal and no acknowledgment is expected. Basically the same information will go to the State Dept re the formal channels.

We arrived on Monday evening after leaving S.C. on Sunday. The living quarters are most comfortable and the staff seems capable and well informed. (The help doesn't speak English so Lois has already learned Kitchen Arabic!)

The King received me on Wednesday and that was unheard of in terms of speed. Some ambassadors have had to wait several months — (Mr. Porter, my predecessor, some 6 weeks because of the Saudi's displeasure at the firing of Jim Akins by Kissinger)

At any rate it was a good start, thanks to your credibility as established by the Fahd visit and your public position on peace in the Mid-East.

Throughout his ambassadorship to Saudi Arabia, West regularly conveyed handwritten letters to President Carter about issues and conditions in the desert kingdom. Presented here are the beginning and the closing of the first such communication to President Carter, a three-page letter dated July 1, 1977. The full text of the letter is contained in Appendix 2. Courtesy of the John C. West Papers, South Carolina Political Collections, University of South Carolina

JOHN C. WEST
AMERICAN EMBASSY
APO NEW YORK 09697

for a peaceful solution.

In all frankness there is skepticism
shared by both the Sandis and the
veteran foreign service people that
we may not carry forward as
we have begun because of 1) the
tremendous pressure that is already
being built up to modify the announced
policy; and 2) your ability and that of
the Congress to withstand it.

I've reported that you are less
susceptible to political pressures than
any elected official I've ever dealt with –
and that together we must provide the
understanding that will insure the
support of Congress.

Thank you again for the opportunity
of serving in an exciting, challenging
position. I will do my best to justify
your confidence.

Lois joins me in warm regards to
you + Rosalyn – she was most gracious
to show us around the White House.

Faithfully,

John

dramatic part took place at departing when Fahd grasped Javits with both hands and said, 'I am delighted that you came—I feel that we have a friend, and I now have a strong ally in the search for peace in the Mideast.'" It was quite a statement to a Jewish senator who would not have been permitted in the country three years earlier. West wrote that "Javits replied by saying he was a friend and that we would work together for peace in the Mideast."[29]

It was quite a moment for West, an ambassador who had been in the country for only two weeks. It gave him some reason to believe that good ol' boy politics could work as well in Saudi Arabia as it did in South Carolina. Things were off to a good start, and West fired off letters to Carter and Vance declaring as much.

Vance would be paying a state visit to the Saudi kingdom in a month. His visit would provide West with his first opportunity as resident ambassador to be directly involved in the long-range diplomatic initiatives that constituted the Carter foreign policy. West relished the role, to which he brought good spirits and high hopes. Carter, after all, had already established himself as an Arab-friendly president, a distinction not lost on the Saudi leadership.

Carter and West shared the belief that Arab interests had been obscured by the Americans' high-profile support for and protection of Israeli interests ever since the founding of that nation in 1948. A middle ground could be struck, they believed, in which the United States could become an ongoing presence in Middle East affairs and not just a visitor in times of crisis. Without unduly jeopardizing their commitment to the Israelis, West and Carter believed that their friendship with the Saudis could be heightened as part of what had become known as their "special relationship" and that a friendship could be extended across broader diplomatic fields.

Such an extension was built on what was basically an arrangement of convenience between the two nations—restraint on oil prices by the Saudis in exchange for American pressure on the Israelis for a long-term Middle East peace. Carter believed that as the paymaster of major Arab nations and entities —Egypt, Syria, Jordan, and the Palestine Liberation Organization (PLO) among them—Saudi Arabia could exercise strategic leverage to foster a comprehensive approach to stability in the region. The Saudis, in turn, believed that the United States, as a major source of support for the embattled Israeli state, could exercise similar leverage in steering Israel toward a settlement of what the Saudis considered long-standing territorial issues dating back to the 1967 Arab-Israeli war and even to the creation of Israel in 1948.

Historians differ in their opinions on why the Arab and Israeli nations had not found a negotiated path to a peace settlement in the wake of the 1967 war.

A conference of Arab nations in Khartoum, Sudan, shortly after that war and the subsequent Khartoum Resolution of September 1, 1967, are often cited as the bases of those nations' refusals to negotiate with Israel. Included in that resolution are what came to be known as the "Three No's—no peace with Israel, no recognition of Israel, no negotiation with Israel."[30]

The basis of Carter's proposal for an Arab-Israeli settlement—or at least the beginning point of discussion—would be the elusive, and seemingly illusionary, proposition of "land for peace," which formed the basis of United Nations Resolution 242, adopted in 1968. Under that resolution Israel's right to exist would be guaranteed by Arab nations in exchange for the vacating of Arab territory occupied by Israel after that war. For the Carter administration, this seemed reasonable and doable, and it was touted as a more ambitious approach than the "step-by-step" approach of their predecessors, Presidents Richard Nixon and Gerald Ford and their primary strategist, the secretary of state and national security adviser Henry Kissinger. By then Kissinger also agreed that the step-by-step, "shuttle diplomacy" exercise had run its course.[31]

The centerpiece of the Carter plan would be a five-part program proposing (1) that the goal of the agreement would be comprehensive; (2) that the basis of the agreement would be UN Resolutions 242 and 338 (which ended the 1967 war and called for negotiation); (3) that peaceful normalization of relations would be established, with boundaries that would be open and determined by negotiation; (4) that the provisions would be phased in; and (5) that a Palestinian state would be created. The plan was based on an extensive 1975 Brookings Institute project in which Zbigniew Brzezinski, Carter's national security adviser, was an active participant. Among the institute's proposals was that "the United States, because it enjoys a measure of confidence on both sides, and has the means to assist them economically and militarily, remains the great power best fitted to work actively with them [the Arab and Israeli nations] in bringing about a settlement."[32]

FADING HOPES FOR PEACE

Things had gotten off to a rocky start, however, for the new president. During an early tour of the Middle East in February 1977 (five months before West's arrival in Saudi Arabia), Vance discovered how deep the Israeli intransigency was toward the ceding of territory or toward any gestures recognizing the Palestine Liberation Organization. The Arab nations were sharply divided over issues and strategies themselves, and Egypt's Anwar Sadat was pressing for a separate peace with Israel, a move that Carter felt would diminish chances for the kind of comprehensive regional peace he was advocating.

"Vance's discussions with the Arab leaders . . . convinced him that they remained divided and incapable of pursuing a united course of action. All wished to see progress made on the Palestinian issue, although Saudi Arabia alone demanded establishment of an independent Palestinian state; yet all were at odds in one way or another with the PLO. All wished to prevent Egypt from further negotiation with Israel, yet they would not negotiate with Israel themselves," wrote the historian Richard C. Thornton.[33]

A subsequent meeting of Carter with Israeli prime minister Yitzhak Rabin had been testy and unproductive. Thornton wrote, "By the end of the year [1977], the Carter administration's policy in . . . the Middle East . . . had failed. Washington's attempt to combine an Egyptian-Israeli peace treaty with a Palestinian resolution had fallen prey to skillful, if short-sighted Israeli diplomacy, which had brought Anwar Sadat to the verge of a separate peace whose terms would have shattered the larger United States position in the region."[34]

By the time Vance reached Saudi Arabia in February 1978, things had become even more complicated. As divided as he had found the Arab world in his earlier visit, Vance would discover firsthand the deep political fissures inside the stormy parliamentary system of Israel, the only democratic state in the Middle East. Rabin, considered a political moderate as the head of the Labor Party, was replaced in May 1977 by the hard-line conservative Menachem Begin of the Likud Party as prime minister of Israel in a shocking political upset. Begin's presence in the equation shifted the attention and tone of the discussions, and his positions on the ceding of territory, the establishment of a Palestinian state, and the presence of a Palestinian delegation at a peace conference were conspicuously less negotiable than those of Rabin. Begin even suggested to Vance procedural changes that would prevent open discussion of certain portions of the Carter plan, a suggestion that Carter and Vance rejected. In light of Begin's positions, including his refusal to consider a Palestinian state or to permit Palestinian presence at a peace conference, it was obvious that some basic changes to Carter's plan, at least on an intermediate basis, were in order.

"In each of the Arab capitals," Vance later wrote, "I presented Prime Minister Begin's procedural proposals, which were rejected with varying degrees of specificity and heat. I also introduced the five-draft principles, as well as our suggestions for dealing with the Palestinian representation issue. After explaining that Israel had rejected the principles on withdrawal on all fronts and on a Palestinian entity, I elaborated on our thinking about the nature of a transitional arrangement for the West Bank and Gaza."[35]

In the weeks prior to Vance's arrival, West spent time making the rounds of the Saudi hierarchy and bureaucracy, concentrating much of his attention on

West maintained a lively relationship with the Princeton-educated Saudi foreign minister Prince Saud al-Faisal. West called some of their heated discussions "meetings of the Princeton Debating Society." Courtesy of the John C. West Papers, South Carolina Political Collections, University of South Carolina

Saud al-Faisal. It was West's thought that the young foreign minister could play a pivotal role in any upcoming negotiations, particularly among the other Arab nations and interests. Like his father, King Faisal, Saud was assertive and could deal across political and tribal lines. He had the charm and sophistication to work effectively with Western nations, but he was also the Saudis' point man in dealing with the rambunctious PLO, whose terrorist and guerrilla activities made it reviled among most of Israel's Western friends. Even so, the PLO and its leader Yasir Arafat had standing among the Arab states, and its influence played into the overall political and security strategies of the region. Saud was a savvy diplomat, and while he and West sparred often and vigorously, they became friends, and along the way Saud gained the confidence of Secretary Vance as well.

Saud and West bounced ideas back and forth, toying with language of a proposed resolution that they believed might get the PLO interested and involved in the peace-seeking process. As Vance's visit neared, West exchanged their ideas with the secretary of state, and Vance later wrote,

> When I arrived in Taif [the Saudis' mountain resort] to meet with King Khalid, Crown Prince Fahd and Foreign Minister Prince Saud, I had prepared [this] specific language:
> "The PLO accepts United Nations Security Council Resolution 242, with the reservation that it considers the resolution does not make adequate reference to the question of the Palestinians since it fails to make any reference to a homeland for the Palestinian people. It is recognized that the language of Resolution 242 relates to the right of all states in the Middle East to live in peace."[36]

As it turned out, the Vance visit produced dubious outcomes for the Carter peace plan, but it proved useful to the new ambassador. Describing Vance's meeting with the Saudi leadership, West wrote, "At his conclusion, Vance gave one of the most magnificent presentations I have ever heard. He came down foursquare for the U.S. positions that they would not back down and in essence said that the Israeli pressure groups were not going to be the controlling factor. This of course strengthened my credibility substantially since that has been the unseen and unasked question hovering over all of my talks with all of the Saudis."[37]

The carefully crafted language offered to the PLO was designed to draw it closer to the negotiating process. It was rejected, however, in a scenario that would be repeated periodically in subsequent peace efforts over the years. Vance gave this account of the effort:

> Prince Saud, a wise and skillful foreign minister whom I came to admire greatly, said that he would communicate the language I had given him and that he hoped we would get a positive response from Arafat before I left Taif. Saud was optimistic, saying that the Executive Committee of the PLO was meeting that night and would consider our proposed language.
> The next morning, when I met Saud at the airport, his face was clouded with gloom. He told me that our suggestion had indeed been considered last night and had failed to muster the necessary votes for approval. The opposition was led by the extreme elements within the PLO. I departed Taif with a heavy heart as I felt that an important opportunity had been missed because of the deep division within the PLO.[38]

The one outcome that seemed positive for Vance and West was the unintended impact of Begin's stubborn resistance to the peace plan. His positions had, in essence, caused more cohesion among the Arab states. West wrote that with a little persuasion, "all of the Arab states . . . could present a unified position on all five of the points [of the Carter peace plan]."[39] West's optimism for Arab unity in support of the U.S. initiatives probably reflected more the naive enthusiasm of an ambassador who had been on the job only a matter of months than it did a realistic assessment of the political condition in the region at the time. About the only thing that could generate and sustain unity among Arab nations at that point was their opposition to Israel and their dislike for Begin. This sentiment never translated into unified support for Carter's peace plan.

SAUDIS' GROWING TENSIONS

Vance left one other message with West the evening before he departed from Saudi Arabia. "Cy invited me up for a private drink and we discussed the overall situation," West wrote. "He told me that Jimmy Carter had agreed to go to the mat—even if it cost him a second term—on this issue, namely that he would not succumb to Israeli pressure."[40]

The initiative undertaken by Saud toward the PLO had come at some risk to the Saudis. In the aftermath of the hardening of the Israeli position and the rejection of the Vance proposal by the PLO, there was some diplomatic shuffling among the Saudis to affirm their position among Arab states and to shore up any flanks left exposed in the process. West was summoned to an extraordinary meeting during Ramadan that included only him, Crown Prince Fahd, and Prince Saud and in which Saud acted as interpreter. West noted that after an hour and forty minutes of cordial but direct conversations, "The significant message being imparted was that the Arab world is uneasy about the loss of momentum in peace negotiations and [it hoped] desperately for some indication or move by the United States to restore the forward pace. There was evident Saudi disappointment of the failure of the PLO, although this point was not addressed directly. Fahd said in his opinion . . . that a resolution of the PLO question was the first prerequisite of any lasting peace and the attempt by the Israelis to join the Palestinian entity to Jordan was not acceptable."[41]

There was also the implicit message for West in the protocol of the meeting that Khalid, the king, would be the ceremonial leader who would conduct the *majilis* (public meetings in which the king would hear grievances or concerns directly from Saudi citizens) and who would serve as the public face of the Saudi kingdom. When it came to the business of governing and determining the tough issues of domestic policy and international affairs, Fahd and

Saud and others of the younger Saudi leadership would be calling the shots. West would become familiar with dominant elements within the Saudi family, such as the "Sudeiri Seven," the seven sons of the kingdom's founder, ibn Saud, by his wife, Hussah-al-Sudeiri, of whom Fahd was the most prominent member at the time. Also emerging as a powerful family unit within the House of Saud were the fives sons of King Faisal by his wife, Iffat, among whom the most prominent were Saud and Turki. (Turki served as ambassador to the United States and Great Britain.) Fahd, Saud, and Turki would become West's closest associates during his years in Saudi Arabia, along with Bandar, a onetime ambassdor to the United States who was the son of the defense minister Sultan, one of the Sudeiri Seven.[42]

West's meeting with Fahd and Saud was followed a day later by a meeting with oil minister Zaki Yamani, the most powerful of the nonroyal leaders in the kingdom at the time. It began with a report, which was probably based on a recent trip by Saud to Egypt, to the effect that "President Sadat cannot survive in Egypt unless there is noticeable progress to peace in the immediate future . . . radical elements are creating an opportunity to overthrow him [and] the Russians will move in and consolidate their position in Egypt as soon as Sadat is unseated." Once Anwar Sadat falls, the report continues, Syria's Hafez al-Assad "would either be overthrown or become radical [again]."[43]

At that point Yamani's language became almost threatening. "Prince Fahd can't tell you and Prince Saud won't tell you," West quoted Yamani as saying, "but I can tell you unofficially as your friend and as a friend of the United States that there is no possibility of maintaining our relationship in the event these things happen. I am known as a friend of the Americans . . . and I do not deny that part of my friendship is based upon what I perceive to be the best interests of Saudi Arabia, and I am a Saudi first, last and foremost. I do not think that Saudi Arabia can survive as an island of Islam and a symbol of the free enterprise system surrounded by the hostile environment which will inevitably come about if we do not obtain peace."[44]

ENCOUNTERING JEWISH DISILLUSIONMENT

As the hopes for a comprehensive Mideast conference appeared to be fading, so too were West's hopes for maintaining a delicate balance between the Arab-friendly stances being taken by him and the Carter administration and the pro-Israeli interests in the United States. West had long counted among his friends and political supporters some powerful Jewish leaders in the ranks of South Carolina Democrats, including state senators Isadore Lourie and Hyman Rubin of Columbia, as well as the Columbia businessmen Norman Arnold and

Samuel Tenenbaum, a major financial supporter and policy adviser to the party. Since the early days of his ambassadorship, West had met periodically with a cross section of Jewish leaders at the Harmony Club in New York in meetings coordinated by Tenenbaum. The group included high-ranking members of the Anti-Defamation League (ADL) and the American Jewish Congress; the prominent rabbi Israel Miller; Edgar Bronfman of Montreal, chairman of the board of Seagrams; as well as Tenenbaum and Arnold. Tenenbaum later recalled that

> in the beginning, it looked like it was very hopeful. West had had our support while he was being criticized nationally during the confirmation process because we had great expectations that he could duplicate what he had done in South Carolina in bringing divergent groups together for peaceful settlement of civil rights issues. We hoped he could do likewise in the Middle East in bringing the Israelis and the Arab nations together peacefully.
>
> As the meetings went on in New York over a period of time you saw the change—that he [West] really became their ambassador to us and no longer our ambassador to them.[45]

The group's first two meetings, held in May and October of 1977, particularly reflected that emerging tension. In a letter following the first meeting, one of the group's prominent members, Aaron Gold of Philadelphia, wrote to West, "I believe that what we were all trying to say was that all of us . . . are concerned about the fate of Israel, and beyond that, the fate of Jewish people everywhere. . . . John, do all you can to see that Israel survives in honor and peace, so that it need not shed the blood of its sons and daughters in yet another war."[46]

As the group convened with West again on October 17, 1977, the tone had stiffened. By then Carter's five-point peace plan built around United Nations Resolution 242, the "Land for Peace" arrangement, had been aired, and lines had been drawn rhetorically and politically over the notion of yielding land in exchange for a promise of peaceful coexistence among Jews and Arabs in the Middle East. West wrote about the October meeting: "It was not as cordial as the first meeting, mainly because of a Mr. Krupp from Boston, who is the most ardent Zionist I have ever seen. He said the Jews would not give up an inch of the West Bank and he started cussing President Carter. I told him I wasn't there to defend either the United States or President Carter. I was an American first. . . . It's hard to believe that these responsible citizens have such an allegiance to Israel that they will put the interests of that country above those of the United States."[47]

In the exchange of letters between West and Aaron Gold, the tone was distinctly more somber than it had been earlier. Gold acknowledged the tumultuous nature of the meeting in his letter, writing, "It is difficult to write a civilized and urbane letter after the conversation took place. The fact of the matter is, the issues are so intense that it is hard for me to keep my cool." With regard to the Carter peace plan, Gold wrote, "There is absolutely no way that the Israelis are going to sit down with the Palestinians. . . . It is unwise and unkind to expect that sensible people would sit down to plot their own destruction. And yet the Carter government has seemed to put that sitting down together with Israel's enemies as a first condition for continued support."[48]

West responded that he shared Gold's pessimism: "I doubt that either of the negotiating sides, Israel as well as the Arabs, will make sufficient concessions for there to be a negotiated peace. I doubt that the United States will attempt through pressure on both sides to impose the terms of a peace, and even if that were possible, the wisdom is still very much in doubt."[49]

On the same U.S. trip when he met with the Jewish group in New York, West hoped to strike a conciliatory note with some of his southern friends and political allies by inviting Prince Saud to speak to the Southern Center for International Affairs in Atlanta. It was through this organization, which was founded by the Georgian Dean Rusk, secretary of state under both John F. Kennedy and Lyndon B. Johnson, that West had become acquainted with Cyrus Vance as a fellow board member. Saud's speech, drafted by a former staffer from West's governorship days, was an exercise in rhetorical diplomacy that tied together several themes, including Woodrow Wilson's boyhood days in Columbia, South Carolina; his presidency at Saud's alma mater, Princeton; and Wilson's striving for world peace during his presidential terms. In the audience were several of West's Jewish friends from Columbia, including state senator Isadore Lourie. West later proclaimed that the speech "was very good" and that Saud "was particularly effective in the question and answer period."[50]

There ensued in the Middle East a restless and testy standoff while the Israelis fumed, the Saudis fretted, and the PLO dithered. Then came Anwar Sadat's stunning declaration that he would go to Israel himself. He announced to the Egyptian People's Assembly on November 9 that he was "ready to go to the ends of the earth" and that "Israel will be astonished when it hears me saying now . . . that I am ready to go to their own house, to the Knesset itself, to talk with them."[51]

CONSEQUENCES OF SADAT'S BOLD STEP

Sadat's initiative rocked the Carter administration and sent the Saudi leadership into a quiet rage. In a matter of hours and days, the Saudis' hopes to build Arab unity were upstaged by an exclusionary Egypt-Israel linkage, and President

Carter's plans for a comprehensive five-point Geneva peace conference similarly suffered. While the Saudis seethed quietly, Carter regrouped, offering a quick endorsement of Sadat's plan and dispatching West to gain Saudi support. It would prove to be a tough sell. It would also prove to be a defining moment and a turning point in Carter's strategy and West's role in Middle East diplomacy. Weeks earlier Saudi Arabia had seemed to be the key player in trying to bring the PLO to the bargaining table. It was the Saudis' initiative to the PLO, using a proposed resolution drafted by Vance, West, and Saud, that had held the promise of making the PLO a party to the broad peace initiatives envisioned by Carter's five-point plan.

Rejection of that proposal and Sadat's bold move shifted the spotlight and attention away from the Saudis and away from the comprehensive Carter plan to the Sadat-Begin axis. This strategic change would eventually lead to the Camp David Accords and would leave the other Arab states in various defensive stances, reacting with mild approval or outright disapproval. The Saudis' response to Sadat's initiative was described as "cautious and circumspect as ever," but scarcely concealed was their distress that the "modicum of unity at the heart of the Arab world, very much the work of the Kingdom's patient diplomacy in 1976, should now be about to fragment. . . . Khalid and the Saudi leadership were . . . sullen, feeling that they, as much as the Arab cause, had been betrayed."[52]

Vance wrote, "The Saudis, the Jordanians and other moderate Arabs exercised public restraint while they awaited the results of his [Sadat's] attempt to change political attitudes in Israel. It was clear, however, that the Saudis could resist pressures to denounce Sadat only if he achieved speedy and noteworthy results."[53]

"It was almost a unanimous feeling [among Mideast Arab states] that Sadat was a traitor when he went to Jerusalem," West later said, noting that the Saudis were particularly peeved that Sadat had met with Saudi officials immediately prior to his announcement and had said nothing of his plans. "He simply did it on his own . . . that was sort of in keeping with Sadat's personality and his method of operation," West recalled.[54]

In one of his handwritten letters to Carter, dated November 20, West wrote, "When the news [Sadat's visit to Jerusalem] became public, King Khalid sent a letter to Sadat (a very polite letter, according to Saud) asking what its purpose was and what he hoped to accomplish. According to Saud, Sadat had as of yesterday failed to give the King the courtesy of a reply."[55]

West's criticism of Sadat did not go unnoticed in Cairo. In an account published in *The American House of Saud* by onetime Senate Foreign Relations

Committee staffer Steven Emerson, West was accused by Hermann Eilts, U.S. ambassador to Egypt, of adopting the "Saudi position hook, line and sinker." Eilts, a onetime ambassador to Saudi Arabia himself, was quoted by Emerson as saying that West was operating "a public relations firm for the Saudis."[56]

Two weeks after Sadat's statement that he would go to Jerusalem, Arab opposition to the Egyptian leader became tangible with the organization of the Left-leaning "Steadfastness," or what Vance called the "rejectionist bloc," of Syria, Libya, Iraq, South Yemen, Algeria, and the PLO. Pressure was building on the "moderate" Arab states, and Vance could feel the clock ticking. "Saudi Arabia and Jordan, torn between private hopes for Sadat's initiative, fears that he would fail, and intense desire to restore Arab unity," he wrote," turned to us for help in building on Sadat's initiative before he was so discredited in the Arab world that they would be forced to break openly with him."[57]

According to Rachel Bronson, in her book *Thicker Than Oil,* "Saudi Arabia's Prince Fahd was livid when he heard about it [Sadat's initiative], mostly because he was caught by surprise, but also because he believed that the Middle East crisis would continue in perpetuity unless the Palestinian problem was effectively solved, and for that a united Arab front was needed." Fahd believed that the United States had been complicit with Egypt and had kept Saudi Arabia in the dark, but he was told otherwise by the CIA. "Fahd did not at that moment sever Saudi Arabia's relationship with Egypt," Bronson wrote. "Within two years, however, Saudi Arabia would slice its aid to Egypt and lead the Arab world in an anti-Egypt boycott."[58]

The Sadat move caused a quick and thorough reshaping of American strategy. Carter's visit to Saudi Arabia, originally scheduled for November 1977 to mobilize support for his comprehensive five-point peace plan and a Geneva conference, was moved to January 1978 to drum up support for Sadat's initiatives and an Israel-Egypt agreement. A bargaining point, in that moment of some White House urgency, became the sale of F-15 jet aircraft to the Saudis, or—more specifically—the timing of the sale. Brzezinski had hoped to delay the actual sale, knowing that there would be a heavyweight investment of Carter's political equity in gaining approval of the sale by Congress.

West thought otherwise. He advised the president in a January 2 letter, and in a personal conversation, that Saudi support could now be tied to the sale of F-15 fighter jets and that a discreetly placed message about the warplanes could be useful. "I emphasized to the President . . . that the F-15s and the self-determination issue [for the proposed new Palestinian state] were the issues," West wrote. "He agreed that he would handle both of them, which he did. He told the King he was submitting the F-15 proposal to Congress as soon as it reconvened. Sultan [the Saudi minister of defense and aviation] really began to smile."[59]

Impatience over the sale of the F-15s was, in fact, becoming a contentious issue for the Saudis, who believed the commitment made to them dated back two years to the Ford administration. Combining that with their uneasiness over the Sadat initiatives, it seemed that things were getting downright chilly for Americans in the warm desert sun. "Carter received a cool, albeit polite, response in Riyadh during his brief stopover on 3–4 January," Holden and Johns noted. "His exchanges with Fahd, Sultan and Saud were sticky. The Saudis were not prepared to give any blessing to Egypt's new approach to a settlement of the Arab-Israeli conflict."[60]

Then came Carter's decision—at West's behest—to expedite the F-15 sale, and it changed everything. Rachel Bronson wrote, "Carter's meeting with Khalid . . . produced one of the most controversial and time-consuming problems faced by his administration. Impressed with Khalid's flexibility over Palestine, Carter agreed to support a long-standing Saudi request for F-15 planes."[61] Brzezinski later wrote dolefully, "We had hoped to delay this matter [the sale of the fighter jets] while going ahead with our peace strategy, but Saudi demands of the planes, as well as Egyptian insecurity about their defense relationship with the United States, compelled us to make the public announcement in mid-February. . . . we did tell the Saudis that we would like to delay this matter, and their reaction was most adverse."[62]

The Saudis were not over their snit with the president, and shortly after his departure, Foreign Minister Saud issued a statement to the effect that any Middle East settlement must be based on a complete Israeli withdrawal from occupied territories, including Arab Jerusalem, and fulfillment of the legitimate rights of the Palestinian people.[63] They did, however, have the opportunity to see that the ambassador did indeed have direct access to the president and that he could use that access to wield some influence.

A PROTOCOL "FIRST"

If there was only grudging progress on the diplomatic front, there was a significant breakthrough in the area of Arab tradition and protocol as it applied to Ambassador West and his family. This had to do with Lois West and her role in welcoming President Carter and his party upon their arrival at Riyadh Airport, and it involved a conflict with some deeply rooted Arab traditions. West had been told in no uncertain terms by the Saudi royal protocol office that Lois could not appear at the airport as part of the greeting party. He wrote, "Lois' situation had created a real problem. . . . [For] never in the history of Saudi

Arabia had a woman been allowed to greet anybody at the airport when the King was present and they wouldn't make an exception."[64]

For West it was hardly acceptable treatment for the woman who had steered Ku Klux Klan night riders away from him on the back roads of Kershaw County, whose wartime marriage to him had made her the first married student to graduate from Winthrop College, and who had served as South Carolina's First Lady for four years. She had been special in his life and deserved special treatment by the Saudis, he decided.

"They called a meeting of the cabinet and finally Saud took the matter directly to the King," he wrote. "The solution worked out [was] that Lois would be in the back waiting room at the airport to greet them after they came off the plane."[65] All went according to plan, and the greeting party gathered in the back waiting room prior to the arrival of the plane. When the plane landed, the greeting party departed, leaving Lois and the king in the waiting room.

"The King asked why she wasn't out there," West wrote.

> She told him she wasn't supposed to go. The King then ordered her to go, and I was standing at the foot of the plane when all the commotion started. Protocol didn't know what she was doing there, but the King had given the order, so she broke the segregation barrier and became the first woman in history—for whatever that's worth—to be present with the King in greeting somebody to Saudi Arabia.
>
> Jimmy and Rosalynn spoke to Lois before they spoke to the King, so I guess that further shattered Protocol. I thought it was funny, but Lois said it was humiliating. I've never seen her get so upset about anything before.[66]

Protocol aside, the advancement of U.S. peace initiatives and the job of the U.S. ambassador to Saudi Arabia were becoming a lot more complicated, and they were beginning to take something of a physical toll on the U.S. ambassador. Late in December, in fact, West recorded in his journal a visit to the doctor for a shot, during which he discovered that his blood pressure had risen to 156 over 96. "Somewhat disturbing," he wrote. "Despite the problems in the Governor's office, my blood pressure was never above 130 to 135 so I guess either age or the problems here are getting to me a little more than I would like to think."[67]

There would be no letup in the pressure and stress of the job, however. Upon the departure of the president in early January, attention swung to the dual issues of (1) gaining congressional approval for the sale of F-15 fighter jets and (2) developing Saudi interest and support for the Begin-Sadat peace initiative, which had by then become a full-blown Jimmy Carter enterprise. The issues were inextricably bound together, and West became the point man in much of the activity.

RUN-UP TO THE F-15s CLASH

For the next month the U.S. Embassy in Saudi Arabia became crowded with official American visitors: three congressional and Senate delegations; Carter's energy secretary, James Schlesinger; and Lucy Benson, the undersecretary of state for security assistance, who became Cyrus Vance's key operative in the F-15 matter. She was tough, and West thought she made a good addition to the support team. Among those congressional visitors calling on the Saudis was the third of the Jewish senators, Abraham Ribicoff of Connecticut, a gruff, no-nonsense type who made no secret of his displeasure with arrangements in the Saudi kingdom. Others in the party were Senators Harrison Williams of Pennsylvania, Ted Stevens of Alaska, Howard Cannon of Nevada, and West's old South Carolina friend Fritz Hollings. All were accompanied by their wives. "Ribicoff and Stevens began raising hell about the schedule," West wrote. "Ribicoff was particularly nasty—said that in his forty years' experience he had never seen such a tough [busy] schedule."[68]

With Hollings's help West managed to calm the Connecticut senator, and by the time the Senate party was treated to a "gracious dinner" at the home of oil minister Zaki Yamani, West said, things were "beginning to smooth out." Ribicoff was still feisty, however, as West led him and his colleagues through rounds of meetings with various Saudi officials, capped off by a session with Crown Prince Fahd. The discussion centered on oil production, and then— as West sensed things were ending—he said to Fahd, "Your Royal Highness, what about the F-15s?" After thanking West for the reminder, Fahd proceeded to deliver what West described as an eloquent plea, at the end of which the grumpy Ribicoff rose. "Your Royal Highness," he said, "you are a good persuader. You have won your case." Hollings, according to West, uttered a stunned "What?" and West said, "Let's go." He later wrote in his journal, "It looks like Ribicoff made a commitment."[69]

The House delegation, headed by the longtime Democratic loyalist and Carter ally Clement J. Zablocki of Wisconsin, chairman of the key House International Relations Committee, also provided encouragement to West and the Saudis. Their visit included a meeting with Fahd and produced what West considered a "very productive session," in which he "made more friends for the F-15." Among those impressed, according to West, was then congressman Christopher Dodd of Connecticut. "He even shook Chris Dodd," West wrote, who "had been putting articles in the Congressional Record opposing the sale."[70]

The run-up to the congressional debate seemed to be going smoothly, although West's persistent recommendation to the Saudi leadership that a public relations initiative be launched to counter the powerful lobbyists had been set aside on numerous occasions. Then, on January 25, came word that a letter was being circulated in the Senate asking that the president hold up submission of the F-15 sale. West passed the word among Saudi leaders—and just about anybody else of interest, including a business-seeking group from Litton Industries—and paid a visit to Saud to give him the news about the letter. West wrote:

> He was livid. I reminded him that they had not done their homework with the Congress and that was one of the problems. He said they would do anything we asked for the Congress. He insisted that the President could push the matter through if he really wanted to.
>
> I pointed out to him that the President had made a commitment and in the message to be delivered to the Crown Prince [transmitted by Carter to West earlier in the day], he would proceed and live up to his promise. He [Saud] wanted me to go right on down . . . to see the Crown Prince, which I did.[71]

In a later conversation with Hollings after he had returned to the Senate, West was told that "the Jewish lobby was active and they were the only ones exercised about the F-15s." It was midnight before West got home that night, "completing the toughest day I've had yet in this position."[72]

THE FORMING OF AN UNUSUAL TEAM

A week later West renewed his plea for public relations support to Saud and Turki al-Faisal, the security chief who would organize and coordinate Saudi involvement in the promotion of the F-15 sale. Within three days West had his long-awaited answer. The Saudis were ready to move on the public relations initiative, and the firm chosen to manage that effort was Cook, Ruef, Spann and Weiser of Columbia, South Carolina, headed by West's longtime friend and political associate Crawford Cook.

Cook, who had managed Marshall Parker's race for lieutenant governor in 1962 and was manager of West's run for governor in 1970, had subsequently served on Hollings's staff in Washington and was well known in congressional circles. His firm, initially organized with the Columbia TV newsman Lee Ruef, had developed a reputation for political toughness and effectiveness in circles inside and outside of South Carolina. Cook's selection helped to flesh out a support team that would eventually include Saudi princes, Ambassador West himself, and Lucy Benson, the State Department coordinator who had already clashed with Prince Saud over the practice of separating men from women at dinner parties. Benson and Fahd had hit it off well, though, and West described her as "sharp, and I do mean tough. She has an excellent grasp of the entire situation . . . [and] is full of spirit and is a good listener."[73]

On February 1, West received word informing him that the president had formally decided to submit the F-15 proposal to Congress. That same day West had extensive conversations with James E. Akins, the former U.S. ambassador to Saudi Arabia, who had been summarily dismissed by Henry Kissinger at the end of the Ford administration, reportedly for being too friendly with the Saudi regime. Akins told West that he and Carter were on the right track with the F-15 proposal but that he could not testify at the congressional hearings "because of his Quaker background."[74]

Over the first seven months on the job, West had learned that the Middle East was like a giant political Rubik's Cube. An alignment of Egyptian and Israeli interests would predictably set off serious repercussions within the fractious Arab world. The courtship of Arab interests toward the PLO similarly chased away Israeli support for peace strategies. Within the Muslim nations there were deep divisions and suspicions, which made the term "Arab unity" something of an oxymoron. In addition, while it might have seemed that Saudi financial support for its impoverished Arab neighbors could cut across political and diplomatic lines, that support was proving not to be the leveraging force that Carter and West had anticipated and hoped for. Most of the Arab nations would not behave as "client states" to the Saudis any more than Israel would accept that role in its relationship with the United States. Leverage was proving to be a scarce commodity in Middle East diplomacy.

On the social side of their lives, the Wests were learning that Saudi Arabian civilization was not as forbidding as the advance billing would have indicated. Shelton's friendship with Carmen bin Laden and others would help her see a lesser-known side of Saudi society—a society of Christian Dior gowns, tennis parties, and frequent jaunts to European capitals. Shelton said, "Everybody always says, 'Oh, look at those poor [Saudi] women.' and I say, 'Wait a minute. Step back a minute.' Probably every Saudi girl I met had gone to college in the U.S., and they had been to the major capitals of the world. They probably spoke two or three languages. I found a lot of these women to be very well-educated."[75]

On the diplomatic front, change was coming rapidly, and roles had to be adjusted to accommodate that change. As events evolved, the Carter administration was finding itself cast not so much as the leader or organizer of peace efforts but as their enabler, coordinator, or convener. The Carter peace plan, with its five carefully drawn principles leading to a conference in Geneva, was giving way to something more haphazard. For all its commitment to a comprehensive approach to Middle East peace, the Carter administration was finding itself at times undertaking the step-by-step approach and eventually even a shuttle-style role, which it had earlier eschewed. The administration was riding ferocious diplomatic and political tigers from which it could ill afford to be thrown, and from which it dared not dismount.

In all of that West was finding himself less inclined to pursue the role of peacemaker between Israeli and Arab interests. The hardening of American Jewish sentiments and the inability of the Saudis to marshal any moderate Arab support for Carter's peace initiatives were polarizing things. Unlike earlier days, when he could—in his capacity as ambassador to Saudi Arabia—foster conversations and the exchange of ideas among Arabs and American Jews, West was finding his job increasingly becoming one of making either/or decisions. In making those choices, he began more and more to believe that buttressing Saudi interests in the diplomatic free-for-all he was witnessing was, in essence, the best way to protect U.S. interests, and he was neither apologetic nor defensive about it. The smooth, Westernized Saudi leaders and diplomats he had come to know and trust were riding tigers of their own, which included the rival forces within the House of Saud, the dangerous Islamic tide and temper abroad in the desert kingdom, and the unstable Arab world that lay just outside their borders.

In that swirling atmosphere, the sale of the F-15 jet fighter planes to Saudi Arabia became more than a strategic military move on the part of the Carter administration. It also placed West squarely in the Saudi camp and became an article of faith designed not merely to shore up the Saudi nation but also to empower within that nation the pro-Western element that was holding the line on oil prices, restraining the more volatile elements of the Arab communities, and resisting the cold-war threats from communist-inspired interests on the kingdom's flanks. Those forces threatening the pro-Western Saudi leadership would remain in place and would flare into open conflict at crucial stages of West's ambassadorship.

THE SHIFTING SANDS OF
SAUDI FRIENDSHIP

> To put it in very simple form, we needed their oil and they needed
> our security.
>
> *John West*

On February 15 Ambassador West got official word from Secretary
Vance that the proposal for fighter jet sales had been submitted to
Congress. The legislation bore the earmarks of a nifty piece of political handiwork, reportedly crafted by Brzezinski and Deputy Secretary of State
Warren Christopher. It was not simply a vehicle for the sale of fighter planes to
the Saudi kingdom. That, the Carter people realized, probably would not have
sufficient support in either house of Congress to prevail. Instead it came in the
form of a package that included fighter planes for Egypt and Israel as well as
for the Saudis.

The strategy was no mystery. The package offered an opportunity for those
legislators who did not wish to become embroiled in the bitter Israeli-Arab
fight to cast a vote "for both sides." Its message of Saudi friendship was also
unmistakable. Those who chose to take sides in the fight would have no difficulty identifying the issues and the potential consequences.

Zbigniew Brzezinski wrote, "We settled in late January on the strategy of
combining the proposed plane transfers for all three countries into a single package, making it known that we would not permit the omission of any one country by a congressional veto. The strategy was designed to paralyze the powerful
Israeli lobby on the Hill. Privately, I urged the President not to give more planes

As ambassador to Saudi Arabia, West regularly conferred with (left to right) Carter's chief of staff Hamilton Jordan, secretary of state Cyrus Vance, and national security adviser Zbigniew Brzezinski. Courtesy of Roderick M. Todd Jr.

to the Saudis and Egyptians together than to the Israelis, but the President, increasingly irritated by Begin's provocations on settlements, on his own decided to increase the number of planes to Egypt to a total of fifty. I suspect that his relationship with Sadat influenced his decision."[1]

As West had been informed earlier, the package contained sixty of the prized McDonnell Douglas F-15 Eagle fighter jets for the Saudis for $2.5 billion. Israel would get fifteen of the F-15 planes and seventy-five of the less effective F-16s at a cost of $1.9 billion. Egypt would receive fifty of the smaller, less expensive F-5E jets at a cost of $400 million. As Washington observers knew, the Saudis got everything they had requested, and the Israelis received only about half of what they had hoped to acquire.[2]

The news that Carter's legislative package had been submitted to Congress came as no surprise in Saudi Arabia, where West had kept the princes closely informed along the way. "We . . . received from the Secretary [Vance] an announcement of the proposal to sell the Saudis 60 F-15s, with 50 F-5Es to go to Egypt and Israel being cut from 250 to 75 F-16s and from 25 to 15 F-15s," West wrote. "I was pleased," he said, "and [Crown Prince] Fahd seemed properly appreciative."[3]

In a handwritten letter West told President Carter that "the news of the F-15 sale was the best thing that's happened to us since we've been here. Prince Fahd was extremely pleased. . . . The Saudis have chosen the F-15 as the litmus test of the 'special relationship.' The fact that you moved forward despite the pressures has given a fresh new dimension to that relationship. Had you not done so, I'm afraid to think what the consequences may have been. . . . the Carter administration's credibility is at an all-time high."[4]

Three weeks after Carter's announcement of the package, West arrived in Washington for regular consultation with the State Department and to undertake an active role in Congress promoting the fighter jet sale. This was a role, in fact, that some did not think appropriate for an ambassador, as the Columbian Samuel Tenenbaum would later observe.

The career foreign service officer James A. Placke, who served as deputy chief of mission under West in Saudi Arabia, disagreed. "This business about the American ambassador representing his country of assignment: that's not unique to Saudi Arabia or to John's tenure there," he later said. "The common phrase is 'localitis.' It's just endemic in the nature of things. Washington doesn't want to hear about why you can't do this, or why they [the country of assignment] don't agree with us, . . . they just want them to agree with us, and they're not really interested in why. . . . That's true of any administration, any ambassador, in any significant country around the world."[5]

THE AMBASSADOR AS ADVOCATE

Over the next two and a half months West would work—in his best southern style of personal politics—through the hallways and offices of senators and House members in order to maintain liaison with a sometimes cranky State Department, to stay in close touch with a stubborn president and an anxious White House staff, and to help keep the enthusiastic but somewhat disorganized contingency of Saudi princes from falling into disarray. It would also be West's burden to protect his own flanks against personal attacks designed to discredit the Saudi cause.

The latter vulnerability was articulated to him by a former U.S. ambassador to Saudi Arabia, James Akins, whose crude dismissal by Henry Kissinger late in the Nixon-Ford administration was still on the minds of the Saudis and their friends. In a letter dated January 10, 1978, Akins wrote to West that "the lobbying against Carter in the Congress is fierce and all stops are being pulled out. . . . A friend of mine in the Senate told me last week that you are going to be brought into it, too." Akins went on to write, "I am constantly asked by newsmen how I think you're doing; yesterday at lunch correspondents of the *Washington Post, Time* and CBS brought up the subject. I told them you were doing a superb job; that you were responsible for restoration of relations which had soured under Kissinger/Porter and that the nation owed you a debt of gratitude."[6]

Within the days and weeks after his arrival in Washington, West would find Akins's letter to be an accurate forewarning of the intensity of the attacks on the Carter legislation as well as the personal attacks on his own character. On the legislative front, the first skirmish to be brought to light came in the form of a letter to President Carter from members of Representative Clem Zablocki's House International Affairs Committee opposing the fighter jet sale. Zablocki himself did not sign the letter, and he remained loyal to Carter, but twenty-one of his thirty-seven committee members did line up against the sale.

According to a press account published on March 11, the letter "represented a clear endorsement of the Israeli and organized American Jewish opinion's critical view of the proposed package deal." The article stated, "The letter contained no threat to seek a congressional veto of the proposed package deal, but the threat was implicit, and the large number of signatures suggested that Carter's plan is in serious trouble on Capitol Hill. . . . Many Jewish groups and other friends have begun a determined campaign to block the package deal. Their intense opposition to it is the most obvious outward sign of the tensions that now grip large sections of the American Jewish community and its political allies." The article also carried a passage reporting that Ambassador West had paid a call on the staff of the Senate Foreign Relations Committee and told them, "Saudi Arabia might let the price of oil rise if it does not get its F-15s."[7]

The anti-Saudi letter from the House committee members was like a shot fired across the bow as the political engagement began to take shape. A more direct shot was fired directly at West less than two weeks later in the form of a request from Kansas senator Robert Dole that West be investigated because he "has engaged in questionable activities." It was "questionable," a news account noted, that "Saudi Arabia has hired a public relations firm headed by Crawford Cook, a political ally of Mr. West, to lobby on behalf of proposed jet aircraft sales to the wealthy Middle Eastern nation."[8]

Dole was quoted two days later as saying, "It is alarming to think that an Ambassador would consent to perform a liaison function for commercial interests in this country and the government to which he has been assigned."[9] The conservative *New York Times* columnist William Safire joined the fray, attacking West's "business fixing [as] being grossly unethical."[10]

Dole and Safire were, in fact, attacking something near and dear to West's heart—helping Americans do business in Saudi Arabia—and with which West saw nothing wrong. For most of his career in public life, West had never drawn much of a jurisdictional line between his personal interests, his moral convictions, and his political life, and he was not going to change those values in Saudi Arabia. "I haven't done anything I am ashamed of," he told a reporter for his home state paper the *Columbia Record,* "and I would do it all over if I had to do it again. . . . Just because people are my friends, I don't think I should have to turn a cold shoulder."[11] West later wrote in his journal, "I can't understand it—how someone can criticize for helping to promote business—but I guess that's politics."[12]

THINGS GET PERSONAL

In a letter to the writer Edward Sims, West called Safire's column "a low blow" and said, "There was certainly never any suggestion on my part which could, in my judgment, even be remotely considered as undue influence to select the Cook firm." He admitted that he did tell the Saudis of his successful experience in the 1970 election with "the very excellent firm" [Cook-Ruef] but said that the Saudis "made an independent judgment."[13]

West checked out the severity of Safire's and Dole's attacks with journalist sources and was told that the story was probably ended for the moment.[14] President Carter, who was feeling pressure himself at the time because of his Atlanta banker friend Bert Lance's troubles, later told West, "If there is anybody in the world you wouldn't mind charges being made by, it was Senator Dole." West wrote in his journal after Carter's comment, "I felt better about it."[15] Dole never got his requested investigation from Clem Zablocki's House committee, and the flap eventually came to a close in late April after an internal State Department investigation by Robert M. Sayre. Sayre, a career diplomat and onetime ambassador to Panama, was serving as inspector general of the Foreign Service and would subsequently become ambassador to Brazil. West wrote that Sayre's report "was basically good. In fact, he commended me for trying to help with the balance of payments and said that the Embassy was not giving me enough support. It was a relief to know that at least that was behind us."[16] On May 23 Senator John Sparkman of Alabama, chairman of the Senate Foreign Relations Committee, received a letter from Herbert Hassell of the State Department's legal department informing Congress that the State Department had found no fault with West's actions regarding the public relations firm selection.[17]

If there was relief on the personal front, however, there was no letup in the attacks on the Carter fighter jet package. A letter to West dated March 20 from Dr. Seymour Piwoz of Pennsylvania stated the case against the legislation: "This proposed sale is yet another step in the continued tilt away from support of Israel toward the Arab position. In this respect, Israeli and American Jewish public opinion speak as one. Over the years the U.S. has looked to the realistic defense needs of Saudi Arabia and will certainly continue to do so. This proposed sale of F-15 planes, however, has as its most likely potential, a threat to the Israeli heartland. The concerned American Jewish community and its constituent organizations are united in this aspect of the area's problems."[18]

Piwoz's letter foretold the issues and extent of the political conflict that lay ahead. As he had stated, the resources of the Jewish lobby, including the formidable American-Israeli Public Affairs Committee (AIPAC), were being mobilized for full combat. Ranged against them would be the improbable team that included the president, an assortment of Saudi princes, a South Carolina public relations firm, various elements of the State Department, the U.S. and Saudi ambassadors, the Saudi lobbyist in Washington (Fred Dutton), and a few legislators who had become allied to the cause.

By April 17 the forces opposing the aircraft sale had reached across the hall and included strong Senate voices. "A majority on both the Senate Foreign Relations Committee and House International Relations Committee oppose the sale," it was reported in *U.S. News and World Report*.[19] By statute it took both houses of Congress to adopt a resolution disapproving, or vetoing, the arms sale in order for it to be blocked. The Carter administration, seeing the strength of the opposition gathered on the House International Affairs Committee, chose to concentrate its forces in the Senate. Senate rejection of the "veto" resolution disapproving the jet sale was all that would be required for the Carter administration to win and to proceed with the sale.

As the combat intensified, the *New York Times* reporter Steve Roberts wrote that "the best lobbyist for the Saudi side was President Carter himself. . . . But the Saudis felt strongly that they wanted to speak for themselves."[20] Roberts went on to describe how Crawford Cook had regularly pelted key leaders with Saudi-friendly printed materials, including reprints of advertisements taken out in *Time* and *Newsweek* magazines by the Saudi kingdom.

What gave the campaign additional flair was what the *Times* called a "blitz." Identified in the extraordinary enterprise were "Saudi officials, ranging from Ghazi Algosaibi, Minister of Industry, to Prince Bandar ibn Sultan, a squadron commander in the Saudi Air Force."[21] The *Washington Post* reported, "Almost every morning these days, the black limousines pull up to Washington's

Madison Hotel to collect their Saudi Arabian passengers. Their destination, very often, is Capitol Hill, where the battle of the F-15s unfolds."[22]

The *Times* writer Roberts had this description of the blitz: "In more than 50 talks with members of Congress, the Prince [Bandar] and the Saudi Ambassador [Ali Alireza] have described Saudi defense problems and how the F-15 fighters could help. Much of their attention has been focused on figures like Frank Church, Democrat of Idaho, of the Foreign Relations Committee. The Saudis have also visited many pro-Israeli members of Congress, including Jews such as Jacob K. Javits, Republican of New York."[23]

PRINCELY LOBBYISTS

The Saudi participation was coordinated by Prince Turki al-Faisal, the kingdom's security chief, who went on to become Saudi ambassador to Great Britain and later to the United States. In an interview with the author in 2004, Turki described the formation of the team and said he was well aware that Bandar had the kind of personality to take a lead role in the lobbying effort. "He was much more outgoing than I was," Turki recalled twenty years later. "It only took one phone call to line him up. I called his father [Sultan bin Abdul-Aziz], who was my uncle, and he was immediately agreeable."[24] Bandar was not only an effective conversationalist but also had flown the F-5 in the Saudi air force and was likely to fly the F-15. Bandar could talk mechanics and military strategies as well as politics.

Bandar went on to become ambassador to the United States in the 1990s, reportedly at the urging of John West. Crawford Cook later recalled, "Prince Bandar [was] ambassador to the United States because John West beat on the Saudis until they finally made him ambassador . . . every time he would see Prince Saud or Prince Turki, he would say, 'You need to make Bandar ambassador to the U.S.' . . . He wouldn't let up, and they finally made him ambassador."[25]

Bronson wrote, "Saudi Arabia dispatched its best and brightest to lobby for the sale. Saud and Turki, two sons of the late King Faisal, descended on Washington. There, they met up with their first cousin . . . Prince Bandar bin Sultan, a favorite of King [then Crown Prince] Fahd and the Gatsby-like son of the Saudi minister of defense and aviation. The princes were the epitome of a new breed of Saudi diplomat—outgoing, sociable and articulate."[26]

On the other side, the pro-Israeli lobby "pulled out all the stops," according to a book later written by Republican congressman Paul Findley of Illinois. Findley, who supported the arms sale, wrote that the Israeli lobby "coordinated a nationwide public relations campaign which revived, as never before, memories of the genocidal Nazi campaigns against European Jews during World War II. In the wake of the highly publicized television series, 'Holocaust,' Capitol Hill was flooded with complimentary copies of the novel on which the TV series was based. Accompanying the book was a letter from AIPAC which said, 'This chilling account of the extermination of six million Jews underscores Israel's concerns during the current negotiations for security without reliance on outside guarantees.'"[27]

In that swirl of heated and emotional combat, West spent much of his time calling on senators and holding out hope that he could generate some Jewish support for the arms sale. He renewed his contact with Senator Javits, whose meeting with Crown Prince Fahd had produced some hope for Arab-Israeli friendship months earlier for the new ambassador. Under the strain of the congressional fight, West found Javits willing to say only that "he would try to work something out." A meeting with another Jewish senator, Richard Stone of Florida, who had visited Saudi Arabia just prior to West's arrival there, was even less encouraging, producing behavior by one of Stone's staff that West described as being "tough, to the point of being rude."[28]

West also paid a visit to New York for a third meeting set up by Samuel Tenenbaum with Jewish leaders at the Harmony Club. "They were not as violent as I thought," West later wrote. "In fact, one of them said that the F-15 sale ought to be approved. He got up and left and the rest of them raised hell!"[29]

Hopes for a peaceful resolution were further damaged by news on March 12, less than a week after West's arrival in Washington, that seventy Israelis had been killed in a PLO terrorist attack on a bus. There were further reports that Saudi radio had called the attack "a noble act."[30] The Saudis quickly denied reports of the radio commentary praising the terrorists, but the incident only deepened the gulf between Arab and Jewish interests on Capitol Hill.

Any doubts about President Carter's intensity on the issue, in fact, were removed during a visit by West and Brzezinski to the president a few days later to discuss the Saudis' reaction to the PLO attack on the Israeli bus. "The President was very positive," West wrote. "Zbiggie was raising the question about the statement from the Saudis condemning terrorism. . . . Zbiggie wanted to know if it had been broadcast in Riyadh, and I said I didn't know and the President said it didn't matter a damn to him. His hackles were really up. We had a good meeting."[31]

For the next two months the battle for the Saudi jets was waged in the manner of hand-to-hand combat in the Senate. The ebb and flow of the commitments seemed to be less about partisan or regional issues and more about individual or personal interests. Senator Wendell Anderson of Minnesota, with whom West had served as a fellow Democratic governor in the early 1970s, was one such case. At a dinner arranged by Senator Hollings on March 9, West learned that Anderson had a Jewish opponent running against him and key Jewish people on his campaign staff. "Wendy has a problem," West wrote in his journal.[32] At the same dinner West had a chance to meet Senator Frank Church of Idaho, chairman-to-be of the Senate Foreign Relations Committee, who was noncommittal, and Florida senator Lawton Childs. Childs asked West if he had talked with his fellow Florida senator, Richard Stone. "I told him I had been cross-examined by him," West later wrote.[33] West considered the meeting to be "constructive."[34]

In mid-April, West returned to Saudi Arabia, but as the date for the scheduled hearing on the fighter jet sale before the Senate Foreign Relations Committee (May 8) neared, West returned to Washington. In the days of early May he was able to confirm the support of Senator Strom Thurmond as well as that of Arkansas senator Dale Bumpers, with whom he had also served as a fellow Democratic governor. West recorded in his journal that a visit with William Proxmire, the veteran Democrat from Wisconsin, was "one of the most pleasant surprises of the day. He was very gracious and listened very attentively." West's meeting with Illinois senator Paul Simon produced a reluctant pledge "if we need his vote."[35]

Beneath the uncommon grind and pressure of lobbying on both sides of the issue lay the prospect of a compromise that could head off a direct fight on the floor of the Senate. *Time* magazine reported that Senator Howard Baker, a Republican from Tennessee, and Democratic senator Abraham Ribicoff of Connecticut had explored the possibility of finding some flexibility in the number of airplanes that would be allocated to each country.

Church of Idaho, fuming that President Carter had not allowed his committee such flexibility, indicated reluctant support for a deal, and Baker explored interest among his fellow Republicans. *Time* reported that Carter had shown some interest in pursuing a compromise, and Vance convened a meeting of Senators Ribicoff, Javits, Baker, and West Virginia Democrat Robert Byrd. The deal, according to *Time,* was that the sales would be submitted separately for each nation, but if any of them was rejected, Carter would veto the whole package.

Another, later gathering with Vance included the retiring Foreign Relations Committee chairman John Sparkman of Alabama, and at the ensuing committee meeting Senators Church, Charles Percy of Illinois, and John Glenn of Ohio spoke in favor of the sale. Speaking against it were Senators Joseph Biden of Delaware, Richard Stone of Florida, and Paul Sarbanes of Maryland. Javits expressed doubts, and Church began to waver. As the committee vote was taken, Church switched to oppose the deal, and the committee was dead-locked. Instead of killing the bill, which would have been tantamount to adop-tion of Carter's proposal, the committee deadlocked, 8–8, and the bill went to the floor of the Senate.[36]

"UNBELIEVABLE" PRESSURES

Debate was set for ten days hence, on Monday, May 15. West wrote, "The pres-sures are unbelievable; 40,000 telegrams and letters to each Congressman, they say." To undergird Thurmond's support, he solicited South Carolinians Roger Milliken, Fred Dent, and George Dean Johnson to call Thurmond the week-end before the vote, and to confirm his support, West paid a call on Thurmond himself on the Monday morning the resolution was to be addressed. "He has indicated he is going to vote for it," West wrote, "and finally George Dean [Johnson] and Warren Abernathy [a Thurmond staffer] came over to the hotel and told me I had convinced Strom. Of course, I knew the others had been on him, too, but it was nice to have him in our corner."[37]

West recorded this account of the day: "It was ten hours of debate and I sat through most of it. It began to swing about midday very noticeably. Several of the waverers came over to our side and the slippage stopped. Finally toward late afternoon Howard Baker came in and told Cy [Vance] that the vote was going to be ample, with a half dozen or so in reserve. As it ended up, it was 55 to 44. It was a great victory. [We] had a late dinner at Hugo's. . . . All in all, it was a great day and everybody is happy."[38]

For West, the euphoria lasted for a few days. The next day he wrote, "The papers were all very kind to Crawford and indicated that the Israeli lobby had been dealt a big blow."[39] *Time* magazine called the vote a "milestone" and observed, "It was the worst defeat suffered in Congress by Israel and its U.S. supporters. It was an indication that the Senate now agreed with three succes-sive U.S. presidents that the U.S. should pursue a more evenhanded Middle East policy, one that protects Israel's interests and supports its moderate Arab neighbors, as well."[40]

West even had the opportunity to try out the F-15 plane himself. Ten days after the sale of the plane passed its Senate test, West strapped himself into the fighter jet and was taken on an outing by Major Jim Newsome, an air force pilot. "Jim asked me if I would agree to a power takeoff and I said yes, so he turned on the afterburners and shot the plane straight up to 10,000 feet. He rolled over and said, 'Look over your right shoulder.' I looked down and there was the end of the runway!" West even flew the plane himself for a while. "I

One of the historic moments of West's tenure as U.S. ambassador to Saudi Arabia was approval by the U.S. Senate of President Carter's proposal to sell F-15 fighter jets to the Saudi kingdom. After the sale was approved, West was given a spin in an F-15 and even took a turn flying the powerful jet. Courtesy of the John C. West Papers, South Carolina Political Collections, University of South Carolina

flew for about 10 or 15 minutes and did, among other things, a loop, which was quite an experience. Held the stick to the extreme right and felt the plane completely roll over with the ground coming up at me and then righting itself. We went about twice the speed of sound, breaking the speed barrier on at least two occasions."[41]

West had had the satisfaction of seeing the commitment made by Ribicoff in Saudi Arabia stand up to the stress of Senate combat over the fighter jet sale. Otherwise, however, his hopes for Jewish-Arab reconciliation were in shambles. Javits, his swimming partner in Jeddah, became embittered and cried out from the floor of the Senate during the debate, "What do we want to do with the Israelis? Sap their vitality? Sap their morale? Cut their legs out from under them?"[42] Brzezinski described Ribicoff as "a tower of strength, in marked contrast to the [incoming] chairman of the Senate Foreign Relations Committee, Frank Church, who, though he privately promised us support, was extraordinarily susceptible to signals from the Israeli Embassy and in the end failed to come through."[43]

Among the supporters of the Israeli position, Senator Daniel Patrick Moynihan of New York was particularly vocal after the vote sustaining the airplane sale to the Saudis, saying, "The bond of trust has been broken."[44] The Carter administration quickly embarked on damage control and peace-keeping missions. White House officials reportedly issued a "no gloating" order, and top aide Hamilton Jordan said, "We take pleasure in winning, but not in beating the group of friends we had to beat."[45]

Whatever the downside of the fighter jet battle in Congress may have been, President Carter believed that his championing of the Saudi Arabian cause would give him extraordinary access to the inner circles in Riyadh. On May 24 he dispatched a message through State Department channels to Crown Prince Fahd describing his expectations in the coming Egypt-Israel peace initiatives he anticipated during the summer of 1978. He wrote, "I am grateful for your thoughtful letter of May 17 on the occasion of the Senate's action in support of the aircraft sale to Saudi Arabia. I agree with your assessment that this new indication of the deep friendship between our two nations will be beneficial to increased cooperation in pursuit of common interests. As I wrote his majesty [Khalid] on May 16, I am particularly anxious to get on with the urgent matter of seeking a comprehensive and durable peace in the Middle East. In this endeavor, I will continue to value deeply the advice and support of the government of Saudi Arabia."[46]

ELEVATED EXPECTATIONS

Carter's expectations of the continuing "advice and support" of the Saudi Arabian government would be translated into recurring and increasingly intense pressures on West to deliver Saudi support at crucial stages of the upcoming round of peace talks involving Carter, Begin, and Sadat. Those pressures would weigh heavily on West as an insider in both Washington and Riyadh, for—as Jim Placke observed—the White House "just wanted them to agree with us."[47]

As West was soon to learn, the Saudis also had their expectations. Upon his return from the United States in early June, he was welcomed with warmth and enthusiasm by his close associates Turki and defense minister Sultan, who was the father of the energetic lobbyist Prince Bandar. He even got a hearty greeting from the conservative Prince Abdullah, the head of Saudi Arabia's national guard, who was next in line to the throne after Fahd. Abdullah, whose linkages to the Saudi tribal interests had made him less than enthusiastic about the king-dom's Western inclinations and influences, met with West on June 4 in what the U.S. ambassador called "practically a love feast." West wrote, "He was effu-sive in his praise of the President and all concerned about the F-15s." Accord-ing to West, Abdullah said, "This is the United States we used to know—we thought she no longer existed."[48]

Abdullah's friendship was particularly sought by West. As Jim Placke later recalled,

> Abdullah, even though he was the third ranking member in the hierarchy, was an outsider. He was the son of King Abdul Aziz [ibn Saud], as they all were. But . . . he was the only son of his mother, and his mother was from a different tribe . . . which is a very, very large tribal confederation covering northern Saudi Arabia and going off into eastern Syria and southern Iraq.
>
> He had no full brothers and was semi-isolated within the family. But John West saw his future importance and made a point of cultivating Abdullah. And Abdullah was flattered because he . . . would often be over-looked, especially by foreigners.[49]

West also paid a postcongressional victory call on oil minister Zaki Yamani, and—as he had come to expect—he got more than a perfunctory assessment of things. "Zaki was in good form," West wrote, "and we covered the whole area of international relations. He is extremely concerned about the Mid-East peace prospects—a pessimism which I share. The troubling thing is that he thinks that the United States can do more to pressure Israel and that of course just isn't so, and I said so."[50]

Unfolding on a larger canvas was the vast Carter peace plan built around the Egypt-Israel linkage. It was a fragile plan fraught with peril, not the least of which would be the leadership role he expected from the Saudis, a role with which they were never comfortable. Not only were the Saudis diplomatically bashful, preferring a low-profile background role, but they also felt threatened by various trouble spots on and near their borders, including the Yemen states to the south, the African "Horn" across the Red Sea, and the ongoing turmoil among their feuding Arab brethren. Saud al-Faisal and Zaki Yamani, two of West's closest friends, were careful to keep the U.S. ambassador informed of their anxieties, the kind of troubling messages that occupied much of his nor-mal workdays.

In addition the Saudis had something of a diplomatic chip on their shoul-ders for other reasons. Unlike the Egyptians, the Syrians, and the Israelis, whose civilizations and traditions stretched back thousands of years, the Saudis as a nation were the new guys on the block. While the various tribes dated back into distant history, their existence as a nation was only a few decades old, the outcome of Saudi tribal victories over their rivals in desert combat earlier in the century. Their traditions were still largely built around those of individual tribes and that of the highly conservative Wahabi version of the Muslim faith. As the oil resources beneath their desert kingdom made them wealthy beyond imagination, they assumed the unexpected role of financial supporter of some of their Arab brethren, among them older civilizations whose identities and visibility were far better known around the world than were those of the emerging Saudi kingdom. This made the Saudis hypersensitive to their perceived status among the hierarchy in the Middle East, and it made them downright cranky over what they might view as disrespect or snubs from anyone, whether from Anwar Sadat, Jimmy Carter, or any other world leader.

For that reason West found himself carefully monitoring the actual wording of dispatches being translated between English and Saudi interpreters for optimum sensitivity. He admitted that messages were occasionally softened for Saudi consumption, presumably without distorting the actual meaning of the messages.

Beyond the issues of external sensitivity, West had to pay attention to the rivalries within the House of Saud, the feelings that might exist between the Sudeiri Seven and the five sons of Faisal, and the differences between the Westernized princes and their more traditional brothers such as Abdullah, who still identified with tribal and Bedouin interests. West's cultivated friendship with Abdullah was a diplomatic coup for the United States and would stand the nation in good stead long after the Carter administration. Had he lived that long, West would have gotten pleasure from the efforts by Abdullah, as Saudi king in 2008, to loosen the tightly restrictive travel regulations governing the closed kingdom and to open its doors very carefully to tourists from the outside world.[51]

A SUMMER OF ANXIETIES

During the summer of 1978 the Saudis turned their attention to other matters. On their southern border a troublesome conflict between Soviet-backed South Yemen and the Saudi ally North Yemen threatened to expand into a regional fight that could involve Saudi territory. Sadat's bold initiative for a settlement with Israel seemed to be foundering, and while Arab fears that he would be overthrown had not materialized, there was still unrest that the initiatives had fallen into deadlock. Meanwhile, Fahd still had hopes of reviving the Saudi ambitions for Arab unity, and he embarked on a mission to Egypt and Syria in late July. Things went well for Fahd, and he extended the trip an extra day to visit Baghdad.

Arab unity, it turned out, was not what the Carter administration was promoting at the moment, particularly if it was Arab unity against an Egypt-Israel agreement. It seemed, in fact, a distraction from the primary U.S. goal of supporting Anwar Sadat in his peace initiatives toward Israel. On August 4 West received a message from Washington, which he described as "plain and, I think, as offensive as any I've ever seen. It in effect told the Saudis to stop messing up Sadat's peace efforts and leave the leadership to us."[52]

West was able to dilute what he considered the peremptory tone of the note, but when he tried out the message on his touchy friend Saud al-Faisal, he said the foreign minister was "belligerent" and that their conversation resulted in a "knockdown drag-out" tussle.[53] Three days later the White House had calmed itself sufficiently to recognize that the Saudi allies deserved better treatment. West was summoned to Alexandria, Egypt, to be told by Secretary Vance that the Camp David talks involving Carter, Begin, and Sadat had been scheduled and that he was to carry the news directly to King Khalid in person.

West's meeting with Vance was an early-morning affair in the secretary's suite, which West described as follows:

> [I] went up to see Cy and found him still in pajamas eating breakfast. He told me that he had met with Sadat for about 2 hours and the news was good. [He] got us all in at 9:30 then and told us that a meeting had been arranged among Sadat, Begin, and Carter at Camp David on September 5.
>
> Sadat had finally agreed. The President is evidently going to make an all-out last-ditch effort to get them together. We discussed various aspects and it was decided that I would leave immediately to notify the Saudis before the announcement is made.[54]

According to a report in the *Washington Post*, Vance may have actually been caught by surprise by the ease with which Sadat agreed to the meeting. He accepted the invitation "seconds after . . . Vance extended it to him without asking for any assurances of new Israeli concessions, a senior state department official said last night." Sadat's quick acceptance, the *Post* story speculated, "suggested that the Egyptian leader was eager to find a way . . . to keep alive the peace progress he set in motion eight months earlier."[55]

In his 1991 book *The Carter Years*, Richard C. Thornton speculated that from the beginning, "Anwar Sadat was eager to align Egypt with the United States. In effect, Sadat's scheme was to have Washington negotiate with Israel on Egypt's behalf."[56] There was more than Middle East diplomacy on the minds of Sadat and other occupants of that politically delicate part of the planet. Disruptions in the nearby Horn of Africa between the Somalis and the Ethiopians were causing major anxieties among the Egyptians, Saudis, and others and were making American involvement a matter of practical and immediate military interest, as well as political expediency.

Whatever the motives and intrigues behind Sadat's behavior may have been, West beat a hasty return to Saudi Arabia to smooth feathers that might have been ruffled in the scuffling before the announcement. He found the kingdom's princes scattered in various locations and difficult to reach. At about ten o'clock that evening, he tracked down Saud. According to West, Saud "had already heard about it by then, but realized we had made an extraordinary effort to inform him before the news was made public. I also reassured him that the President and the Secretary were not backing away from anything they had said."[57]

A day later West called on Fahd after being told by Saud that he would recommend that a statement of Saudi support for the Camp David meeting be issued. The meeting with Fahd, according to West, turned out to be cordial and productive, and Fahd agreed to issue the statement of support. "He was agreeable to almost everything and the meeting lasted almost an hour and a quarter," West wrote in his journal. "He started out by taking the offensive, castigating those who would start rumors about the Saudis trying to undermine the peace process. Everyone was elated at the outcome."[58] Less than a week later, West wrote, "He [Saud] gave us a letter from the King giving further support to the Camp David summit so the Saudis are really going all-out."[59]

A FRIENDSHIP IN JEOPARDY

These would prove to be among the few remaining moments of elation during the West ambassadorship. For the man who enjoyed nothing more than celebrations, friendships, and the politics of the cocktail hour, the gulf was deepening between the Carter administration's urgency on the Egypt-Israel peace effort and the Saudis' growing interest in Arab unity and the security of its borders with neighboring states. For all the acclaim given the Sadat-Begin peace breakthroughs as shepherded by the Carter administration, those labored parleys would actually drive a wedge between the American and Saudi leaders and would place West in an uncomfortable position politically, diplomatically, and personally.

By August 21 the Saudis were becoming peevish at the White House expectations over the Camp David meeting, and Saud told West bluntly that the Yemen trouble was more important than Camp David. West began devoting more attention to the festering trouble on the Saudis' southern border and became embroiled in another tug-of-war with the State Department over U.S. military aid to the Saudi ally North Yemen. West, curious about the extent of Saud's concerns, set about planning a trip to the ancient kingdom of North Yemen, but a response was passed through State Department channels that such a visit might not be a good idea at the time.

The message enraged West, who attributed it to one of his adversaries within the department. He later wrote that he "raised hell" and passed it along that "I was going privately, paying my own way, and [I] just wanted to know if the department was telling me I couldn't go! [I] asked to find out if Mr. Vance were in town." West got a call back in an hour telling him to go ahead to North Yemen.[60]

The ambassador spent three peaceful days in the ancient desert kingdom. In the ensuing days he nursed along an agreement from Carter that the United States would extend the maximum military aid it could to the small nation, absent a mutual defense treaty. However, he wondered in an entry in his journal if the Saudis were not exaggerating the dangers in the Yemens. The whole affair took on the appearance of something of a charade, given the smallness of the two sheikdoms and their armies. The Saudis' complaints seemed intended to draw attention away from the Egypt-Israel peace talks; later the Carter administration would use the Yemen threat as reason for the Saudis to buy into large new U.S. defense commitments.

In the tense run-up to the Camp David meeting, a report appeared in the August 28 *Newsweek* that West had been involved in a secret initiative by Israel to set up a meeting between Israeli foreign minister Moshe Dayan and Crown Prince Fahd. The initiative, it was reported, was part of Israel's quiet effort "to build bridges to the Arab world's political moderates. . . . The Saudis apparently viewed the Israeli overture as an attempt to split the Arab ranks and they told West they weren't interested," according to *Newsweek*.[61]

For whatever reason—West's growing friendship with the Saudis, his pessimism about overall chances for an Arab-Israeli settlement, his friction with the State Department, or any other factor—Camp David received little attention from West in his journal during the historic September 5–17 summit. On the opening day of the talks, September 5—which West recorded as Lois's birthday—he met with King Khalid, Fahd, Saud, and Abdullah. After a brief discussion over an exchange of letters with President Carter over Camp David, the conversation turned more lengthily to the Yemen crisis and the potential threat from Soviet and Cuban armed forces. Later in the week the Wests and office staff spent a couple of days with Zaki Yamani and his family at the oil minister's mountain home in Taif. In conversations with Yamani, West wrote, "We covered all the problems, from oil production to the Russian threat, women working, etc."[62] However, there was no mention of Camp David. On September 10 West made a simple eight-word entry in his journal: "No news of any importance about Camp David."[63]

On Monday, September 18—the day after the signing of the historic accords—West made another brief entry. He wrote, "We had news from Camp David—it seems to be a success—and a letter from the President to the King also [includes] the invitation for Fahd to come to Washington," an idea, West noted, that had originated with him and Isa Sabbagh.[64]

That night Carter made his historic report to Congress describing the two outcomes of the Begin-Sadat conference:

(1) "A Framework for Peace in the Middle East Agreed at Camp David," which Carter described as dealing with "comprehensive settlement between Israel and all her neighbors, as well as the difficult question of the Palestinian people and the future of the West Bank and Gaza," and

(2) "A Framework for the Conclusion of a Peace Treaty between Egypt and Israel," a treaty which would call for Israel turning over control of the Sinai to Egypt and Egypt extending full diplomatic recognition to Israel. Such an agreement would be concluded in three months, Carter said.[65]

All manner of sensitivities were loosed by the accords and the president's speech. Critical to acceptance of the agreement by moderate Arab states such as Saudi Arabia and Jordan had been the belief that Begin would agree to a freeze on Israeli settlements on the West Bank and Gaza Strip, an agreement that Carter believed Begin would convey by letter immediately after the signing of the accords. The letter, as it turned out, contained an agreement to freeze such settlements for only three months. Other unresolved issues dealt with the governance of the West Bank as a Palestinian homeland, which was seen in the accords as emerging from a future Egypt-Israel-Jordan agreement. There was no mention made of Jerusalem or the Golan Heights, Syria's critical issue. The overall impact was one of disappointment among America's Arab friends.

ARAB BACKLASH TO CAMP DAVID

Unleashed by that disappointment were powerful forces that would dim the "special relationship" of the United States and Saudi Arabia and cloud West's credibility and effectiveness. Hermann Eilts, the U.S. ambassador to Egypt who had also served in Saudi Arabia, called the breakdown of the agreement on

West Bank settlements "an ignominious collapse of the U.S. position." He said, "It destroyed the last chance of obtaining moderate Arab support."[66]

The Saudi response was strong and critical. While diplomatically thanking the United States for making the effort, the kingdom took the position that the accords were "an unacceptable formula for a definitive peace" and enumerated its complaints about the issues of West Bank–Gaza settlements, Jerusalem, self-determination for the Palestinians, and PLO recognition, among others. Jordan called the accords "a fig leaf" and "pure sugar coating." The PLO condemned it as "the most disastrous sell-out of the Palestinian cause ever," and the "stead-fastness" (called "rejectionist" by Vance) states of Syria, Algeria, Libya, and South Yemen were equally virulent in their criticism.[67]

For all the high-octane language being flung around the diplomatic hall-ways, West and the Saudis worked to keep their cool. West called the Saudi statement "somewhat negative" and said that the Saudis were "shocked that we didn't like it. I told them it was discourteous because they prejudged the sum-mit results before the Secretary could explain it to them."[68] Immediately upon making his address to Congress, Carter had dispatched Vance on the difficult mission of restoring confidence among key Arab allies, Saudi Arabia and Jordan.

West paid a call on Fahd later that day and later wrote, "He was the usual ole' smoothie. He did not once mention the statement, but said that he wanted more ammunition, primarily on the Palestinian question. I told him that we knew as much as anyone about the Palestinian question because Isa [Sabbagh] was our most senior advisor, and he was a Palestinian and had lived the prob-lem since its inception. Fahd immediately recognized that."[69]

Despite the worrisome statement, Vance felt that the Saudis were leaving their options open on the Camp David issues and that there was still "a slen-der chance that the Camp David accords might make the basis of a compre-hensive settlement." However, he also sensed that the Saudis felt caught in the middle of an Arab world that "was in danger of being polarized by the Camp David accords."[70]

Vance wrote that most of the Jordanian and Saudi ire was directed toward Sadat. "They believed he had given them an explicit commitment before the summit to negotiate a comprehensive settlement in which the rest of the Arabs could join, at least support, without unacceptable political risk," Vance wrote. "Instead, they told me, most of the Arab world was attacking Sadat. . . . [He] had let them down for making a separate peace in exchange for the return of the Sinai."[71]

On that shaky note negotiations were launched in follow-up to the Camp David accords to create an actual Egypt-Israel peace treaty. What had been envisioned as a three-month process stretched into a six-month ordeal, which became a test of tolerances among all the parties involved. At issue were the same questions that had snarled the Camp David meetings and had been left largely unresolved: Israeli settlements on the West Bank, governance of a Palestinian state, the Golan Heights, and the status of Jerusalem.

Overshadowing the fragile Israel-Egypt activity, however, loomed a development that threatened to reshape the entire political landscape of the Middle East and to strike a serious blow to U.S. influence in the area. For months political unrest had threatened the government of Shah Reza Pahlavi of Iran, the monarch whose twenty-five-year reign atop the Iranian throne was directly attributable to an August 1953 coup backed by the United States and Great Britain. That coup resulted in the overthrow of the popularly elected prime minister Mohammad Mossadeq and his replacement with a monarchy friendly to U.S. and British interests. In the anticommunist frenzy of the cold-war 1950s in the United States, Mossadeq had seemed too friendly with the Russians, and he was threatening to nationalize the British-dominated oil production in the country.

The shah's regime had survived over the years largely as a client state of the United States, providing what American leaders considered the upper geographical tier of defense against the Russian threat and serving increasingly, along with Saudi Arabia, as one of the major sources of oil for the United States and other Western nations. The shah's rule, however, had never been popular with many Iranians, who still viewed him as a colonial sachem of U.S. interests being imposed on the nation. As the influence of the Shiite cleric Ayatollah Ruhollah Khomeini increased in the shaky kingdom, the Carter administration found itself divided on a strategy to deal with the threat to the shah. On the one hand, Vance was favoring a negotiated support for a coalition government including Khomeini; on the other hand, Brzezinski, who was increasingly becoming Vance's rival for Carter's attention and influence, favored an internal military takeover of Iran. As the United States groped for a position, opposition to the shah grew. On September 8, 1978, some twenty thousand Iranians gathered in Tehran to protest the shah's regime. Iranian armed forces killed hundreds and wounded thousands of the demonstrators in what became a landmark moment for Iranian dissidents.

The decline of Iranian stability placed new pressures on Saudi Arabia and its American allies. There was the ready perception that the same anti-American Islamic militancy that was driving the shah from power in Iran might be replicated in the Saudi desert kingdom. There was also the immediate concern that a cutoff of Iranian oil supplies to the United States and other Western nations would place increased reliance on the Saudi oil fields. On Friday, January 26,

1979, as the Iranian situation grew more desperate, Carter's secretary of commerce, Juanita M. Kreps, made a stop in Saudi Arabia during a Middle East tour.

West wrote that Kreps brought "a message from the President about a possible increase in the oil prices applicable to the increased production the Saudis were doing to offset the Iranian situation." West's inside sources had informed him that such a position would be ill-advised at the time. West called Washington and suggested that "the priority of the Kreps trip should be to see Fahd and present the message asking for a freeze—or at least not an increase—on the oil prices."[72] West's entreaties went largely unheeded, and he reported the next day, "She had instructions from Washington to make a strong pitch to keep production up and prices down. Isa [Sabbagh] and I thought the message was very abrasive and tried to soften it, but succeeded only partially. We went to the palace and waited for nearly an hour, but Fahd saw us—and Juanita made her pitch."[73]

According to Holden and Johns, Kreps claimed in an interview with the Jeddah newspaper, the *Arab News,* that the Saudis had given assurances that production would be maintained at 10–10.5 million barrels a day, while the Saudi policy was actually limited to 9.5 million barrels a day for the first quarter of 1979. This was reminiscent of a December 1978 visit by Treasury Secretary Michael Blumenthal during which Saudi officials promised that they would hold the line on oil price increases, only to turn around a month later and support an OPEC price rise from $12.70 a barrel to $13.34.[74]

Zaki Yamani's biographer later wrote that the meeting of Kreps and Fahd actually proved damaging not only to the increasingly delicate U.S.-Saudi friendship but also to the long-term relations between the oil minister and the crown prince. "According to an ex-official at the US Embassy," Jeffrey Robinson wrote,

> Fahd made some wild promises to Kreps, presumably regarding the increase in production, regarding Saudi oil policy towards the four Aramco companies. He then drafted a formal letter which he sent to Yamani, ordering his oil minister to make good on those promises. Copies of that letter were widely circulated at the time around the Embassy and in Washington. But Fahd's pipe dreams were never put into effect. Yamani refused.
>
> After [King] Faisal, Yamani didn't always do what he was told to. In fact, that's one of the reasons he became an irritant to Fahd.[75]

The actual exchanges between West and Yamani and their outcomes are uncertain. However, the growing pressures from Washington, West's increasingly delicate role as intermediary, and the stress being felt within the Saudi leadership reflected the darkening days of Saudi-U.S. relations and foretold the deepening Middle East schisms that would leave the Carter administration and its Middle East ambitions seriously strained.

SHOCKS AND TREMORS IN THE MIDDLE EAST

Across a broad range of issues and events, the early days of 1979 were becoming especially troubling ones for the Saudis. On January 23 the shah departed from Iran, leaving a fragile and unstable "regency" government and suspect army in his place. A little more than a week later Ayatollah Khomeini returned to Iran, sending shocks and tremors through the Persian Gulf area and leaving the Saudis "alarmed and aghast at what was happening."[76] Pro-Israeli interests in Washington, led by Senator Frank Church of Idaho, were unhappy with the Saudis' lukewarm attitude toward the Camp David accords and were threatening to revisit the decision to sell the F-15 jets to the Saudis. As the treaty negotiations labored onward with Carter, Begin, and Sadat, the Saudis fretted that their longtime ally Egypt was becoming too friendly with their longtime opponent Israel. On top of all that, Crown Prince Fahd, on whom much of the burden of day-to-day leadership had fallen, was beginning to fade in that role. "Fahd was listless, tired and unwell," wrote Holden and Johns. "He was overweight and suffering from diabetes, both of which conditions were aggravated by his consumption of up to sixty cups of sweet tea a day."[77]

Things began coming to a head in late February. Carter was taking the offensive in seeking Saudi support for the Egypt-Israel treaty. Besides Secretary Kreps, Carter dispatched Defense Secretary Harold Brown and National Security Adviser Brzezinski during the weeks leading up to the anticipated completion of the treaty. He also extended an invitation to Crown Prince Fahd to visit Washington, an invitation the Saudis reportedly accepted provisionally.

The invitation turned out to be a tempest of surprising diplomatic proportions. As tensions grew over the prospective Egypt-Israel treaty, the Saudis fretted over the potential awkwardness of having their crown prince subjected to heavy pressure in Washington to support the treaty. The Carter White House, in turn, did not wish to suffer a public snub from the Saudis on what it hoped would be the eve of the treaty signing. Amid confusing and mixed signals, a story appeared in the Washington press that the Fahd visit had been cancelled for reasons of the crown prince's health. The report infuriated Saud, who lashed out at West. The ambassador, in turn, blamed Saudi sources in Washington for the leak, and another West-Saud tirade ensued.

"I told him that if the leak reflected anything like the present relationship between the U.S. and Saudi Arabia, then I had been badly fooled—that I had been telling my government that despite the problems we were still in a good relationship, but according to this story it was completely bad and the cancellation was for that reason," West wrote.[78] The exchange cooled, but the situation did not get much better for West in the weeks ahead. Saud was making the rounds of the Saudis' best friends among the Arab nations—Iraq, Syria, and Jordan—and even suggested at one time that the kingdom might consider a relationship with the Russians. "My conclusion was that he was sending the United States a message—and a part of our testing," West wrote.[79]

In early March, Carter decided to resort to shuttle diplomacy to push Sadat and Begin toward agreement on a peace treaty, and on March 7 he made trips to Egypt and Israel with new proposals. Holden and Johns called this strategy "a breathtaking gamble."[80] Fahd felt diplomatically ignored and trapped between his increasingly restive Arab friends, the pressure from Carter, and his diminishing hopes for some sign of friendship from Egypt. On March 8 West was summoned by a worried Fahd and an angry Saud and was told "how gravely Riyadh regarded Carter's initiative."[81] West was asked by Saud "to deliver personally an invitation to the U.S. President, who was still in Egypt, to come to the Kingdom before proceeding, as he had planned, straight to Jerusalem."[82] West got nowhere with that proposal.

It was a time of deepening annoyance and even some self-doubt for the chronically upbeat West, the happy warrior who had spent his political life winning friends and finding ways to pull enemies together. This time, it seemed, nothing he did seemed to reconcile the differences between his bosses—the Carter administration—and his friends—the enigmatic Saudi leaders. Three days before he had been called on the carpet by Fahd and Saud (on March 5) he paid a call on Prince Turki al-Faisal and laid out his frustrations. "I told him that I was becoming concerned about my effectiveness as an ambassador," West wrote, "that while I recognized differences in policy, I did not think that the relationship was as strained as reports in the newspaper . . . had indicated, and that I had so reported to the White House that the continued Saudi insistence that the postponement [of Fahd's trip to Washington] was because of pique and dissatisfaction was causing me great concern, and if this were true, and I had not been able to sense it, then my usefulness was probably ended."[83]

West said that Turki was animated and complimentary toward the U.S. ambassador. "I told him I wasn't looking for compliments, I was just looking for facts and that I considered our special relationship to be based on mutual self-interest. . . . [For] to put it in very simple form, we needed their oil and they needed our security."[84] Years later, while serving as Saudi ambassador to Great Britain, Prince Turki recalled West's concerns and affirmed that the Saudis did not wish to lose their good friend John West as U.S. ambassador. They made their feelings known to the Carter administration.[85]

Through all the shifting strategies, new leverages emerged. Brown and Brzezinski were arriving with beefed-up guarantees of defense protection for the Saudis, protection from the South Yemen–Soviet threat, as well as protection from as yet undefined communist enemies. From Brown came the proposals, as West wrote in his journal, that amounted to "an all-out commitment of help in any way Saudi Arabia wanted it."[86] Such defense guarantees would be by inference the prize for Saudi support of the Egypt-Israel peace treaty. The Saudis, however, had their own new leverages. It hardly took a Princeton or Georgetown degree to figure out that with the probable removal of Iran as one of the two major American sources of Mideast oil, the Saudis were the big kids on the block in oil production for American customers. They had the United States over an oil barrel.

So the Saudis could remain coy, and they did, greeting the various emissaries with courtesies and offering guarded encouragement. They also were aware that Carter's negotiations with Begin were not going well. The Israeli prime minister was pulling back from the table and threatening to terminate negotiations with no treaty at all. He stonewalled Carter on a number of critical issues and wound up yielding little beyond what he had begrudgingly offered at Camp David months earlier. The Arabs' hopes for movement in addressing the issues of Palestinian statehood, West Bank settlements, and Jerusalem were still unfulfilled. The president would have little to show for all the effort other than the extraordinary image of a light-skinned Jew and a dark-skinned Arab agreeing to still largely undefined conditions of peace—although this image was so powerful that it would propel all three toward Oslo and Nobel Peace Prizes. Much of the treaty still had the aspects of a gentleman's agreement, and the Saudis were not buying anything that ephemeral. At the moment when Carter most wanted his "special relationship" with the Saudis to show solidarity to the world, he would wind up with only some friendly "attaboys," some privately conveyed good wishes, and tantalizing requests for more substance to pass along to their Arab allies.

The peace treaty was signed on March 26 to the acclaim of a world hopeful that it represented a breakthrough in Middle East diplomacy. In Saudi Arabia, however, West reported little more than a few personal congratulations to him from various sources. Tensions were high, and security around the U.S. ambassador was stepped up. The Saudis, however, were officially quiet until two months later, when a disgruntled Prince Fahd said that "there are many doors open to us and we can replace the Americans any time we want." There were, he said, "few wise men in the United States who realize the importance of their interests with Saudi Arabia . . . [to] ask themselves if the American line is identical to that of Israel."[87]

In May 1980 another stinging statement came from Fahd, combating perceptions that U.S. and Saudi relations had grown warmer. Fahd denied such speculation and declared that "a just and comprehensive solution cannot be achieved unless Israel withdraws from all the Arab territories occupied in 1967, including, first and foremost, Holy Jerusalem. No solution of the Palestinian issue can achieve peace unless it is based on recognition of the Palestinian people's legitimate rights to return and to self-determination, including the setting up of an independent state on their territory."[88]

A cruel irony was being played out in a scenario in which the U.S. president, his ambassador to Saudi Arabia, and all the forces at their command could not bring together America's best friend in the Middle East—Israel—and its best friend among the Arab nations—Saudi Arabia. Years later President Carter wrote of the frustration of the elevated expectations and pressures placed on the Saudis at the time. "We expected them to moderate the Arab condemnation of Sadat after his peace initiative, to support strongly the Camp David accords, [and] to induce the Jordanians and the Palestinians to join the peace talks. . . . We were often disappointed—and even at times angry—when our expectations were not met." The lesson, Carter wrote, was that "Americans and many others expect too much from them and fail to recognize that, with all their wealth and prestige, the Saudis do not have unbounded influence in the Middle East."[89]

It was a lesson learned in the heat of combat. For West and Carter, it was particularly painful to observe that the special brand of southern politics they hoped would create a new diplomatic idiom for the region—that mixture of personal engagement, friendship, and goodwill—had met its match in the form of the ancient Arab invocation of *Inshallah,* that shadowy, fatalistic term meaning "If Allah wills." In a matter of months the elation and euphoria in Riyadh over approval of the F-15 jet sales had been replaced by disillusionment and shattered expectations of the Camp David accords and the Egypt-Israel treaty. Questions would be raised as to the long-term price the United States had paid for that treaty.

DANGEROUS TIMES FOR AMERICANS

It was my damn neck, and if I felt safe, I didn't see why [the State Department] kept worrying us with all the paperwork.

John West

As disappointed as President Carter may have been with the Saudis over their tepid reception of the Egypt-Israel treaty, his reaction was mild compared to the uproar from Arab nations upset that the Saudis did not denounce the treaty more vigorously. The Saudis were living up to the pledge they had made quietly to the United States not to harm Egypt materially, and it was proving to be a painful experience for them. At an Arab summit meeting in Baghdad, which came only days after the treaty signing, PLO chairman Yasir Arafat told Saud al-Faisal, who represented the kingdom at the meeting, that he was a "disgrace to his father [King Faisal]." He also reportedly said, "Do not force us to become a band of assassins." The Saudis found themselves to be in an awkward position. Holden and Johns wrote, "Saudi Arabia's will, as well as its ability to resist [increases in oil prices], had been weakened by its dissatisfaction with the Egyptian-Israeli peace treaty and its disillusion with the U.S."[1]

Ambassador West had similar reports about the tumultuous meeting and the rifts among the Arab states. He wrote, "Seems as though Arafat had said that the late King Faisal had lived and died for Islamic traditions and now they were being betrayed by Saudi Arabia. Of course, Saud got very mad and insisted that Arafat listen to his answer—which Arafat refused to do—and walked out, followed by the Libyan and Syrian delegations. Saud talked for an hour and a half anyhow."[2]

With the usual exercise of Arab ambivalence, Arafat had passed a message to West a day earlier through Jihad Khazan, former editor of the *Arab News*. According to West, he "wanted to tell me that we needed understanding—that as long as the Syrians surrounded the PLO there was nothing he could do about helping the peace process. A very conciliatory message—particularly in light of his public statement yesterday of cutting the President's hand off along with Begin and Sadat for signing the peace treaty."[3]

By then, dealing with the rhetorical extremes and emotional eruptions of Middle East politics was almost a matter of business as usual for West. He had become a seasoned filter for many of the intemperate diatribes that passed for communications in those overheated days, and he could step back from the fray far enough for all parties involved to take deep diplomatic breaths. In the days after the treaty signing, Crawford Cook reported to him that the U.S. press was characterizing Saudi Arabia as having caved in to the Islamic radicals in its diffidence toward the peace treaty, and Prince Saud went into seclusion for a week after the fury of the Baghdad conference. West spent some time drafting a paper containing his thoughts about the future of U.S.-Saudi relations and what he was viewing as a crisis in the "special relationship" that had existed between the nations.

By April 3 some sense of normalcy was being restored. West visited his friend Prince Sultan, the Saudi defense minister and Bandar's father. He stated "positively that nothing that happened at Baghdad should prejudice our [U.S.-Saudi] bilateral relationships." West was also able to resume contact with the prickly Prince Saud and to continue what was by now their familiarly contentious relationship. "It was the Princeton Debating Society all over again," West wrote, referring to Saud's alma mater, Princeton University. "Two hours—on what the U.S. ought to do with respect to the Mid-East peace—namely pressuring Begin."[4]

Later in the month West met with the Policy Review Committee in Washington: President Carter's top-level advisers Vance, Brzezinski, Energy Secretary James Schlesinger, Treasury Secretary Michael Blumenthal, and Defense Secretary Harold Brown. He wrote of that meeting, "We had quite a go-around and the net result was much as I had wanted—namely a period of cooling off with repairing of personal relationships, etc., with the Saudis—not pushing them any harder on support until and unless we had something tangible to offer them."[5]

LOOMING CRISIS IN IRAN

In the meantime events unfolding elsewhere would occupy much higher priorities for Americans and Saudis in the months ahead. Even as Carter, Begin, and

Sadat were applying their signatures to a document they hoped would open doors to regional peace, deteriorating conditions in Iran were producing nightmarish diplomatic prospects for the United States and unsettling options for anyone in the Middle East who professed friendship or support for American interests.

The early days of 1979 brought the simmering Iranian troubles to a crisis point. Two weeks after the departure of the beleaguered Shah Reza Pahlavi on January 16 to self-imposed exile in Morocco, Ayatollah Ruhollah Khomeini made a triumphant return to Iran. On February 9 the last government resistance to his revolutionary forces collapsed, and the remnants of the Iranian army declared themselves neutral in the uprising. By February 11 the revolutionaries had control of Tehran. Prime Minister Shapour Bakhtiar went into seclusion, and a provisional government was created under Khomeini's designee Mahdi Bazargan.[6]

Khomeini's power lay not only in the antisecularism he had been promoting since his earliest days as a student in Muslim seminaries in Iran; he was also a leading Shia scholar and represented a powerful voice in the centuries-old schism within Islam between the Sunni and Shia beliefs. The argument went back to the disagreement at the death of Muhammad as to whether the succession should be only through members of the family, as the Shia believe, or the succession should be elected, as the Sunni believe. The Shia outnumbered the Sunni throughout the Muslim world, but in Saudi Arabia the Wahhabi faith was Sunni and was therefore favored by the House of Saud. Within each Muslim nation, regardless of which belief was supported by the leadership, the Sunni-Shia division was a source of tense and often violent encounters and contributed to an ongoing sense of instability.

Compared to the gradual pace in the decline of the shah's government during 1978, the resolution of affairs in Iran within a matter of days in early 1979 shocked the Carter White House and produced deepening rifts between National Security Adviser Brzezinski and Secretary of State Vance. Brzezinski had advocated a military coup in support of pro-Western interests, while Vance had been prodding the shah toward accommodation with opposition elements. Even as Khomeini's presence drastically changed things, Vance held out for a flexible U.S. role in support of a transitional coalition government. As it turned out, the unexpectedly swift turn of events left the United States seemingly indecisive and virtually powerless. In a matter of days the onetime staunch American ally was being transformed into an Islamic republic whose leader would call the United States the "Great Satan." The fall of the shah, in the words of Brzezinski, was "a political calamity" for President Carter and had implications far beyond the Middle East. It contributed "centrally" to Carter's political defeat in 1981.[7]

For West, the rapid changes in Iran would have personal and painful ramifications. During 1978 he had added to the embassy staff a particularly promising young career diplomat by the name of John W. Limbert. Equipped with B.A., M.A., and Ph.D. degrees from Harvard University, Limbert had extensive experience in Iran, having served there as a Peace Corps volunteer (1964–66) and as an English instructor at Shiraz University in southern Iran (1969–72). He had married an Iranian woman, Parveneh, and was fluent in Farsi, the dominant language in Iran.

West and Limbert hit it off well, and the ambassador handed his young staffer important writing and analysis assignments over the course of his early months in Saudi Arabia. As things grew grimmer in Iran in early 1979, West noted, the State Department was advised to "clean out" the Iranian embassy and to solicit volunteers for the hazardous post. "I knew that John Limbert couldn't resist . . . so he volunteered, and he was selected."[8]

At that point, however, the status of Limbert's family became an issue. West remembered Limbert telling him that he had no family in the United States to care for Parveneh and their two young children, and the hazardous duty in Tehran required that Limbert take up the post alone. Under those circumstances Limbert would be forced to resign, and West recalled telling him, "You're too valuable to resign. Let me see what we can do."[9]

The solution turned out to be another unorthodox John West maneuver. "There was an old building on the [U.S. Embassy] compound and we got the General Services Office to go in and redo it as a two-bedroom apartment [for Limbert's family]." West remembered that he was able to get Parveneh Limbert a position with the embassy as an interpreter to justify her housing, and he worked out an arrangement for Limbert to travel to Jeddah frequently to visit his family. "I went to the Saudi Airlines and for the amount of money that he would get to make two trips a year from the States, they gave him a pass that would allow him to make two visits a month [from Iran to Saudi Arabia]."[10]

THINKING THE UNTHINKABLE

Limbert took up his new post on August 18, 1979. Only months earlier the United States had gotten a preliminary taste of the kind of brutal realities the diplomatic corps would be facing in that unstable city. On February 14, less than a week after Khomeini's return to Iran, the U.S. Embassy in Tehran was overrun by students, and recently appointed ambassador William H. Sullivan and embassy staff were held hostage for several hours. Even though the hostages were freed by the end of the day, the event was sufficient to elevate the level of alarm at the embassy to full-blown crisis proportions. Sullivan, a State Department veteran of Southeast Asia service, conveyed the sense of desperation by telling the White House that it was time "to think the unthinkable." John Limbert recalled that the term "unthinkable" had been used in embassy messages as early as the autumn of 1978 in reference to the possible downfall of the shah.[11] Its usage in this instance won Sullivan no friends among jittery Carter officials at the time, but it would prove to be a gruesomely accurate assessment of things as they stood and an ominous foreboding of the "unthinkable" calamity that lay only months down the road.[12]

On February 14, the day of the first U.S. Embassy takeover in Iran, Adolph Dubs, the U.S. ambassador to Afghanistan, was kidnapped, and a day later he was killed in an incident that the Carter administration linked to Soviet interests in the Marxist-controlled country. The sudden escalation of terror and danger for U.S. personnel in the Middle East came home clearly to the affable American ambassador in Saudi Arabia. During the course of a meeting with the ambassador to Great Britain, John Wilton, West made this notation, "He [Wilton] made a great comment having to do with the death of Ambassador Dubs and the capturing of Ambassador Sullivan on yesterday. 'You know, the general perception of us Ambassadors as guzzling tax-free gin most of the time is bound to be reassessed somewhere in the world today in light of yesterday's events.'"[13]

About that time West got word that Limbert had been accepted for the Tehran assignment. Two days later he wrote in his journal, "The Iranian situation [is] blowing up and we got permission to use Saudi Arabia as an evacuation point [for U.S. citizens in Iran]."[14]

Speculation that the Saudi Arabian monarchy might be the next to topple was stirring among Western journalists, and West traced at least some of that accelerated speculation to reports from the Central Intelligence Agency (CIA) in Jeddah. West said in an interview years after his experience in Saudi Arabia:

It turned out that right after the Shah fell, suddenly—why, of course—the CIA got a lot of criticism, much of it probably undeserved. They didn't foresee [the] fall of the Shah, so the agency in Saudi was asked to do an assessment of the strength of the Saudi [regime]. Would it go [the way of] the Shah?

Well, we had some real problems at the time. Fahd's health wasn't good, and we had some minor problems that had created some difficulties. But the CIA wrote a report which said that the Saudis were [in] much the same situation that the Shah of Iran was . . . they didn't think the Saudi government would last six months to a year.

I did a memo saying that I disagreed with them, that [while] we had difficulties with the Saudi government, [it] had widespread support among the people and did not have any particular unrest. So this fellow had access [to] the CIA report and did a major article on it. . . .

He said the only dissenter was President Carter's political appointee, John West, [who] had no background in the Mideast and had obviously been brainwashed by the Saudi royal family.

West recalled months later meeting the writer of the article at a reception in New York and offering to buy him a drink. According to West, "I said that part about me being brainwashed by the royal family . . . I had [it] translated into Arabic and sent it to every member of the royal family. [It] did more for my credibility than anything else you could have done. So, I said, I owe you a drink."[15]

Another account of the CIA assessment of Saudi stability came from the *Wall Street Journal* correspondent Yaroslav Trofimov in his book *The Siege of Mecca*. In the wake of the Iranian takeover, Trofimov wrote, "the CIA . . . saw little reason to worry about Saudi Arabia's stability. The agency, which found it extremely difficult to procure information in the tightly knit and pathologically secretive Saudi kingdom, had no inkling of Juhayman's agitation [to seize the mosque at Mecca], and discounted the Iranian threat."[16]

A *Time* magazine article published in early 1979 gave three reasons why Saudi Arabia would not suffer the fate of Iran: (1) the Saudis' closeness to the people of the kingdom; (2) Saudi attention to its fundamentalist religious roots in the Wahhabi sect of Sunni Muslims; and (3) the Saudis' use of the country's vast petrodollar fortunes to prop up moderate Arab regimes in the area. "Unlike the Shah, a stern, remote and isolated figure, the huge Saudi ruling family, with its estimated 5,000 princes, has its roots in the lives of its people," the article conjectured. "Its members are married into the families of commoners all over the country. They take their places in the chain of command below non-royals in the civil service. Saudi rulers take their 'desert democracy' seriously, [and] even the lowliest citizens can approach King Khalid or Crown Prince Fahd with a complaint during their daily *majilis* (councils)."[17]

Sandra Mackey wrote, "There is a golden road between the crown and the tribal sheikhs, paved with gracious hospitality, various economic rewards, and direct entrée to the king. But access to the king is not limited to the ulema (Islamic hierarchy) and the sheikhs. At the king's weekly *majilis,* his lowliest subjects kiss his cheeks, then his nose, and finally his shoulder as they press their crumpled pieces of paper with their request on his majesty. And every Saudi realistically expects the king to deliver."[18]

IRANIAN IMPACT IN SAUDI ARABIA

For all his bravado, West was becoming deeply concerned about Iranian developments. Five days after the fall of the Bakhtiar government in February, West met the first refugees from Iran. Three Iranians, partners in an architectural and engineering firm in Tehran, along with the brother of John Limbert's wife, Parveneh, had fled and were staying with the Limberts in Jeddah. "They were very discouraged," West wrote.[19]

Shortly after that and less than a week after the U.S. Embassy in Tehran had been attacked, West had a heart-to-heart with Prince Bandar about the potential Iranian impact on the Saudi kingdom:

> I started out by telling him I wanted to help them unofficially and as a friend, not as a representative of the government . . . that we had, of course, been doing exhaustive analyses of the similarities between Saudi Arabia and Iran, and we found a lot of dissimilarities, along with some similarities. I told him the differences outweighed the similarities, but there were several things that disturbed me.
>
> He interrupted me to say that they were concerned, too, and he listed many of the dissimilarities, pointing out that the Saud family had won its right to the Kingdom over a period of 400 years.
>
> I told him that the legitimacy of the monarchy was certainly a strength, but the trend of the times was against monarchies. I pointed out that it was his generation that would have to face the pressures and it was a question of survival of them, their lifestyle, and their Kingdom. . . . [I told him] that in my judgment, unless some steps were taken to transform the government into a constitutional monarchy, that it would not survive for more than five years. He said he agreed—that he felt five years a safe time in terms of stability, but that he and others recognized that something had to be done. Rather surprisingly, he told me that his father [Prince Sultan] had drafts of a constitution which had been worked on and was being worked on by bright young scholars. He said it included plans for a consultative assembly.
>
> Evidently, they had had some recent discussions but had decided that now was not the time to institute it as it would look [like] a fear reaction from Iran. I told him I was delighted to hear—that I knew it was going to be difficult, but at least they were going about it in the right way.[20]

As West and the Saudis pondered the messages and signals coming from the Iranian experience, Washington's efforts to find some stability in dealing with

Tehran were becoming an ever-changing proposition, reflecting both the anarchic conditions created by the revolution and the limited effectiveness of the Carter diplomatic corps. Initial support by the United States of the shah's government under Bakhtiar backfired as that government collapsed and was replaced by the Khomeini-supported provisional government under Bazargan. Through the months of March and April 1979, Iran moved further toward the theocratic state envisioned by Khomeini, and the United States found itself uncomfortably trying to deal with a virulently anti-American regime.

Increasingly, a major issue of contention became the status of the exiled shah. Upon his departure from Iran in January, he had chosen to remain in the politically friendly Arab settings of Egypt and, later, Morocco, perhaps hoping that events in Iran might swing to his advantage and make possible his return to the country. An invitation had actually been extended for him to come to the United States upon his leaving Iran on January 16, a move that attracted no particular controversy at the time. As tensions mounted, however, particularly over U.S. support for the government under Bakhtiar, Khomeini found it politically advantageous to heat up anti-American sentiment and, in turn, to demand the return of the shah to Iran "to face revolutionary justice."[21]

On March 17, a scant two months after he had left Iran, the shah was informed that President Carter had withdrawn his invitation to come to the United States, in the interest of protecting the safety of Americans in Iran. The former Iranian leader was subsequently shunted off to the Bahamas and eventually Mexico. All the while American friends of the shah, including Henry Kissinger, David Rockefeller, John McCloy, and others, made known their continuing belief that the shah should be permitted to come to the United States.

In other diplomatic scuffles, Khomeini reacted to a U.S. Senate resolution protesting human rights violations in Iran by refusing to accept the newly designated U.S. ambassador Walter Cutler, who had been named in June to replace the departed William Sullivan. The Carter administration then sought to placate Khomeini by withdrawing Cutler's appointment and seeking to make a nomination acceptable to the Khomeini regime. According to one account, the name of Bruce Laingen, chargé d'affaires in Tehran in the absence of a permanent ambassador, was offered to the Iranians as a prospective ambassador, and on October 7 the Iranian government announced that it would accept him. A veteran of twenty-eight years in the Foreign Service, Laingen had served as ambassador to Malta for two years prior to being assigned to the Iranian post in 1979. John Limbert, who was serving at the Tehran embassy at the time, recalled that Laingen had actually been offered the position as ambassador to Iran in September by Bruce Newsome, a Vance deputy, and had turned it down.

"I don't think the U.S. government ever submitted Laingen's name to the Iranians," Limbert said.[22]

ACCOMMODATING THE SHAH

Whatever opportunity there may have been for Iranian-U.S. negotiation in early October, it was short lived. On October 18 came news that the shah was terminally ill with cancer. Refusal to admit him for treatment at the advanced American medical centers in New York, his backers insisted, had become a humanitarian as well as a political issue. Vance wrote: "On October 18, David Rockefeller's staff told us that the shah's condition was worsening, and that his illness could not be properly diagnosed and treated in Mexico . . . we were faced with a decision in which common decency and humanity had to be weighed against possible harm to our embassy personnel in Tehran."[23]

At that critical moment Vance believed there was sufficient political stability in Iran to withstand a strong public reaction against the admittance of the shah to the United States. With its diplomatic fingers crossed, the Carter administration decided to admit the shah, and on October 22 he arrived in New York.[24] Vance wrote, "The initial public response in Iran seemed to bear out our assessment that the Iranian government could maintain control of the situation."[25]

Meeting informally with Iranian government officials on the occasion of an independence celebration in Algeria a week later, Brzezinski had conversations with Prime Minister Mehdi Bazargan, Foreign Minister Ibrahim Yazdi, and Defense Minister Mustafa Ali Chamran. He even broached the subject of the shah, and while there was some contention, Brzezinski reported to the president and Vance that the "discussion ended very amiably, and actually throughout, the Iranians were surprisingly cordial."[26]

What neither Vance nor Brzezinski seemed to have factored into their assessment at the time was the fragility of the Bazargan government. While Washington was keeping up its hopes that the Iranian response would remain moderate, staffers inside the U.S. Embassy watched in stunned apprehension as conditions worsened around them. One of them, William J. Daugherty, the third secretary of the U.S. Mission, wrote in a 2003 article that the decision to admit the shah to the United States "utterly astonished" the embassy staff. "Not only had they [the embassy staff] warned Washington over the previous summer of the various dangers associated with such a decision, but some had even been told by Washington seniors that the consequences of the shah's admission to the United States were so obvious that no one would be 'dumb enough' to allow it."[27]

Similarly John Limbert believed that the United States misread any signal that seemed to assess the Iranian response as "moderate." He later said that "the Iranians were informed of the decision [to admit the shah] as a fait accompli. You can hardly call their response 'we'll-do-the-best we can' positive."[28]

Both Brzezinski and Vance detected sudden changes for the worse in a matter of days. By the time the Iranian officials had returned from Algeria, their meeting with Brzezinski was being used to stir up even more anti-American fervor, and—according to Vance—this contributed to the substantial weakening of the Bazargan government. When swarms of militants overwhelmed security and broke into the U.S. Embassy on November 4, there was little in the way of Iranian governmental authority in force to protect the Americans.

One hundred hostages were seized, sixty-six of them Americans, including Bruce Laingen, William Daugherty, and John Limbert, at the embassy and at the foreign ministry. According to Vance, he was awakened at 3:00 in the morning, or about 11:00 A.M. Tehran time, with the news that the U.S. Embassy had been attacked by a street mob. Elizabeth Ann Swift, chief of the embassy's political staff, gave him an account of the siege by telephone, describing how the assault had taken rioters onto the lower floor, where U.S. Marine guards were seized, and how the students worked their way to the upper floors. According to Vance, Swift lost telephone contact at 4:57 A.M. Washington time, or about 1:00 in the afternoon in Iran. Shortly thereafter she told her colleagues, "We are going down [to surrender]."[29] Swift was one of two female hostages.

Anxiety in Saudi Arabia had been building for months as the Iranian crisis unfolded. Much of that anxiety spilled out during a head-to-head exchange between West and Crown Prince Fahd a month before the seizure of the American hostages in Tehran. In his 2007 book *The Siege of Mecca*, Trofimov wrote, "Crown Prince Fahd impressed the Saudis' frustration on Ambassador West during a late-night meeting October 2, 1979, in his palace on Jeddah's Red Sea beach."[30] As West later recorded, the significance of Fahd's message was increased by the presence of the U.S. ambassador to Ethiopia, Fred Chapin, who was the Wests' guest at the time. West wrote, "We got a call from the Crown Prince's office that he wanted to see Chapin, Isa [Sabbagh, the interpreter], and me. We had suggested that might be a good thing. We left about 9:30 [in the evening], got back about 12:30. Fahd was in an expansive mood. I guess it was a fresh audience [Chapin]. At any rate, he lectured us on the American credibility as a friend and then the Arab-Israeli thing. Of course, I responded at equal lengths and it took about two hours."[31]

FAHD'S ANXIETIES

In Trofimov's version of the exchange, Fahd became heated and launched a broadside against U.S. ineffectiveness. "As Fahd saw it," Trofimov wrote,

> the Soviets, with their support for Khomeini and mischief from Ethiopia to Afghanistan, were making a push for controlling the Persian Gulf, while America manifested "seeming indifference or impotence."
>
> "Instead of pressuring the Shah into bringing his thoughts and actions up to date so as to pull the rug from under the Communist agitator, you let him go," Fahd lamented. "Look at what has happened in Iran. They have killed the cream of their society—the best brains in the military, the professions, and the civil service have all been executed or forced into exile." And after all this, Fahd continued, there had been "not a word of caution to Iran from President Carter."
>
> Fahd went on to say that other regimes were vulnerable—Pakistan among them—and that other Arab nations were anxious to see an American show of strength. "Three quarters of the Arab regimes are really with you," he [Fahd] told West, Chapin, and Isa Sabbagh, "they all await, expect and hope for their powerful, wise and morally adroit friend, the U.S., to send out the message loud and clear: enough is enough."[32]

After West "responded in equal length,"[33] Fahd had more to say. "The crown prince wouldn't relent," Trofimov wrote.

> All he had received from the United States so far were vague words instead of a "firm, unequivocal stand."
>
> "The stakes for the kingdom were just too high," he explained, and the dangers seemed far more immediate from Riyadh than from Washington. "To count the lashes is one thing, but to feel them is something else."[34]

For his part, it was probably a message West had heard before, but never so firmly. He had been on the receiving end of lectures from Yamani, Saud, and Fahd about the Saudis' vulnerability in an Arab world they considered to be made more dangerous by Carter's Camp David initiatives. West had been told, particularly by Saud in their "Princeton Debating Society" conversations, of Saudi frustrations that the United States was not more effective in pressuring the Israelis on key Arab issues such as the status of the PLO, a homeland for Palestinians, the city of Jerusalem, and other matters. Chapin's presence, as U.S. emissary in Ethiopia, a nation that was particularly worrisome to the Saudis, gave the event added dimension, and while West wrote playfully in his journal that the discussion was "all in good fun," it was clearly a moment in which the accumulated frustration of the Saudis was pouring forth. Sandra Mackey wrote that "the House of Saud interpreted the hesitancy of the United States to prop up the regime of the shah as treason against its allies. . . . If the United States were willing to desert the shah of Iran, with whom it enjoyed a far cozier relationship than with Saudi Arabia's leaders, what were the Americans to do if the House of Saud were threatened? These were profound questions for the defenseless oil producer." Saudi anxieties, Mackey wrote, "were ignored by Western governments and the presses alike."[35]

In the nineteen months since Congress had approved the sale of the F-15 jets to the Saudis and the two nations had joyfully proclaimed their "special relationship," things had gone sour and the relationship was on the rocks. Within the next two months each nation would suffer unimagined disasters that would test even further the tenuous political alliance and the personal friendships John West had built to support that alliance. For West, the happy warrior from South Carolina, his role changed, and he found that while the U.S. Embassy in Jeddah continued to be a place for socializing and cocktail-hour politics, it also increasingly became a place of refuge, solace, and even some intrigue during the nervous times that lay ahead.

West was on leave at his Hilton Head home when the embassy in Tehran was overrun by Iranian militants on November 4. Like many others at the time, he was concerned, but he believed that the trouble would be of relatively short duration. There was only a brief entry in his journal that day, which read: "The most disturbing thing [of the day] was the news that they had seized the Tehran Embassy. John Limbert is undoubtedly among them, and the students are holding them until the shah's return."[36]

The brief journal entry, however, did not reflect the deep concern or the significant commitment and involvement he had already made to Limbert's family, which included bringing Parveneh and the children to the embassy and assigning her staff duties. Over the months of the hostage ordeal, West and his family worked to keep up the spirits of the Limbert family, and in his journal are several entries that record trips to the souk (market) to soothe Parveneh's nerves. West later recalled that Limbert "became a spokesman for the hostages because he spoke the language. . . . She [Parveneh] would listen to the media broadcasts and they [the Iranians] would say that [the hostages]were all CIA operatives and traitors and so on," West said. "The one thing that would divert her," he remembered, "was to go down to the souk [market] and negotiate for rugs and other things . . . she loved to negotiate."[37]

In her book *Inside the Kingdom,* Carmen bin Ladin wrote, "All Saudi Arabia became mesmerized by the political volcano in Iran, and its fallout in the

Middle East. It was all we talked about. One of our occasional guests, John Limbert, an American diplomat, played tennis with us one Thursday in October, [on leave visiting his family at the time] and told us he would be leaving for Iran the next day. Then, a few days later, he was taken hostage in the U.S. Embassy in Tehran. He and dozens of others were paraded before the TV cameras to demonstrate the might of Islamic insurgents on the godless Americans. John was among the group of fifty-two hostages who were held in captivity for 444 days. Lois West tried to comfort his [Limbert's] wife, Parvenai, through the terrible ordeal; we were all shaken."[38]

A MONTH OF VIOLENCE

The brutal events in Tehran proved to be only the beginning of a month in which the Middle East would erupt in violence and mayhem. Sixteen days after the U.S. Embassy in Tehran was seized—on November 20, 1979—Islamic extremists stormed the Grand Mosque in Mecca, the pride of Saudi Arabia and the holiest shrine in the Muslim world. "As possessors of two of the three holiest sites of Islam, Mecca and Medina [Jerusalem is the third]," Sandra Mackey has written, "the Saudis see themselves as having a certain birthright as defenders of the faith."[39] Mecca, the birthplace of the founder of the faith, Muhammad, was the "epicenter of the Islamic faith, the point to which all Moslems turn in prayer five times a day," Mackey wrote.[40] The Saudis were not only the territorial possessors of the cities; they were also stewards for the entire Muslim world of these holy shrines.

While some precautions had been taken to deal with possible disruptions growing out of the Tehran embassy takeover, the boldness of the Mecca attack caught the Saudis off guard. Crown Prince Fahd and Prince Turki al-Faisal, head of the kingdom's General Intelligence Directorate, were in Tunis attending an Arab League summit meeting, and Prince Abdullah, next in command after Fahd and head of the Saudi national guard, was on vacation in Morocco. News of the takeover, in fact, may have first been communicated to Jeddah from the Bin Laden Organization. For all the notoriety associated with the name because of Osama bin Laden's terrorist activities, the Bin Laden Organization was one of the largest and most powerful private companies in Saudi Arabia, and among its responsibilities was the oversight of public works in Mecca and al-Medina. For decades it had been the foremost construction company in the kingdom, building everything from highways and power plants to mosques and libraries in the growing nation. Carmen bin Laden wrote,

> The extremist forces had sneaked into Mecca using Bin Laden Organization trucks, which were never searched.

We must have been the first to know. The Bin Ladens kept a permanent staff of employees in a maintenance office in Mecca. When the rebels stormed the Grand Mosque, a Bin Laden worker immediately phoned the head office in Jeddah, and reported that violence had broken out. Then the insurgents cut the phone lines. Incredibly, it was the Bin Laden Organization that informed King Khaled that rebellion had broken out in Islam's holiest city.

One of the King's first decisions was to cut all phone lines in the nation. . . . The newspapers didn't dare report the attacks for days. But the rumors spread anyway. There was tumult.[41]

In those disorderly moments after the takeover, as rumors and speculation spread quickly, the United States was fingered by some as a culprit in the emotional fury that was beginning to sweep much of the Islamic world. Within hours after the seizure of the Grand Mosque, a wildfire of anti-American sentiment broke out. A mob attacked the U.S. Embassy in Islamabad, Pakistan, killing two Americans and four Pakistanis. There was a subsequent attack on the consul general in Lahore, India, and in the next two days, November 22 and 23, there were disturbances in Turkey, Bangladesh, and India.

It was a terrifying time to be an American in the Middle East, and it was a particularly dangerous time for the man who served as U.S. ambassador in the vulnerable kingdom of Saudi Arabia. Among other things, John West was worried that his embassy in Jeddah might be overrun as the U.S. Embassy in Tehran had been. At his request, patrols around the embassy were increased by the Saudi national guard and peripheral gates were closed. Even the "Welfare" [church] services were suspended, and West ordered the shredding of classified files, something the Tehran embassy staff had not been able to complete before the student takeover sixteen days earlier.[42]

"Washington called and [said] to take particular care," West wrote in his journal. "Therefore, I am staying in the compound. They have added a lead car to the chase car [for Embassy auto trips] and of course they have tripled the forces around the compound."[43]

Callers to the U.S. Embassy in Jeddah were read a statement from Ambassador West that, in essence, there had been a disturbance in Mecca but that there was no indication that Americans or other Westerners had been involved. Americans were advised to stay in their homes or at their places of employment.[44] The security measures were of such a drastic nature that West decided not to tell his wife, even though Lois had been his security escort years earlier, eluding the Ku Klux Klan in a 1950s chase across the back roads of Kershaw County. "All in all, an interesting day," the ambassador noted.[45]

KEEPING AN EYE ON MECCA

At the moment no one was quite certain what had happened in Mecca, who had caused it, or why. Communication into the mosque was nonexistent after the Saudis had cut telephone lines early in the conflict, and official and unofficial versions of the event were inconsistent and in conflict. With his embassy located only about forty-five highway miles from Mecca, John West was acutely sensitive to the possibility of an insurrection spilling down the road to Jeddah and overwhelming the American compound there. As rumors swirled that Iranians had been involved in the takeover, West was made aware of reconnaissance photos taken during a helicopter flyover shortly after the seizure of the mosque. The photos were taken by an American expatriate flying for the Saudi air force and were provided to the embassy through a staff member who knew the pilot. They gave the worried ambassador a first look at actual conditions at the mosque.[46]

Based on what the photos showed—and did not show—and other information gathered from conversations among embassy sources, contacts, and accounts from the helicopter pilot, West was able to piece together a carefully worded telegram to Washington, which read in part: "Embassy is continuing to receive information—some of it conflicting—concerning occupation of the Grand Mosque in Mecca. It is still not known for certain who is occupying the mosque, although it appears that they are very well-armed. We have received reports indicating occupiers could be Iranian or Yemeni, although reports from Saudi sources state occupiers are Saudi tribesmen supporting as yet unidentified group of Islamic fundamentalists."[47]

West's cautious but insightful dispatch arrived hours before a crucial meeting of Carter's National Security Council and was one of many telegrams that came to the council's attention. The remarkably accurate description of conditions at the mosque provided by West went largely unheeded, however, and was superseded by a Pentagon assessment that those carrying out the takeover were "believed to be Iranian" and "quite likely . . . fanatical followers of the Ayatollah Khomeini."[48] The next day's *New York Times* headline read, "Mecca Mosque Seized by Gunmen Believed to Be from Iran," and the president ordered the supercarrier *Kitty Hawk* to the Persian Gulf.

West kept up his surveillance and inquiries, including contact with Zaki Yamani; thirty to forty-five relatives of Yamani's were at the mosque at the time of the takeover but had escaped before their identities were detected. "It was not until I went to see Zaki Yamani about 1:00 [P.M.] that we got the first real insight into what happened. Zaki reported that a young religious fanatic named Mohammad Abdullah, who had been [imprisoned] at one time by Saudi authorities, had represented himself with about 300 followers as the new Mahdi . . . a sort of John, the Baptist type."[49]

The actual organizer and leader of the assault on the mosque was Juhaiman ibn Mohammad Utaibi, described as "a wild-eyed man with a heavy, matted beard."[50] His forces numbered between two hundred and three hundred heavily armed men and were identified as being part of an anti-Saudi faction known as the Ikhwan, many of whom resided in the northern region of Saudi Arabia. They were the remnants of the last major rivals to the Saudis' supremacy on the Arabian peninsula, a tribal force that was defeated in a 1929 battle that all but decimated the Ikhwan and their influence.

They were not Iranian; that much was certain. The Ikhwan had survived in small numbers and harbored bitterness against the Saudis, clinging to the fundamentalist Wahhabi faith, which they believed the Saudi kingdom had defiled in its accommodation of automobiles and television sets and other emblems of modernity. Some of the leaders of the mosque takeover were descendants of tribesmen who had been defeated in the 1929 showdown with ibn Saud.

The mounting tensions over the Mecca takeover were enough to convince West that if the United States had been perceived as abandoning its friend the shah of Iran in times of stress, the same would not hold true for the Saudis. Working with Prince Bandar and Prince Turki, who had become the de facto head of the Saudi troops at Mecca, he made available what military equipment he could, including tear gas, which was used to rout the insurgents from the upper floors of the mosque during the latter days of the siege.

As the siege of the mosque continued into its second week, West became increasingly perplexed over the protraction of the crisis and the inconsistency of reports coming from various sources. The Saudis, anxious to downplay the event, proclaimed victory prematurely on several occasions, including a pronouncement from the information minister Ahmed Yamani on Thursday, November 22—two days after the siege began—that "this group, which is deviating from the Islamic religion, is under the control of the security forces."[51] The announcement was in stark contrast to the information West was continuing to get from the clandestine photos being provided by the American helicopter pilot.

Another problem too was troubling the American ambassador. Washington's decision to link the siege of the mosque to the Iranians had touched off a counterattack from Khomeini, whose office issued a communiqué stating, "It is not far-fetched to assume that this act [the takeover of the mosque] has been perpetrated by the criminal American imperialism so that it can infiltrate the solid ranks of Muslims by such intrigues. It would not be far-fetched to assume that . . . Zionism intends to make the House of God vulnerable."[52]

AMERICANS' VULNERABILITY

West was feeling vulnerable. He was observing how the ayatollah's anti-American statements had touched off violence at embassies in Turkey and Pakistan, and his worries over the security of his embassy in Jeddah were becoming acute. In a conversation with Zaki Yamani, West said that the Iranian statements were "putting in jeopardy the lives of American citizens, as well as American diplomats, throughout the world,"[53] and he urged the Saudis to refute them publicly. In the disorder of the early days of the mosque takeover, West—with the help of Prince Bandar—had been able to put together an official, but tentative, statement intended to absolve the United States from involvement in the takeover. The statement was described by West as being "not as clear as we wanted, but it was the best we could do—with Fahd in Tunis, and everyone confused and not knowing what was going on."[54]

A day later, under pressure from the State Department, West visited Zaki Yamani again. After learning that the oil minister's family members had safely escaped the Grand Mosque, he told Yamani, "we desperately need a more definitive statement on no U.S. involvement [in the Mecca uprising]. Zaki said he would call Sultan [the defense minister] and call me back, which he did, and the statement was forthcoming."[55]

Secretary Vance, in the meantime, was making contact with Foreign Minister Saud al-Faisal in Tunis, expressing the same urgency for the new, stronger statement. Prince Saud met with Crown Prince Fahd; West met again with Yamani; and the decision was made for the Saudis to issue a stronger statement. Early that afternoon the statement came from Prince Nayef, the interior minister: "Neither the United States, Iran nor any other countries have had anything to do with the attack on the Holy Kaaba [Grand Mosque]. News reports alleging U.S. involvement in the incident were absolutely untrue and baseless."[56]

For all the clarification the statement may have provided for U.S. security purposes, West's anxieties over the contradiction of reports coming from Mecca were not resolved. Trofimov describes how the American ambassador even authorized a spy mission by two staff members into Mecca and the area of the Grand Mosque to determine the status of things in the holy city. Whether because of his old instincts as a would-be journalist, his experience as a military intelligence officer, or just plain anxiety over the security of U.S. interests and his Saudi friends, West decided on a drastic, and characteristically unorthodox, course of action. To his mind there were still significant questions as to whether the mosque had indeed been secured or fighting was still under way at the shrine.

According to Trofimov's account, West authorized Mark Hambley, who had uncovered the first leak of information from Mecca, and his colleague Richard Ryer to sneak into the holy Muslim city disguised as pilgrims in order to determine the nature of the situation at the time. Wearing Arab garb and utilizing Hambley's facility in the Arabic language, the pair blended in with the flow of Muslim traffic heading toward the mosque, a number enlarged by Saudi reports that the fighting was over. Hambley and Ryer found, however, as they approached the vicinity of the mosque, that the fighting was indeed continuing, and they took photographs to prove it. "West," Trofimov wrote, "safe in his friendship with Carter, decided in the end that he could—and should—authorize a quick trip to Mecca for an embassy employee or two without necessarily informing the jittery State Department brass back in Washington."[57]

The escapade worked, and Hambley and Ryer returned to the embassy with photographic evidence that West wanted. According to Trofimov's account, however, the inability of the embassy equipment to transmit the photos to Washington electronically kept them from being useful to the State Department at the time. Subsequent high-altitude photos confirmed that fighting was continuing, and Washington had its own source, which finally established the extent of hostilities continuing in the Muslim shrine. West was also getting a regular "insider" account of the events in Mecca from Bandar, including a candid description of interrogation techniques. According to West, Bandar "said they had captured a few people and interrogated them, using truth serum, and starvation, and no water, etc., but 'no torture such as pulling out their fingernails.'"[58]

For all the reassurances West may have been receiving from his Saudi friends, however, political and diplomatic impatience was growing in Washington over the magnitude of the terror raining down on America and its allies in places such as Tehran, Islamabad, Izmir, and Mecca. On November 28, eight days after the siege of Mecca began, West got a message from Washington "strongly suggesting that we give consideration to a phase-down of American personnel, looking toward an eventual evacuation."[59] This message was eerily similar to that delivered to Ambassador Sullivan in Tehran nine months earlier. West wrote, "I figured it can mean only one thing—that military action was being contemplated in Tehran . . . that caused me great concern."[60] Secretary Vance had been told a day earlier by the Senate Foreign Relations Committee "either to protect Americans or see that they were protected or get them out."[61]

West told the State Department that he felt safe, but he was reminded that a similar message had come from U.S. personnel in Islamabad the day before they were attacked. West then alerted Bandar to the possibility of military action to protect the U.S. hostages in Iran. He was told that "Saudi Arabia would support any military action if the hostages were in fact harmed."[62]

There then ensued an extraordinary exchange, as West recorded it, in which Crown Prince Fahd "agreed to give us every protection possible and . . . agreed to call the other Gulf States and offer them Saudi security forces and equipment if needed to protect Americans."[63] This was a message of such urgency that Bandar wanted to take it directly to President Carter. Fahd gave it such priority that he even agreed to serve as an intermediary with the Saudis' longtime rivals, the Egyptians, in assuring Americans' safety. It was quite a reversal from a conversation West had held with Fahd only two months earlier in which the crown prince had criticized the United States for its lack of attention to its Middle East allies.

Anxieties were piling up for the ambassador, and stress was again beginning to show. Wearily at the close of a particularly hectic day, West wrote in his journal that an hour-long interview with NBC "didn't go . . . well because I had just come in from Bandar's and had about a dozen things on my mind—find my brain gets swamped—but I guess it's understandable."[64]

"MY DAMN NECK"

West was subsequently told by the State Department to proceed with evacuation plans, and it set off a steamy reply from the ambassador. After hearing to what remarkable extent the Saudis would go to protect Americans in the gulf region, West said that even the planning for evacuation "would be taken by the Saudis as a sign of a lack of trust in their administration. We pointed out that if [we] evacuated, it would wreck the armed forces, oil production, transportation, etc., and that would lead to an overthrow of the Saud administration."[65] As news of the State Department plans for Middle East evacuation spread, West spent much of the rest of the day denying any such plans for the United States in Saudi Arabia.

All this led to another tug of war between West and the State Department, this time over evacuation plans. The ambassador wrote that Washington "still [has] the panic button on" in its security concerns, "and I got a little impatient. [I] told them it was my damn neck and if I felt safe, I didn't see why they kept worrying us with all the paperwork."[66]

The security issue, however, was becoming larger than a dustup between West and the State Department. As the Mecca seizure stood unresolved against the backdrop of the Iranian standoff, an institutional nervousness set in. It was felt not only within embassy and other official circles but also within the expatriate business community in Saudi Arabia. According to a December 5 *New York Times* report, West told American business leaders that they had "nothing to fear as a result of recent turmoil" in the country.[67] However, in a journal entry West noted that he was being told in no uncertain terms that people were worried: "Jim Lewis of Raytheon says he has already started [on evacuation plans]. Most of the other companies have, too. He says one more incident and he's going to send his [people home]."[68]

The Mecca incident was not the only worry within the Saudi kingdom. Shiite uprisings in the eastern areas of the kingdom, where most of the oil production was centered, had provoked concerns, and the U.S. consul in Dhahran, the major city in that region, had told Americans "to stay out of sight as much as possible."[69] While official Saudi statements were denying such outbreaks of violence, West quoted Prince Bandar as telling him that they "would keep it under control as long as we didn't complain too much about human rights violations."[70] The *Times* article reported that five marchers had been killed when Saudi national guardsmen fired into the crowd at one of the Shiite protests.[71]

In all it took two weeks for the Saudi army to overwhelm the rebel contingent at the mosque, and the siege ended at 1:30 A.M. on Tuesday morning, December 5, with the surrender of Juhaiman and the last remaining dozens of his warriors.[72] The Ikhwan leader was asked by one of the Saudi troops, "How could you do all this? How could you?" Juhaiman reportedly responded, "This was God's will."[73]

Even after the uprising was quelled, however, there was still the matter of dealing with misinformation that had come out of the Mecca uprising, and West made these observations in his journal:

> there were two incidents that received widespread publicity in the press that I knew to be false. . . . The first was the story that French troops had been brought in with special anti-riot equipment, including tear gas, and it was through their efforts that the mosque was finally cleared. I added that the press had emphasized that these non-Muslims were allowed to go into the Holy City. I told him, of course, the opposite of that was true—that we in the United States had furnished sophisticated anti-riot equipment, including gas, and had brought a special team into Taif to train the Saudis how to use it—and of course that was the true story.
>
> The other incident was the story that Prince Saud had hastened back from Tunis to lead the charge. Fahd laughed and said, "Yes, that was a good one—Saud was with me." I said yes, that despite our respect for Saud as an

intellectual and foreign minister, no one ever accused him of being a military leader or commander, and the undoubted purpose of the news plants was to create division between the sons of Faisal and the present rulers of the Kingdom. [Crown Prince Fahd was the senior member of the Sudeiri Seven.] Fahd acknowledged that this was so.[74]

Casualties were high on both sides of the mosque incident. Numbers varied from source to source, and Mackey's account listed 127 Saudis killed and 461 injured. Rebel losses, she wrote, were estimated at 117 dead, although she said, "The figures for both sides were probably higher."[75]

On January 9, 1980, sixty-three of the rebels were beheaded, and to maximize the impact of the events, the executions were held in eight cities across the Saudi kingdom. Of the sixty-three, forty-one were identified as Saudi citizens, ten were Egyptian, six were South Yemeni, three were Kuwaiti, one was Sudanese, and one was Iraqi. The nationalities and identities of those found dead in the mosque were not established.[76] Among those identified, it was confirmed that there was not a single Iranian.

SOVIETS ENTER AFGHANISTAN

By the time the mosque siege ended, however, more things were complicating the Middle East scene. On December 25, 1979, the Soviet Union—emboldened by American and Saudi disarray in such places as Pakistan, Iran, and the Grand Mosque in Mecca—sent troops into Afghanistan, toppling the existing government in Kabul and installing its own regime. Suddenly what had been a series of confrontations within a remote region among warring factions of political and religious foes escalated into a major cold-war event. Lukewarm Saudi interest in exploring a stronger U.S. military presence in the region only weeks earlier became transformed into a fearful awareness of its long-dreaded communist threat.[77] Along the way the influence of Brzezinski toward a more militant U.S. role in the region was beginning to take hold. A day after the Soviet invasion, Brzezinski told Carter in a memo, "If the Soviets succeed in Afghanistan, and if Pakistan acquiesces, the age-long dream of Moscow to have direct access to the Indian Ocean will have been fulfilled. It could produce Soviet presence right down on the edge of the Arabian and Oman Gulfs."[78] Prince Turki echoed Brzezinski's alarm, saying, "It was obvious that the invasion of Afghanistan was one step toward reaching other countries, especially Pakistan, and then moving on to the Gulf and the Arabian Peninsula."[79]

Within a matter of weeks President Carter said in his State of the Union address, "Let our position be absolutely clear. Any attempt by an outside force to gain control of the Persian Gulf will be regarded as an assault on the vital interests of the United States of America and . . . will be repelled by any means necessary, including military force."[80] This amounted to a Monroe Doctrine for the Middle East, and it reflected the ongoing polarity of world affairs in the 1970s and the two decades before that. Unlike the isolationist position it took in the years following World War I, the United States was pursuing a vigorous policy of challenging the territorial ambitions of nations it viewed as unfriendly to its own national interests. In most cases those challenges were directed toward the Soviet Union and those states it identified as part of the Soviet Bloc of nations in Eastern Europe.

Cold-war tension had led the United States and its Western allies to fight off the Soviet attempt to blockade the city of Berlin in 1948–49 with an airlift that brought four thousand tons of food and supplies into the city every day for almost a year. Similarly the United States led the resistance to the North Korean invasion of South Korea in 1950, invoking what had become known as the "domino theory"—responding to each territorial challenge lest neighboring nations fall in a domino-like collapse. The United States was still worrying about dominos when it became stuck in the quagmire of Vietnam, an experience that disproved the theory and also left a deep wound on U.S. domestic and foreign policies. The Korean and Vietnam wars proved to be bitterly divisive within the United States and are generally credited with costing both Harry Truman and Lyndon Johnson their presidencies.

The cold war was in full sway as the Carter administration addressed its Middle East issues. One of the reasons for Sadat's popularity with the United States was his bold action in drawing his nation away from the Soviet sphere of influence and lodging it squarely with the United States and its allies. In a world where nations were expected to take sides—East or West, communism or democracy, Russia or the United States—the Sadat defection was a major coup for the West. If Carter seemed to be risking Middle East alliances with his support of Sadat, he was not about to let the Egyptian friendship go sour on the larger stage of the cold war.

As the Soviets moved their forces into Afghanistan, it set off alarms in the East-West struggle, and Brzezinski articulated what by then had become an activist, international U.S. position of resistance against the Soviet threat. Carter subsequently dispatched Brzezinski and State Department deputy Warren Christopher to the Middle East for meetings in Pakistan and Saudi Arabia, and they arrived with a message of cold-war toughness on Afghanistan and distinctly anti-Russian strategies. This message was welcomed by the worried Saudis, whose anxieties over instability among their neighbors and within their own borders had heightened their already acute sense of alarm. "Brzezinski did a good job of outlining the Cold War," West wrote. "He is . . . a hawk on Russia and that appeals to the Saudis."[81] The Saudis, according to Thornton's account, were receptive "both in terms of improving their own defense capabilities and approving a greater American presence in the region—a marked change from a year ago, when they had publicly denounced American policy over the Egypt-Israel treaty and threatened to shift away from Washington."[82]

Amid the grind of day-to-day pressures, West had time for an occasional chuckle. Such a moment arose during the visit of the Carter insider Charles Kirbo, who met with various Saudi officials, including West's friend Prince Sultan, the minister of defense. West recorded this exchange: "In introducing Charlie Kirbo to Sultan, I said he was the President's long-time friend and attorney and in political and legal circles, he was reputed to have more influence with the President than any other living human being save and except possibly Mrs. Carter. The translator, much to Isa's [Sabbagh] horror, said, 'He has great influence on President Carter, but none on Mrs. Carter.'"[83]

As West worked to maintain stability in U.S.-Saudi affairs, things were getting no better in Iran, and chances for a negotiated settlement of the hostage stalemate were fading. At that point the Carter administration began actively exploring other options. Brzezinski, who was regularly scheduled as President Carter's first meeting every day, was exerting increasing influence with the president. As the hostage crisis deepened, he began having regular meetings with a task force to develop rescue plans for the Tehran captives.

CARTER'S DECLINING POPULARITY

There were other pressures building on the Carter administration. Polls by the Harris and Gallup organizations showed drastic drops in the level of public confidence in the president. The Harris survey showed a reversal of his 66–32 percent approval rating in December to a 65–24 percent disapproval score in early April. Similarly the Gallup poll had his 77–19 percent approval rating in December declining to a 49–40 percent disapproval rating in April, both attributable to the Iranian stalemate.

Clearly the Carter presidency was entering a "no more Mr. Nice Guy" phase. Brzezinski began talking up a "cooperative security framework," which would offer U.S. friendship to Muslim nations where there existed "no irreconcilable differences."[84] This was intended as an invitation from the United States to explore relations with nations that might have been previously considered off-limits for American interests and initiatives but now might prove helpful in the U.S. standoff with Iran. The prospect attracted the attention of Iraq's Saddam

Hussein, who had become president in July 1979 after more than a decade as a behind-the-scenes strongman. Hussein was becoming something of a political wild card in the shifting Middle East diplomatic shuffle, and he and the United States had maintained an on-and-off relationship over the years. His strong anticommunist stand and his Sunni Muslim beliefs made him valuable to the Saudis, and he had used the vast Iraqi oil fortunes to build strong, modern education, health care, and social service systems. Hussein, however, had also been a pan-Arabist follower of Egypt's Gamal Abdel Nasser as a youth, and his support of Palestinian interests was an ongoing threat to Israel. He held strong nationalist beliefs, and the seizure of the Iraqi oil fields by his Ba'ath Party government in the 1960s made him anything but a friend of Western nations.

For the moment he was best known in U.S. circles as a long-standing enemy of Ayatollah Khomeini, and that was about all that counted. After an exchange of carefully worded public statements, Brzezinski said on a public television news program, "We see no fundamental incompatibility of interests between the United States and Iraq. We feel that Iraq desires to be independent, that Iraq wishes a secure Persian Gulf, and we do not feel that American-Iraqi relations need to be frozen in antagonism."[85] The thawing of relations between the United States and Saddam Hussein set in motion a further initiative by Jordan to seal a Saudi-Iraqi understanding, and in short order the United States had created a Jordan-Saudi-Iraq entente to match up with the Soviets' Iran-Syria-Libya lineup. The Carter administration hoped that where negotiation had failed with Iran, the pressure of a military conflict with Iraq would force Khomeini to loosen his hold on the hostages and take a less hostile stance toward the United States.

As the Iraq-Iran war cranked up in early October, however, the military outcomes were not as had been hoped by the United States, and Iran more than held its own against the Iraqis. By the middle of the month, three weeks before the 1980 presidential election, the United States called for an end to hostilities and immediate negotiations.[86] The truce held for only a short time, and for the next eight years the two neighboring countries waged one of the most brutal conflicts of the twentieth century. It ended in 1988 in a stalemate.

The disappointing outcome of the early stages of the Iraq-Iran war came about six months after an earlier effort to rescue the hostages had failed. In late April 1980 the United States launched a complicated military expedition involving 209 men, six C-130 transports, and eight helicopters from the aircraft carrier USS *Nimitz* in the Gulf of Oman. Among other elements, the plan required helicopters to take off from the carrier deck and fly six hundred miles to a rendezvous in the desert some three hundred miles from Tehran. Two of the helicopters never reached the rendezvous, and a third developed a hydraulic fluid leak. Scarcely before phase one of the mission had been carried out, it was aborted on direct orders from the White House. In the ensuing scramble to withdraw from Iranian territory, a transport plane collided with a helicopter. For all President Carter's hopes to avoid or minimize bloodshed, eight American soldiers were killed and three were injured in the rescue attempt. The mission failed; the withdrawal was a disaster; and the whole episode became an international tragedy.[87]

There was yet another casualty of the failed rescue mission. Secretary of State Cyrus Vance, who had been losing ground in his strategic and philosophical disagreements with Brzezinski, decided to resign as a result of the decision to attempt the hostage rescue. He later wrote, "I recognized that the president was in political trouble, and I wished I could stand by him. But . . . I knew I could not honorably remain as secretary of state when I so strongly disagreed with a presidential decision that went against my judgment as to what was best for the country and for the hostages. Even if the mission worked perfectly, and I did not believe it would, I would have to say afterward that I had opposed it, give my reasons for opposing it and publicly criticize the president. That would be intolerable for the president and for me."[88]

Vance's departure came as a blow to John West, whose personal friendship with the secretary of state had been important strategically and politically to him. For all his tussles with the State Department, West knew he could always make a personal appeal to Vance, as he did on occasion. Without Vance, West lost an important power source during the last year of his service in Saudi Arabia.

West wrote, "News came in that Cy Vance had resigned. Quite upsetting to us all. Later Joe Twinam [high-ranking State Department officer Joseph W. Twinam] called and said Cy had resigned in opposition to the military expedition to rescue the hostages. Submitted his resignation before the operation, but of course agreed to keep it secret. He's a good man and I hate to see him go."[89] By then another of West's avenues of access was being at least partially blocked. Brzezinski was intercepting West's treasured handwritten letters to Carter and was briefing the president on their contents.

While West actually had little direct involvement in the efforts to dislodge the hostages from their captivity in Tehran, he continued his effort to keep spirits as high as possible for John Limbert's wife, Parveneh, and their two children, particularly in the face of ongoing depressing news about the status and potential fate of the American captives. A final issue, however, occupied much of his attention in the waning months of the Carter administration.

DEATH OF A PRINCESS

That issue was the British-made television drama-documentary based on the public execution of a nineteen-year-old Saudi princess and her lover in a Jeddah parking lot in July 1977, two months after West arrived as U.S. ambassador. Accounts vary as to the actual events leading up to the brutal slaying of the two young Saudis, but it was known that Princess Mishaal bint Fahd bin Mohammad had eloped with her commoner lover, Khalid Muhallal, nephew of the Saudi ambassador to Lebanon, in defiance of her arranged marriage. Upon learning of what he deemed to be adultery within his family, the princess's grandfather Prince Mohammad bin Abdul-Aziz had ordered the execution of his granddaughter and her lover under traditional tribal law. Mohammad was the older brother of King Khalid and was known as a power within the inner circle of senior princes and also as a man of strong temper and imperious personality.

Although the executions were carried out in public, they received little international attention until the spring of 1980, when it became known that a British corporation (ATV) in conjunction with a Boston public television station had produced a two-hour "dramatic reconstruction of the events leading up to the 1977 [executions]." According to one account, "Even before the broadcast, Saudi officials, who had been given an opportunity to preview the film, were livid. They were simply not going to tolerate such an unflattering portrait. The royal family saw the film as an attack on them, and by extension—owing to the logic of a family understandably obsessed with maintaining itself in power—as an attack on the Islamic world."[90]

The bigger issues for others were matters such as the prince's right to order the execution without trial under tribal law and the general status of women in a twentieth-century Islamic state. "Under tribal custom, Prince Mohammad as the senior member of the family, had every right to kill any woman in the family who violated her *ird* [chastity] in order to restore the honor of the family. The executions were a matter of his honor, not a matter of the courts," the historian Sandra Mackey wrote. "Women continue to be trapped in an exaggerated male mystique sanctified by a culture thousands of years old and extending back centuries before the Prophet, that decrees that women exist solely to serve men."[91]

Most of the Saudi ire was directed toward the British, whose ambassador was expelled from the kingdom amid a flurry of diplomatic and economic measures designed to express Saudi displeasure and to punish the nation they saw as the perpetrator of an international indignity. West absorbed his share of the reaction as well. For all the rage that was being expressed elsewhere, however, he heard a reasoned argument from Prince Turki. West recorded the conversation as follows:

> We talked largely about the Death of a Princess film—his original judgment was to do nothing—but he said the incumbent publicity had already increased the viewing audience potential to two-to-three-times what it would have been ordinarily. He said they would have to make a decision.
>
> He went into great detail to say the reason they were unhappy with Britain was because Britain had taken a lackadaisical attitude; that other governments had responded very positively, very quickly . . . France, Spain, Australia, etc., Sweden. . . . Britain had simply said they could do nothing.
>
> I told him I would draft a letter [requesting a U.S. position against airing of the film], which I would use if necessary. He said that he and the [Saudi] government did not want to make a request that would be turned down and further exacerbate the problem. . . . I felt strongly that we should make an effort. He seemed impressed.[92]

West spent the next week in back-and-forth meetings with Turki, Saud, and others discussing the film and possible avenues of protest, at one point commenting that all the attention going to the controversy was going to result in "Death of an Ambassador."[93] Similar exchanges were taking place among the White House, the State Department, and the Saudi embassy, including a Carter statement asking PBS to give "appropriate consideration to sensitive religious and cultural issues."[94]

South Carolina ETV president Henry Cauthen, son of West's longtime friend John Cauthen, agreed to pull the program, as did a station in Jacksonville, Florida, and two in Texas. In speaking for ETV, Pat Dressler was quoted by author Steven Emerson as saying that the film had been canceled not only because it was considered "offensive" to the royal family but also because "the Saudis are people we are relying on for economic resources and we want to be friendly to them."[95]

The show aired in the United Kingdom on April 9, 1980, and most public broadcasting stations in the United States carried it on May 12, 1980. PBS chairman Newton N. Minow acknowledged the controversy and said that PBS would have seriously considered rejecting the program had it not been for the reverse effect of a high-pressure pro-Saudi ad taken out in the *New York Times* by Mobil Oil. PBS subsequently sought to balance its position by producing a one-hour, postbroadcast discussion program that featured John West's friend Jim Akins, the former ambassador to Saudi Arabia.[96]

A LESSER ROLE

With Vance gone from the State Department and Brzezinski calling most of the shots with Carter, West's voice became somewhat diminished. In the context of growing American vulnerability in the Middle East, he spoke up vigorously on behalf of the U.S. sale of AWACS surveillance planes to the Saudis in 1980. However, he—like most of America—was a witness to the downward spiral of President Carter's fortunes in the run-up to his presidential contest with Republican Ronald Reagan in November 1980. Prior to the outbreak of the Iran-Iraq war in October, West sent a confidential memo to Vance's successor as secretary of state, Edmund Muskie of Maine, saying, "The United States Policy in the Mideast has created a sense of disillusionment and despair throughout the Gulf area. The role of the United States as a leader as well as our credibility is being seriously questioned even by those leaders who heretofore have been our strongest allies and supporters. There is a general agreement that the Camp David accords have failed and a new life cannot be breathed into the process without a major move by the U.S. to break the intransigence of [Israeli prime minister Menachem] Begin and his Government."[97]

Bad news was piling up for the Carter presidency. Aside from the calamitous problems in the Middle East, factors closer to home were making his bid for reelection a troublesome business. America was mired in serious inflation; unemployment was high; the robust economy of the early 1970s was weakening; and gasoline shortages were once again creating lines of automobiles waiting at the pumps in some parts of the nation. John West was told by Reagan insiders Casper Weinberger and George Shultz that they believed a Ronald Reagan presidency would offer him the opportunity to stay on in Saudi Arabia. In July, however, as political matters worsened for Carter, West wrote, "The election news is all bad. . . . All we can do is make plans to pack in January, I guess, but I hate to be negative."[98]

West was in South Carolina for the election. He voted in his Charlotte Thompson precinct in Kershaw County and then traveled to Hilton Head to look over his newly constructed home in the Palmetto Dunes section. The following day, as the full extent of the Carter defeat was apparent, he wrote, "A horrible situation. President only got about 50 electoral votes."[99]

Carter carried six states, including his native Georgia, and the District of Columbia, and he got 49 electoral votes, to Reagan's 489. The popular vote was 43.9 million (50.7 percent) for Reagan to 35.5 million (41 percent) for Carter. Carter's margin of support fell from 64–34 percent in his victory over Gerald Ford in 1976 to a narrow 45–39 percent in his loss to Reagan. He would later claim that the Jewish vote "cost me the election," although Jews constituted only 5 percent of the electorate in the 1980 election.

Reagan was inaugurated as president on Tuesday, January 20, 1981, the day chosen by Ayatollah Khomeini and the Iranian leaders to release the embassy hostages being held in Tehran. That ordeal had occupied a total of 444 days, and the moment of the captives' release was not lost on West politically or personally. "It was a pleasant day, made so in the middle by the news that the hostages had finally been released and were on their way," he wrote.

> The Iranians waited until after Reagan's inaugural address. He finished at 12:30 and they let them go at 12:33. They really played the string out, as Parveneh said they would. I told her that the Iranians were good traders, as was she, and they knew how to squeeze the last bit of goody out of any transaction, including a rug sale or a hostage delivery.
>
> I talked to Parveneh and of course, she was ecstatic. It was a very moving, emotional moment.[100]

The next day there was a champagne celebration at the embassy over the hostages' release. West wrote, "We let Parveneh cut the yellow ribbon off the flagpole." She talked to her husband, John Limbert, for about an hour, and after the festivities, she was driven to the Jeddah airport at one A.M. to depart for her trip to be reunited with her husband. "She was happy," West wrote, "complete with children and dog."[101]

Several days later West talked to Limbert and then wrote:

> He told me that he was on his way to the souk on November 4—the day the raid came—that if he had been an hour earlier leaving the Embassy things would have been different. Also, on his way down to the airport he told the captives that he would like to stop by the rug souk. They said he was crazy. . . .
>
> He sounded good and he is flying on tomorrow to see Parveneh and sounds quite excited.[102]

West remained as ambassador for almost two months into the Reagan administration. A *Washington Post* article reported "informed sources" as having said, "West may be needed in the immediate future to conduct the Saudi end of discussions on upgrading the F-15s, which the Saudis see as a litmus test of their relations with Washington."[103]

In his interim status West spoke up frequently and candidly about his concerns over U.S.-Saudi relations, hitting often at themes that had emerged from pro-Saudi positions he had taken during his three and a half years in the desert kingdom. On January 23 he was quoted in a *Washington Post* article as saying, "I feel very strongly . . . that our failure to even want to talk to the PLO or to even engage in any dialogue is very difficult to explain or justify to Saudi Arabia and other Arabs. Today, there is no doubt in the Arab world that the PLO has got to be involved in any ultimate negotiations or discussions. . . . Until we recognize that, then, frankly, in my judgment, there is a stalemate."[104]

Ten days later he directed his remarks to the Reagan administration, telling the *New York Times* that the new president would have a "real problem unless he addresses two key issues, Jerusalem and the Palestinian problem. The relationship between the United States and Saudi Arabia is as good as it has ever been in my judgment. But we are walking on a very tight rope, and we are on the edge of a cliff, and the relationship could deteriorate very rapidly."[105]

Reagan was in accord with West's beliefs, but the sales of the AWACS planes and the upgrading of the F-15 fighter jets proved to be a greater task than his administration had anticipated. That political battle lasted much longer than West's tenancy in the role of ambassador. As it had been with Carter's initial struggle in 1977 over the sale of the planes, Reagan's fight took place in the Senate. It was nine months into his administration—on October 28, 1981— before he was able to eke out a 52–48 vote supporting the sale of the AWACs, Sidewinder air-to-air missiles, and fuel tanks for the F-15s.[106]

By that time West had long been back home in Camden, having returned to the practice of law with an additional office at Hilton Head. He told his hometown newspaper, the *Camden Chronicle-Independent,* "I'm probably the luckiest man that ever lived. I had four good years, highly satisfactory years. I left just at the right time."[107]

EPILOGUE

Had he lived long enough, John West would have seen the fulfillment of some of his fondest Utopian dreams. He would have been thrilled by the victory and inauguration of Barack Obama as president in 2009. For a man who promised in 1971 to make South Carolina government "color-blind," West would have gloried in the message of racial triumph that the 2008 election reflected. In addition he would have applauded the ambitious "Yes, we can" social agenda put forward by Obama, a set of initiatives that would have reminded him of his own history-making speech of thirty-eight years earlier, when he described to an eager state the things "we can, and we shall" do.

He would have beamed as Jim Clyburn stepped onto the inaugural platform on the historic day January 20, 2009, at the head of the official delegation of the U.S. House of Representatives. He would have cheered the ascendancy of Clyburn through the ranks of congressional leadership to become the House majority whip, the third-highest position in the Democratic House of Representatives. West would have told friends that he had "known Clyburn when" and that he had been smart enough not to impede the swagger of his young, aggressive staff member in the 1970s.

He would have watched with great joy the surprising emergence as a reformer of Saudi Arabia's King Abdullah bin Abdul-Aziz, a man dismissed by many as an old conservative Bedouin during the pro-Western reign of Fahd bin Abdul-Aziz. West had sought out and cultivated the friendship of Abdullah during his years as U.S. ambassador to Saudi Arabia and would have applauded the major reforms initiated by the aging monarch after he assumed the throne, at age eighty-one, upon Fahd's death in 2005.

West's daughter, Shelton West Bosley, believes that West would have appreciated the peacemaker role played by U.S. senator Lindsey Graham in providing a bridge between the two political parties in Congress and voting occasionally with the Democratic majority. "He would love Lindsey Graham," she said.[1]

As with most Utopias, John West's quest was more about the journey than the destination. The state did not become truly "color-blind," nor did it solve the problems of poverty that had wracked its people for centuries. He lived, in fact, to see South Carolina caught up in antigovernment, tax-cutting political sprees that he believed seriously damaged the state's economic and educational well-being and reversed some of the initiatives of his administration.

John West said only months before his death in 2004:

I guess this is where my partisanship was reflected because I do think government can help solve problems. When prosperity came, and the Republican Party suddenly adopted the philosophy—the style was particularly favored by Reagan—that government is a part of the problem, I simply disagreed with that very strongly. To have a president elected on a theory that government is the problem is completely wrong. It changes the whole attitude.

In South Carolina, the fact that we're not funding the public schools or the universities adequately is almost treason. And those who take a no-tax increase pledge and stick to it regardless of what services have to be cut or what educational opportunities have to be eliminated are not very good public servants.[2]

West also lived to see the fragile Middle East order he and President Carter had worked so diligently to sustain and stabilize torn apart by the U.S. invasion and occupation of Iraq under President George W. Bush. West had strong feelings about that action also and said:

The Bush foreign policy is a disaster—in my judgment—almost immoral. The idea of a preemptive strike on any nation that has not molested us reinforces the international view that America is a bully, that we rely on military strength to achieve objectives that aren't necessarily the right ones.

I have asked my former colleagues, many of them senior diplomats, and I have found not a single one of them agrees with the preemptive strike concept of Mr. Bush. [To] the old foreign service hands, the idea of going into Iraq without broad support—mainly the United Nations—was considered a disaster. They [the Bush administration] overlooked history and over-looked the advice of old-time Mideast scholars.

The brain trust of [Dick] Cheney, [Donald] Rumsfeld, [Paul] Wolfo-witz and [Richard] Perle was just absolutely wrong, and they didn't want to admit it.[3]

For all the stress between him and President Carter during the various instances of Middle East crisis and conflict, West never lost his sense of admi-ration for his Georgia friend and said:

Had it not been for the Iranian hostage situation, he would have been re-elected President.

Carter was probably the most honest, straightforward person who has been in the Office of President. He was not devious. He would take a posi-tion that he thought was morally right regardless of the political implica-tions. He was truly a good man, and I'm glad that history has treated him better than the electorate did.[4]

Carter and West made good—if sometimes feuding—partners. Their dif-ferences seemed to arise because they both practiced the kind of southern poli-tics in which personalities and loyalties played a major part. Carter's friendship with Sadat was a strong and personal one, as was West's feelings for the Saudis. The two nations—Egypt and Saudi Arabia—were not enemies, but they were rivals for leadership in an Arab political world where alliances shifted like the sands. Both West and Carter knew that the Middle East was not a place for declaring winners or losers. It was a place where stability was a daily goal, and Egypt and Saudi Arabia were not only America's best friends among the Arab nations; they were also countries whose collective influence could go a long way toward assuring that stability. Whatever their differences may have been, West and Carter understood the diplomatic rhythm of the Middle East, and they knew that it was not a place for sudden turns and twists.

The spring of 1981 brought West back to South Carolina as a private citi-zen, and according to Lois West and their daughter, Shelton, the transition was a smooth one. Part of the reason for this was that he never really accepted the notion that—at age fifty-nine—he should fall into a slow pace of life. "He was always into something," Shelton recalled. "He found excitement in everything he did."[5]

In the ensuing years West found any number of ways to stir up excitement and to reinforce his role as former governor, former ambassador, all-round troubleshooter, practicing attorney, occasional entrepreneur, and family man.

Although he never really left public life, John West allotted much of his time for golf after retiring to Hilton Head. Decked out in dapper plus fours, he is ready to tee off with his good friend Bob Onorato. Courtesy of the John C. West Papers, South Carolina Political Collections, University of South Carolina

He and Lois built a sprawling home on Hilton Head Island beside a Palmetto Dunes golf course, where he could hone his skills on a lush green layout instead of the expanse of sand fairways of Saudi Arabia. The new house had the characteristics of his former embassy home: one wing devoted to comfortable family quarters and another wing with guest lodgings, where West could continue to practice what Lois had dubbed his "invite-itis." Also as there was at the embassy, there was a swimming pool, which West used regularly until the final weeks of his life.

His first love continued to be the practice of law, and Shelton said, "If he did nothing but practice law, he would have been happy."[6] West had occasion to handle some cases with his son Jack, and in 1988 he signed on as "of counsel" with his old friend and colleague Bob McNair and the McNair firm. Five years later he joined the Hilton Head law firm of Bethea, Jordan and Griffin, a legal position he maintained for the rest of his life.

The Hilton Head years were family times for a clan that had known little other than the fast-paced, tension-filled days of elective office and diplomatic service for almost four decades. The Wests' daughter, Shelton, married a Hilton

Head commercial real estate broker, Bill Bosley, and their older son, Jack, married a Camden schoolteacher named Flonnie. Jack remained in Camden with his law practice, and Shelton worked for the Hilton Head Hospital Foundation. The younger West son, Doug, married Sue Broadbent and settled at Hilton Head as a booker of rock bands. Lois continued her work with the Muscular Dystrophy Association ("Jerry's Kids"), serving as national president one year and remaining active with the organization well into the twenty-first century.

These were also times for West's family to reminisce about life with a good-natured, warmhearted father who was always on the go. John West was an inveterate letter writer, whether it was a matter of urgent state importance to President Carter or a personal sentiment to family. "You never got a letter from Daddy that was critical," Shelton said. "It was always positive and upbeat. It was wonderful. I got a letter the day we moved out of the governor's mansion—him telling me how much it meant that I was around and how proud he was . . . beautiful letters." Like the letters to Carter, the family letters were all hand-written. "And he signed them JCW," Lois recalled, "love, JCW."[7]

In the West household the role of disciplinarian went to Lois. "Disciplinarian, he wasn't, bless his heart," Shelton said.[8] "Momma was the one who wielded the flyswatter," Jack recalled.[9] The family also recalled John West's long absences—by necessity—during his legislative years, and they remembered the special nickname they had for him during those times. "Let's put it this way," Lois West recalled, "the children called him 'Uncle Daddy.'"[10]

As he had been as governor and ambassador, West was at his best when there was a cause to champion. On at least two occasions he was involved in rescue missions involving business enterprises where a high degree of public interest was at stake. One such mission was close to home, at a time when Hilton Head was awash in real estate bankruptcies. An account published in the *New York Times* in March 1987 said, "Last year was a bad one for the elegantly casual oceanfront retirement and vacation town. . . . A wave of bankruptcies washed over the island. 'Things were so bad that . . . suppliers would not deliver golf balls to the pro shops,' said Charles E. Fraser, founder of the island's oldest real estate and resort company, the Sea Pines Company."[11]

Fraser's company had been sold to Ginn Holding Company, headed by E. R. "Bobby" Ginn, which owned three of the largest developments on the island. In December 1987 the federal court stepped in and appointed a trustee to organize an orderly way out of the chaos, disposing of disputed assets in the various bankruptcy proceedings, lawsuits, and countersuits. John Curry became the trustee, and John West was named legal adviser. The federal judge overseeing it all was Sol Blatt Jr., son of West's sometime nemesis and longtime House Speaker Sol Blatt. It was, in the words of a well-known cinematic closing moment, the beginning of a beautiful friendship for West and Blatt. Lois West later recalled, "Sol Blatt Jr. was his best buddy. I thought they were joined at the hip. They were on the phone at least once or twice a day."[12]

Even though their lives and careers had some parallels in the small state of South Carolina, the Blatts and Wests did not connect socially and personally until their Hilton Head days. "They all ran in the same circles, but I don't think they were ever close friends," Shelton West Bosley recalled. "They didn't get to be friends until later in life and then they were inseparable."[13]

Blatt and West teamed up on the Hilton Head bankruptcy, with West providing much of the fund-raising effort. "He and Sol worked a lot of things out between them," Lois West said.[14]

Among the steps taken were the creation of Sea Pines Associates, to own existing resort properties; Community Services Associates, to own common properties; and the Heritage Classic Foundation, to sustain one of West's favorite events, the Heritage Golf Classic. In a Sea Pines history published in 2009, the company is described as having "emerged [from its 1986 bankruptcy] within a year better and stronger for the most part."[15]

Another rescue mission came in the wake of Hurricane Andrew, a 1992 storm that swept through southern Florida and central Louisiana killing sixty people, causing over $20 billion in damages, and forcing two million people to evacuate their homes. Among the casualties of the storm was an old Columbia-based insurance company, Seibels-Bruce, which suffered heavy financial losses largely as a result of Andrew as well as Hurricane Hugo three years earlier. As claims piled up, the company's reserves dwindled, and by 1994 it was in serious financial trouble.

At that time a Saudi Arabian investor, Saad Alissa, was recruited by a Hilton Head broker to provide a financial infusion to shore up the company. Jack West recalled that his father was not directly involved in making the Saudi connection, but West was invited to become the company's chairman of the board and to head up its restructuring effort. Working with Dr. Susie VanHuss, at the time dean of business administration at the University of South Carolina, the new board leadership brought in a team of faculty and consultants to reshape the company. One of those faculty members was a Romanian refugee named Ernie Csiszar, who had caught the attention of VanHuss as a rising star in USC circles. West offered Csiszar the presidency of the company in May 1995, shortly after the company had reported a $2 million loss for the first quarter of that year. By the second quarter of 1995 the company showed a small profit, and

Csiszar observed in a 1997 USC publication, "We have been profitable ever since."[16]

Csiszar later wrote of his experience with West: "He became Chairman at Seibels-Bruce and I became his CEO. He was a man who, in many ways, changed my life. He was a gentleman. He was as honest as daylight. He was a very bright, talented human being. He had a true feel for people and for listening. I would hope I have as much patience, and the listening skills, and the talent that John brought to the state."[17] Csiszar went on to serve as S.C. commissioner of insurance in the administration of Governor James H. Hodges, 1999–2003.

West never lost the sense of racial fairness that had shaped much of his political career. When an effort was launched in 1999 to bring the Confederate battle flag down from the State House dome—where it had flown since 1962— he joined right in. West was one of fifty-one members of the 1962 General Assembly who had voted to raise the flag in celebration of the state's Confederate heritage, and thirty-seven years later—at age seventy-seven—he declared that it was time to take it down. Dubbing themselves the "Has-Been Brigade," West and his colleagues insisted that the initial hoisting of the flag was intended to end in 1966 and that it remained atop the dome through an "oversight." West said, "The flag on top of the State House is, in a sense, meaningless, because a flag represents sovereignty. To honor the flag, it should be in its own surroundings. I personally would like to see it in the [State] Museum with some sort of history of the Confederacy."[18] The flag eventually did come down from the dome, but it still occupies a prominent place on the Gervais Street side of the capitol building. The new location seems to satisfy no one in particular, and the NAACP, which initiated a business boycott of the state in an attempt to force the lowering of the flag, continued the boycott long after the flag was relocated. In hindsight West later said that one of his mistakes as governor was not taking down the flag.[19]

Another powerful influence motivated West on a personal basis during most of his years of political service. He never lost sight of the role that the philanthropy of Colonel Clark Williams played in his life and career, making possible his education at the Citadel through the grant of an academic scholarship. In 1974—during his last year as governor—West established the West Foundation as a nonprofit corporation to provide grants to institutions and to individuals, and to foster the opportunities for would-be John Wests of the future to have doors opened to college education. Foundation moneys not only provided undergraduate scholarships to students but also endowed a chair in political science at the Citadel.

At the invitation of Governor Jim Hodges, the West family returned to the Governor's Mansion after its renovation. Left to right are Doug West; Bill Bosley, husband of Shelton; Shelton Bosley; the Bosleys' son, Zan; and Jack West and his wife, Flonnie West. Governor John and First Lady Lois West stand at the rear. Courtesy of Lois R. West and Shelton W. Bosley

At his other alma mater, the University of South Carolina, West Foundation funds helped with the creation of the West Forum in 2002, an entity designed to promote civic education and citizen participation in government. To the dismay of some of West's Jewish critics, the West Forum also provided a platform from which he could continue his advocacy of Saudi Arabian and other Arab interests before South Carolina audiences. He became Distinguished Professor of Mid-East Studies at USC, a position that gave him further opportunities to educate and enlighten new generations of South Carolinians on the complexity of the Middle East world he had experienced and that he had come to know so well.

In 2008 the West Forum was moved to the campus of Lois West's alma mater, Winthrop University, to continue its role—according to a Winthrop statement—to "begin the training of a new generation of civic leadership."[20] The forum took its place along with the Lois Rhame West Health, Physical Education and Wellness Center as memorials to the young couple, who had challenged precedent and gotten married during the tumultuous early days of World War II six decades earlier.

The Hilton Head years were mellowing and fulfilling ones for the Wests. They were also years in which an emerging family tragedy left a permanent mark on each of them. Their younger son, Doug, had married Susan "Sue" Broadbent of Camden, and their marriage was only a few years old when she contracted a deadly form of cancer. For fourteen years she waged a battle against the disease before dying in 1995. The ordeal, as the Wests soon discovered, did not end with Sue's death. It had also taken an unforeseen toll on Doug over the course of those years. He never recovered physically or emotionally from the experience and died on September 19, 2006—eleven years after Sue died and three and a half years after the death of his dad. Doug was fifty-four.

John West's own struggle with cancer began in 2003 with the discovery of liver cancer at the Hilton Head hospital. Subsequently he received the prognosis of metastatic melanoma at the Medical University of South Carolina. "The cancer had metastasized to his liver," Shelton recalled. "They never did find the primary site. They just determined that it was somewhere inside the body."[21] After the initial finding, the Wests chose to seek further diagnosis and opinion at the renowned M. D. Anderson Cancer Center in Houston, Texas. There the news was no better.

Jack West recalled the experience. "He found out [he had cancer] in May 2003. They had done a CAT scan at the Medical University and found some cancerous growths. We decided to hold off everything until Judge Blatt's party and he went to [that] party for the last time and had a good time."[22] Sol Blatt

Jr.'s party was an annual affair that included former and current governors, other VIPs and friends, and a good cross section of the state's political community. West, Bob McNair, and Fritz Hollings were regular attendees, and it had not been uncommon for West—in his days as ambassador to Saudi Arabia— to receive a middle-of-the-night phone call in Jeddah from the revelers at "Sol Junior's Party."

After Blatt's party Jack West accompanied his dad to the Anderson Center in Houston. According to Jack,

> We wanted a second opinion [on West's cancerous growths] and I was fortunate enough to borrow a friend's plane both times so that the flight was easier for Dad.
>
> The second flight back, after we got the bad diagnosis, I fixed him a drink and we held hands for about an hour. It was a tough day.[23]

During those remaining months John West resisted stubbornly what he knew by then was the inevitable. "He continued going to the office," Lois recalled, and Shelton said, "He truly worked until the week before he died."[24] He also kept up a practice that dated back to his days in Saudi Arabia. "He continued swimming laps," Lois recalled. "I heated the pool and built a little portal out there where he could go out and step right into the pool."[25] Shelton stated, "He was doing whatever he needed to do to keep himself healthy."[26]

West also paid homage to a ritual he had honored for most of his adult life, the five o'clock cocktail. Even after he was confined to his home in his final weeks, it was a regular occurrence, and by then he had struck up a strong friendship with Lois's little dog King Kong. Years later, after she and King Kong had taken up residence in a suite in the Bosley home she dubbed "The West Wing," Lois remembered,

> The dog and John would have martinis and green beans.
>
> He loved the dog, and they were best buddies. At the end of every day at five o'clock, they'd sit down, have a drink [for West] and a snack [for King Kong].[27]

In his final months West kept a busy schedule, granting interviews, receiving visits from friends and former colleagues, and keeping up on world affairs on a daily basis. One of the most insightful interviews of West came from Aaron Gould Sheinin, then a reporter for the *State* newspaper, who visited with West six months before his death. Sheinin's article quoted West as saying, "My whole ambition and my whole thrust was to get the state's racial relationships in better order." Sheinin sought out an opinion from I. S. Leevy Johnson,

28 ∇ 10
JOHN C. WEST
BOYHOOD HOME
This farm was the boyhood home of
John Carl West (b. 1922), governor
of South Carolina 1971 - 75. West,
a graduate of the Citadel and the
University of S.C., served as
an intelligence officer in World
War II, as state senator 1955-66,
and as lieutenant governor 1967-71
before his term as governor. He
was later U.S. ambassador to Saudi
Arabia 1977 - 81.

A roadside historic marker on Cleveland School Road near Camden marks the location
of the farm where John West grew up. It stands next to the cornfield where he decided
that farming was not going to be the life for him. From the author's collection

a Columbia attorney who had become one of three blacks elected to the General Assembly the year that West became governor, 1971. West "changed the course of South Carolina history," Johnson told Sheinin. "People recognized him as a person who believed strongly in good." Jim Clyburn had told the *Charlotte Observer*, as quoted in the same article, "We were breaking ground. No southern state was doing what John West was doing. None."[28]

If there were to be a benediction to the Utopian journey of John West, it came from his friend Jimmy Carter. During his race for president in 1975, Carter recalled,

> There were 49 other governors, and John West was my favorite of them all.
>
> He was and has always remained way ahead of his time, not only in race relations, but also in a deep commitment to make sure that every citizen of South Carolina was given an opportunity for good education and health care.[29]

John West, eighty-one years old, died at about three o'clock in the afternoon of March 21, 2004, at his Hilton Head home with family nearby. His funeral attracted hundreds to his home church of Bethesda Presbyterian in Camden, and he was buried in a family plot north of town. He was widely hailed as a crusader in his native state. His old friend Prince Turki al-Faisal of Saudi Arabia said some time later, "He left us too soon."[30]

For all his acclaim as a reformer, John West was, in fact, a traditionalist at heart who saw racial justice not so much as a radical notion but rather an idea whose time had come. Freeing the energies of a long-oppressed segment of the population simply made sense to him. "I felt that if we could unleash that potential, it would be a great boon to the state," he told Sheinin in his last public interview. "I think I was right about that."[31]

West was right about a lot of things, as it turned out, and his Utopian quest left a permanent, undeniable, and irreversible impact on a state whose residents ordinarily did not much like the idea of change. He was, to the end, that good man who got elected governor of South Carolina. His son Jack West had perhaps the best description of his father's role: "He was a combination of John C. Calhoun and Atticus Finch."[32]

APPENDIX I

Inaugural Address of His Excellency the
Honorable John Carl West, Governor

State of South Carolina, Tuesday, January 19, 1971

Nineteen hundred-seventy was the year that the citizens of South Carolina marked the 300th anniversary of the founding of this state, and we now move with confidence and optimism into the Fourth Century of our stewardship of this land. Our Tricentennial year was a time of new awareness of the essential character and strength of the people of this state.

It was also a time to gain new understanding of our particular moment in history, and to view the past and the future with a new degree of sensitivity and perspective.

It was a time to realize that no state has produced more greatness in the character of its individual leaders; no state has given more freely of itself in the building of this great nation. But it was also a time to understand that ours is a history of people—of people who have known struggle and survival, disappointment and endurance, frustration and despair. We have emerged as a state in the twentieth century still limited in material attainment. But out of the trials and tests of the past, we have built a wealth of human and spiritual resources with which we can now look to our Fourth Century, a new Century of Progress for People.

As never before, we can look forward with confidence to a new era of achievement, to new milestones of accomplishment for our people, to a reawakened spirit of unity which should project our state to new heights of greatness, unparalleled in this state, or in any state at any time in history.

I make these statements not in the sense of the politician reaching for the easy superlative on a most memorable day. Instead, I speak with the assurance of one who senses an elevation of the spirits and the renewed confidence of the people in themselves. I speak as one who has observed and experienced the resurgence of our state in recent years, and has detected the new energy and new determination present within the fiber of our people.

In the last decade, South Carolina has made more progress in every meaningful way than at any comparable period in her 300-year history. In fact, I challenge historians of today or tomorrow to match the progress that South Carolinians have made in the last ten years with that made by any state—including our own—in any hundred year period of the past.

If there has been a single factor which has influenced this phenomenal growth and progress more than any other, it has been the quality of leadership our state has had in the Office of Governor.

I should like to say especially to our retiring Governor, Robert E. McNair, that yours has been a period of unusual service and unprecedented accomplishment. You have served more consecutive years as Chief Executive than any Governor in the history of our state, but your place in the history books will be for reasons other than length of term. Yours will be recorded as a period in which this state experienced its greatest human advancement. By reason of your distinguished service, you will unquestionably be accorded a well deserved place as one of the greatest governors who has ever served the State of South Carolina.

I would be remiss if I did not mention also the one who has not only been your helpmate, but one whose years as First Lady have brought new dimension to that position and a new and lasting sense of pride for the people of South Carolina. Through such accomplishments as the restoration and furnishing of the Governor's Mansion, you have not only won national acclaim but with your charm, grace and dignity, Mrs. McNair . . . Josephine . . . a lasting place has been won for you and your family in the hearts of all South Carolinians.

Thanks to the caliber of leadership South Carolina has experienced, the decade of the sixties was one of unparalleled progress for our people. But more importantly, it was a period in which the foundation was laid for the seventies —a foundation giving us the capacity to reach for and attain any goals to which we as a people may aspire.

Therefore, it is appropriate on this occasion marking the beginning of the New Century in South Carolina that we set for ourselves certain goals, goals whose urgency and priority at this moment in our history cannot be questioned The time has arrived when South Carolina for all time must break loose and break free of the vicious cycle of ignorance, illiteracy and poverty which has retarded us throughout our history.

If to some these goals seem too lofty, impossible of achievement, or unrealistic, I submit that nothing is impossible if we unite together with energy, determination, and dedication toward a common cause.

We can, and we shall, in the next four years eliminate hunger and malnutrition, and their attendant suffering from our state.

We can, and we shall, in the next four years, initiate new and innovative programs which will in our time provide adequate housing for all our citizens.

We can, and we shall, this year initiate far-reaching programs to provide more doctors, nurses and health personnel as well as better systems for delivery of health care to each citizen. Our goal shall be that each citizen may live with proper protection from disease and proper treatment of illness for his full life expectancy.

We can, and we shall, in the next four years, eliminate from our government any vestige of discrimination because of race, creed, sex, religion or any other barrier to fairness for all citizens.

We pledge to minority groups no special status other than full-fledged responsibility in a government that is totally color-blind.

We can, and we shall, accelerate programs of industrial and agricultural development until every citizen who is underemployed has the opportunity for full and rewarding employment, and every young person has a job opportunity that is productive, meaningful and challenging.

We can, and we shall, strengthen our law enforcement system by providing better training, better pay and better equipment for our officers; by strengthening our laws and court procedures dealing with criminals; and by working for the removal of the root causes of crime.

We can, and we shall, seek and channel the energy, dedication and social consciousness of our young people into solving the problems of our times.

We do not need—and we cannot afford—an alienation of the generations, and I pledge that this will be an administration that actively seeks the involvement of the young and old alike.

We can, and we shall, in the next four years take whatever action is necessary to ensure the preservation of our living environment, and to provide the type of resource management which will make it possible for all interests in our society to live in harmony with each other. There need not be and there shall not be—economic or ecological sacrifice in the progress of South Carolina in the next four years.

Finally, and perhaps most important of all, we can, and we shall, provide a better educational opportunity for all citizens of whatever age or status, from a comprehensive preschool program for the very young to a continuing educational program for adults ranging from basic literacy to sophisticated advanced research-oriented graduate programs.

These goals, admittedly ambitious, are no more impossible of achievement than those articulated by the brave young President, John F. Kennedy, who stated so eloquently in 1961 that we could perform the seemingly impossible task of placing a man safely on the moon and returning within the decade of the sixties—a dream of man for untold centuries.

It has been just as much a dream that man one day could conquer the plague of human hunger and privation, and could live in peace and dignity with his fellow man. The fact that these conditions have been a part of man's recorded lot since Biblical times should make us no less determined to attack them with all our energy and capabilities in this decade.

The setting of these goals is in itself an important first step toward their ultimate accomplishment, and—in all candor—this first step is perhaps the easiest. Certainly it is the simplest. But if these words can launch our state into positive action, if they can unleash the energies of our people and their government toward solutions, then they will have proved to be a valuable first step.

More important than action and good intentions at this point must be the establishment of guiding principles to direct and channel our efforts in this undertaking. Basically, I see three principles to be of immediate and primary importance.

First, the goals, as stated, must be accorded priority status. In today's complex society with constantly increasing demands and expectations of people, there is a tendency to overlook fundamental problems, and to scattergun society's thrust on less essential, but more glamorous functions. In a state with limited financial resources, we must concentrate with laser beam accuracy on the basic human problems using the constant criterion of Progress for People toward stated goals.

Second, the achievement of these goals can become a reality only if the people of this state unite and work together putting aside differences of race, politics, generation, or other. Two thousand years ago, the greatest philosopher and teacher who ever lived said, "And if a Kingdom be divided against itself that Kingdom cannot stand, and if a house be divided against itself, that house cannot stand." The politics of race and divisiveness have been soundly repudiated in South Carolina.

We are all one—God's people, and our differences—whether they be age, sex, religion or race—should be considered as blessings and strengths. As we work toward the elimination of discrimination, as we build toward a better life for all, as all the people of our state join together in this most noble of undertakings, perhaps we shall begin to realize the truths as expressed in the words of the hymn:

God moves in a mysterious way
His wonders to perform.
Ye fearful saints, fresh courage take;
The clouds you so much dread
Are big with mercy and shall break
In blessing on your head.

Third, in directing our efforts toward achievements which have eluded man throughout his time on this earth we must have the active involvement of all citizens. Government is but the instrument of the will of the people—having no power in and of itself; deriving not just its power but its will and effectiveness from its citizens. It is not our purpose to change that relationship; it is our goal to strengthen it. What we outline today in terms of human progress are not simply governmental projects. If we are to eliminate hunger, provide better housing, improve the delivery of health care for all, we must have the deep involvement and commitment of the private sector working in close cooperation with the public sector and providing necessary support from our whole free enterprise system.

If we are to bring the generations together, if we are to eliminate discrimination, it requires more than a law or mandate from government. Basic to all our hopes and aspirations is the willingness of our people to accept change, and to gain a new respect for the opinions and the rights of all people.

Providing a better education for all, especially within our present limited tax sources, requires new and innovative concepts, the most important aspect of which will be the voluntary involvement of citizens in the educational program.

As we address ourselves to Progress for People, it is implicit that I am also talking about Progress by People. It is most important that each citizen recognize his responsibility and his opportunity to participate in Progress for People and to make the years ahead rewarding and fulfilling, and . . .

I pledge to each of you, my fellow South Carolinians on this the most important day of my life, every ounce of strength, every talent which I possess, to move with you toward these goals for a better life for all South Carolinians and a new and brighter era in the history of our state.

APPENDIX 2

Letters from John West to President Jimmy Carter

Dear Mr. President: *July 20, 1977*

Lois and I have spent the last two days in Riyadh—my first visit here since presenting my credentials to the King some 2 weeks ago. We have been reviewing the activities of the Corps of Engineers and the Defense Dept. in assisting Saudi defense efforts, including the Saudi National Guard (SANG). This group is the Royal Family's private security guard and is composed mostly of Bedouins from the desert who are fierce fighters, intensely religious and loyal to the king. It is headed by Prince Abdullah, who is the second deputy Prime Minister after Prince Fahd.

As you perhaps know, Prince Abdullah is more conservative than Prince Fahd, but in temperament and ideology very close to King Khaled. The fact that we have a military mission to train and modernize SANG has been a major factor in helping quiet internal Royal Family opposition (led by Abdullah at one time) to Prince Fahd's pro-western, liberal policies.

This afternoon I spent an hour or so with Sheikh Abd-al-Aziz, who is deputy commander of the SANG. He describes himself as a desert Bedouin—and he looks the part. Probably in his sixties, weather-beaten with a hawk face, he has had no formal education but is extremely well-read and has a wide reputation as a philosopher as well as Prince Abdullah's chief adviser and no. 1 assistant.

He told me that he won a bet from Prince Abdullah on your election. That he bet on you because he felt you were a man of peace whose mission was to bring order and sanity to a troubled world.

"I felt that Allah sent President Carter to make peace in our lifetime," he said, "and by his actions thus far, he has made me almost a prophet among my people."

"If he will continue to move for peace based on justice and individual rights, we will have a lasting peace which will benefit all mankind."

An eloquent expression by one who might be considered less than sophisticated by some standards!

Our chief representative here is Skip Gnehm from Macon—a nephew of Dave Garrett of Delta—he is one of the best young Foreign Service officers I've ever seen.

Faithfully,
John

Dear Mr. President   *October 29, 1977*

Since you and your staff were overly generous in your comments over my letters, it hasn't taken any more persuasion to continue them, and even to expand their frequency and length!

First of all, I want to congratulate you on the way you handled the meeting with Prince Saud. It was most effective. He and Alirezia were both impressed and persuaded. Riding with them to the State Dept. afterward, Ali said, "that man makes my adrenalin flow." Saud said, "He gives me new hope."

You made them feel that we are depending on Saudi Arabia as a full partner with equal responsibility for peace in the Mid-East and economic stability in the world. That is the most effective point which can possibly be made. As I've pointed out before, they seek recognition and attention for something other than the money which they have. They are much like a newly-rich family trying to break into the blue blood social circle in Charleston. Until you came along they were ignored by the U.S. except for their money.

This same theme will be the most effective approach you can use during your visit here with the King and the Crown Prince. It will be the one point which will do more than anything else to get them to oppose an oil price increase.

Anyway, I will write you in more detail on that point before your trip, in accordance with your request. Sufficient to say, we had some excellent meetings with Sec. Blumenthal, Zaki Yamani, the King and Prince Fahd yesterday. I'm sure that Sec. Blumenthal has reported those meetings to you by now. The commitment given us by Fahd and Yamani that the Saudi position is for no increase at all was most encouraging. The only question is how strongly they will hold out at the December meeting. That's why your visit here is so important. It will give them hopefully the motivation to take a strong, even implacable, stand, on this issue at Caracas.

My two weeks in the States were busy and informative. I felt that it might be helpful to share with you some of the events and impressions from Prince

Saud's visit to Atlanta, my meeting with the Jewish leadership in New York, and several meetings with senators and Congressmen.

Saud charmed the Atlanta audience. Peter White has assembled a good group from the southeast—and even the Jewish groups who were well represented couldn't seem to make much headway with their tough questions. Saud told Paul Austin and Sam Aycock that his country would support an Egyptian motion to take Coke off the boycott list—which made them very happy. (It was a private meeting and this was given in confidence.)

The meeting with the Jewish group in New York was helpful to me—and I hope worthwhile. I recognize that an occupational hazard of an ambassador is to become too imbued with the point of view of the country he represents, and certainly meetings such as this are helpful from the point of view of perspective. The meeting included Ben Epstein, lay head of ADL, Arnold Foster, Vice-Chairman and general counsel of ADL, Rabbi Israel Miller, past pres. of presidents of all Jewish organizations and about eight others.

The major point at issue is the P.L.O. The more reasonable, less emotional members—and there were some—accept the premise that the Palestinian question has to be addressed and a solution found before a lasting peace can be had. But all took exception to our dealing with the P.L.O. They can't accept the fact that there is at present no other group with any claim or basis to speak for the Palestinians other than the P.L.O.

Fritz Hollings told me of an interesting conversation he had with Begin at the Senate breakfast—when Fritz asked him why he wouldn't talk to the P.L.O. if they accepted Res. 242. Begin gave him a lengthy lecture on how they were nothing but a bunch of terrorists—Fritz asked him again and the lecture continued—Mr. B. didn't know that Fritz doesn't take kindly to being lectured. At any rate, Fritz then said, "But Mr. Begin, don't some revolutionaries, even terrorists, gain respectability once their goals are obtained—even to the point of becoming heroes and Prime Ministers?" He said Begin grabbed his stomach and said, "Oh!"

We have several good meetings with Congressmen and Senators. I had lunch with Wendell Ford, Wendie Anderson, Fritz and Dick Stone. Sen. Stone, is, of course, the biggest spokesman for Israel in the Senate. The other three listened and were not particularly persuaded—they all think your Mid-East policy is right although the pressures from the constituent groups are strong.

Alizeria had a stag dinner for about a dozen senators at which I was included. Prince Saud is at his best in such a group and gave them a lot to think about. Those present included Jackson, Javits, Hollings, Bumpers, Morgan,

Stone, Nunn, Lugar and Hansen. The talk after dinner was largely on the proposed F-15 sale. Even Jackson and Javits seemed to soften and Javits asked if we had considered a mutual defense treaty with Saudi. Hollings said, "My God, how can you even consider that when you can't go along with selling them 50 or 60 F-15s for cash?" At any rate, the exchanges were good for all.

I went with Saud on successive mornings to the Hill for meetings with the Senate Foreign Relations Committee and House International Affairs Committees. Again, the F-15s were the principal subject. I was pleased that representatives from both groups plan to visit here after Congress adjourns. Congressman Zablocki has a list of 20–25 Congressmen who want to come. Depending on adjournment they hope to be here in early December.

Senator Byrd, Baker and Hollings will leave on Jan. 2 along with some 4 to 6 others. I think this group will be especially important. (I have visited with Senator Church and invited him to come here—he has been non-committed up to now, but I have some of his friends working on him.)

If we get enough of the decision-makers from the Congress here, I believe it will help in getting support for your Mid-East policy—which is being proven to be right with every passing day and event.

I enjoyed my visits with you and the staff—I'll write you again in the next few days—maybe it won't be as long as this one.

Faithfully,
John

P.S. Lois is indeed pleased that Rosalyn is coming along.

NOTES

I. A SOUTHERN GOVERNOR IN THE COURT OF THE SAUDIS

1. Mackey, *Saudis,* 93.
2. George Ballou in Robinson, *Yamani,* 119–20.
3. John West in Robinson, *Yamani,* 120.
4. Jimmy Carter, interview by the author, January 21, 2004, Jimmy Carter Presidential Library, Atlanta, Ga.
5. Ibid.
6. Lippman, *Inside the Mirage,* 312.
7. John C. West to Jimmy Carter, October 27, 1977, John C. West Papers, box 40, South Carolina Political Collections, University of South Carolina, Columbia (hereafter SCPC).
8. Vance, *Hard Choices,* 163–77.
9. John C. West Journal, May 24, 1977, West Papers, SCPC.
10. Shelton West Bosley, interview by the author, February 20, 2008.
11. West Journal, May 24, 1977, West Papers, SCPC.
12. Ibid.
13. Carter, interview by the author, January 21, 2004.
14. West Journal, May 24, 1977, West Papers, SCPC.
15. Carter, interview by the author, January 21, 2004.
16. West Journal, May 24, 1977, West Papers, SCPC.
17. Vance, *Hard Choices,* 178.
18. Ibid., 179.
19. John West, conversation with the author, January 16, 2003.
20. Robinson, *Yamani,* 235.
21. Vance, *Hard Choices,* 163.
22. Strong, *Working in the World,* 185–86.
23. *Washington Post,* May 14, 1977.
24. Ibid.
25. Long, *Saudi Arabia,* 13–14.
26. Powell, *Saudi Arabia,* 165.
27. Ibid., 14–15.
28. Ibid., 80.
29. Carter, interview by the author, January 21, 2004.
30. Ibid.
31. John C. West, interview by the author, August 1, 2003.
32. Ibid.
33. West Journal, May 24, 1977, West Papers, SCPC.
34. Lois West, interview by the author, February 20, 2008.

35. Eddy, "FDR Meets Ibn Saud," 45. Despite the diplomatic rebuff, the Saudis chose to regard the meeting at the Suez Canal as the beginning of the U.S.–Saudi Arabia friendship. In the article cited above, an account of the 1945 meeting was provided by the American interpreter at the session, William A. Eddy. He recorded the dissent over the issue of the Jewish state, but the account of the Suez meeting deals largely with the personal friendship developed by the two heads of state. In his 2006 book *Saving the Jews,* Robert Rosen uses the Eddy material in describing the meeting and Roosevelt's disappointment. Prior to departing for the long trip, the president had told a close associate and adviser, Rabbi Stephen Wise, and members of his cabinet that he hoped to engage ibn Saud to "try to settle the Palestine situation." Rosen, *Saving the Jews,* 409–10. Upon his return, he told his wife, Eleanor, that the meeting was "one complete failure," and he reported to Rabbi Wise, "I most gloriously failed where you are concerned." Ibid., 414.

Roosevelt was probably aware that Saudi discontent over the prospect of a Jewish homeland predated Hitler and the Holocaust. It was articulated as early as 1917 when ibn Saud's son Faisal traveled to Great Britain to articulate Saudi opposition to the "Balfour Declaration," a policy position issued by British foreign secretary Arthur Balfour, which favored the establishment of a "National Home for the Jewish people" in Palestine. Faisal argued that acquiring Arab land for a Jewish national home amounted to "bald-faced banditry." Powell, *Saudi Arabia,* 264–65.

Thirty years later the Saudis opposed the United Nations resolution establishing the nation of Israel in 1948 and were offended by the U.S. support of the resolution. "Relations between the two countries became strained over the question of Palestine," the historian William Powell wrote. "President Truman had chosen to ignore Roosevelt's promise to Abdul-Aziz [ibn Saud] that the United States would take no position without first consulting with the Saudi monarch." Powell, *Saudi Arabia,* 265.

36. John West inaugural address, January 19, 1971, West Papers, SCPC.

37. Ibid.

38. John West, remarks to twenty-fifth anniversary dinner of the S.C. Human Affairs Commission, West Papers, SCPC.

2. WHERE THE NEW SOUTH WAS BORN

1. "Democrats' Comeback in South—a Political Key to '72," *U.S. News and World Report,* March 29, 1971, 22.

2. Ibid., 23.

3. Senator Beauregard Claghorn was a popular character on the radio program *The Fred Allen Show* in the 1940s. He was a blustery southern politician with a humorously portrayed obsession with the South.

4. Harvey, *Question of Justice,* 4.

5. "Democrats' Comeback in South," 24.

6. Carter, *An Hour before Daylight,* 19.

7. Harvey, *Question of Justice,* 7.

8. Bumpers, *The Best Lawyer,* 10.

9. Autobiographical fragment, West Papers, SCPC.

10. Ibid.

11. Dale Hudson, "Baptism by Fire," unpublished manuscript, 329. Copy in author's possession; cited with permission of Dale Hudson.

12. Ibid., 361.

13. Autobiographical fragment, West Papers, SCPC.

14. Ibid.

15. Hudson, "Baptism by Fire," 399.

16. Ibid., 444. The site of the Cleveland School is marked by a monument listing all the victims and their ages and a small replica of the wooden school building. It is located on Cleveland School Road, a short distance from Interstate 20 east and south of Camden.

17. Autobiographical fragment, West Papers, SCPC.

18. John C. West, interview by the author, July 25, 2003.

19. Autobiographical fragment, West Papers, SCPC.

20. Ibid.

21. John C. West, interview by the author, July 25, 2003.

22. Autobiographical fragment, West Papers, SCPC.

23. Ibid.

24. Ibid.

25. Ibid.

26. John C. West, interview by the author, July 25, 2003.

27. Ibid.

28. Autobiographical fragment, West Papers, SCPC.

29. Ibid.

30. Ibid.

31. Ibid.

32. Lois West, interview by the author, February 21, 2006.

33. Ibid.

34. *Charleston Post-Courier,* March 23, 2004.

35. Autobiographical fragment, West Papers, SCPC.

36. Lois West, interview by the author, February 21, 2006.

37. Autobiographical fragment, West Papers, SCPC.

38. Ibid.

39. John West to General Charles P. Summerall, April, 11, 1938, the Citadel Archives and Museum, Charleston, S.C.

40. Ibid., June 16, 1938.

41. Autobiographical fragment, West Papers, SCPC.

42. Papers of Dr. Madison Langley Bell, 1943–46, the Citadel Archives and Museum.

43. Autobiographical fragment, West Papers, SCPC.

44. Ibid.

45. Lois West, interview by the author, February 21, 2006.

46. Autobiographical fragment, West Papers, SCPC.

47. Ibid.

48. Ibid.

49. Clark Williams to General C. P. Summerall, April 18, 1942, the Citadel Archives and Museum.

50. George McCarty, head, Department of Speech, South Dakota State College, to President Summerall, April 17, 1942, the Citadel Archives and Museum.

51. *The Sphinx,* 1942, the Citadel, Charleston, S.C.

52. Autobiographical fragment, West Papers, SCPC.

53. Lois West, interview by the author, February 21, 2006.

54. Ibid.

55. Ibid.
56. Ibid.
57. Autobiographical fragment, West Papers, SCPC.

3. THE CODES OF WAR

1. D.H. White Jr., "Oral History Transcript of an Interview with the Honorable John C. West, Hilton Head Island, South Carolina, July 14, 2000," Revised 1/27/2003, p. 8, West Papers, SCPC.
2. Ibid.
3. Ibid.
4. Ibid., 1–2.
5. Autobiographical fragment, West Papers, SCPC; White, "Oral History Transcript," 2.
6. White, "Oral History Transcript," 2.
7. Ibid.
8. *Camden (S.C.) Chronicle,* September 12, 1942. The wedding announcement in the *Camden Chronicle* recorded that the service was held at 8:00 P.M. at Post Chapel 4, Fort Monmouth, New Jersey. The bride was given away by her brother Lt. Robert L. Rhame, and Charles G. Whitmire was West's best man. The wedding ring, it was noted, was an heirloom from the bridegroom's family, having been worn for four generations. It was reportedly made of gold dug in 1849 from a mine in California owned by the bridegroom's great-great-uncle, who made the ring for his wife.
9. Autobiographical fragment, West Papers, SCPC.
10. Ibid.
11. Ibid.
12. Ibid.
13. Ibid.
14. Ibid.
15. Ibid.
16. Ibid.
17. John C. West to Col. Williams, December 20, 1943, the Citadel Archives and Museum.
18. Lois West, interview by the author, February 21, 2006.
19. Autobiographical fragment, West Papers, SCPC.
20. Ibid.
21. Ibid.
22. Ibid.
23. Ibid.
24. Ibid.
25. Ibid.
26. World War II Military Intelligence, U.S. Army Center of Military History, Washington, D.C. (hereafter WWII Military Intelligence), chap. 5, 4.
27. McCormack, *History of Special Branch M.I.S.,* 9.
28. WWII Military Intelligence, chap. 5, 4.
29. Ibid., 10.
30. Russell is described in State Department documents as being among those who provided "outspoken dissent and undermining efforts" against McCormack's recommendation. "Russell and the heads of the geographic bureaus, arguing that 'intelligence is only as good as it is translated into action' by the geographic units, lobbied for a decentralized structure under

their control . . . while McCormack favored a more centralized organization in the Department that would be 'free of operations or policy involvements' and could serve other units as well as the geographic bureaus. . . . Because it soon appeared that the whole Department was deadlocked on the intelligence issue, the military increasingly decided to take the lead on the issue." Wrangling over responsibility for foreign intelligence among the departments continued in the postwar years until President Truman issued a directive asking that the secretaries of state, war, and the navy create an independent Central Intelligence group whose director would be appointed by the president. See U.S. Department of State, Foreign Relations of the United States, Emergence of the Intelligence Establishment, Office of the Historian, 4–5.

31. WWII Military Intelligence, chap. 5, 4.

32. *Washington Post,* May 26, 2002.

33. Autobiographical fragment, West Papers, SCPC.

34. Ibid.

35. A fond recollection of West's in later years was a story about his final days at the Citadel and a lecture from a Major Tasker, professor of military science and tactics, ROTC. "I well remember one of the last things he said in our final lecture at The Citadel," West recalled. "'Now, fellows, when you get to your first post, the one thing we don't want you to do is go to the officers' club on Saturday night, drink too much beer, and sing Citadel songs.' Well, of course, we did exactly that, and we drank many a beer toast to Major Tasker on that first Saturday night at Camp Stewart." See White, "Oral History Transcript," 4.

36. Autobiographical fragment, West Papers, SCPC; White, "Oral History Transcript," 4.

37. Autobiographical fragment, West Papers, SCPC.

38. White, "Oral History Transcript," 5.

39. Autobiographical fragment, West Papers, SCPC.

40. Graham's wartime experiences were noted by his wife Katherine Graham in her autobiography, *Personal History:* "Phil had maneuvered to jump over to a more exciting and challenging milieu in the Special Branch. So, after another month-long school program on intelligence training, he was transferred to Washington to go into the Special Branch, a super-secret part of Intelligence run by an ex–Cravath, Swaine & Moore lawyer, Colonel Al McCormick [*sic*], who had commandeered many of our friends, as well as many others who were to become friends. I never knew, and probably none of the spouses knew, what Phil and the other men did. Only much later, when we learned that early in the war the secret codes used by Germany and Japan had been broken, did we understand that Special Branch had been engaged in reading messages being sent back and forth from the field." Katherine Graham, *Personal History* (New York: Alfred A. Knopf, 1997), 153.

41. McCormack, *History of Special Branch M.I.S.,* 29–30.

42. Finnegan, *Military Intelligence,* chap. 5, 4–5.

43. *Enigma and the Code Breakers,* 1–2, Imperial War Museum, London, England, http://www.iwm.org.uk/upload/package/10/enigma/enigma7.htm (accesseed October 13, 2010). Finnegan, *Military Inteligence.*

44. Finnegan, *Military Intelligence,* chap. 5, 6.

45. Ibid.

46. Autobiographical fragment, West Papers, SCPC.

47. McCormack, *History of Special Branch M.I.S.,* 61–62.

48. Ibid., 57.

49. White, "Oral History Transcript," 7.

50. Ibid., 14.

51. Ibid.

52. Ibid., 8.

53. Autobiographical fragment, West Papers, SCPC.

54. "The Incendiary Bombing Raids on Tokyo, 1945," Eyewitness to History, http://www.eyewitnesstohistory.com/tokyo.htm (accessed August 2, 2010).

55. White, "Oral History Transcript," 15.

56. Ibid.

57. Ibid., 8.

58. Ibid., 9.

59. John C. West Jr., interview by the author, April 17, 2009.

60. White, "Oral History Transcript," 8.

61. Ibid., 9.

62. Ibid., 8.

4. THE MAKING OF AN ADVOCATE

1. Autobiographical fragment, West Papers, SCPC.

2. Ibid.

3. See http://www.pbs.org/wnet/jimcrow/stories_events_smith.html (accessed August 2, 2010). In its *Smith v. Allwright* decision, the U.S. Supreme Court ruled, "The right to vote in a primary for the nomination of candidates without discrimination by the state, like the right to vote in a general election, is a right guaranteed by the Constitution." South Carolina governor Olin D. Johnston responded to the *Smith* ruling by calling an "emergency" session of the General Assembly in April 1944, and in six days legislators wiped out all statutes relating to the primary and ruled it to be a "private" apparatus. The Columbia black businessman George A. Elmore challenged the action in federal court, and on July 12, 1947, in his *Rice v. Elmore* verdict, Judge J. Waties Waring ruled in Elmore's favor, nullifying the Johnston initiatives and erasing the legislative maneuvering to keep the Democratic primary all white. See Carolyn Click, *State* newspaper, http://www.thestateonline.com/civilrights/day2/civilrights03.php (accessed August 2, 2010).

4. Autobiographical fragment, West Papers, SCPC.

5. Ibid.

6. Ibid.

7. Ibid.

8. Ibid.

9. Ibid.

10. Ibid.

11. Ibid.

12. Ibid.

13. Ibid.

14. Ibid.

15. Ibid.

16. Ibid.

17. Ibid.

18. Ibid.

19. Ibid.

20. Ibid.

21. Ibid.

22. Ibid.

23. Ibid.

24. Ibid.

25. Ibid.

26. Ibid.

27. Ibid.

28. Ibid.

29. Ibid.

30. Ibid.

31. Ibid.

32. Ibid.

33. Ibid.

34. Ibid.

35. Ibid.

36. Coit, *Mr. Baruch,* 5–17, 45. Baruch's interest in health care was spawned by his father, Simon Baruch, a doctor who had immigrated to the United States from Prussia in 1855 and served as a field surgeon on the staff of Confederate general Robert E. Lee during the Civil War. Bernard Baruch was born in Camden in 1870, and in 1881 the family moved to New York, where he graduated from City College in 1889. Although he became internationally known as a successful financial adviser to U.S. presidents, Baruch retained an interest in Camden and South Carolina, spending time at his 17,500-acre Hobcaw Barony on the South Carolina coast above Georgetown, where he hosted distinguished guests such as President Franklin Roosevelt and British prime minister Winston Churchill. By the early 1950s, however, Baruch was spending less time at Hobcaw and more time at "Little Hobcaw," his 1,000-acre estate near Kingstree. Ibid., 646.

37. Autobiographical fragment, West Papers, SCPC.

38. *Camden (S.C.) Chronicle,* January 12, 1954.

39. Autobiographical fragment, West Papers, SCPC.

40. Lois West, interview by the author, February 21, 2006.

41. Autobiographical fragment, West Papers, SCPC.

42. Ibid.

43. *Camden (S.C.) Chronicle,* May 3, 1954.

44. Ibid., May 25, 1954.

45. Ibid.

46. Ibid.

47. Autobiographical fragment, West Papers, SCPC.

48. A longtime friend and campaign worker in the 1954 race, Harvey Teal described West as "a good campaigner. He understood the psychology of the voters and what motivated them. He was not a rip-snorter or an orator . . . he was more of a reason person . . . actually a calming person" (Harvey Teal, interview by the author, June 25, 2005).

49. *Camden (S.C.) Chronicle,* May 25, 1954.

50. Ibid., June 1, 1954.

51. Ibid.

52. Autobiographical fragment, West Papers, SCPC.

53. Teal, interview by the author, June 25, 2005.

54. *Camden (S.C.) Chronicle,* March 23, 1954.

55. Autobiographical fragment, West Papers, SCPC.

56. Ibid.
57. *Camden (S.C.) Chronicle,* June 11, 1954.
58. Ibid., June 15, 1954.
59. Ibid., June 11, 1954.
60. Ibid., June 11, 1954, and June 25, 1954.
61. Grose, *South Carolina,* 131.

5. POLITICS IN THE ROUGH

1. Halberstam, *The Fifties,* 9.
2. Workman, *Bishop from Barnwell,* 252.
3. Lachicotte, *Rebel Senator,* 84–85.
4. Workman, *Bishop from Barnwell,* 251–52.
5. Rembert Dennis, personal interview, Oral Histories of the McNair Gubernatorial Administration, S.C. Department of Archives and History, Columbia, S.C., 6.
6. Workman, *Bishop from Barnwell,* 252.
7. Ibid., 248.
8. Ibid., 249.
9. Ibid., 250.
10. Cohodas, *Strom Thurmond,* 256–57.
11. Workman, *Bishop from Barnwell,* 253.
12. Ibid., 254–55.
13. Ibid., 259.
14. Ibid., 256.
15. Cohodas, *Strom Thurmond,* 262.
16. Ibid., 264.
17. Lachicotte, *Rebel Senator,* 88.
18. Cohodas, *Strom Thurmond,* 264.
19. Autobiographical fragment, West Papers, SCPC.
20. Workman, *Bishop from Barnwell,* 256.
21. Autobiographical fragment, West Papers, SCPC.
22. Lander, *History of South Carolina,* 197–98.
23. Cohodas, *Strom Thurmond,* 264.
24. Ibid., 263.
25. Autobiographical fragment, West Papers, SCPC.
26. Ibid.
27. Ibid.
28. Workman, *Bishop from Barnwell,* 270.
29. Ibid.
30. Autobiographical fragment, West Papers, SCPC.
31. Ibid.
32. Ibid.
33. Ibid.
34. *Camden (S.C.) Chronicle,* March 13, 1956.
35. Lander, *History of South Carolina,* 203.
36. Autobiographical fragment, West Papers, SCPC.
37. Ibid.
38. Lander, *History of South Carolina,* 202.

39. Ibid.

40. *Camden (S.C.) Chronicle,* March 23, 1956.

41. Ibid., January, 27, 1953.

42. Ibid., February 10, 1956.

43. Ibid., February 14, 1956.

44. Ibid., July 31, 1956.

45. Ibid.

46. Ibid.

47. Autobiographical fragment, West Papers, SCPC.

48. *Camden (S.C.) Chronicle,* December 31, 1956.

49. Autobiographical fragment, West Papers, SCPC.

50. *Camden (S.C.) Chronicle,* December 31, 1956.

51. Ibid.

52. Jim Clyburn, interview by the author, January 20, 2006.

53. *Camden (S.C.) Chronicle,* December 31, 1956.

54. Autobiographical fragment, West Papers, SCPC.

55. *Camden (S.C.) Chronicle,* February 1, 1957.

56. Ibid., January 14, 1957.

57. Ibid.

58. Ibid., January 7, 1957.

59. Ibid., March 11, 1957.

60. Ibid., June 1957.

61. Autobiographical fragment, West Papers, SCPC.

62. Ann Hutchins, interview by the author, May 4, 2006.

63. *Clemson World Magazine,* December 1981.

64. *Camden (S.C.) Chronicle,* July 21, 1997.

65. Autobiographical fragment, West Papers, SCPC.

66. Lois West, interview by the author, February 21, 2006.

67. Autobiographical fragment, West Papers, SCPC.

68. Lois West, interview by the author, February 21, 2006.

6. A QUIET VOICE OF REASON

1. Autobiographical fragment, West Papers, SCPC.

2. Ibid.

3. Ibid.

4. Ibid.

5. Ibid.

6. Ibid.

7. Ibid.

8. Ibid.

9. Ibid.

10. Frank Best, WDIX editorial, box 1, Public, S.C. Senate, Topical, Education, Higher, General, West Papers, SCPC.

11. Report of the Governor's Committee to Lend Support and Leadership to Nursing in South Carolina, p. 3, box 1, West Papers, SCPC.

12. WBTW editorial, February 12, 1965, box 1, West Papers, SCPC.

13. West to Tom Waring, February 6, 1958, box 1, West Papers, SCPC.

14. George C. Rogers to West, January 8, 1958, box 1, West Papers, SCPC.

15. Report of Public School Curriculum Committee, box 1, West Papers, SCPC.

16. Autobiographical fragment, West Papers, SCPC.

17. Ibid.

18. Ibid., 115.

19. In its report to the General Assembly, West's study committee observed that

> only about one-third (⅓) of our high school graduates enter college. . . . When we further consider (1) that only about one-half (½) of the students who enter school in the first grade ultimately receive the high school diploma and (2) that there are many dropouts in college after the first or second year, we conclude that less than five (5%) percent of our school population finishes college.
>
> Therefore, approximately 95% of our citizens at present are faced with the problem of earning a livelihood without the benefit of a college degree. The vast majority of our youth present to the state a real challenge to provide them a quality program of technical training which will better prepare them to earn a livelihood and assume the responsibilities of good citizens (John West files, 1961 Report of Committee Studying the Needs of the State Development Board on the Subject of Vocational and Technical Training, p. 3, SCPC).

20. 1961 Report of Committee Studying the Needs of the State Development Board on the Subject of Vocational and Technical Training, p. 16, West Papers, SCPC.

21. Ibid., 2.

22. Autobiographical fragment, West Papers, SCPC.

23. Ibid.

24. Ibid.

25. Ibid.

26. Ibid.

27. *Camden (S.C.) Chronicle,* June 9, 1958.

28. Ibid.

29. Ibid.

30. *Camden (S.C.) Chronicle,* June 11, 1958.

31. C. T. Graydon to West, October 19, 1960, box 1 (1954–60), West Papers, SCPC.

32. Ibid., West to Graydon, October 22, 1960.

33. Ibid., letter from William D. Workman Jr., January 2, 1962.

34. Ibid., West to William D. Workman, January 5, 1962.

35. Ibid.

36. Ibid., Estellene Walker to John West, March 26, 1956.

37. Ibid., Robert C. Tucker to John West, March 27, 1956.

38. *Charlotte (N.C.) Observer,* May 15, 1961.

39. Autobiographical fragment, West Papers, SCPC.

40. *Charlotte (N.C.) Observer,* May 15, 1961.

41. Ibid.

42. Autobiographical fragment, West Papers, SCPC.

43. In 1963 the North Carolina General Assembly passed the Speaker Ban Law, an effort to prevent communists from appearing on state-owned college and university property. The law was passed without legislative debate, so its origins remain obscure. There were many

civil rights demonstrations going on in 1963, and while these demonstrations were not known to be communist inspired, some legislators tended to see communism behind racial unrest.

In 1966 the campus chapter of Students for a Democratic Society (SDS) invited Herbert Aptheker (an avowed communist) and Frank Wilkinson to speak at UNC–Chapel Hill. After exchanges among the university trustees and administration over the application of the Speaker Ban Law to the appearances of Aptheker and Wilkinson, it was decided that they should be banned. The speakers addressed the students over the wall on the perimeter of the campus. After a subsequent lawsuit by students and banned speakers, the Speaker Ban Law was declared unconstitutional in 1968. See https://www.unctv.org/60s/speaker_ban.html (accessed September 27, 2010).

44. West to Julia Post, March 18, 1965, box 1, West Papers, SCPC.

45. Autobiographical fragment, West Papers, SCPC.

46. Ibid.

47. Robert E. McNair, personal interview, Oral Histories of the Robert E. McNair Gubernatorial Administration (1965–71), South Carolina Department of Archives and History, Columbia, tape 5, 6.

48. Ibid.

49. Autobiographical fragment, West Papers, SCPC.

50. McNair, personal interview, Oral Histories, tape 5, 7.

51. John C. West Jr., interview by the author, April 17, 2009.

52. Autobiographical fragment, West Papers, SCPC.

53. Ibid.

54. McNair, personal interview, Oral Histories, tape 5, 7.

55. Autobiographical fragment, West Papers, SCPC.

56. McNair, personal interview, Oral Histories, tape 5, 8.

57. Grose, *South Carolina,* 131.

58. Autobiographical fragment, West Papers, SCPC.

59. Ibid.

60. McNair, personal interview, Oral Histories, tape 5, 24.

7. AN EXPLODING POLITICAL UNIVERSE

1. Workman, *Bishop from Barnwell,* 238.

2. Ibid., 270.

3. *Columbia (S.C.) State,* June 20, 1968.

4. Supplemental Report of the Secretary of State to the General Assembly, 1968, courtesy of the South Carolina State Election Commission.

5. *Camden (S.C.) Chronicle,* 1964, undated clipping, West Papers, SCPC.

6. *Columbia (S.C.) Record,* June 19, 1965.

7. McNair, personal interview, Oral Histories, tape 11, 14–15.

8. West to John L. Hall, April 8, 1965, West Papers, SCPC.

9. Dent, *Prodigal South Returns,* 288–89.

10. Ibid.

11. Autobiographical fragment, West Papers, SCPC.

12. Ibid.

13. Ibid.

14. Ibid.

15. *South Carolina Legislative Manual* (1967), 364–65.

16. *Greenville News,* October 17, 1966.

17. *Charleston (S.C.) News and Courier,* June 17, 1966; reprint from *"Had Enuff?" News, Florence (S.C.) Morning News,* undated clipping, Joseph O. Rogers Papers, SCPC.

18. *Charleston (S.C.) News and Courier,* October 23, 1966.

19. *"Had Enuff?" News,* undated clipping, Joseph O. Rogers Paper, SCPC.

20. *Florence (S.C.) Morning News,* August 21, 1966.

21. *Greenwood (S.C.) Index-Journal,* November 3, 1966.

22. Ibid.

23. *Columbia (S.C.) State,* November 4, 1966.

24. Ibid.

25. Vote totals from the *South Carolina Legislative Manual* (1967).

26. *Columbia (S.C.) State,* December 14, 1965.

27. Autobiographical fragment, West Papers, SCPC.

28. West Journal, May 17, 1967, West Papers, SCPC.

29. Ibid., June 29, 1967.

30. Ibid., June 30, 1967.

31. Blatt to West, in the presence of reporters, including the author.

32. West Journal, June 7, 1967, West Papers, SCPC.

33. Ibid., June 15, 1967.

34. *Columbia (S.C.) State,* July 9, 1967.

35. *Camden (S.C.) Chronicle,* 1964, undated clipping, West Papers, SCPC.

36. *Columbia (S.C.) State,* March 8, 1968.

37. Ibid., March 14, 1968.

38. Leroy Davis to West, March 29, 1968, West Papers, SCPC.

39. Andrew Hugine Jr. to West, March 29, 1968, West Papers, SCPC.

40. Rubin F. Weston to West, April 22, 1968, West Papers, SCPC.

41. C. H. Thomas Jr. to Governor Robert E. McNair, March 6, 1968, SCPC.

42. WDIX editorial, April 1, 1968, West Papers, SCPC.

43. John West address at S.C. State, February 20, 1968, West Papers, SCPC.

8. "WE CAN, AND WE SHALL"

1. Address to public hearing on desegregation rules and regulations conducted by Minnesota State Board of Education, St. Paul, Minnesota, December 2, 1972, manuscript in the possession of Cyril Busbee.

2. Panetta and Gall, *Bring Us Together,* 21–22.

3. *Charleston (S.C.) News and Courier,* January 24, 1970.

4. Dent, *Prodigal South Returns,* 121.

5. In his letter to Jeryl Best, West said, "I regret that a previous commitment will make it impossible for me to attend the rally scheduled for Sunday afternoon. However, I want to assure you and the other concerned citizens of Darlington County of my sympathy and concern for their cause. The disruption of the educational processes of your children by the tyranny of the federal courts is the most senseless judicial act that I have ever seen in my nearly twenty-five years as a practicing attorney. Such an action can only hurt the educational process of all children, black or white." West to Jeryl Best, February 20, 1970, West Papers, SCPC.

6. *Columbia (S.C.) State,* February 23, 1970.

7. *Camden (S.C.) Chronicle,* February 23, 1970.

8. *Charlotte (N.C.) Observer,* March 22, 1970.

9. *Washington Post,* March 7, 1970.

10. *Charleston (S.C.) News and Courier,* July 5, 1970.

11. Undated Associated Press clipping, West Papers, SCPC.

12. *Charlotte (N.C.) Observer,* July 9, 1970.

13. Undated Associated Press clipping, West Papers, SCPC.

14. In an interview two years later with Jack Bass, West said that his comments "weren't intended to have racist overtones." Bass wrote that after such episodes, citing "other sources," West "told campaign aides, who urged otherwise, that he would make no more [comments] like them because if he had to yell 'nigger,' he didn't want the job." Bass, "John C. West of South Carolina," 9–10.

15. Jim Clyburn, one of the founders of the United Citizens Party, contended that the party was founded to run candidates for the legislature from the state's ten majority black counties, and not for statewide office. "We didn't realize that you can't stop anybody from going out and announcing what they were going to run for," Clyburn said. Broadwater's decision to run caused significant divisions among black political leaders. James Clyburn, interview by the author, October 11, 2005.

16. Clyburn, interview by the author, October 11, 2005.

17. *Columbia (S.C.) State,* October 16, 1970.

18. Ibid.

19. Jay Latham, transcript of October 16, 1970, press conference, University of South Carolina, in the author's possession.

20. Hathorn, "The Changing Politics of Race," 233.

21. *Florence (S.C.) Morning News,* September 25, 1970.

22. *Columbia (S.C.) Record,* November 11, 1970.

23. Clyburn recalled, "The night of the vote about ten o'clock in the evening I was declared the winner. Then about three-thirty in the morning, I got a visit from a TV reporter. . . . [He] told me . . . something had gone wrong at the courthouse, I'd better get down there. So we went down to the courthouse and found that rather than being a 500-vote winner as I was declared to be at ten o'clock in the evening, I was a 500-vote loser. . . . Somebody adding up the votes had forgotten to carry a one." Clyburn, interview by the author, October 11, 2005.

24. Ibid.

25. West, conversation with the author.

26. *Columbia (S.C.) State,* January 20, 1971.

27. John West inaugural address, January 1971, West Papers, SCPC.

28. *New York Times,* January 20, 1971.

29. Undated *New York Post* clipping, West Papers, SCPC.

30. *New York Times,* January 22, 1971.

31. *Charlotte (N.C.) Observer,* January 20, 1971.

32. *Columbia (S.C.) State,* January 20, 1971.

33. John West inaugural address, January 19, 1971, West Papers, SCPC.

34. Ibid.

35. West Journal, January 19, 1971, West Papers, SCPC.

36. *Columbia (S.C.) State,* January 28, 1971.

37. Beazley, *South Carolina Human Affairs Commission,* 8–9.

38. Ibid., 8.

39. Members of the Advisory Commission on Human Relations were J. W. "Bill" Travis of Columbia, Dr. Benjamin F. Payton of Columbia, Elliott E. Franks of Columbia, Susan Goldberg of Charleston, Barbara Paige of Aiken, William Saunders of Charleston, Fred Sheheen of Camden, Mrs. Charles Wickenberg of Columbia, Dr. Joseph Stukes of Due West, Arthur M. Williams of Columbia, Rev. James T. McCain of Sumter, Cooper White of Greenville, John R. Hall of Great Falls, Dr. R. N. Beck of Florence, Malcolm Havens of Charleston, Andrew Hugine of Orangeburg, Bobby Leach of Spartanburg, John H. Lumpkin of Columbia, and Andrew Teszlar. Ibid., 9–10.

40. Bass, interview with West, *South Today,* July–August 1972, 9–10.

41. "Schizophrenia," *Columbia (S.C.) State,* undated, in Grose, *South Carolina,* 195.

42. Not until the year 2000, forty-five years after the alleged shooting incident and twenty-five years after the death of Reverend De Laine, was the issue resolved. At the initiative of Governor Jim Hodges, the state's Probation, Parole and Pardon Board issued a posthumous pardon to Reverend De Laine, clearing him of all charges in the 1955 shooting. This was the same year that the Confederate battle flag was removed from the dome of the South Carolina State House. See *Washington Post,* October 11, 2000.

43. Beazley, *South Carolina Human Affairs Commission,* 18.

44. Members of the first Human Affairs Commission were the holdovers Elliott Franks, Barbara Paige, William Saunders, Bobby Leach, Margaret Wickenberg, Arthur Williams, Benjamin Payton, Malcolm Havens, Andrew Hugine, and John Lumpkin. Newly appointed members were John Hagins of Greenville, Guy Hutchins of Camden, Lachlan Hyatt of Spartanburg, W. E. "Buddy" Myrick of Allendale, Ray Williams of Columbia, and Marian Green of Charleston. The commission also had a new chairman, the attorney Harry M. Lightsey Jr., who had chaired West's 1966 campaign for lieutenant governor and went on to become dean of the University of South Carolina Law School and president of the College of Charleston. *South Carolina Legislative Manual* (1972).

45. *New York Times,* May 26, 1973, in Beazley, *South Carolina Human Affairs Commission,* 27.

9. MAKING THINGS HAPPEN

1. *Columbia (S.C.) State,* January 4, 1973.

2. Byrnes, *All in One Lifetime,* 411.

3. John West, State of the State Address, 1972, West Papers, SCPC.

4. *Charleston (S.C.) News and Courier,* October 27, 1970.

5. Ibid., October 24, 1971.

6. John West, State of the State Address, 1972, West Papers, SCPC.

7. *Columbia (S.C.) State,* January 13, 1972.

8. *Charleston (S.C.) News and Courier,* January 14, 1972.

9. *Anderson (S.C.) Independent,* January 13, 1972.

10. *Charlotte (N.C.) Observer,* February 13, 1972.

11. *Columbia (S.C.) State,* March 1973.

12. Saunders, *To Improve the Health of the People,* 102.

13. Ibid., 132.

14. *Sandlapper* 7 (January 1974): 7–8, 12–18.

15. Robert E. "Jack" David, in conversation with the author.

16. *Charlotte (N.C.) Observer,* January 23, 1973.

17. Ibid., June 27, 1974.

18. Ibid., July 2, 1974.

19. Ibid., January 17, 1973.

20. John West, State of the State address, January 16, 1973, West Papers, SCPC.

21. Lois West recalled: "There hadn't been any married students at Winthrop. Most people got married and left, just didn't come back if they got married. So I had to get my degree because I knew I had to put John through law school . . . I went to the Dean of Women, Mrs. Hardin, and asked her if I could come back and finish. She said, 'Lois, nobody ever asked me that before.' And so I said, 'Well, I've got to get a degree.' So I came back and finished it." Lois West, interview by the author, May 14, 2009. The Wests' daughter, Shelton, later enrolled as a freshman at Winthrop, and she commented to a reporter about her mother's position on the coeducation issue. "Her reason behind it," Shelton West said, "is that she'd like to see Winthrop's football team beat Clemson and Carolina—she's pretty cool about stuff like that." *Columbia (S.C.) State,* undated clipping [ca. 1972], West Papers, SCPC.

22. *Columbia (S.C.) State,* May 15, 1972.

23. Ibid., October 3, 1972.

24. Douglas H. Carlisle, "The Administration of John Carl West, Governor of South Carolina, 1971–1975," 1975, typescript, 3:9, box 25, West Papers, SCPC.

25. Thurmond was up for reelection in 1972, and a Democratic state senator, Eugene N. "Nick" Zeigler of Florence, entered the race against him. West hoped that Wallace could provide some conservative credibility and support for Zeigler's campaign, and he persuaded the Alabaman to agree to the language of a Zeigler newspaper ad that ran statewide proclaiming that if George Wallace lived in South Carolina, he would vote for Nick Zeigler. In the landslide Nixon victory of 1972, Zeigler lost by a 64 to 36 percent margin. Zeigler, *When Conscience and Power Meet,* 267–68..

26. *Charlotte (N.C.) Observer,* March 5, 1972.

27. *Columbia (S.C.) State,* June 22, 1972.

28. *Gulfport-Biloxi (Miss.) Daily Herald,* September 13, 1972.

29. West, in conversation with the author.

30. *Columbia (S.C.) State,* February 21, 1973.

31. West Journal, February 20, 1972, West Papers, SCPC.

32. *Columbia (S.C.) State,* July 1974.

33. Ibid., September 29, 1974.

34. Ibid.

35. A staff member's conversation with the author.

36. Carlisle, "Administration of John Carl West," 4:2, West Papers, SCPC.

37. *Camden (S.C.) Chronicle,* November 15, 1972.

38. Carlisle, "Administration of John Carl West," 2:5, West Papers, SCPC.

39. *Greenville (S.C.) News,* January 1972.

40. *Columbia (S.C.) State,* April 8, 1973.

41. *Charlotte (N.C.) Observer,* January 14, 1973.

42. *Orangeburg (S.C.) Times and Democrat,* January 14, 1974.

43. *Florence (S.C.) Morning News,* January 15, 1974.

44. *Greenwood (S.C.) Index-Journal,* January 15, 1974.

45. *Columbia (S.C.) State,* August 23, 1974.

46. *Columbia (S.C.) State,* quoted in the *Camden Chronicle,* undated, 1974.

47. West Journal, October 29, 1974, West Papers, SCPC.

48. West, Memorial services for Edgar Brown, June 29, 1975, box 35, West Papers, SCPC.

49. Autobiographical fragment, West Papers, SCPC.
50. *Columbia (S.C.) Record,* May 23, 1977.
51. Ibid., May 25, 1977.
52. Associated Press clipping, November 13, 1977, West Papers, SCPC.
53. *Economist,* July 9, 1977.
54. *Columbia (S.C.) Record,* June 25, 1977.

10. AN ARABIAN ADVENTURE

1. The *Wall Street Journal* correspondent Yaroslav Trofimov wrote in his 2007 book, *The Siege of Mecca,* "For decades, al Saud forbade infidels from staying overnight in the kingdom's conservative desert capital [Riyadh]. By the 1970s this restriction was lifted, but the royal family still preferred to transact most of its business with foreigners in opulent palaces on Jeddah's seashore. The diplomatic community was allowed to transfer to the capital only in 1984—and even then it was largely segregated in a special embassies neighborhood" (88).

2. Powell, *Saudi Arabia,* 14.

3. "A unique adventure living and working at the King Faisal Specialist Hospital and Research Center," Hospital Corporation of America, International Division, 1976.

4. Ibid.

5. Lois West, interview by the author, February 20, 2008.

6. Betty Bargmann Hunter, interview by the author, September 12, 2007.

7. Lois West, interview by the author, February 20, 2008.

8. West Journal, June 27, 1977, West Papers, SCPC.

9. Ibid., June 29, 1977.

10. Lippman, *Inside the Mirage,* 141.

11. Prominent among those in attendance at Faisal's funeral were Anwar Sadat, Egypt; Houari Boumedienne, Algeria; King Hussein, Jordan; Ahmed Hassan, Iraq; Jaafar Nimairi, Sudan; Muhammad Daourd, Afghanistan; Zulfiqaar Bhutto, Pakistan; Prince Juan Carlos, Spain; and Idi Amin, Uganda. Holden and Johns, *House of Saud,* 385.

12. Ibid., 381.

13. Mackey, *Saudis,* 202. Always the storyteller, John West offered this anecdote demonstrating Khalid's sense of humor. West had been dispatched to deliver a message from President Carter to the king and arrived during a function associated with the Islamic *hajj.* After apologizing for interrupting the function, he recalled the king being in a jovial mood, and West proceeded to recount what Khalid said on that occasion. "I was having a *majili* just before you came in," West recalled Khalid telling him, "and two old ladies came up to me and they had some dispute about some land . . . I tried to give them through to my assistants. Finally, one of them cracked her veil and said, 'Now Khalid, you just sit there, listen and decide this just like your daddy would have done.' That is the tough part of being King." John West, conversation with the author, August 1, 2003.

14. The ban on Jewish visitors to Saudi Arabia came to an end with the visit of Secretary of State Henry Kissinger in 1974. A year later Representative Henry Waxman of California became one of the first American Jewish lawmakers to visit the kingdom. Even so, Waxman found his meeting with Faisal to be testy. "The King told me he regarded all Jews as friends of Israel and therefore enemies of Saudi Arabia," Waxman said. "King Faisal said that Jews, regardless of nationality, had no business in Saudi Arabia as visitors." Lippman, *Inside the Mirage,* 221–22.

15. Part of West's handwritten record of his first meeting with Khalid reads as follows:

> After opening pleasantries as to the King's health, etc., I told him President Carter sent his best wishes and appreciation for his responsive attitude and action taken thus far by Saudi Arabia in these beginning months of the new administration. I also extended to him the President's thanks for sending Crown Prince Fahd and his accompanying delegation to the United States. I told him that it was the unanimous view of all of the U.S. officials involved that the visit was a complete success.
>
> The King replied that he, too, was pleased with the results of the visit and hoped that more such visits by SAG [Saudi Arabian Government] could be arranged.
>
> I thanked him for seeing Senator Stone [Senator Richard Stone of Florida, one of three Jewish senators in the U.S. Congress] and told him that the Senator was much impressed by the courtesies extended to him and by the warmth of hospitality and sincerity of the Saudi officials and peoples. I told him that Senator Javits [Senator Jacob Javits of New York, another of the Jewish senators] was arriving next weekend. I felt the visit was important as the Senator was a key member of the Foreign Relations Committee. The King commented at length on the fact that his country welcomed Senator Javits and he regretted the fact that so many people thought that SAG discriminated against Jews when in fact that was not the case—only against Zionists. He dwelt at length on the subject, explaining that the Jews who were Zionists had brought an undeserved stigma on those Jews who were not Zionists.
>
> I told him that I thought that such things as the King Faisal Foundation financing the solar energy systems at the Terrasett School in McLean, VA were excellent actions to show the concerns of the Saudi people for major problems such as alternative sources facing the world.
>
> The King then started talking about the problems in Africa. He said talks had begun even before Fahd's Washington visit and that he was extremely interested in the new and emerging countries. West Journal, June 29, 1977, West Papers, SCPC.

16. Mackey, *Saudis,* 94.

17. Mackey provided this detail of the "ground rules" of the agreement: "There could be no public organization that even faintly resembled a church; there could be no publicity connected with any religious function; there could be no proselytizing among either Moslems or non-Moslems; the availability of Christian religious groups could not be used in recruiting Western labor, nor could new employees be informed of the existence of Christian worship by an employer. In return, the Christians could meet as long as the purpose of their meetings did not become known to the Saudi population. The Christians were permitted to bring in ministers for the major cities of Riyadh, Jeddah and Dhahran. For the political purposes of the House of Saud, the visa for the Protestant minister in Riyadh listed him as an employee of Lockheed, and the Catholic priest was a social worker with the British consulate." Ibid.

18. *Christian Science Monitor,* August 8, 1983.

19. Ibid.

20. West Journal, July 1, 1977, West Papers, SCPC.

21. bin Laden, *Inside the Kingdom,* 100.

22. Shelton West Bosley and Lois West, interview by the author, February 20, 2008.

23. Shelton West Bosley, interview by the author, February 20, 2008. Shelton's trip from the United States to Saudi Arabia proved to be an adventure in itself. Delayed from traveling

with her parents because of a wedding, she set forth from Kennedy Airport in New York only to have a harrowing experience on takeoff. "The engine blew up," she recalled. "There's a loud explosion and the stewardesses were running up and down, saying, 'Is there a fire? Can you see a fire?' We were flying at a strange angle, and I decided the good news was that I was going to die calmly because I was holding the hand of a nervous Italian woman next to me and I was saying to her, 'It's okay.' We finally leveled off, dropped all the fuel, came in and landed. But it messed up all my flights. I ended up getting into Saudi Arabia a day and a half later."

24. John C. West Jr., interview by the author, April 17, 2009.

25. West Journal, July 7, 1977, West Papers, SCPC.

26. Ibid., July 10, 1977.

27. Ibid., July 6, 1977.

28. Ibid., July 7, 1977.

29. Ibid.

30. The historian Walter Laquer wrote that the Israelis were prepared to relinquish territories gained during the 1967 war and were "waiting for the phone call from the Arab leaders to start negotiations. Those hopes were dashed in August 1967 when Arab leaders meeting in Khartoum adopted a formula of three no's." Walter Laquer, *The Road to War, 1967* (London: Weidenfeld and Nicolson, 1969), 207.

31. There was optimism among the Saudis, at least partially because of the accession to power of "an idealistic chief executive." The historians Holden and Johns note, "Carter's choice for the key post of National Security Adviser was Zbigniew Brzezinski [who] had been involved in the preparation of the Brookings Institute study on American policy in the region, which was reckoned to have established guidelines for Carter. It concluded, as Kissinger had done, that the scope for 'step-by-step' diplomacy was probably exhausted. The goal should be a comprehensive settlement, it recommended." Holden and Johns, *House of Saud*, 453.

32. Brzezinski, *Power and Principle*, 85–86.

33. Thornton, *Carter Years*, 137.

34. Ibid., 136.

35. Vance, *Hard Choices*, 187.

36. Ibid., 188.

37. West Journal, August 8, 1977, West Papers, SCPC.

38. Vance, *Hard Choices*, 189.

39. West Journal, August 5, 1977, West Papers, SCPC.

40. Ibid., August 8, 1977.

41. Ibid., September 8, 1977.

42. The Sudeiris' roots went back to the Sudeiri tribe, whose friendship with the Saudis was sealed by the marriage of the dynasty's founding king, ibn Saud, to Hussah al-Sudeiri. She was described as "King Abdulaziz's [ibn Saud's] most powerful and influential wife . . . (who) . . . remained one of the closest women to the old monarch right up until his death." She was said to have trained her sons "to be fiercely loyal to each other" and to have "held regular meetings with her seven sons to discuss the political status of the royal family." See Powell, *Saudi Arabia*, 291.

The "Sudeiri Seven" sons were Fahd, who became crown prince and king; Sultan, who became crown prince and served as minister of defense; Abdul Rahman, vice minister of defense; Turki, onetime vice minister of defense; Naif, who headed the Ministry of Interior, which oversaw most police and security operations; Salman, governor of Riyadh; and Ahmed, vice minister of interior. See Robinson, *Yamani*, 175.

During the reign of King Faisal, Iffat would become viewed as "Saudi Arabia's queen" and was described as "the most powerful woman in Saudi Arabia." She and her aunt, the widow of Ahmed al-Thunaiyan al-Saud, came from their home in Turkey to Saudi Arabia at the invitation of King Faisal after the death of Ahmed. Both had experienced the Western influences of Kemal Ataturk's reforms in Turkey and were literate and fluent in three languages. They were also outspoken advocates of the emancipation of women in Islam.

Lois West and her daughter, Shelton, had occasion to visit with Iffat in December 1977. In his journal West referred to her as "Queen Iffat" and wrote, "They had a great time with Queen Iffat. The Queen is very gracious, speaks English somewhat haltingly, but all in all made them feel very welcome. Said Shelton was the spitting image of a Russian princess that she and her daughter had known. They came back all aglow." West Journal, December 3, 1977, West Papers, SCPC.

Lois West had this description of "Queen Iffat": "She had a whiskey voice and had a long cigarette holder, and she wore a metallic silver dress with heels and metallic pumps. She reminded me of Tallulah Bankhead." Lois West, interview by the author, April 20, 2008.

Iffat is credited with influencing Faisal to send their sons to the United States for their education, for both prep school and college. In addition to Saud al-Faisal, who was a Princeton graduate, the other sons were Turki al-Faisal, a graduate of the Hill School and Georgetown University; Abdul Rahman, a military officer; and Muhammad, a businessman. See Powell, *Saudi Arabia,* 267–68.

43. West Journal, September 9, 1977, West Papers, SCPC.

44. Ibid.

45. Samuel Tenenbaum, interview by the author, February 28, 2006.

46. Aaron Gold to West, May 17, 1977, West Papers, SCPC.

47. West Journal, October 19, 1977, West Papers, SCPC.

48. Gold to West, October 21, 1977, West Papers, SCPC.

49. West to Gold, November 9, 1977, West Papers, SCPC.

50. West Journal, October 22, 1977, West Papers, SCPC.

51. Holden and Johns, *House of Saud,* 480.

52. Ibid., 481.

53. Vance, *Hard Choices,* 195.

54. John C. West, interview by the author, August 22, 2003.

55. In the same letter West wrote to the president:

> Aside from the understandable furor of hurt feelings and damaged egos, the real problem—and opportunity—posed by the Sadat visit is reasonably clear. The Arab world since 1974 has been drifting more and more into two camps—one of which Sadat is the spokesman, if not the leader—has (pinned its hopes) for the future of the Mideast on U.S. leadership. Saudi Arabia has provided the financial assistance as well as what political support they could muster for this group. The other group has maintained that the U.S. is so committed to Israel that no just peace can ever be forthcoming following U.S. leadership. Since they are in the minority, they're just 'agin' everything the other crowd (us) does and they're very vocal about it.
>
> A failure of the Sadat mission will discredit our whole crowd here, including Saudi Arabia. West to President Jimmy Carter, November 20, 1977, box 11, West Papers, SCPC.

56. Emerson, *American House of Saud,* 364.

57. Vance, *Hard Choices,* 195.

58. Bronson, *Thicker Than Oil,* 142.

59. West Journal, January 3, 1978, West Papers, SCPC.

60. Holden and Johns, *House of Saud,* 485. In a December 1, 1977, dispatch to the White House marked "Top Secret-Sensitive," West was reported as having informed the president, "Prince Sultan said that Saudi Arabia has not been able to satisfactorily determine the U.S. position on Sadat's recent moves, but he expressed appreciation for U.S. policy support in the Middle East. The Prince also expressed his chagrin with regard to U.S. policy towards arms sales to Saudi Arabia, stating that the F-15 case had been in the mill for over two years and has yet to be resolved." Zbigniew Brzezinski daily report file, December 1, 1977, Jimmy Carter Presidential Library.

In a similarly marked dispatch dated December 27, 1977, West was reported as noting, "Prince Saud said that the issue of the sale of F-15s to Saudi Arabia would be the first priority in the King's and Crown Prince's mind during their meeting with the President." Brzezinski file, December 27, 1977, Jimmy Carter Presidential Library.

61. Bronson, *Thicker Than Oil,* 142.

62. Brzezinski, *Power and Principle,* 248.

63. Holden and Johns, *House of Saud,* 485.

64. West Journal, January 3, 1978, West Papers, SCPC.

65. Ibid.

66. Ibid.

67. Ibid., December 31, 1977.

68. Ibid., January 7, 1978.

69. Ibid., January 8, 1978.

70. Ibid., January 9, 1978.

71. Ibid., January 25, 1978.

72. Ibid.

73. Ibid., February 11–14, 1978.

74. Ibid., February 1, 1978.

75. Shelton West Bosley, interview by the author, February 20, 2008.

11. THE SHIFTING SANDS OF SAUDI FRIENDSHIP

1. Brzezinski, *Power and Principle,* 248.

2. The F-16 was about half the size of the F-15 and did not have the long-range capability of the F-15. It was designed largely for close-range dogfight combat. The F-5E was also smaller than the F-15 and was also designed for close-range combat. It had a relatively low cost and was easy to maintain. Saudi Arabia and Jordan already had about 150 of the F-5Es. See *Congressional Quarterly,* April 8, 1978, 835–40.

3. West Journal, February 14, 1978, West Papers, SCPC.

4. John C. West to President Carter, February 19, 1978, White House Central File, Jimmy Carter Presidential Library.

5. James A. Placke, interview by the author, September 18, 2003.

6. James E. Akins to West, January 10, 1978, West Papers, SCPC. Holden and Johns provide this account of Akins's departure: "In August [1976], the Saudis were disturbed by Kissinger's abrupt and cynical dismissal of James E. Akins, who had won the friendship and trust of the ruling hierarchy. The Secretary of State leaked his decision to the *New York Times,* from which Akins first learnt of his recall. His outspoken honesty perhaps was

too much for Kissinger. More important may have been the Secretary of State's resentment of Akins'[s] consolidation of his position as accredited representative of the President of the United States. That, together with the distrust Kissinger himself had engendered in Feisal, made it impossible for him to bypass normal diplomatic channels in Saudi Arabia, or to establish the same kind of link he had forged with Sadat, who was wont to call him 'Dear Henry.'" Holden and Johns, *House of Saud,* 419.

Another perspective of the Akins-Kissinger relationship came from the author Jeffrey Robinson in his biography *Yamani.* Quoting a "long time Kissinger friend and associate," Robinson wrote: "Jim [Akins] thought he knew the Arabs better than Kissinger, better than anyone else, and when he disagreed with policy, he didn't always follow Henry's direction. At the same time, Henry was always undercutting his ambassadors. He was a great one for that." Robinson, *Yamani,* 119.

7. *Washington Post,* March 11, 1978.

8. *New York Times,* April 1, 1978.

9. *Columbia (S.C.) Record,* April 3, 1978.

10. *New York Times,* March 20, 1978.

11. *Columbia (S.C.) Record,* April 3, 1978.

12. West Journal, April 2, 1978, West Papers, SCPC.

13. John West to Edward H. Sims, April 17, 1978, SCPC.

14. West Journal, March 10, 1978, West Papers, SCPC.

15. Ibid., April 13, 1978.

16. Ibid., May 2, 1978.

17. Ambassador to Saudi Arabia files, box 12, West Papers, SCPC.

18. Seymour Piwoz to Ambassador John C. West, March 20, 1978, West Papers, SCPC.

19. *U.S. News and World Report,* April 17, 1978.

20. *New York Times,* May 12, 1978.

21. Ibid.

22. *Washington Post,* May 7, 1978.

23. *New York Times,* May 12, 1978.

24. His Royal Highness Prince Turki al-Faisal, interview by the author, July 27, 2004.

25. Crawford Cook, interview by the author, June 28, 2005.

26. Bronson, *Thicker Than Oil,* 142–43.

27. Findley, *They Dare to Speak Out,* 102.

28. West Journal, March 8, 1978, West Papers, SCPC.

29. Ibid., March 15, 1978.

30. Ibid., March 12, 1978.

31. Ibid., March 15, 1978.

32. Ibid., March 9, 1978.

33. Ibid., March 8, 1978.

34. Ibid.

35. Ibid., May 4, 1978.

36. The essence of this account came from *Time* magazine, May 29, 1978.

37. West Journal, May 15, 1978, West Papers, SCPC.

38. Ibid.

39. Ibid., May 16, 1978.

40. *Time* magazine, May 29, 1978.

41. West Journal, May 25, 1978, West Papers, SCPC.

42. *Time* magazine, May 29, 1978.

43. Brzezinski, *Power and Principle,* 248.

44. *Time* magazine, May 29, 1978.

45. Ibid.

46. State Department outgoing telegram, May 24, 1978, White House Central File, Jimmy Carter Presidential Library.

47. Placke, interview by the author, September 18, 2003.

48. West Journal, June 4, 1978, West Papers, SCPC.

49. Placke, interview by the author, September 18, 2003.

50. West Journal, June 2, 1978, West Papers, SCPC.

51. The *New York Times,* February 24, 2008, Travel sec., p. 3, reads, "The ruler of Saudi Arabia, King Abdullah, is instituting a number of well-publicized reforms to diversify the country's economy and insulate it against changes in the oil market. International tourism isn't part of that program, but domestic tourism is. The government estimates that Saudis who might take holidays in Saudi Arabia are an untapped $15 billion market, and that the international tourism market is tiny by comparison. Still, international tourists do have value to the government as part of a public relations campaign."

Picking up on a message West had pounded into his Saudi friends decades earlier, Prince Sultan bin Salman bin Abdul-Aziz, secretary general of the Supreme Commission of Tourism of Saudi Arabia, is quoted in the *Times* article as saying, "Saudi Arabia today faces a big challenge which is its image. It is very important for us that people come and see it as it is. Seeing is believing."

52. West Journal, August 4, 1978, West Papers, SCPC.

53. Ibid., August 5, 1978.

54. Ibid., August 8, 1978.

55. *Washington Post,* August 8, 1978.

56. Thornton, *Carter Years,* 145.

57. West Journal, August 8, 1978, West Papers, SCPC.

58. Ibid., August 10, 1978.

59. Ibid., August 15, 1978.

60. Ibid., August 23, 1978.

61. *Newsweek,* August 28, 1978.

62. West Journal, September 7, 1978, West Papers, SCPC.

63. Ibid., September 10, 1978.

64. Ibid., September 18, 1978.

65. Executive, CO1–7, White House Central File, Jimmy Carter Presidential Library.

66. Holden and Johns, *House of Saud,* 490.

67. Ibid., 491–92.

68. West Journal, September 20, 1978, West Papers, SCPC.

69. Ibid.

70. Holden and Johns, *House of Saud,* 492–93.

71. Vance, *Hard Choices,* 230–31.

72. West Journal, January 27, 1979, West Papers, SCPC.

73. Ibid., January 28, 1979.

74. Thornton, *Carter Years,* 319.

75. Robinson, *Yamani,* 70.

76. Holden and Johns, *House of Saud,* 498.

77. Ibid., 500.

78. West Journal, February 24, 1979, West Papers, SCPC.

79. Ibid., March 5, 1979.

80. Holden and Johns, *House of Saud,* 502.

81. Ibid., 503.

82. Ibid.

83. West Journal, March 5, 1979, West Papers, SCPC.

84. Ibid.

85. Prince Turki, interview by the author, July 27, 2004.

86. West Journal, February 10, 1979, West Papers, SCPC.

87. Thornton, *Carter Years,* 340.

88. Ibid., 341.

89. Carter, *Blood of Abraham,* 177.

12. DANGEROUS TIMES FOR AMERICANS

1. Holden and Johns, *House of Saud,* 505, 507.

2. West Journal, March 29, 1979, West Papers, SCPC.

3. Ibid., March 28, 1979.

4. Ibid., April 3, 1979.

5. Ibid., April 27, 1979.

6. According to John Limbert, the provisional government remained in place from February until November 1979. Limbert, e-mail communication with the author, September 30, 2008.

7. Brzezinski, *Power and Principle,* 398.

8. John C. West, interview by the author, August 1, 2003.

9. Ibid.

10. Ibid.

11. John Limbert, e-mail communication with the author, September 30, 2008.

12. Sullivan's comment can be found in several sources, including Kaufman and Kaufman, *Presidency of James Earl Carter,* 157.

13. West Journal, February 15, 1979, West Papers, SCPC.

14. Ibid., February 11, 1979.

15. John C. West, interview by the author, August 1, 2003.

16. Trofimov, *Siege of Mecca,* 59.

17. *Time* magazine, January 19, 1979.

18. Mackey, *Saudis,* 207.

19. West Journal, February 16, 1979, West Papers, SCPC.

20. Ibid., February 19, 1979.

21. Vance, *Hard Choices,* 344.

22. John Limbert, e-mail communication with the author, September 30, 2008.

23. Vance, *Hard Choices,* 371.

24. In a *New York Times* obituary of Undersecretary of State David Newsom published on April 5, 2008, David Rockefeller recalled being told by Newsom that the U.S. Embassy in Tehran would be overrun if the shah were admitted to the United States. Rockefeller was asked to convey to the shah that President Carter thought it was "not convenient" for him to come to the United States at the time. When Rockefeller refused to deliver the message to the shah, Newsom went to Henry Kissinger, who also refused to deliver the president's message.

Eventually, the obituary reported, the shah's friends prevailed, and the president reversed himself. *New York Times,* April 5, 2008.

25. Vance, *Hard Choices,* 372.

26. Brzezinski, *Power and Principle,* 476.

27. Williams J. Daugherty, "Jimmy Carter and the 1979 Decision to Admit the Shah into the United States," http://www.unc.edu/depts/diplomat/archives_roll/2003_01-03/dauherty_shah/dauherty_shah.html (accessed August 2, 2010).

28. John Limbert, e-mail communication with the author, September 30, 2008.

29. Vance, *Hard Choices,* 373–74.

30. Trofimov, *Siege of Mecca,* 60.

31. West Journal, October 2, 1979, West Papers, SCPC.

32. Trofimov, *Siege of Mecca,* 60.

33. West Journal, October 2, 1979, West Papers, SCPC.

34. Trofimov, *Siege of Mecca,* 61.

35. Mackey, *Saudis,* 228–29.

36. West Journal, November 4, 1979, West Papers, SCPC.

37. Ibid., August 1, 2003.

38. bin Laden, *Inside the Kingdom,* 123.

39. Mackey, *Saudis,* 13.

40. Ibid., 63.

41. bin Laden, *Inside the Kingdom,* 123–24.

42. Trofimov, *Siege of Mecca,* 93.

43. West Journal, November 20, 1979, West Papers, SCPC.

44. Mackey, *Saudis,* 230.

45. West Journal, November 20, 1979, West Papers, SCPC.

46. Trofimov, *Siege of Mecca,* 91–92.

47. Ibid., 94.

48. Ibid., 94–95.

49. West Journal, November 21, 1979, West Papers, SCPC.

50. Mackey, *Saudis,* 230.

51. Trofimov, *Siege of Mecca,* 136.

52. Ibid., 108.

53. Ibid., 138.

54. West Journal, November 21, 1979, West Papers, SCPC.

55. Ibid.

56. Ibid., November 22, 1979; Trofimov, *Siege of Mecca,* 138–39.

57. Trofimov, *Siege of Mecca,* 146.

58. West Journal, November 27, 1979, West Papers, SCPC.

59. Ibid., November 28, 1979.

60. Ibid.

61. Ibid.

62. Ibid.

63. Ibid.

64. Ibid.

65. Ibid., November 30, 1979.

66. Ibid., November 29, 1979.

67. *New York Times,* December 5, 1979.

68. West Journal, December 4, 1979, West Papers, SCPC.

69. *New York Times,* December 5, 1979.

70. West Journal, November 28, 1979, West Papers, SCPC.

71. *New York Times,* December 5, 1979.

72. Holden and Johns, *House of Saud,* 525.

73. Trofimov, *Siege of Mecca,* 213.

74. West Journal, March 13, 1980, West Papers, SCPC.

75. Mackey, *Saudis,* 233–34.

76. Holden and Johns, *House of Saud,* 527–28.

77. A week before the Soviet invasion of Afghanistan, West recorded in his journal that a meeting with Prince Turki proved to be "somewhat of a shocking situation. The *Washington Post* had written a story saying that the delegation [two Pentagon officials] was coming out to get bases from Saudi Arabia, which of course was completely wrong, but Turki was real upset about it. . . . The meeting started off awfully cool but [the Pentagon officials] immediately explained we were not here to get bases, etc., but simply to inform the Saudis that we were going to Oman, Somalia [and] Kenya to talk to them about bases. That mollified Turki." West Journal, December 18, 1979, West Papers, SCPC.

78. Trofimov, *Siege of Mecca,* 236.

79. Ibid.

80. Ibid., 237.

81. West Journal, February 4–5, 1980, West Papers, SCPC.

82. The Brzezinski-Christopher mission produced several specific outcomes, according to Thornton:

> The Saudis now sought to enhance the capabilities of their newly-acquired F-15s and to purchase AWACS [high technology surveillance aircraft] while agreeing to greater cooperation with Pakistan, including the provision of funds for Islamabad's weapons purchase.
>
> Regarding a larger American regional presence, the Saudis endorsed Washington's plans to gain base rights in Oman, Somalia and Kenya, but continued to demur on the question of providing bases in Saudi Arabia for American forces. The growing threat, however . . . prompted them to make two substantial concessions in the matter of bases. First, they agreed that the United States could use Saudi bases in a military emergency. Most important for the long run, however, was Saudi agreement to construct, according to American specifications, a greatly enhanced military base structure—over two dozen bases costing some fifty billion dollars (Thornton, *Carter Years,* 520).

83. West Journal, March 9, 1980, West Papers, SCPC.

84. Thornton, *Carter Years,* 519–21.

85. Ibid., 521.

86. Ibid., 523–24.

87. Ibid., 499–500.

88. Vance, *Hard Choices,* 410.

89. West Journal, April 28, 1980, West Papers, SCPC.

90. Emerson, *American House of Saud,* 152, 153.

91. Mackey, *Saudis,* 141, 142.

92. West Journal, April 29, 1980, West Papers, SCPC.

93. Ibid., May 2, 1980.

94. Emerson, *American House of Saud,* 160.

95. Ibid., 164.

96. Ibid., 161.

97. *New York Times,* October 26, 1980.

98. West Journal, July 30, 1980, West Papers, SCPC.

99. Ibid., November 5, 1980.

100. Ibid., January 20, 1981.

101. Ibid., January 21, 1981.

102. Ibid., January 24, 1981.

103. *Washington Post,* February 21, 1981.

104. Ibid., January 23, 1981.

105. *New York Times,* February 2, 1981.

106. Bronson, *Thicker Than Oil,* 160–61.

107. *Camden (S.C.) Chronicle-Independent,* August 31, 1981.

EPILOGUE

1. Shelton West Bosley, interview by the author, May 14, 2009.

2. John C. West, interview by the author, August 22, 2004.

3. Ibid., October 24, 2003.

4. Ibid.

5. Shelton West Bosley and Lois West, interview by the author, May 14, 2009.

6. Shelton West Bosley, interview by the author, May 14, 2009.

7. Lois West and Shelton West Bosley, interview by the author, May 14, 2009.

8. Ibid.

9. John C. West Jr., interview by the author, April 17, 2009.

10. Lois West and Shelton West Bosley, interview by the author, May 14, 2009.

11. *New York Times,* March 15, 1987.

12. Lois West and Shelton West Bosley, interview by the author, May 14, 2009.

13. Ibid.

14. Ibid.

15. "A History of Sea Pines," Memories of Sea Pines 50th Anniversary Web Site, www
.seapines50thanniversary.com/history_of_sea_pines.php (accessed September 27, 2010).

16. University of South Carolina, *Business and Economic Review,* June 22, 1997.

17. *Business Insurance,* January 5, 2009.

18. *Camden (S.C.) Chronicle-Independent,* December 15, 1999.

19. Associated Press in *International Herald Tribune,* March 23, 2004.

20. Winthrop University, *Education News,* October 10, 2008.

21. Shelton West Bosley, interview by the author, May 14, 2009.

22. John West Jr., interview by the author, April 17, 2009.

23. Ibid.

24. Lois West and Shelton West Bosley, interview by the author, May 14, 2009.

25. Ibid.

26. Shelton West Bosley, interview by the author, May 14, 2009.

27. Lois West and Shelton West Bosley, interview by the author, May 14, 2009.

28. *Columbia (S.C.) State,* September 23, 2003.

29. Ibid.

30. Prince Turki al-Faisal, interview by the author, July 27, 2004.

31. *Columbia (S.C.) State,* September 23, 2003.

32. John West Jr., interview by the author, April 17, 2009.

BIBLIOGRAPHY

ARCHIVAL SOURCES

Camden Archives and History, Camden, S.C.
The Citadel Archives and Museum, The Citadel, Charleston, S.C.
Jimmy Carter Presidential Library, Atlanta, Ga.
South Carolina Political Collections, University of South Carolina, Columbia

INTERVIEWS

Bosley, Shelton W. Interview by the author, February 20, 2008, and May 14, 2009.
Carter, President Jimmy. Interview by the author, January 21, 2004.
Clyburn, Congressman James E. Interview by the author, October 11, 2005, and January 20, 2006.
Cook, Crawford. Interview by the author, June 28, 2005.
Faisal, His Royal Highness Prince Turki al-. Interview by the author, July 27, 2004.
Hunter, Betty Bargmann. Interview by the author, September 12, 2007.
Hutchins, Ann (Mrs. Guy, Jr.). Interview by the author, May 4, 2006.
Placke, James A. Interview by the author, September 18, 2003.
Teal, Harvey. Interview by the author, June 25, 2005.
Tenenbaum, Samuel. Interview by the author, February 28, 2006.
Todd, Roderick. Interview by author, April 24, 2006.
West, Governor John C. Interview by the author, August 22, 2002, July 25, 2003, August 1, 2003, and August 22, 2003.
West, John C., Jr. Interview by author, January 19, 2010.
West, Lois (Mrs. John C.). Interview by the author, February 21, 2006, February 20, 2008, April 20, 2008, and May 14, 2009.
Whitmire, James M. Interview by author, July 25, 2007.

PUBLICATIONS

Aburish, Said K. *The Rise, Corruption and Coming Fall of the House of Saud.* London: Bloomsbury Publishing, 1994.
Bass, Jack. "John C. West of South Carolina: His Emphasis on Health, Hunger, Race Relations Reflects Changed Tone of State's Politics." *South Today* 2 (July–August 1972): 9–10.
Beazley, Paul W. *South Carolina Human Affairs Commission: A History (1972–1997).* Columbia: State of South Carolina Human Affairs Commission, 1997.
bin Laden, Carmen. *Inside the Kingdom: My Life in Saudi Arabia.* New York: Warner Books, 2004.
Boyd, Carl. *Hitler's Japanese Confidant: General Oshima Hiroshi and MAGIC Intelligence, 1941–1945.* Lawrence: University Press of Kansas, 1993.

Bronson, Rachel. *Thicker Than Oil: America's Uneasy Partnership with Saudi Arabia.* New York: Oxford University Press, 2006.

Brzezinski, Zbigniew. *Power and Principle: Memoirs of the National Security Adviser, 1977–1981.* New York: Farrar, Strauss, Giroux, 1983.

Bumpers, Dale. *The Best Lawyer in a One-Lawyer Town: A Memoir.* New York: Random House, 2003.

Byrnes, James F. *All in One Lifetime.* New York: Harper, 1958.

Carter, Jimmy. *The Blood of Abraham: Insights into the Middle East.* New ed. Fayetteville: University of Arkansas Press, 1993.

———. *An Hour before Daylight.* New York: Simon and Schuster, 2001.

Cohodas, Nadine. *Strom Thurmond and the Politics of Southern Change.* New York: Simon and Schuster, 1993.

Coit, Margaret L. *Mr. Baruch.* Cambridge, Mass.: Riverside Press, 1957.

Coll, Steve. *The Bin Ladens: An Arabian Family in the American Century.* New York: Penguin Press, 2008.

"Democrats' Comeback in South—a Political Key to '72." *U.S. News and World Report,* March 29, 1971, 22–24.

Dent, Harry S. *The Prodigal South Returns to Power.* New York: John Wiley and Sons, 1978.

Eddy, William A. "FDR Meets Ibn Saud." Special issue, *Middle East Insight* (1995): 38–46.

Edgar, Walter B. *South Carolina: A History.* Columbia: University of South Carolina Press, 1998.

Emerson, Steven. *The American House of Saud: The Secret Petrodollar Connection.* New York: Franklin Watts, 1985.

Findley, Paul. *They Dare to Speak Out: People and Institutions Confront Israel's Lobby.* Westport, Conn.: Lawrence Hill & Company, 1985.

Finnegan, John Patrick. *Military Intelligence.* Army Lineage Series. Washington, D.C.: Center of Military History, U.S. Army, 1998.

Grose, Philip G. *South Carolina at the Brink: Robert McNair and the Politics of Civil Rights.* Columbia: University of South Carolina Press, 2006.

Halberstam, David. *The Fifties.* New York: Villard Books, 1993.

Harvey, Gordon E. *A Question of Justice: New South Governors and Education, 1968–1976.* Tuscaloosa: University of Alabama Press, 2002.

Hathorn, Billy B. "The Changing Politics of Race: Congressman Albert Watson and the S.C. Republican Party, 1965–1970." *South Carolina Historical Magazine* 89, no. 4 (1988): 227–41.

Holden, David, and Richard Johns. *The House of Saud: The Rise and Rule of the Most Powerful Dynasty in the Arab World.* New York: Holt, Rinehart and Winston, 1981.

Kaufman, Burton I., and Scott Kaufman. *The Presidency of James Earl Carter, Jr.* 2nd ed., rev. Lawrence: University of Kansas Press, 2006.

Lachicotte, Alberta. *Rebel Senator: Strom Thurmond of South Carolina.* New York: Devin-Adair Company, 1966.

Lamb, David. *The Arabs: Journeys beyond the Mirage.* Rev. ed. New York: Vintage Books, 2002.

Lander, Ernest M. *A History of South Carolina, 1865–1960.* Chapel Hill: University of North Carolina Press, 1960.

Lewis, Bernard. *The Crisis of Islam: Holy War and Unholy Terror.* New York: Random House, 2003.

Limbert, John W. *Iran, at War with History.* Boulder, Colo.: Westview Press, 1987.

Lippman, Thomas W. *Inside the Mirage: America's Fragile Partnership with Saudi Arabia.* Boulder, Colo.: Westview Press, 2004.

Long, David E. *Saudi Arabia.* Washington Papers 39. Beverly Hills, Calif.: Sage Publications, 1976.

Mackey, Sandra. *The Saudis: Inside the Desert Kingdom.* New York: Meridian, 1988.

McCormack, Alfred. *The History of Special Branch M.I.S. in World War II.* Laguna Hills, Calif.: Aegean Park Press, 1994.

Panetta, Leon E., and Peer Gall. *Bring Us Together: The Nixon Team and the Civil Rights Retreat.* Philadelphia: Lippincott, 1971.

Pollack, Kenneth M. *A Path Out of the Desert: A Grand Strategy for America in the Middle East.* New York: Random House, 2008.

Powell, William. *Saudi Arabia and Its Royal Family.* Secaucus, N.J.: Lyle Stuart, 1982.

Robinson, Jeffrey. *Yamani: The Inside Story.* New York: Atlantic Monthly Press, 1988.

Rosen, Robert N. *Saving the Jews: Franklin D. Roosevelt and the Holocaust.* New York: Thunder's Mouth Press, 2006.

Saunders, Donald E., Jr. *To Improve the Health of the People: An Insider's View of the Campaign for the University of South Carolina School of Medicine.* North Charleston, S.C.: Book Surge, 2005.

Schwartz, Stephen. *The Two Faces of Islam: The House of Sa'ud from Tradition to Terror.* New York: Doubleday, 2002.

South Carolina Legislative Manual. Columbia: General Assembly of South Carolina, 1967, 1972.

Strong, Robert A. *Working in the World: Jimmy Carter and the Making of American Foreign Policy.* Baton Rouge: Louisiana State University Press, 2000.

Thornton, Richard C. *The Carter Years: Toward a New Global Order.* New York: Paragon House, 1991.

Trofimov, Yaroslav. *The Siege of Mecca: The Forgotten Uprising in Islam's Holiest Shrine and the Birth of al Qaeda.* New York: Doubleday, 2007.

Vance, Cyrus. *Hard Choices: Critical Years in America's Foreign Policy.* New York: Simon and Schuster, 1983.

Vitalis, Robert. *America's Kingdom: Mythmaking on the Saudi Oil Frontier.* Stanford, Calif.: Stanford University Press, 2007.

Winterbotham, F. W. *The Ultra Secret.* New York: Harper & Row, 1974.

Workman, William D. *The Bishop from Barnwell: The Political Life and Times of Senator Edgar A. Brown.* Columbia, S.C.: R. L. Bryan, 1963.

Zeigler, Eugene N., Jr. *When Conscience and Power Meet: A Memoir.* Columbia: University of South Carolina Press, 2008.

INDEX

DATE			